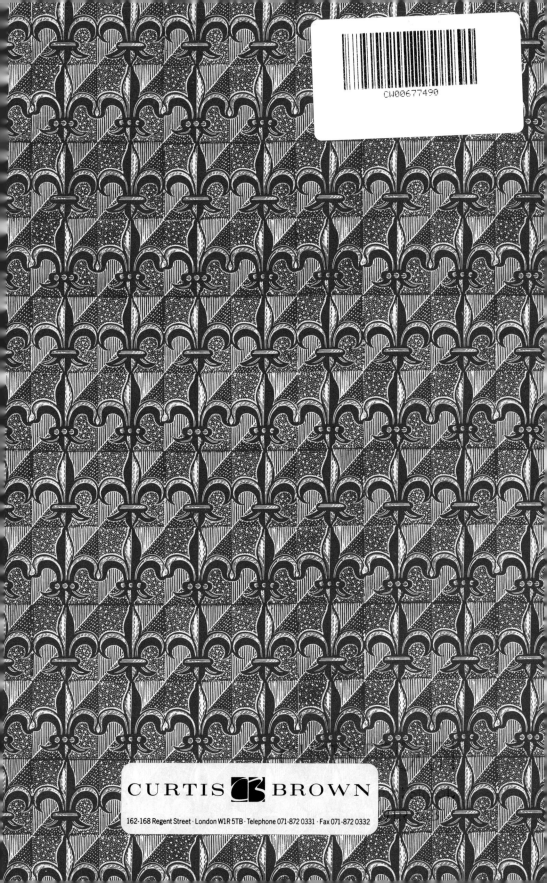

CURTIS ⬛ BROWN

162-168 Regent Street · London W1R 5TB · Telephone 071-872 0331 · Fax 071-872 0332

The Cedar Story

CURTIS BROWN

162 - 168 Regent Street,
London, W1R 5TB

Also by Charles Gordon

The Two Tycoons

For John and Elizabeth

CHARLES GORDON

The Cedar Story

The Night The City Was Saved

SINCLAIR-STEVENSON

CURTIS BROWN
162 - 168 Regent Street,
London, W1R 5TB

First published in Great Britain 1993
by Sinclair-Stevenson
an imprint of Reed Consumer Books Ltd
Michelin House, 81 Fulham Road, London SW3 6RB
and Auckland, Melbourne, Singapore and Toronto

A CIP catalogue record for this book
is available at the British Library
ISBN 1 85619 217 2

Typeset by Wilmaset Ltd, Birkenhead, Merseyside
Printed in Great Britain
by
Mackays of Chatham plc.

Contents

Acknowledgements

First and foremost my deepest thanks to Nadia; her support was undeviating.

A special pleasure in researching and writing the *Cedar Story*, indeed as it was with the *The Two Tycoons* was seeing old friends and making new ones. I was given help and assistance in nearly every instance and in many unexpected ways. What I found particularly interesting, was that nearly all of the participants in the Cedar marathon at the Bank of England remember their experience of over twenty years ago, vividly, though not in all details, as an indelible event in their lives. Many of course have sadly died, and perhaps I miss most of all Sir Kenneth Cork, an endearing new friend, who could strike terror or a chord of friendship whenever he chose.

The men of the Bank of England were particularly helpful, Lord Richardson above all, whose intellectual clarity and integrity was an inspiration from the beginning in providing me with the right focus; also Sir Jasper Hollom, the unsung hero of the crisis as Dennis Healey described him, and who I hope will not abjure me for singing his praises; to Rodney Galpin and Roger Barnes; to John Keyworth, Carol Pearce and Roger Mayes; to Ray Simpson and Ian McQuire.

Of the bankers, stockbrokers, lawyers, accountants, I express my gratitude to Godfrey Chandler, Sir Michael Richardson and Michael Belmont, to John Gillum and William Sadleir, to Brian Pitman, Rupert Hambro, Geoffrey Bell, Nigel Tapley, Derrick Hanson, Ray Wheeler; to David Higginson, David Bolton, Richard Coleman, Cyril Peach, Frank Woodowson; and to Gerald Drew and Tony Pinckney.

Many others have asked that I do not make an acknowledgement and to them I would also wish to record my thanks.

Of the men of the institutions, I owe particular thanks to William Broadfield, Cob Stenham, Hugh Jenkins, Burton Johnson, Lord De L'Isle and to Eric Rogers, Rafe Langham, Alan Urwin, Sydney Cowtan, Bill Harris, Ron Bishop and Brian Oram.

Of the executive directors, I wish to pay special thanks to Alan Glass, Alan Watt, Yusuf Ahmed and Philip Johnstone.

I received help from some members of the Morrison family and have not named them in order to respect their confidence.

I am particularly grateful to John Plender of the *Financial Times* for reading the manuscript at an early stage and Lord Rippon and Lord Lever for reading and correcting certain chapters.

I also received help and wish to thank Lord Wolfson, Sir Kenneth James, Sir Nigel Mobbs, Edward Erdman, Norman Bowie, Geoffrey Tucker, David Gordon, Brian Banks, Richard Law, Alexander Stone, John Roberts, John Dillworth, Ian Pitt and Lady Morse, whose book *Square Mile Walks*, a masterpiece of intelligent description is a most readable account of City history, and who very kindly read the chapter 'The Evergreen Lady'.

I wish to record my appreciation to the members of the 'aviation division' of Cedar, Harry Green, Roger Seymour and Al Thomas, and an especial mention of thanks is due also to Brian Gates who publishes the unique book on the ownership and registration of private jets.

In addition I would also like to thank Paul Walton, Shaun Davitt, A R North of the V&A, Keith Wilson, the Press Association, the *Glasgow Herald and Evening Times*, the *Yorkshire Post*, the *Financial Times*, Universal Pictorial Press and Agency Ltd, EPR Architects Ltd, Barclays Bank and Sotheby's.

Finally, I wish to record what a pleasure it is to be published by Christopher Sinclair-Stevenson and to have had the ever-ready, always courteous, support of his colleagues. It is a pleasure to have been edited by Jenny Parrot, and my thanks are due also to Julie Scott-Bayfield for her advice.

The Leading Cast at the Bank of England on the night of Wednesday 19 December 1973

The Bank of England	Lord Richardson	The Governor
	Sir Jasper Hollom	The Deputy Governor
	James Keogh	Principal of the Discount Office
	Rodney Galpin	Deputy Principal of the Discount Office
	Ray Simpson	First Parlour Steward
The Institutions	Lord De L'Isle	Phoenix Assurance
	Ronald Bishop	
	Hugh Jenkins	Coal Board
	David Clement	
	Burton Johnson	Electricity Supply Industry
	George Cumming	
	Cob Stenham	Unilever
	William Broadfield	
The Morrisons	Jack Morrison	Chairman of Cedar
	Michael Morrison	Co-managing Director of Cedar
	David Fischer	Co-managing Director of Cedar
	Arnold Ziff	Son-in-law of Jack Morrison
The Bankers	Sir Timothy Bevan	Barclays
	Deryk Vander Weyer	
	Douglas Horner	
Financial Advisers	John Gillum	Samuel Montagu
	William Sadleir	
	Ray Wheeler	Hambros
The Stockbrokers	Michael Richardson	Cazenove
The Liquidator	Kenneth Cork	Cork Gully
The Lawyers	David Higginson	Herbert Smith
	David Bolton	
	Paul Boyce	Coward Chance
Officers of Cedar	Yusuf Ahmed	Executive Director
	Alan Watt	
	Alan Glass	
	Philip Johnstone	
	John Eames	
	Michael Grinling	
	Reg Edward	
	Ronald Stanley	Secretary
	John Bailey	Accountant

ix

Prologue

On Wednesday, 19 December 1973, two separate groups of people were invited to the Bank of England by the Governor, Lord Richardson, and the Deputy Governor, Sir Jasper Hollom. Their purpose in issuing these invitations, more in the nature of a summons than a polite request, was quite simply to make plans to prevent the collapse of the entire banking system. Potentially the country's worst-ever bank crisis, few outside the City of London were aware of the extreme dangers, and even in the City, although alarm bells had been set off, they were not yet shrieking. The Governor looked unflinchingly into the eye of the storm, and quickly and firmly decided that it was essential to stamp out, before it was too late, what he later described in a memorable phrase as 'the contagion of fear'.

A major run on deposits had begun. Smaller banks on the fringe of the banking establishment were already under extreme pressure. Three weeks earlier a notorious fringe bank, London and County, had set off the actual alarm. Now Cedar Holdings, impeccable in contrast to London and County, was in deep trouble – despite having four of the country's most powerful investment institutions as substantial shareholders. In fact Cedar was bleeding to death.

Of the two separate groups invited to the Bank, one was made up of the chairmen of the four major clearing banks. They met the Governors in the afternoon; their meeting was not confidential; it was secret and it was short and sweet, with everyone in accord on what had to be done and that it had to be done with the utmost urgency.

The second group, invited early in the morning on that fateful Wednesday, comprised the heads of the four institutional supporters of Cedar and its lead bank. The four institutions were Phoenix Assurance, and the nationalised pension funds of the coal and electricity supply industries, and of the Unilever pension fund. The lead bank was Barclays. The Governor spelt out the dangers: if Cedar was not able to open its doors for business the following morning, the domino effect could cause the collapse of the banking system. He indicated that he would like his guests to stay in the Bank until they had worked out between themselves the terms of a rescue for Cedar. It was not stated, but it was thought, that all would be settled by lunchtime.

However, this early-morning meeting of the second group, to everyone's astonishment, developed into an unprecedented eighteen-hour cliff-hanging series of discussions, wrangles and arguments between the four institutions themselves – the Fabulous Four as they became known – between them and Barclays, between all of them and the Cedar directors and also between the Cedar directors themselves. It was only after the great liquidator, Kenneth Cork, adviser to Barclays, finally had his say, that the rescue was assured. The agreement was eventually signed just before 3 am on Thursday morning, by which time there were over thirty cold and hungry participants; some of them resentful, some deeply angry, some baffled, some just plain petrified, but all of them weary out of their minds. Nor were they mollified to read in the *Economist* after Christmas, that this was 'How The City Was Saved'.

*   *   *

The country itself was enduring a period of extreme national crisis, and nothing as severe had been experienced since the Second World War: labour forces were militant, there was a rail and a coal go-slow, there was an energy crisis, oil had recently tripled in price, and emergency measures had been imposed – a three-day week at factories, lighting restricted in shops and offices, none at all in the streets, no television after 10 pm, and just two days before, drastic interim budget measures had been announced. The economy was out of kilter, and social and commercial life was deranged.

And now if not sufficiently plagued, a financial storm was blackening the horizon with daunting turbulence, threatening to block the nostrils of the banking system. To a critical extent the avoidance of this looming financial crisis depended upon the rescue of Cedar. This in turn depended upon whether the four institutions would agree to come to its rescue, which in turn depended upon whether the executive directors of Cedar would agree to the terms of any such rescue.

The chairman of the board of directors was Jack Morrison. He and his son Michael were perhaps the most personally affected of all those who were involved in this unique marathon at the Bank. They were founder directors of Cedar and with their family trusts, their shareholdings matched the combined shareholdings of the institutions, the balance being owned by the public. Before entering the Bank, Morrison had been a very rich man by any standards: when he left in the small hours of the next morning, he was virtually bust. His reaction was cataclysmic. To be wiped out at all is a tragedy, but to be wiped out in hours is outrageous bad fortune.

Yet the financial portcullis which severs the yoke from former wealth and grandeur is not only activated by external events, there are also internal self-instilled causes, signalling warnings long before the killing severance. But whatever the cause, come Armageddon, close colleagues, advisers and friends of the stricken principals are not slow in proclaiming very soon after the gory event that they had, of course, seen it all coming, and that the victims, now the culprits, thoroughly deserved what was happening to them. These people are faithful adherents of hindsight, which can provide valuable lessons if applied with intellectual honesty; but far too frequently hindsight becomes the iniquitous alibi of the survival process, part of the scapegoating, part of detaching and untainting oneself, of removing the evidence, the muck, of one's direct or indirect association, of not being around, when whatever it is hits the fan. Hindsight of this nature is a corrupting disease which destroys the cells of loyalty and the bonds of friendship and, particularly in the realms of business life, glibly erases the shame of recent events from the memories of its more craven adherents.

Whatever had been the previous state of the relationship between the Morrisons and their four supporting institutions, it came to a dead stop on Wednesday 19 December. From the moment the Morrisons entered the Bank of England, they were regarded by their erstwhile associates as second-class citizens, or worse. Together with the other executive directors the Morrisons were put into a single small room on the ground floor, whilst their old friends, the directors representing the institutions, joined by a supporting cast of lawyers, stockbrokers, bankers and financial advisers, milled around upstairs in comfortable splendour, in what was to all of them the most hallowed of all City enclaves, the great Court Room of the Bank of England, with its

3

adjoining Anteroom and Octagon Room, sitting, talking, whispering, arguing, negotiating, cowed if not overwhelmed by what seemed to them a stately home. Exercising their brains and their wits as to how this crucial fringe bank should be saved – if at all – their loyalties to each other, to the Bank of England, to the City, to the country, were evident in their separate ways; but any semblance of loyalty from those on the first floor of the Bank to the shivering Morrisons down below, seemed to vanish without any trace and without any remorse, though one or two felt a twinge of guilt and one or two felt a shiver of shame.

When Jack Morrison finally emerged from the Bank in those grim hours of Thursday morning, someone remarked that he had aged twenty years in as many hours. He was completely broken and decimated. Frozen in shock, he later lost any remaining vestiges of spirit when he found that support from friends and even some of his family was either tepid or cool. During this period of unmitigated misery, what undoubtedly sustained him was the undiluted love of his son Michael, who for a long while was himself like a broken reed.

Though inherently not deserving his swift unremitting karate-like downfall, it could not have been a surprise to those who knew Jack Morrison well. For a man of boundless ambition, he possessed a fierce pride which he had firmly laminated to an overweening, almost paranoic distrust of others, which was even directed at the four institutions which had been his and Michael's constant supporters for years. It was this noxious element of distrust, gnawing at the roots of Jack Morrison's relationships with others, which fundamentally destroyed him. But the most ironic twisting of the knife in the Morrisons' undoing, arose from a fairly obsessive, undeviating, persistent endeavour – to inject the family's very valuable property company, Amalgamated Securities, into Cedar. The reasoning behind this was his determination to increase the percentage of his family's shareholding in Cedar beyond that held by the Fabulous Four. Amalgamated was the means of doing so and, with his mind set on being in control, Jack Morrison in fact only achieved his single-minded objective a mere six months before their summons to the Bank. The sheer awfulness of his plight, should be seen as a terrible nemesis which need never have happened. Had he kept Amalgamated independent, even if Cedar had gone under, he would still have been of substantial independent means; the totality of his ruin was actually sealed by his own misguided distrust of others, rather than by an external catastrophe.

4

I was also a prime target of his distrust. He may well have had some cause, for he not only knew that my loyalties to the institutions took precedence over any due to him and that I was totally opposed to a takeover of Amalgamated by Cedar. He also knew that my personal aspirations were not, by any means, dedicated as he would have wished, to his own unrelieved self-seeking. Until some two or so years before his ordeal at the Bank, I had been for nearly a decade his and his son's closest business associate, responsible for conceiving and establishing the financing strategy of Cedar and for introducing the Fabulous Four and Barclays bank. Then in June 1971 I had a confrontation with the institutions whom I had brought into Spey Investments, a banking, property and investment group I had founded and which I controlled, and Jack Morrison immediately grasped the opportunity to force me out of Cedar. The Spey tentacles, my close association with the Morrisons and its rupture, and my relationship with my friend Sir Charles Clore, all form an integral part of the Cedar story.

An underlying theme in this book, as it was in my earlier *The Two Tycoons*, is the relationship between entrepreneurs and institutions. Entrepreneurs cannot exist without being underpinned by institutions, whether they be banks or pension funds or insurance companies or government agencies; institutions cannot avoid sinking beneath their monolithic bureaucracy, without a full measure of entrepreneurial dynamism. All commercial activities need to combine discriminating entrepreneurial enterprise with institutional financial and management follow-through, and though confrontations have inevitably occurred and will occur, there is not – nor should there be – a hostility between the essential spirit of the entrepreneur and of the institution. Indeed the well-being of any country's economy, depends to a material extent, on a responsive working marriage between the two cultures.

The rise and fall of the secondary banks in the 1960s and early 1970s constituted an amazing era in Britain's banking history. Why do banks have crisis after crisis, whether they be primary or secondary banks? Why do banks keep making unsound loans? Why were the secondaries, the fringe banks, allowed to proliferate? How did they get to the point where they could undermine the country's banking system? Who was at fault? Such questions form part of the Cedar Story. But an over-riding truism is that the successful outcome of any human endeavour depends upon the right men being in the right place at the right time. Led by the Governor, the Deputy Governor and the chairman of the four clearing banks, the country was saved from the dire consequences of the domino effect, of the contagion of fear, of a major banking crash, but only just, and only because true leadership was available when it was most needed. These heroes in the City – they were nothing less – launched a support plan called 'The Lifeboat'. It was off the slipway before dawn, they were at its helm for month after month, displaying rare determination, stamina, courage and professionalism, and though many like the Morrisons, were drowned or beached, many more were brought into a safe haven. It all began on the night that Cedar was saved.

*　　　　　*　　　　　*

The phone calls from the Bank of England started on the afternoon of the previous day, on Tuesday 18 December. First to be called was Lord De L'Isle, chairman of Phoenix Assurance. Could he meet the Governor tomorrow morning before the others? Yes. Just after 8.30 am? Thank you. Then Hugh Jenkins, the director general of the coal industry pension fund. He was out of town on business, but when he arrived late that evening, there was a message for him from his office. The Bank of England had phoned; a meeting with the Governor on Cedar at 9.00 am next morning, confirmed in his absence. A call to Burton Johnson, chairman of the electricity supply pension fund. Tomorrow? On Cedar at 9 am? A meeting with the Governor. Yes. Then Cob Stenham, financial director of Unilever and chairman of its pension fund. A meeting on Cedar at 9 am. Could Mr Stenham see the Governor at 9 am. Yes. Confirmed. Finally Barclays, Cedar's bankers. Here the phone thoroughfare from Threadneedle to Lombard was on familiar ground. Timothy Bevan, deputy chairman of the country's largest bank and chairman of the UK division, and also Deryk Vander Weyer, Barclays' senior general manager. Tomorrow morning at 8.45? Cedar? Yes.

Phoenix first, then Barclays, then the three pension funds, Coal, Electricity and Unilever. An adroit sequence. All of them, top men. No assistants. An unambiguous echelon. Very hush-hush; their colleagues were either not informed at all or were told to keep it confidential. Each person invited, already well aware of Cedar's travails, appreciated that if the Governor thought it necessary to have a meeting at such short notice, the Cedar problem had become alarming. Very alarming. What only the Governor and the Deputy

6

Governor fully appreciated was that the alarm was not only over Cedar, but over the whole banking system.

The same quiet persistent reverberations, were targeted elsewhere. The modulations of the arrangements were relaxed, the enquiries were confidential and very low key. At Samuel Montagu, Cedar's merchant bank, John Gillum was called. Days earlier he had been in touch with Jim Keogh, Principal of the Bank's Discount Office, and he had been ruffled by Keogh's response, which seemed out of touch with the stark reality of a deposit run, and Gillum had told him so. Now he received a call. Mr Gillum, can you be at the Bank of England tomorrow? Yes, of course. Also your clients. All the executive directors? Yes. Would you please advise them. Mr Gillum did, and with native merchant banking instinct he also advised Michael Morrison and his cousin David Fischer, the joint managing directors to be prepared to attend before the others.

Discreet calls were made elsewhere directly and indirectly: to Hambros, the financial advisers, and to Coward Chance, the lawyers, both acting for the institutions; to Cazenove, the stockbrokers; to Herbert Smith, the lawyers acting for Cedar – each with the same exceedingly polite request, could they please make themselves available? The assemblage was in formation. The preparation for the rescue of Cedar had commenced. And with the most sensitive calls of all made to the four clearing-bank chairmen, the preparation to deal with the onslaught of the banking crisis was underway.

*   *   *

The storm had broken in the City of London.

ONE

The Seeding of Cedar

One can easily be equivocal about immigrant families, yet man was always a migrant, the wafts of human evolution having shaped the most fabulously varied races, creeds and sects; always impelled by a supreme gift for enquiry, he has wanderlusted with the instincts of a true nomad over hills, mountains, plains and deserts and across rivers, lakes and oceans, on rafts and canoes, on boats and ships, reaching new lands and new worlds, surviving, seeding, settling, assimilating and eventually becoming wholly indigenous. Emigrants evolved into immigrants and within a winter or two they became settlers, and within a generation or two they became endemically home-grown with ever-fading memories of their ancient customs.

An extraordinary culmination of these varied restless wanderings over the centuries, was the mass of huddled Europeans who, at the turn of the nineteenth century sailed on promises and hopes from the old to the veritable New World. It was a phenomenal period of human migrancy and it included a large exodus of Jews, mostly from Russia and Poland, who were forced to seek haven in a less harsh political and economic climate. The largest number of these Jewish emigrants went to the United States; a small but significant number fled to England.

In Britain until the turn of the century, the number of Jews was relatively small; most of the native English population had probably never met one, though a few may have heard of Rothschild or Disraeli. But as their numbers enlarged three-or four-fold, as the dark-clad Goya-like passengers disgorged from the boats clasping their shapeless bundles, they were welcomed, received and looked after by their own, by the previous recent influx or by the small community of Anglo-

Jews who had been in the country since Cromwell. These early seventeenth- and eighteenth-century Sephardic Jews originally deriving from Spain and Portugal considered themselves superior to the later arrivals, the Ashkenazy Jews of the more Eastern reaches. Undernourished bewildered survivors, the new arrivals were a ragbag, hollow-eyed flock, literally spilling on to the surrounding London docks and soon germinating a few hundred yards further on, in the Jewish East End, now legendary for the nourishment of its special culture – the sanctity of family life, the survival of the fleetest and not only the fittest, the veneration for creativity and learning, and not least, the striving for material success. Sir Marcus Samuel, founder of Shell Oil and of his family bank M. Samuel, Sir Jack Cohen, the founder of Tesco Stores, Sir Charles Clore and Lord Rayne were outstanding examples of this strain of Ashkenazy East End Jew.

The small Baltic states of Estonia, Latvia and Lithuania were somehow set apart from the rest of Eastern Europe and concentrated more upon scholasticism and less on trade. My own father and mother were products of this Baltic stock, emigrating to South Africa before settling in London. They were Lithuanian born and bred, reared in Vilna, a university town (the oldest in the Soviet Union) and a respected seat of Christian and Jewish learning, where Gordons had lived for hundreds of years; Vilna, now Vilnius, the capital city of Lithuania, which for centuries housed the greatest Jewish library in the world, produced over the years an extravagant number of scholars, teachers, writers, musicians, philosophers, businessmen, and, it must also be said, the largest number of educated blockheads in the diaspora, amongst whom it must also be said, I include one or two of my own brothers.

In our family the Vilna mores have faded, although I have generations-old letters written in precise Russian calligraphy by my mother, describing Vilna activities, new plays, new marriages and new books. One of the most gracious and delightful telephone calls I have ever received was from John Ogdon who telephoned me from Vilna before his piano recital to tell me, in his halting unintrusive manner, what a lovely town I had originally come from and how charmed he was by its lazy river and sturdy villas. Another Baltic city of similar renown is the celebrated port of Riga, which like Vilna also has its grand progeny, its most distinguished being Isaiah Berlin, whose father and mother, endowed with great intelligence and culture, were friends of my parents; and it was Shaie, as his parents called their only child and as we knew him, who unfolded the exquisite wonders of a truly profound intellect for my wife Nadia and I one summer on the beach of Santa Magharita.

And it was from Riga that Jack Morrison's parents came as immigrants at the turn of the century, sojourning in Leeds and Manchester for a while, before settling in Glasgow, and in no time at all becoming leading citizens of 'their' city, whose dynamism and thrustful spirit has long been unduly and unfairly overshadowed by the stigma of the Gorbals.

In Glasgow, the Morrisons were different, and what made them different was Jack's mother, Edith Morrison. No ordinary matriarch, she was a full-time wife, a full-time business lady, a full-time social worker, and with seven children – four daughters and three sons – a full-time mother, each child having to show unstinting respect towards their father for, although Edith Morrison ruled the roost at home and in the business, Edith Morrison never let them forget, in her constant determination to stabilise family life, that he was after all, the head of the family.

Apart from her family, and her family business, she had two passions – sewing and music. She was already a court dressmaker in Riga before the age of fifteen, and it was through her sewing that she was able to build up her formidable family dressmaking business, until the Morrison dress shops proliferated throughout the country. It was also through her sewing that she performed her social and charitable work, concentrating on training girls and women in dressmaking and helping to save those fortunate enough to come within her encompassing largesse from the worst exigencies of the Glasgow scrapheap.

It was through her passion for music, however, that she derived her greatest pride and contentment. Few events gave Edith Morrison more happiness than to listen to her three sons playing trios at the Glasgow Athenaeum; the oldest, Peter, played the piano, the middle son, Hymie, the cello, and the youngest, Jack, the violin. All three were exceptionally fine musicians, with Peter himself having sufficient talent to become the first Scot – his Glasgow accent is as rich today as it ever was – to win a scholarship to the Royal College of Music, becoming over the years one of its most generous benefactors.

Nadia and I first met the matriarch when she was already in her eighties, residing in a luxurious flat in Grosvenor Square overlooking the American Embassy. It was the violinist who introduced us. Her priorities were as usual in order: I was involved with her son Jack and grandson Michael in some business called Cedar; I was merely a man who worked in a City bank. But Nadia, a world-famous ballerina, an artiste, was different. She was something special; so Jack had scored in his mother's eyes.

*   *   *

Having introduced Jack Morrison, the central character of the Cedar Story, it is now time for me to introduce my wife Nadia and myself.

I first met Nadia when I was an undergraduate at Cambridge. The Sadlers Wells, the pre-cursor of the Royal Ballet Company, was appearing at the Arts Theatre in a mixed repertoire which included Fokine's *Carnival*. Nadia danced the role of Columbine and her radiance spread through the entire theatre. Afterwards I gave a party for the company; all of us, dancers and undergraduates, were aged under twenty, and the dancers could not understand how we could lounge around without jobs and we could not understand how they had become artistes and money earners when they were so young. As we grew older, we were to learn that perceptions have a reality of their own and bear little resemblance to the true facts of life.

Michael Mendelsohn, later my best man, and later still a poet and an anthropologist, was already known as being as knowledgeable and erudite as any ballet critic, and it was he who introduced me to Nadia saying, 'She is going to be one of the world's great dancers'. As I was to learn to my own great admiration and that of many others, he had not exaggerated.

At Cambridge I read English and Law. When I first came down, I travelled to New York and worked there for a shortish while in my father's office. I wrote him to say that I thought he should close it down. His New York associates put me on a boat to Cape Town – then the longest sea voyage possible without touching land. In South Africa, where Nadia was born, I travelled throughout the country and then worked in my father's office in Cape Town. I wrote my father to suggest that he should sell out to his partner before he was cheated out of everything. I was soon put on a boat at Cape Town for South-ampton.

I had already decided what I wanted to do: to work in the City. But my father felt that I should work with him in the family engineering business. It was located in Wembley and our arguments were a fair match to the roar of the nearby football crowds, although our affection for each other was too precious to allow serious differences of opinion on business to intervene. After some accountancy, when the only thing

I learnt was that I had a passion for reading balance sheets, I joined the *Investors' Chronicle*, the sister paper of the *Financial Times*, then the most superior journal of any for analysing balance sheets and valuing shares. For me it was a stepping stone to joining a merchant bank, and the *Chronicle* only took me on because I was prepared to work at no salary. Whilst there I learnt that I also had a passion for property structuring; not buildings but financial engineering. I became the *Chronicle's* first property editor, and it became the first UK news or investment journal to have a dedicated property section. I stayed there for about eighteen months, until I had to leave because I had been showered with an embarrassing number of offers from stockbrokers, jobbers, property companies and banks to join them. I decided to accept one particular offer, which was to join the largest property development company, City Centre Properties, as its financial consultant. The company was headed by two *anciens* tycoons, Jack Cotton and Charles Clore. They had merged their great property interests, and their sensational property marriage ended in an even more sensational divorce three years later. I wrote an account of their relationship in *The Two Tycoons*.*

The loudest and most enjoyable laugh I had at the *Chronicle* was nothing to do with the journal, but everything to do with my rapport with my father and his sense of humour. One day he asked me to have lunch with him, an enjoyable occasional occurrence. This time, in describing why he particularly wanted to see me, he was laughing so much, I too started to have the giggles. You advised me to close down the New York office, he said. I didn't, I was wrong. You told me to sell out in South Africa; I didn't till too late. I was wrong. Now do you remember you said I should check the wages system at Wembley.

I thought; I did what? Then I remembered. During my accountancy, in an early lesson, we were told that a good auditor should enquire whether the wages clerk had ever taken a holiday and if you found that he had not then you knew there was a problem. I recalled asking my father after that early lesson, whether his wages man at Wembley had been on holiday recently and received a flea in the ear from him, for being such an irreverent instant expert. Amid the laughter, my father told me that, being bored one recent afternoon, he idly asked his wages manager – it was not a small job, there were several hundred on the

---

* Published by Hamish Hamilton whose then Chairman and Chief Executive was Christopher Sinclair-Stevenson.

payroll – where he was going on holiday. The wages manager replied that he was not taking one. My father insisted that he should do so and promptly asked the auditors to come in to check the figures. They found (it was not easy, being cleverly and ironically hidden on false holiday payments) that around £25,000 had been taken. My father was particularly cross, he told me, because he had not only lost a very nice wages manager, but as the profits had been understated, there was an additional tax liability. By then we were both in hysterics.

The Royal Ballet's vintage period was during the 1950s and 1960s, until its remarkable founder, Dame Ninette de Valois retired at the age of sixty-five, at least twenty years too early. In the 1950s the maturity of the company was brilliantly reflected in the way it was able to perform the classics, *Sleeping Beauty*, *Swan Lake*, *Giselle*, *Coppelia*, with such abundant rich talent, that for example a different Swan Queen, a genuine ballerina, appeared each night in a single week. In the early 1960s the great excitement at the Royal Ballet was the success of Frederick Ashton's *La Fille Mal Gardée*, which was not only an instant masterpiece, but an instant classic, with Nadia creating the role of La Fille.

It was around this time that we first met Edith Morrison. She admired anyone who could achieve things on their own, and she and Nadia took to each other, although it was to Edith Morrison's repeated regret that Nadia never found the time to visit her famous sewing circle held every Monday afternoon in a special workroom off Lower Oxford Street; this was her special joy in her last years and when she described the way she taught her ladies the intricacies of dressmaking, mainly childrens' clothes sent to the needy in Israel, her eyes would light up with youthful enthusiasm. On no occasion that I ever saw her did she look or talk like an old woman. Short and stout, she had a very handsome appearance and was extremely well turned out in every detail, as if she was on her way to have tea at Buckingham Palace with the old Queen Mary. In possessing a quiet but firm propriety, she raised standards of behaviour without raising so much as an eyebrow or a voice. She had an endearing old-world sense of decorum, extolling personal achivement, particularly artistic, above any other, emanating from the old traditions of her Baltic upbringing from which she had learnt to derive more pleasure from music-making than from money-making. On her ninetieth birthday, two years before she died in 1966, she was given a lavish dinner party at Claridges by her children. She sat in her honoured place with calm tranquillity and pride, and even Sir Isaac Wolfson, one of Glasgow's greatest progenies felt it was a special privilege to be in attendance at the celebration of this great lady.

Much earlier, however, an event of lasting sorrow had occurred which was to haunt her for the rest of her days. It arose from an explosive intermingled family scandal implicating the spouses of not one, but two of her children – Jack, her youngest son, and Rosemary, her second daughter.

The actual scandal was a bizarre entanglement. Jack and his wife Anne, both in their early forties, had parted and divorced. It was a messy separation leading to possible court action, an aggrieved Scottish wife – Jack had strayed and had been found out – was entitled to half her husband's property and a third of the movables (only the Scots could have sustained into modern usage such a delightful legal term), something which cut raspingly against Jack's mercenary grain. A settlement was finally agreed after bitter arguments; this in itself caused sufficient disruption. But then his ex-wife decided to re-marry, and the man she chose was Rosemary's estranged husband, who was himself on such bad terms with Jack that it was said their mutual dislike of Jack brought them to the altar. The resulting distress and acrimony sent tremors in all directions, taking many years for the disturbing oscillations between the various children to abate. It was doubtful whether the matriarch ever got over the shock. With a trio of sons and a quartet of daughters she managed to keep the incipient family turbulence under control, and allied to her childrens' respect and affection for her, a working family relationship was reimposed. Notwithstanding, her special motherly feelings and watchful anxieties for Jack remained steadfast throughout the shockwaves and was visibly demonstrated by her having him to stay with her until he was well into his fifties.

In Jack's ever-sensitive, uncertain relationship with his two brothers, Peter and Hymie, the incident from beginning to end was a fraternal disaster. In physical appearance the trio looked very much like brothers, the same short stature, the same baldish round faces, the same bustling alive expressions, however the other two had always looked on Jack as a difficult brother who, though ebullient and eloquent, was showy and a talker, and though more successful and more wealthy, was not quite a fool – he was far from being a fool – but foolish. In Jack's restless aspirations, it was always his two brothers whom he wanted to impress. This need was evident in all his activities, whether business or social; he had a constant nagging desire to persuade his brothers that they had misjudged him. To my mind much of Jack's conceit and high-handed ways were a gloss covering a deep-felt anxiety that no matter how much he tried, no matter how much he achieved, he was unable to dislodge the brotherly disdain – which, after his divorce, was totally irreversible. He fought for a respect he felt was his due, but he was not to earn it, though they were not able to hide their jealousy when he was on the crest in the immediate years before the Cedar collapse.

In 1957, by which time there were hundreds of Morrison dress shops throughout the country, the family decided to sell up. Until then for most of their working lives, the brothers worked well enough within the stable structure of their mother's remarkable commercial and family constraints, though there had been many arguments. There were regrets and tears over the decision to sell, and different reasons have been given by different people. Jack told me it was to allow each member of the family to go his or her own way. That may be part of the story; it is far more likely to have been the wise judgement of the matriarch seeking family harmony. At any rate, after the sale of the business Peter and Hymie stayed on, working for the new owner, and it was Jack who went his own way. The family received more than £50 million in today's terms and each child had their portion, the three boys taking the lion's share.

The new owner of the famous Morrison business was the inimitable Sir Isaac Wolfson. Wolfson, for my money, has earned a chapter in any history. He was also in effect the patron saint of the Glasgow Jews, many of whom seemed to have a native understanding of the business of credit and lending. Wolfson was a figure who had a long-term overwhelming influence on the Morrisons and he was rarely out of their thoughts. He was one of the greatest entrepreneurs of this century, and not only did he hold the unique distinction of endowing a college in his name in Cambridge as well as in Oxford, he virtually and almost single-handedly established the UK mail order industry. His business credo, on which he built his great business, was simple and direct: 'Don't worry about bad debts because the British public is honest'. He was utterly brilliant in his timing on each transaction and in getting what he wanted; I have described elsewhere the way he purchased Jack Cotton's stake in his company City Centre Properties, to Cotton's permanent surprise. Even Charles Clore paid Wolfson the rare compliment of expressing his admiration for this entrepreneurial colossus. In any business and charity corridor, the name Isaac meant only one person; it was never necessary to add the surname.

In the immediate post-War years he was the most talked-about businessman in the country. He was particularly remembered by all Glaswegians, he was their own home-grown genius, and as he strode onto ever increasing business triumphs, all the other major retailers looked up to him, particularly his shrewd competitor and fellow Scot, Hugh Fraser, the founder of the The House of Fraser and the owner of Harrods, both men similar not only in their blissful marriages but also in their proud acknowledgement that their success was due to their wives. Wolfson was held in awe by all and was made a baronet in 1962: no knighthood for him.

During the mid-1960s, whilst I was at Hambros, I triggered a transaction in which, with Unilever, we purchased a Wolfson-controlled company called Commercial Plastics, and which may have led me to a much closer relationship with the Wolfsons than the one I had with the Morrisons. My father knew Isaac, and I had met him on occasions, originally through his personal lawyer, Alexander Stone, a highly respected Glasgow solicitor. I was also friendly with his son Leonard, for whom I had a great liking, and who, apart from the present Lord Thomson of Fleet, is the only completely normal yet distinguished son of a great father I have come across.

After the Commercial Plastics transaction, Wolfson was clearly impressed with how rapidly we had consummated the deal – he was also impressed with the Hambros' mystique and with the fact that Unilever was even larger than his own company. Wolfson owned, through one of his family trusts, the Anglo-Portuguese Bank, and one day completely out of the blue, he asked me whether I would be interested in leaving Hambros to head up Anglo-Portuguese – as a partner, he was quick to point out. This appealed to me. I said yes, but was equally quick to point out, only if his son were the chairman: 'You see Isaac, I don't know how to put this, but I would feel more comfortable'. He laughed and said, 'What you really mean is that you don't want me to interfere'. I let that pass. More seriously I suggested the name be changed from Anglo-Portuguese to Wolfson and Co. The quicksilver mind behind the handsome quicksilver brow reacted immediately. 'Not Wolfson and Co but Wolfson and Son. Ruth is having another baby. If it's a boy we'll talk again, if it's another girl . . .'

There was no need to finish the sentence. A poignant chord had been struck. His son already had three daughters. A dynastic bank with his son and grandson and the baronetcy, yes of course, but if they had another daughter? They did have another daughter, a delightful girl, now herself a mother, and the Anglo-Portuguese bank was sold to others, a long way from the inspired musings and ambitions and creative wonders of the great Isaac.

Wolfson's decisions were quick and distinctive, and during the 1950s and 1960s he acquired businesses faster than anyone had ever done before. These were the first post-War takeovers, all on agreed terms; he pioneered this non-hostile process as Charles Clore pioneered the first hostile takeovers; whilst Hugh Fraser, his sharp nose also able to smell a deal a mile off, with cigarette drooping from his mouth and trilby on his head, picked up most of their best ideas, always going out of his way to express his personal gratitude, a courtesy which was not welcomed with particular warmth by his two rivals. Wolfson's company, Great Universal Stores, was just that, great universal stores. He acquired mostly family retail businesses, similar to the Morrisons, and he ate them up, one after another, before breakfast. It was said that the more stingy the terms he offered, the earlier the meeting took place in the morning; there was an active appraisal about Wolfson's technique, down to evaluating the price differential between a meeting with him at 7.30 am and one at say 8.30 am. In nearly all the acquisitions the family which sold out stayed on as management.

In the case of the Morrisons, Isaac knew whom he wanted and whom he did not want. He wanted Peter, who spent an increasing amount of his time on the Royal College of Music, and most certainly he wanted Hymie, who subsequently became one of the closest business friends of both Wolfsons, father and son; but for Jack Morrison there was no place. Did Isaac not care for him? When I pressed Jack about Isaac he said he had been asked to stay on but that he had wanted to go his own way with his own son, and when I prodded further, perhaps too pointedly, he said that he most emphatically did not want to work for Isaac, although he encouraged his son Michael to have a learning stint in the Wolfson organisation for a short while.

Jack was fifty-two. Divorced, he was a ladies' man free to exercise his charms without constraint, free to tickle his two happily-married brothers' habitual disdain with a modicum of envy, and now cash rich, free to roam into any business activity which took his fancy. But what business? Hitherto he had spent all his life in commercial harness with his brothers, within the matriarchal dressage. He was now able to trot out on his own for the first time. But into which field?

*   *   *

It was at this juncture that Jack was guided by another Glaswegian, another colt of the Wolfson breed, young Isadore Walton, the chairman and controlling shareholder of Scotland's largest quoted property investment company. Izzy Walton, the progenitor of Cedar, indeed the implanter of its seed.

Walton's father was a successful Glasgow moneylender, an occupation which although not ignoble was regarded as being slightly unbecoming. To young Izzy Walton, in his world, the Wolfsons were near royalty, whilst the rich musical Morrisons were amongst the aristocrats. To know Peter, Hymie and Jack was a social privilege, which also meant, of course, a wonderful business connection, and Izzy was rather proud of his early association with the sons of the eminent Edith. His acquaintance with Jack matured into a sort of friendship, where Jack was somewhat patronising, generally looking down upon the hard-working, not so poor lad, who was doing so well setting up his own property business, making contacts on the veritable shop-floor level, concentrating almost entirely on Scottish cities, working closely with Scottish real estate agents, with Scottish institutions and Scottish bankers. Walton, not surprisingly, named his company Scottish Metropolitan Properties, and by careful acquisition and careful financing, steadfastly allergic to any form of risk taking, he built up a superb property portfolio. By the early 1950s, at the moment when the unreined Jack Morrison was surveying the horizon and considering his options, Walton had achieved a stock exchange quotation and a very respectable reputation.

Walton became one of Glasgow's most highly regarded financial and social stalwarts, admired for his fair dealing, competence and reliability. He was a man who never ventured to take one step forward when half a step would suffice, and when embarking on what was always in his mind an epic exploration, he was always tentative, travelling straight forward on his journey, plodding ahead solidly and painstakingly, never making any mistakes, or if he did, never allowing it to be known. He had an ardour for reading the small print, in fact not only reading and studying it, but understanding it in most respects far better than the lawyers who had done the drafting. He was thorough and meticulous to a fault, turning over every stone whilst determining his judgement. Anyone who met him knew that he was over-fastidious, but accepted it not as a deterrent in doing business with him, but because of the cast of his character, regarded his extreme caution as an old-fashioned virtue. He was a man for whom I had considerable respect.

I had watched and evaluated his progress when I was property editor of the *Investors' Chronicle* and indeed it was through my job there that we met. He phoned me one day to say he had bumped into a friend of mine and could he discuss something I had written about his company, not to question my value judgement (he was too canny and intelligent to be drawn into that grey area, although like many businessmen who avowed no interest in publicity, he had long before come to the conclusion that it was never harmful to be friendly with journalists), but to draw my attention to the small print I had missed on one of his property loan stocks. This was a financing whereby the borrower was able to substitute the security on an ingenious basis which Izzy had himself formulated. What prompted him to phone me was not to point out how clever he was, but to underline for general interest a fresh method of charging property with more flexibility, and on studying it, I found that it certainly did deserve serious comment.

His cleverness and his prudence, reflected in the impressive growth of his company, inevitably meant that his Scottish Metropolitan Company would outgrow its tartan-imposed confines and that he would have to start looking south of the border. This he did, still tentative, still careful, still taking no chances. Many of his Glasgow friends and acquaintances, becoming richer after the war, some extremely rich, had already left Glasgow for London like the Wolfsons and the Morrisons, or were taking flats or permanent or semi-permanent suites in hotels. A favourite was the Grosvenor House Hotel in Park Lane where Walton's son who became chairman of Scottish Met after his father died, still maintains an abode.

Walton had an intellect well above the average for a property man. He was also a man for whom it was easy to feel affection. In the early 1960s, to his permanent surprise – the reaction of a man who preached moderation – he suffered a heart attack. Then, with typical caution, he set about re-tidying his affairs and papers, seeing that all his personal effects were in even more impeccable order, deliberately over-solicitous, like a housewife fussing over an immaculate linen cupboard. He decided to appoint further trustees, and I was astonished when he invited me. I had gone to Scotland to visit some institutions, and arrangements were made to dine with Izzy in the bleak restaurant of Glasgow's leading hotel, after first having drinks with his wife and their son at his home. The heart attack had obviously jolted him, and his unexpected invitation to become a trustee was considered with discrimination. I have always believed that the old-fashioned legal obligations and responsibilities of a trustee are grotesquely out of proportion and so I declined, telling him that I did not feel up to the task of reading all the small print. I still remember his laugh, a sort of chortle, impeded by his sinus.

If it had not been for Izzy's enquiring mind and the knowledge he gained through his father, there would never have been a Cedar. Although brought up in the ambience of the moneylending business Izzy had become addicted to property rather than to lending. Property was his passion, although he was also a fair expert in property financing and property law. In the first-ever conversation I had with him on Cedar he said, 'It's time you fellows down there were taught a little bit of real law, by which I mean Scottish law; in Scotland we are the reasonable man and also the pragmatic man; in England you are just the reasonable man and then not that all of the time', followed by the inevitable Walton chortle or wheeze. Not involved directly in his father's business, he told me that if he had been, he may well have started his own lending business rather than Scottish Metropolitan. Nevertheless, though addicted to the business of property investment, he was intrigued by rules and regulations on lending, particularly lending on second mortgages.

His agile brain was bound by a sinewy curiosity. It was natural, therefore, that he, a Scottish businessman having learnt at his father's knee how people made money out of lending money, would have grasped more quickly and better than most the intricacies of Scottish law and Scottish lending in the borrowing area in general, and in the borrowing area on one's own dwelling in particular, an area where Scotland had traditionally been more advanced, or 'pragmatic', in his words, than England. When Jack Morrison turned to his old friend, still patronising him, even though Walton had by now become Scotland's premier property man, it was not surprising that the distillation of Izzy's thinking would be in two specific areas – property and lending.

It was also not surprising that Jack, motivated by his need to demonstrate his fraternal mettle, to be a success and to make money on his own, should be immediately attracted to going into both these areas. Many of the Morrison shops had been introduced to the brothers by Walton the property expert. Jack Morrison could readily see the money-making possibilities in property, although it must be admitted, he was always the first to admit that he left the intricacies to others, particularly his son, whilst retaining the credit for advising on the bigger matters. And of course lending money on interest appealed to him; it works for you twenty-four hours a day, every day, he once said to me as if he had made a totally new discovery. As soon as the dialogue with Walton began, Jack brought Michael into the discussions. He too bubbled with enthusiasm. This was what he wanted, to work closely with his father.

And so the property area became known under the all-embracing Amalgamated Securities Limited, and the lending area became Cedar Holdings Limited.

Both these Morrison companies were, therefore, to a large extent the brainchild of one Isadore Walton, their fellow Glaswegian and another member of the inner-circle Wolfson club, a small rotund figure, with a bald head and small glittering highly-active intelligent eyes, a strong reed-like voice, rich in its border accent, interspersed with snorts and grunts and catarrhal clearings of the throat; the careful go-one-step-forward man, then pause, then look over your shoulder, once, twice, then go back half a step, pause, think, look down, turn the stone over, scratch the grains, form your judgement, look over your shoulder once, then read the small print again. This was the man who was the catalyst in launching Jack's new career, not only in property but also in banking, who first introduced me to Jack, and who, when it came to the Morrison glory years, was pushed aside and ignored – no more need for Jack and Michael to listen to Izzy insistently proffering his very good advice: to be careful, to be cautious, to be prudent.

The Morrisons were nonchalant, patronising and indifferent; why take a step forward and pause when you can hop, skip or jump three steps forward? And when Jack and Michael fell from financial grace with sickening thuds, Izzy was there, loyal to the end; but the friendship had dwindled to a figment of what it was. Jack could not look Izzy in the eye: advice ignored and subsequently proved to be correct is the poisoned chalice of friendship.

I sat at a reception in the City with other guests to mark the launching of the public quotation of Amalgamated Securities. Although the room was sparsely furnished and distinctly on the meagre side, there was a dias at the top table. Sitting in the centre, was the chairman, Jack Morrison, next to him Michael; also on high were the brokers to the issue and the other directors, one of whom was Izzy. Jack stood up to speak, immaculately dressed, navy blue suit, beautifully cut waistcoat, white shirt, matching blue silk tie, and described in measured tones the quality of his company's portfolio and the careful policy of selecting high-grade properties which were well let and well located. You would have thought that he had been a property man all his life and the chairman of a public company for most of it. He was articulate, a goodish speaker, using his stammer with some deliberation, and was peculiarly effective in his wayward manner of looking in all directions except at his audience.

I had been invited because of my job at the *Investors' Chronicle*. Property was the buzzword at the stock exchange. There was a new issue boom, most of the companies taking advantage of the boom being property companies of differing qualities and sizes. I had become the City's leading expert in this sector and did not have the time nor the inclination to attend all the lunches and presentations of the seemingly endless number of new property companies coming to the market. In the case of Amalgamated Securities, I would have restricted myself to a brief mention in the *Chronicle*, there did not appear to be anything special or unusual about Amalgamated, except that it had Walton, the chairman of a well-respected quoted property company on its board who was, as it happened, the person who had specially asked me to attend.

Financial public relations were just beginning to impinge on the mechanics of a stock exchange quotation. Hitherto the interest of the press was spurred more by advertising possibilities than by editorial potential. The property entrepreneurs, however, were by their very nature more alive to the benefits of good publicity than industrialists and bankers, most of whom, in this period, regarded the press with universal distaste. The press in any event was not nearly as professional and as assured as it is today. In fact it was the property boom of the early 1960s which did much to convert the then advertising-oriented financial press into the news-oriented investigative press of today.

The otherwise humdrum Amalgamated Securities event would have been forgotten, but it has remained a vivid memory not because it was the occasion when I first met Jack and Michael Morrison, but more because of my recollection of the chairman's son: a vivid cameo of a young man who revered his father, listening intently to his every word, watchful and affectionate, and clearly in the grip of some form of father worship.

The formalities of the presentation over, Izzy introduced me. Jack Morrison's response, as always when meeting people who might be useful to him in whatever capacity, whether a banker, girl, journalist or policeman, was instantly over-effusive: yes, he had read my stuff in the *Investors' Chronicle* every week; yes, I had galvanised the property sector in the City; yes, he knew how friendly I was with Izzy; yes, was I free for dinner that night, or the next, or any night the following week? And yes, he and Michael, who was at this moment pushed forward, fresh-faced, pleasant-looking, well-mannered, were both overjoyed that I had attended. I should, he added, be aware that Amal, which is how he referred to his company and which, eventually was what we all called the company, was a very special company and though he did not really wish to talk about money, the fact was that the family, the Morrison family, had substantial outside resources in money and connections, and – an evident master of the non sequitur – as Michael and I were of the same generation, we should be able to understand the many problems of life more easily and we should be able to grow up together in unison and harmony.

As I was to learn later over the years, this was vintage Jack Morrison, rambling and opportunistic. His wish to be an immediate intimate was undisguised, but his declaration of our brotherhood or cousinship was nevertheless wide of its target. I expressed regret that the evenings were not free. He did not seem to mind. Yet soon after, he arrived unexpectedly with a girlfriend in Nadia's dressing room to congratulate her after a performance. This was an unusual occurrence at Covent Garden; many a formidable person found it was by no means easy to get past dear old Joe who secured the Opera House stage door; it was apparent that Jack had sufficient panache to sweep through any guarded entrance. But the image of this son-father adoration has always remained, and Jack was right about Michael and I.

We did become friends, but the fact that we did so was a testimonial to our own personal and business liking for each other rather than to Jack's pushy self-interest. This encounter with Jack and Michael Morrison, comical in some respects, charming in others, at the debut of Amal's existence as a public company, was the result, as I was to discover, of a seed carefully planted by Izzy Walton to bring me into an association with the Morrisons and to play a role in the growth of Cedar.

In *The Two Tycoons* I describe how Nadia and I sailed to New York in the early 1960s. The Royal Ballet's tour was to commence in New York and as there was a merciful gap in Nadia's normally rigorous timetable, we decided to take advantage of this by sailing on the *Queen Mary*, a majestic passenger ship, unlike her cruising cousin, the floating casino code-named *QE2*. A contributory factor was that in those days I did not care to fly; perhaps it was the real reason, and perhaps, without my knowledge, Nadia had arranged it this way.

A few days before sailing, Izzy phoned me at the *Chronicle*. The crackle on the line was not a bad connection but his sibilant wheeze. He was coming to London shortly and wondered if I was free to have lunch with him. I explained I could not make it because we were sailing to New York. I was greeted with a volcanic eruption which, when it subsided, was his ecstatic surmise that Jack Morrison might be sailing on the same ship. I have since wondered if this was one coincidence too many, but have generally come to the conclusion that coincidences are a positive and definite ingredient in the mysterious rhythm of life and the coincidence of Jack Morrison sailing to New York on the same ship as Nadia and myself was, as it turns out, one of the most significant of my business life.

On the ship, Jack in true character, lost no time in leapfrogging cousinhood to brotherhood, not however a brotherhood with Jack – even he would recognise that misrelationship – but a brotherhood with Michael. I was, he was making it clear, the brother Michael never had. Nadia was bemused, especially when Jack, not over-delicately, asked her if she could use her good offices to have him placed at the Captain's table. In those days the Captain's table was reserved for distinguished passengers and the liner's directors, and I have since conjectured that if we had not already been seated there, we might not have been able to escape Jack's vicissitudes at every meal, which in turn might well have led us to being on very much less good terms by the end of the voyage.

In our cabin before the departure there were flowers, fruit and chocolates, from family and friends. There was a particularly large bouquet from Jack Morrison. The card was addressed to Nadia and said something to the effect that it was God's wish that we were all together on the same ship, that it was not only a heavenly blessing but also that the flowers were a small token of his prodigious admiration. There was, too, a large buff envelope addressed to me. Inside was a typed note from Jack dated some days earlier clipped to a few typewritten sheets of figures. The note stated that he was enclosing details of a company he and Michael had started which he would like to discuss with me. These sheets were the profit and loss account and the balance sheet of a company called Cedar Holdings Limited. I glanced at the papers before putting them away. Some decades later, prompted by hindsight and a thousand memories, the wishful thought occurs that perhaps there and then I should have opened the porthole and dropped the papers overboard. Taking subsequent events into account, if I had done so, it may have altered an important course in all our lives.

Hardly out of Southampton Sound Jack collared me on Cedar and, to my great surprise, got me interested in the by-ways of Scottish lending and the second mortgage business. He had, I quickly realised, a very superficial knowledge, most questions were parried by saying that Izzy or Michael would explain. I remember asking Nadia during the voyage whether it was possible that Jack, learning from Walton when we were sailing, had changed his bookings accordingly. She thought this not only far-fetched but overly self-important; I am still dubious. Jack Morrison could go to extraordinary lengths to achieve his ends.

To most people the intricacies of lending and of borrowing are a source of anxiety or of boredom; it need not be the latter. Lending and borrowing are fascinating activities, both part of the mainstream of life. They are also the positive and negative of the same process; the in and the out; each is one side of the same coin; each is the complement of the other; neither can exist without the other; if you are borrowing someone else is lending, and if you are lending somebody else is borrowing. A bank, however, is both a borrower and a lender, trading in confidence whilst using the symbols of money. The very early traders, the merchants, dealing only in tangible goods, were barterers; there was an exchange of one thing for another, rudimentary money as such had other practical uses, it came in the form of pepper, salt, silver or gold, only later in coin or printed paper. There was no such thing as credit until the IOU was created, thus allowing the lender to lend and the borrower to borrow; this was the true beginning of moneylending or banking as we know it today. The IOU was the first manifestation of commercial trust by mercantile man. By exchanging an IOU in return for money or for goods an entirely new *modus operandi* was created: one party was able to re-lend that money, that deposit, to someone else or to give credit on the security of the goods, immovable or movable, on real or personal estate.

In trade there is a buyer and a seller, and the buyer and the seller have to be two different entities: you cannot trade with yourself unless you are knavish or corrupt or just plain stupid. In banking the lender and the borrower are part of the same entity. That is the crux of a bank; it is always both a lender and a borrower, although many customers will hotly dispute the former appellation. Much of a bank's borrowings, its liabilities, are in the form of deposits of one sort or another. A bank must match these deposits, these borrowings, with what it lends out to its customers. If there is mismatching there can be serious problems: the depositors who have accepted an IOU will suffer as will the shareholders. The technique and operation of the inflows, the deposits, are completely different from the technique and operation of the outflows, the advances to the customers. The only common ground, itself an incongruity, is that the same top-level officers make the decisions concerning both these flows.

As both these distinct functions, the two mainstream activities of a bank, are treated as if they are not inimical, it is no wonder that banks get themselves into trouble and no surprise that there are recurrent bank crises. There is an inherent collision course between the two main functions of banking, which bankers traditionally refused to recognise. Banking is not child's play. Yet it is constantly amazing how bankers, even immensely experienced and shrewd bankers succumb to aberrations and from time to time behave like children.

There is only one perfect remedy to forestall a bank crisis and that is for a bank to match its deposits precisely with its loans. In so doing, by matching the periods and the amounts of deposits with advances no bank can go bust – as long as it maintains prudent reserves and maintains elementary ground rules on lending. A bank cannot suffer from mismatching difficulties if it borrows for the same or longer periods than it lends out. If there are no advances or loans to match the deposits and no deposits to match the loans, it would seem a simple rule that deposits should not be accepted or bought, that loans should not be advanced. A prime rule of banking used to be: if you cannot borrow long and lend short – don't borrow and don't lend. If you break this rule on an overall basis, there is a disequilibrium, which could in certain circumstances become an abberation, and the danger to the banking system increases because the inflows and outflows of each bank form part of the cash stream of larger banks, moving into ever wider channels. The flows all interrelate, so a local cash flood caused by a local disequilibrium can cause immediate cumulative damage in the immediate area, then widen regionally, then nationally and finally internationally. When this happens a deposit run affecting one small bank, unless quickly arrested, soon runs into the arterial system of the larger, and then the largest banks.

Matching is fiendishly difficult, both technically and philosophically, because the specific periods required for deposits and loans are almost infinitely varied and even though the rule is broken, not as an exception, but as a rule, the system does work – until there is an unusual occurrence or singularity. The contagion of fear then spreads in a flash and the bank is faced with the dire peril of illiquidity. For the IOU given by the bank to its depositor is only of any value if the depositor does not present his IOU at the same time as everyone else – unless, of course, there has been perfect matching. The banker says 'Your money is safe with us as long as you don't all want it at the same time'. Banking is consequently based on an entirely immoral principle.

Bankers know it and all professionals know it, and at the first whiff of danger it is those professionals who are the first not to renew deposits, the first to withdraw their money; the individual depositor, the member of the public, with inferior intelligence, taking fright, panics in person by physically queuing up outside the door of the bank.

Banking is virtually founded on confidence; yet it is the greatest of all confidence tricks. The banker's prayer is that his depositors will not lose confidence, will not withdraw, will not explode, all at the same time, but inescapably that is just what they will do at the first smell of gas. Bankers are amongst the very few (still) non-bankrupt commercial species whose business logic is based on an untenable premise.

Bankers preach about prudence and security to their customers, about keeping their overheads down, but in not practising what they preach and in refusing to come to terms with their own dilemma, they sit on the horns, crisis after crisis, rationalising their hypocrisy on a mostly true, not a false conclusion, that come the next crisis they will almost certainly be rescued by a bigger brother or the lender of last resort.

*　　　　*　　　　*

The Royal Ballet tour had been an enormous success. The Company had been acclaimed, especially in New York. Nadia in particular, as Lise in *La Fille Mal Gardée*, dancing the role with wonderful tenderness, had enjoyed a personal triumph. There had been many ovations and many parties. Rose Wolfson, the widow of the developer who with Jack Cotton owned half of the Pan Am building, gave a party for the whole of the company in the vast lobby of the building. Dancers skipped and jumped over the marble floors, incredulous that such a small dainty lady could own part of such an enormous building. We sailed back to England on *The France*, a de Gaulle *grand travail*, and soon after my return to the *Chronicle* I joined the Jack Cotton and Charles Clore property development group. I was extremely occupied and it was several weeks before Izzy Walton and I found a convenient time to meet.

As usual it was in his suite in the Grosvenor House. We discussed the property scene in New York, which was an anathema to Izzy who considered an investment in England as venturing into a risky geographical outpost. We talked generally about other matters, about Jack Morrison and of Cedar, and of deposits and matching. I declared that I had an unalterable belief in borrowing long and lending short. Indeed, that I not only abhorred short-term deposits but had an addiction for term loans to the extent that I saw no reason why any lending entity, particularly a small one, like Cedar, had to take in deposits, other than medium- or long-term deposits. Izzy, in turn, explained some aspects to me of Scottish law. There was, he said, a less complicated mechanism for lending money in Scotland than in England. In Scotland an agreement to agree was binding, one only needed an exchange of letters, missives in the vernacular. The mechanics of lending were generally easier, and moneylending did not quite have the same stigma as in England. Any lender was basically a moneylender, like his father, who had to obtain his moneylender's licence; otherwise he could not sue for the recovery of his money unless he was recognised as being in the banking business. But if a licence as a moneylender was taken up, there was certainly a stigma. There had emerged not only in Scotland, he explained, but all over the country, a curious twilight world where many small lenders loathed the idea of being licensed moneylenders, and traded on being recognised as being in the banking business. Recognition is what it is all about, he said. Thinking of his father's business, I asked him pointedly, 'You're so fascinated by the lending game, why haven't you started a lending business yourself?'

Izzy repeated what he had basically told me on previous occasions, that he was dedicated to property investment, not to lending as his father had been, that he was in any case the sort of person who could devote his time to only one business. 'Lending is for Jack. He used to sell dresses on tick in the Morrison shops. He likes all that. He is a true trader and likes being close to the customer. He misses all that. Also he's a real snob. To him banking means Rothschilds. He knows what he wants.' 'What is that?' I asked. 'Business and social success and admiration, especially from his brothers,' replied Izzy, and then smiling broadly, 'and also of course from his girlfriends.' I looked at the tiny pinheads of his eyes, 'What's behind all this? Come on Izzy, tell me the whole story.'

'Believe me,' he said, 'I only want to run Scottish Metropolitan. I'm only interested in my company and my family, apart from my charitable work. You know why I went on the Amal board – only to give it more credibility. Jack implored me. I don't want to be on any board other than Scottish Met. I will get off as soon as I can. Jack asked me for advice. I must admit that I was flattered. After all he is one of the Morrisons. Like many in Glasgow I looked up to them. Jack could never get over my own success. He was always asking me about the property business. When the family sold to Isaac he asked me to help him to get into property. So I did. I was always pleased to be involved with the Morrison family. I advised them on many of Amal's purchases. Let's face it, the association did me no harm.'

'You must understand, Jack wants to cut a figure. He wants something more than property. Which is why Cedar fits in. He and Michael took to it from the very first moment I mentioned the idea to them. They want to be bankers. From the dress trade to property to banking. That's how Jack sees it. But he doesn't want to be a moneylender – he wants to be a Rothschild. He may know what he wants but he doesn't know how to get there. You asked me for the whole story. This is where I believe you come in. It's your sort of thing. We've talked a lot together. I know your mind. I've told Jack and Michael they must rope you into Cedar.'

'The second mortgage business is a natural. The mortgage business is the biggest business in the country. Second mortgages have only just started. It is a wonderful banking business. Very low risk. Cedar could become big. They can't do it on their own. They need you. This is your area. You'll come up with the best way to bring the big money into Cedar. You have done wonders already for Jack Cotton. This is what the whole story is all about.'

It was a long peroration, and I believe I have reconstructed it accurately. I now knew more of the background, of the Morrisons' initiation into property, of Jack's need for social recognition, and I was beginning to understand his hold on Walton. I was also intrigued, I must admit, by the mortgage business. I had seen its sophisticated application in America, how Rayne, guided by the Everest property finance brain of Bill Zeckendorf Snr, had parleyed a genuine fifth or sixth minor mortgage into ownership of what of all things became the New York headquarters of General Motors on Fifth Avenue. I also suspected that Walton had spoken to someone in the Cotton/Clore camp, and had come to the conclusion that I might be interested in something new.

What he did not know, nor did I tell him, was that I had already decided on what I was going to do after my financial consulting stint with Cotton and Clore. I wanted to concentrate on my business activities at Hambros bank and upon Bishopsgate Property and on what eventually became the Bentworth group. Cedar would at the least be a learning curve. But it was premature. And the Morrisons? I was not anywhere nearly as sure of them as I was of Walton. I reasoned that if he was right in assessing their need of me, Cedar and the Morrisons could wait. I decided to go into neutral.

'I've read the Cedar accounts,' I said, 'it has a small capital, it has made a few loans which are of no consequence. Certainly the business is interesting, it needs a lot more consideration.' 'But it is a smashing vehicle, my friend,' wheezed Izzy, pushing me in his friendly way. 'Anyway, please see Jack and Michael. They want to talk to you.' He was the tied emissary. He could not get his youthful fascination for the Morrisons out of his system; to him they were the *crème de la crème*, getting on towards the Wolfson level, so, though a major star himself, he was glad to be of service, to be the marriage broker, to maintain and renew his contacts. It was also evident that Jack and Michael were reluctant to approach me directly in case they were spurned. They knew I was fond of Walton and they had asked him to intercede.

Woods Mews in Mayfair runs from Park Street near Charles Clore's house, to Park Lane near Dudley House; the former is now owned by others, the latter, the most elegant headquarters building in London, has been restored with meticulous care, under the stentorian leadership of Sydney Mason, the chairman and brilliant guiding light of the renowned Hammerson property group which owns and occupies the building, its classical atrium bathed in a cool suave light. The Cedar and Amal office was situated at the Charles Clore end of Woods Mews; Jack Morrison's home was at the Hammerson's end, and it was virtually his first after leaving the maternal sanctuary of his mother's Grosvenor Square flat nearby. Each day Jack took an easy stroll from residence to office, all of one hundred paces. He was proud of his mews house and of its furnishings, proud of its calculated impression that here was the house of a man of taste which, of course, immediately destroyed the effect for which he was striving.

Jack entertained frequently and generously. On one occasion, at drinks before going on to dinner, his partner was Patricia Roc, a well-known film star (clearly Jack had his charm); another occasion, was a reception in honour of James Callaghan, who was out of office but not out of Jack's reach. Our host on every occasion was well dressed, invariably in a dark-blue single-breasted suit, beautifully cut, the waistcoat trim and neat, its owner habitually making the most flowery introductions to his guests. When he introduced me to James Callaghan, Jack described him as one of the greatest politicians of our age and a future prime minister. This seemed to me to be such an intemperate exaggeration, even for Jack, that I remember remarking to Michael that his father must surely have taken leave of his senses. He had not. Mr Callaghan, not only became a prime minister, he was one of Labour's best (happily one can still count them on the fingers of one hand), and Jack's acquaintanceship with this generally underrated political heavyweight, which he carefully nurtured, would have stood him in very good stead in his ever active long-term knighthood pursuit, if Cedar had not collapsed.

A jolly saunter from residence to office, a slightly cocky look, a twinkle of self-satisfaction, a twirling of his long gleaming golden key chain, a proud swagger through the bankerish front door of the semi-mews offices, he would give a cheery smile to the reception girl or to Rose the tea lady on his way up to his own room on the first floor. Inside, Jack's office had winged armchairs, coffee tables, vitrines and silver framed photographs. Michael's office was on the other side of

the corridor furnished in a similar vein; my architect brother Max*
would have described this baroque style as Louis XIV – but not of
France. It was, however, a working office with actual papers on the
desk, with filing trays and with chairs arranged for business meetings
rather than for a tea party.

At our meeting, father, son and I, sat in our comfortable armchairs.
Jack had made his finer points and so had I. Jack had said with typical
exaggeration that I was indispensable for the growth of Cedar, and I
had said with untypical caution that I was too busy at the time working
with Cotton and Clore, having also taken up abode at Hambros bank
and was very engaged setting up Bishopsgate Property, a new property
investment vehicle. Jack implied, stated, suggested (it was not at all
clear which) that there was no hurry, that he and Michael and Cedar
would, or could, or might wait. We were in normal Jack Morrison
focus.

The door opened. A small, dark, barrel keg with a bulbous, balding,
shining forehead, trundled into the room. 'I'd like you to meet my
nephew David,' said Jack.

In the Cedar story there are numerous characters with as many
variations of character. One of them, the Governor of the Bank of
England, was genuinely great; another, the Deputy Governor, was
near great; several were seemingly honourable, who when under
pressure, obliged to display their true nature hidden beneath the
protective shell of normal social buffeting, proved even more honourable; several were seemingly honourable who under pressure proved
less than honourable, even dishonourable; some were decent men
embedded with a sound moral sense, but with weak characters, so they
were not around when needed; others were disagreeable with strong
characters, who were not absent when needed, who could be relied
upon for the simple reason that it was not in their nature to confuse
their moral principles with their innate unpleasantness.

But of all the Cedar characters, there was one – though the shortest
in stature, all five feet of him – who stood out above and beyond all
others, who seemed to be universally disliked, who could have given

---

* In his last years before he died Max made a name for himself in the art world,
particularly for his concept and design of the Saatchi Gallery and his design of a
section of the Queen Sofia Gallery of Contemporary Art in Madrid. He died in
1990 at the age of 59.

Iago* fundamental lessons in how to incite – this nephew of Jack Morrison, always by his side; this cousin of Michael, later always by his side, this deeply loyal family member who, after the Cedar collapse fled out of the country to no one knew where, who had disappeared without trace, severing all family and other London connections in one quick plane trip, who still kept his brave silence even after he was known to have surfaced years later in Miami, who saddened the sweet-tempered Angela, Michael's wife, beyond measure, when she hoped mistakenly that out of some semblance of affection for Michael he might have emerged from his exile to offer his condolences when Michael died of cancer in 1984.

I was now about to meet this man, later described to me by one pension fund board representative of Cedar as the most detestable man he had ever met. The person was called David Fischer.

'Charles, I would like you to meet my nephew David'†, Jack had said and I looked at the roly-poly barrel keg gliding in on his tip-toe castor wheels, with the look of a brimming clever child, his large knowing eyes veiled by an alien innocence, not quite camouflaged by the wide, gleaming, fixed smile, which remained fixed as he started addressing me with an Uncle Jack-like gush of how it was not only a great pleasure to meet me, it was also one of the most important days of his life, how he had seen my mother's paintings which he simply adored and how he had been a fan of Nadia's, oh, for so many years, having been to one of her earliest performances in *Sleeping Beauty* at the Met. I detested him on sight.

I detested him no more and no less throughout all the years of Cedar's proclivities. I suspect, or rather I know, that most of the institutional respresentatives of Cedar had a similar antipathy towards him. I never hid my personal feelings, seeing him as a definite and practical danger to Cedar's progress, going as far on one occasion, as to request Michael to keep him out of Cedar altogether, to restrict him

---

* The Iago thematic interplay is thrilling in its awesome interpretation of the power which one manipulative scheming person can hold over another unsuspecting person, the power possessed by the far lesser figure, adroit and agile in knowing how to exploit the other's weakness. The exceptional situation here was that Fischer the lesser figure, exercised his skill and gained his power over two persons, and not in the dramatically effective Shakespearian time-scale, of days or weeks, or months, but over ten consecutive years.
† And not really a nephew, but a second cousin by marriage to Michael, whose mother was a first cousin of David Fischer's father.

solely to Amal. I was immediately rebuffed. Frequently I would ask him to leave the room or would merely give him an openly hostile glare if I was with Jack or Michael discussing some business matter, and he would in those early years slide out without a murmur. It did not occur to me that I was making an arch enemy and if it had, I would still not have attempted to disguise my enmity or modify my aversion in any way. I squelched him at every opportunity, my opprobrium becoming infectious when I noticed several wider Cedar associates, in addition to one or two of the institutional representatives, demonstrating quite openly a similar antagonism. The fact that he was clearly rubbing people up the wrong way did not perturb the Morrisons.

This was puzzling, and I was given some explanation by Ian Morrison, Peter's son, another nephew of Jack's, and the nicest of all the male Morrisons apart from Michael. Ian had worked in Cedar for a while, and knew the set-up from the inside. What David set out to do, he said, was to make himself useful to Uncle Jack in every way; to stick to him and to Michael like a loving leech. This, of course, was the last attachment one wanted for Cedar. Cedar was striving for credibility, its then eggshell strength could have been shattered by a single mindless comment from a member of the Morrison family.

So, when I first brought Jasper Knight of Unilever to Cedar's offices to introduce him to Jack and Michael, I made it an express condition of that crucial encounter that Fischer had to be kept out, rusticated, sent abroad, sent anywhere but not to be allowed remotely near the premises. I was given assurances, but very reluctantly, that he would not be around.

Fischer was a long-distance campaigner; the metal discs of his agile brain recorded every slight, every offence, and he patiently bided his time; he knew it would come. When it did, years later, he instantly retrieved the full catalogue of all the insults he had endured from my implacable animosity and in return applied his considerable talents to persuading Jack and Michael, although Michael's heart was not in it, to cut me up into small pieces.

This, however, was our first encounter. The new addition to the Morrison family sat down in the remaining winged chair, too podgy to cross his legs, so the heel of one shoe was up-ended clumsily on his knee. I noticed the heel was worn. He, too, was clearly appraising me, his fixed pasty smile like a gleaming toothpaste advertisement beneath a wide-open child's stare, measuring what he was seeing with what he had been told: an unheralded invisible battle was to commence.

Fischer had already begun to weave his presence around Uncle Jack and cousin Michael; invited to be part of their entourage, as a poor relation on his uppers, he became secretary, colleague, butler, friend and confidant; weaving and spinning tighter and tighter around them, employing flattery, incitement, and intrigue as the tools of his trade. He made Jack, already deeply suspicious about other people, ever more suspicious, almost paranoid, and he manoeuvred Michael into depending upon his presence with an almost neurotic compulsion. He would also be as closet a homosexual as possible, as this preference would not be wholly admired in his family circle, but at the same time, as he liked sailing close to the wind, any dangers in these waters would make it all the more exciting. He would be, and indeed became, indispensable to uncle and cousin; the shadow with increasing substance, he was appointed a director of Amal and a director, then joint managing director with Michael, of Cedar.

He accompanied Jack on any venture, a theatre, a lunch, a trip – perhaps to Leeds where Jack's daughter lived – or to Glasgow, or to Tel Aviv, or to the tailor, or to the barber, or to Aspreys, or to the Marlborough Gallery. He pushed Jack's art purchases up-market. He was always around like a popinjay, always in evidence, and during the period before the rescue, his influence had become so pervasive, he had even persuaded Michael that his father was too aged and should be let out to grass and whilst humbling Jack, encouraged him to go on holiday after holiday, David personally perusing the brochures of a wide range of geriatric cruises.

Jack's suspicions for once were stultified. He was not apparently aware of what was going on around him, seeming almost drugged by hearing the daily insidious lopsided accounts from Fischer, the daily incantations of the great successes of Cedar, and not only from Fischer, but also from Michael, whose own injections of enthusiasm had a tendency of bordering on unbridled euphoria.

The stage was finally reached when Fischer was so compelling an influence on Michael that Jack was fully divorced from the day to day affairs, becoming a true figurehead. The elder Morrison stopped looking at memoranda, at balance sheets, stopped attending meetings. Not knowing what was really going on, he nevertheless wallowed in the froth, relishing all the publicity, all the acclaim, all the grand people he was meeting. Jack became a sort of highest-level public relations apostle of Cedar, he spent more time at charity events, at social functions, still articulate and pervasive, so much so that even the more wary amongst his own family started having second thoughts about his achievements.

Jack and Michael were already endowed with excitable temperaments, prone to incoherence when flustered, easily carried away, easily going over the top. What they didn't need was Fischer's continuous buttering of their already unhealthy illusions, his unctuous Brooklyn twang droning in their ears, exhorting them, pushing them, urging them, constantly pandering to their commercial and social fantasies, this insistent drone with its Woody Allen vowels, never slurred, perfectly enunciated, whining on and on, year in year out. Jack and Michael could certainly have done without it. The course of Cedar would certainly have been different without it.

Just after the Cedar collapse, when David disappeared, it brought father and son together again, each leaning on the other for support, Michael ever more compliant and ever more gracious to his smitten parent, now an old man in black despair, eyeless in Gaza, devoid of any strength and devoid of any will, because he was devoid of any money and devoid of any status. During this terrible time, an empty painful void, he fell back on Michael, who was himself for a time in traumatic shock. Jack couldn't even look at his violin, let alone enjoy the solace of playing it, and he wept when this his most prized possession, his Stradivarius, had to be sold.

TWO

The Blueprint

A year after going into neutral, having seen Michael and Jack at various times, it was decided that we would have a more formal meeting at my office at Hambros, to be followed later with a lunch at the Savoy Grill. Amal was growing steadily, and so was Cedar. Jack had bought the old Hamptons store in Kensington. The purchase received much prominence in the newspapers, which pleased him, and he was careful to send me cuttings in case it had escaped my notice. He was more self assured, claiming an expertise in property, even querying a real pro like Walton on some of his own acquisitions. Jack and Michael were strutting over a larger stage. The Cotton/Clore battle having been won in Clore's favour, I was no longer the full-time financial consultant of the two tycoons, but was now a full-time independent at Hambros Bank, Jack Cotton's merchant bank to which he had originally introduced me. In City terms my arrangements with Hambros was unique: though independent my staff was paid by the bank and on any transaction which I instigated, I took up as a principal, a share of the equity or a share of the profits. I was establishing the Bentworth Group (the forerunner of Spey Investments, both of which endeavours I refer to later), taking over the existing Bentworth Trust, and as managing director and deputy chairman had the largest shareholding, other than the bank itself.

Generally I was concentrating on what I liked doing most – property financing, special financial and investment situations and venture capital. Although Hambros was the largest of the merchant banks and amongst the most prestigious, its balance sheet total was only £200 million. It is difficult for the reader to appreciate the true scale of the inflationary changes and of globalisation. The following example may suffice. In 1965 the largest loan ever raised in the entire history of the City was raised by ICI. The enormous, record-shattering amount was £50 million. It caused such a sensation that there were headlines in the general press and dissertations on radio and TV. All of us in the City were generally amazed because the amount was so huge. So was the interest rate. No industrial loan had ever been raised at such a high rate before – 7·25%, yes seven and one-quarter per cent. ICI, the premier industrial company, had profits of £101 million and its market value was £905 million. Today ICI's profits are £843 million, its market value is £9·3 billion. In the mid-1960s a fee of over £5,000 was considerable. A salary of £1,000 for a secretary was almost unheard of. My own secretary, who became Charles Hambro's secretary after I left to start Spey, was the first to receive a four-figure salary; I might add that she was not only worth it but worth a lot more. A loan from a bank in excess of £100,000 was considered sizeable. Few bank managers had full discretion in excess of £5,000. The £3 million received by the Morrisons, from the sale of their business some years earlier, had been an enormous amount of money.

So in going over the figures of Cedar that day in my office at Hambros with Jack and Michael sitting by my desk – a modest but beautifully made sofa-table whose collapsible ends made for a pleasing enlargement when needed for an informal meeting – it was by no means unimpressive that Cedar had an overdraft with its own bank of over £500,000. Cedar had come some way since that buff envelope lay like a time bomb amongst the flowers in our cabin in the *Queen Mary*.

Jack had been quite clever in the way he had set up Cedar. He had not put in a penny but had guaranteed an overdraft. I suspected Walton had a hand in this. As Michael had an outstanding operational and administrative talent, efficient procedures had been laid down, the actual documentation well thought out by Michael and cleverly designed under Fischer's direction. There were a number of innovations in the use of printed forms and in the method of following up slow repayments, later taken up by competitors. Loans still amounted to a dozen or so a week. New business derived from an assortment of brokers who were themselves a new breed, all unregulated and free from any legal restraints. The marketing of new business through these brokers was being built up carefully. Progress was steady and not impeded by the anti-second-mortgage cavils, which arose overtly from the press and less overtly from the financial establishment. The press was quite rightly gunning for those disreputable lenders who some-times doubled up as brokers and who charged exorbitant arrangement fees to get round the moneylending Acts. The *Investors' Chronicle* under its then editor, Andreas Whittam Smith (who later founded the *Independent*) was continuing the investigative traditions started by our legendary alumnus Margot Naylor, in attacking these practices.

There were numerous abuses by lenders; eventually a Royal Commission (Crowther) was initiated, one of whose recommendations was to disclose the true interest rate being charged. The Crowther Report did not go far enough but at least its thrust was in the right direction. Habitually there had been a strong groundswell against second mortgages from the financial establishment, but it was insinu-ated rather than declared outright, because many of the major banks, through their own finance house subsidiaries or through close associations with favoured customers, were themselves guilty by indirect association.

In this problem area of over charging on consumer credit and on second mortgage loans, there had always been ambiguous boundaries. The general disapproval was never quelled. Indeed it was the open wound causing much of the resentment of the clearing banks towards the fringe banks when they had to support them through the Lifeboat during the crisis. The Cedars and their ilk were made to feel that they were commercial climbers trying to scale the traditional banking ramparts by unorthodox if not disreputable means, and were conse-quently disavowed by the banking establishment. It is not easy to comprehend today how rigidly compartmentalised these disapproving financial entities were in their own various manifestations. A bank was either a merchant bank, a high street bank or an overseas bank, each, though not enjoying a legal definition, having its own clearly defined area of activity, each looking down on the other in that order of prestige. In turn, they all looked down upon the finance companies, like United Dominions Trust, Lombard, Mercantile Credit; these in turn looked down their noses upon the Cedars of the world, the distaff progeny, who were in the waif-like financial underworld of almost semi-recognition. However, the high street banks, the clearers, were not only geographically prejudiced and sectarian, but also extremely snobbish and high-minded towards these lowest-rung echelons, helping them with advances because it was good business, but like dog owners looking the other way, pretending that they were not a party to fouling the system.

The commercial nuances amongst the banks were intriguing, yet the banks were only one side of the lending divide, with the legally defined building societies on the other, these building societies looking askance at the fast-breeding second mortgage lenders operating in the financial area between themselves and the banks. Cedar, lending on second mortgages, was not a bank nor was it anything like a building society, which only lent on first mortgages; Cedar was operating in the fringe terrains – a veritable no-man's land between the banks and the building societies, but with an ecology which was remarkably resilient.

It is useful to describe how the banks in the early days of their existence captured their territory and altered the environment to suit themselves. In those days, the high street bank could be likened to a church; it was in charge of and guarded your financial well-being; you were expected to have total confidence and faith in its solid permanent existence. In seeking a meeting to request an advance, it was more of a visitation; you were seeking a form of communion, you were a potential Elder. Borrowing was, of course, a sin, but in borrowing from your bank you were to some extent being condoned because your bank only lent to people who were good enough, good in the moral sense as well as the financial. You could redeem your loan as you could redeem your soul. When you borrowed, you offered in supplication security acceptable to the bank, and such security had to have a value well in excess of the money you were borrowing. An unsecured loan was anathema; it was the devil's own ticket to perdition. Both the bank as lender and you as the borrower had to feel secure in every sense: the bank secure in taking no risk, secure in your steadfastness: you secure in your assets, secure in having been bestowed with the bank's seal of approval. You were part of the nineteenth-century ethic which proclaimed saving an act of worship and borrowing an act of heresy.

The high-minded high street banks prided themselves on their (mostly) successful attempts to look like the bleakest of churches, so there were high-vaulted ceilings, leading to the inner sanctum, to the office of the high priest, known as the manager. He was the ordained official, pinstriped, white stiff collar, smiling sincerely, and as you entered the portals would pat you on the back for having increased your deposits, for having kept your account in credit, and he would give you just that precise stern look of latent reprimand, to remind you the customer, that in making this assignation to request a loan, you were in serious danger of being a Wanderer from the Truth. His handshake was a crisp clasp of slightly-received friendship, for after all you were a customer, a misnomer – more a member, you had taken the vow, you were one of the fold, and as his unsceptred arm directed you to your chair to await the spiritual examination, there was almost a hint that an organ might start playing as he seated himself opposite you, studying your bank statement, the recorded proof of your standing, your probity, your morality, looking up from time to time to give you sharp looks of incredulity.

Your bank manager was respected because he could provide you with status, with assurance of your financial morality or otherwise. He had a form of power over you, for in seeking assistance you were baring your soul, not only your net worth; so the manager, palms together, questioned you closely to make sure that you had performed a thorough soul-searching before deciding that he might make a recommendation to a more important order, to the area or regional officers, those higher, more heavenly invisible bodies who never made an appearance, that you should be privileged with their authorised approval of a loan. It was a very serious ritual.

Of course there was a great subterfuge behind all this. The banks needed your credit balances and deposits in order to make loans. They needed you more than they would ever admit, and what they wanted above all were the credit balances on your current account, your day-to-day involuntary deposits, on which they could make loans without paying any deposit interest. These credit balances provided the real profits of the banks – and what profits. It was even more profitable than printing money because they suffered no costs and as the banks enjoyed the benefits of your credit balances, they zealously safe-guarded their fabulous benefits. It started with Pinstripes instilling in you the basic first commandment of high street banks – Thou Shalt Keep Your Current Account In Credit. To your bank it was a free ride to Eldorado; all these credit balances comprised the protean profits of the banks for generations, they were free gifts from you the customer, entirely free because you paid all the expenses, all the bank charges. And if you wanted to borrow, a special loan account separate from your current account would be opened, with interest set-offs considered – only if requested. These 100% profit margins deriving from your credit balances were the petrol, oil and lubrication of the banking system which opened thousands of branch banks throughout the country. It was the greatest ever golden fleece and the entire customer banking base of the country was fleeced with sanctimonious disdain and vigour. The customer was the sacrificial lamb. It was a very neat form of legal theft, accepted until recently, with incredible equanimity.

If we now move across the lending/deposit divide to the other side of the terrain, to the first-mortgage providers, the building societies, we find that they too had built-in advantages, a series of measures enacted to provide special privileges to building society borrowers and depositers which arose directly from the morally inspired thrift industry. To the Victorians, being thrifty meant being superior, it meant being on the road to posterity, on the road to civic respect and also to abstinence – for thrifty persons were supposedly synonymous with non-drinkers. To Gladstone, thrift was 'the symbol and instrument of independence and liberty', and the very word still enjoys a pensive echo of Victorian morality. The history of the thrift industry is fascinating, for although born out of genuine charity it was motivated by class distinction. The ruling classes, mindful of the French Revolution, had taken such fright that much new legislation was directed to prohibiting groups of workers from getting together and forming unions – hence the notorious Combination Acts, which should have been called Anti-Combination Acts.

On the strongly-held early-Victorian tenet that God helps those who help themselves, the idea of mutual self-help, that one should save together was forcefully put across to the populace. This was the true beginning of the mutual societies, the friendly societies, the affiliated and trades societies, the co-operative societies and the building societies. From these beginnings, thrift and self-help societies took hold with immense success, surging ahead on the booming crest of the industrial revolution of the first truly industrial nation. Hundreds, then thousands, then tens of thousands of these societies were formed, many with members drawn from the same occupation, thus sewing the seeds of the beginning of the trade unions. Almost overnight, savings became an industry, with many convinced that the new savings institutions were manifestations of God's will rather than Man's rectitude.

What were these different institutions, these different societies? There were deposit societies merging into a single enormous entity called the National Deposit Society, with 1.5 million members during the two World Wars; there were dividing societies, whereby at the end of each year the amount remaining after payment for sickness and burial was divided amongst the surviving members, also called Tontines (the accounts were so simple they were put on a slate in the public house, so they were also called slate societies). There were collecting societies, the origin of the assurance societies, with the Prudential being the first to discipline its collectors who, working on commission only, were prone to being over-zealous in increasing their 'book'; the Pru starting in business in 1854 had over one million policy holders only twenty years later. There were the co-operative societies, 1,500 of them by 1815 and because interest on the shares earned compound interest they were like savings banks, and in not selling alcohol they also played an important part in the temperance movement. The most pathetic of all were the burial societies, the worst horror of all being the pauper's funeral which meant a burial in a common grave – not the exit from earth but the entrance to hell – and to avoid disgrace, saving coppers for a private burial was the first savings of any, the tombstone being the most tangible evidence of respectablity, the common grave, being the most damning evidence of shame.

And then there were the building societies. Originally known as terminating societies, because they terminated when they achieved their object, which was simply to enable their members to subscribe until each had acquired his house. By the 1850s, when over seven hundred terminating societies had been formed mostly in the industrial midlands and the north, the building societies started their own great growth in the new industrial areas: Birmingham, for example, doubled in size in the first decade of the nineteenth century. The later emergence of the permanent building society was inevitable, for by being permanent the mortgage loans and withdrawals could be freely available, members were no longer restricted to the original subscribers. But the dominating cause for the extraordinary success of the permanent building society was that it separated the depositor from the borrower. Deposits grew very rapidly. Management soon settled into being essentially middle class, the boards of directors made up mainly of solicitors, land agents, auctioneers and builders, with links forged with assurance societies. The building society movement also attracted strong support from the anti-drink lobby and many of the formal meetings now took place in the more austere temperance hall rather than in a convivial public house. As always in England, class distinction imposed its own rigid unwritten rules.

The building society movement was well conceived but there was a serious flaw: the same inherent collision course as found embedded in the structure of banking, a similar dichotomy on cash in-flow and outflow. The apostolic manager of the building society branch, was the same twig as Pinstripes at the bank branch. 'Now listen, my man, as you have deposited your savings with us you have two great advantages. The first is that the interest you earn is, up to a point, tax free, the second is that as a depositor you will have preferential treatment when you require a mortgage. We do not have to tell you that although our deposits come from you and the likes of you, we are their guardians and we decide with absolute discretion whether you are going to be the lucky recipient of our favours'. Not stated to the quivering borrower was: 'We both, of course, suffer from split personalities. You are split between being a depositor and a borrower; we are split between being a borrower and a lender.'*

Our building societies became unfriendly monolithic ogres to the general public. Some indeed, with ludicrous gall, still call themselves friendly societies, despite the fact that the journey leading to the final destination, the purchase of the house, was a formidable pilgrim's progress of almost overwhelming obstacles. In order to get your loan, you, the applicant, again more a supplicant, had to go through even worse torture than when you had to kneel prostrate in front of Pinstripes. To obtain your building society mortgage you put on your Sunday best and, from the moment of that first interview, you and your entire family were placed in a state of sheer fright until the verdict was handed out, until you were told, 'Yes, you can have a mortgage', or 'No, you cannot'. You had filled out numerous forms, you had answered questions which your own family doctor had not ventured to ask, your employer was quizzed, even to that obsessional class question of whether you were buying above your station, you had obtained all the supporting data, your references, your hobbies, your blood count. And then you were kept dangling in suspense.

* The Danes, those logical Latins amongst the Scandinavians, got it right from the beginning. They have the simplest building societies in the world. They don't take deposits, they only lend money. There is no collision course in the Viking's mortgage business, no two-way flow, only one way. The Danish building societies only provide mortgages. When they need money to make their advances, they merely go into the bond market and raise what they need, matching loans to perfection, paying the going rate for interest and charging the going rate for interest. They have no concern whatsoever on the rate of in-flow of desposits. They are not in a state of conflict as they only borrow what they need. It obviously works commercially as two of the largest Danish building societies are nearly as large as our own Abbey National and Halifax, in a country with a tenth of our population.

If the decision of the building society was negative, no reason was given. That was it. No apology. You were not a fit person. You may have changed your job twice in the last fifteen years – black mark; you may have been divorced – black mark; you may have sent your children to expensive schools – black mark.

If the decision was positive and, buying chain permitting, you went ahead with the mortgage with the building society taking a first charge as its security. Until released you paid your monthly instalment, which was not fixed but fluctuated with interest rates. The main deterrent in moving from one job to another was the fear of jeopardising the mortgage; so job mobility, the muscular strength of a country's vigour, was virtually strangled. This difficulty in obtaining a mortgage, helped to stultify the country's economy for most of this century and is, I believe, an underlying psychological reason for the sluggish attitude to work and lack of productivity. The country had a head start over the rest of the world and sadly it squandered its enormous advantages by concentrating on class warfare instead of economic warfare.

With your mortgage in place, you were tied to your building society whilst the major asset of your net worth was tied to your house; this asset was not negotiable. Topping up your mortgage was considered the same as topping up your criminal tendencies.

It was not so in Scotland. Borrowing was moral; not repaying one's debt was the sin. The Scots have always been united in those matters which were of benefit to them, regarding the appellation, United Kingdom, as an irrelevant political euphemism. Their greatest pride is in being canny – to a Scot being canny means he is charmingly shrewd, but if an Englishman is canny it means he is disgustingly devious – and being canny, the Scots have not allowed their law to be the same as the law of the United Kingdom. Theirs is simple: you buy or you do not buy. There is no confusion in their law. One letter is sufficient for a binding contract. The Scots recognised also that if you wanted to improve your house, indeed, if you wanted money to buy a car, you should be able to borrow against your own asset, against the equity in your own house. Why shouldn't you? After all it was your house, your equity and why should any official be allowed to suggest otherwise? It did not matter that your house was already secured to your building society by way of a first mortgage, you should be able to seek a second mortgage from anyone else who was prepared to offer it to you, a moneylender, a broker or solicitor – as long as the terms were agreeable.

The mechanism of establishing a second mortgage loan was relatively simple. In the first instance, the lender verified the value of your house; he then ascertained that the borrower had the earning capacity to repay the monthly repayments in addition to the building society repayments. All that was required was the approval of the building society. That was the rub. It was extremely unusual for a building society to stop a second-mortgage lender from advancing a loan to its own first mortgage borrower. But the application meant that the borrower was on notice; he was 'short' of money. The borrower now had a question mark on his file.

The amount of the two combined mortgages was usually 80% of the forced sale value of the house. Debts were paid primarily because of the inherent honesty of the British public *à la* Wolfson, and secondarily because of the deterrent of repossession – only the television set was comparable to a house in the emotional and financial priority of avoiding repossession. The differences, therefore, between a first and second mortgage are that the second mortgage ranks after the first, that the period of the second was far shorter, and that the uses of the moneys raised from a second mortgage were varied, not the single purpose to purchase a house. But the most invidious difference was the intangible one: first mortgages were respectable, second mortgages were not. Indeed for a long time second mortgages were dirty words in the City, and it was this intangible aspect, respectability or rather the lack of it, which worried me most in looking at Cedar's business of lending on second mortgages.

*　　　　*　　　　*

In our discussion on Cedar and second mortgage lending in my office, Jack, Michael and I were on the first floor of Hambros Bank, number 41 Bishopsgate. On the Threadneedle side was a major branch of Nat West, the original City headquarters of the very provincial National Provincial Bank before it rushed into a hasty marriage with the wonderfully genteel Westminster Bank; except for its lobby this old headquarters is worth a Michelin detour at any time. On our Liverpool Street side was Palmerston House, no Brownie points for knowing whom it was named after, except that most stockbrokers thought of it as an office building with a well-known City restaurant, unaware that the old political sage's sidewhiskers would have bristled with the ignominy that the only mark of his eminence amongst all the Wren churches which he loved, was a basement restaurant with the most inedible food ever offered to hungry City clerks and brokers. I had my first and only meal there in my *Investors' Chronicle* days, and I sometimes wonder if the urge to have it closed down and transformed into the Hambros bank staff canteen, was not spurred on by that unique meal.

Next door to Palmerston House was the M. Samuel building, the family bank of the Bearsted's, which had held Charles Clore in so much thrall as the East End Jewish lad passed by in the bus which he could ill afford. Further on there was a motley of buildings, since cleared and redeveloped, an area overshadowed by the thirty-storey Hong Kong and Shanghai building. Credit for this huge development must go to my assistant at Hambros, John Spink, and his colleagues Malcolm Yeulet and Michael Boggis, with all three of whom it gives me pleasure to record I am still in touch. Between them, they masterminded the buying in of the various ownerships and the setting up of the subsequent consortium. My role from the beginning was very thin, if not invisible. My friend Felix Fenston, a minor owner of one of the minor buildings, had asked me how he should handle the negotiations. I said the best advice I could offer him was not to underestimate Spink, as I considered him one of the best property finance brains in the City. Norman Bowie, that eminent chartered surveyor, now retired as a senior partner of Jones Lang Wooton, once said that he thought that he, Spink and I, were the foremost City property brains. He was two-thirds right, as they both easily out-classed me, Spink being as formidable as Bowie. He was a perfect foil to Fenston who, though one of the country's most talented property developers, was possibly one of its worst financiers. In any event Fenston, forewarned, did well on Bishopsgate, as did Spink, Yeulet and Boggis for Hambros bank.

But well before this major Bishopsgate development got under way, my own office on the first floor at Hambros, the partners' floor, was actually in Palmerston House, by courtesy of a City gentleman of the old sort. He was almost the sole relic of an old Greek banking family which had settled in England a hundred years earlier, a Mr Rodocanachi who, in a matter of minutes, deftly finessed Sir Charles Hambro and myself out of our objective with such elegance that it is worth describing how he did it. It is also an example of how in those days, a man's word was quite genuinely his bond.

I had suggested that we acquire Palmerston House, owned by a quoted property company whose largest shareholders were the Rodocanachi family. I knew Rodocanachi slightly and invited him to join Sir

Charles and myself for a general discussion, but it was not the discussion that the two of us had had in mind.

The perfect City gentleman, soon after sitting down in the board room at Hambros, referred initially to the business his family had done with the Hambro family over so many generations, and then he referred to Hambros' Greek connections – these were not tenuous, as Hambros had started Hellenic and General Trust after the war to channel investments into Greece, and among the best Hambros lunches I attended was when the then chairman of the Bank of Greece, on his annual visit, regaled us with a range of the wittiest stories, from banking to girls, I had ever heard. Mr Rodocanachi then disclosed that at the board meeting of his property company the day before, the directors had decided to consider appointing Hambros Bank – not *actually* to appoint, that was made perfectly clear – as their financial advisers. In one sentence the dear old boy, as clever as a monkey and with the charm of an ancient Athenian, put us out of court: Sir Charles Hambro gave no glimmer that he was taken aback. He told our visitor it would be a pleasure if, that is, the proposed relationship matured into an actual appointment. Hambro then asked me if I had any questions. Yes, I said, and deliberately rambling – a useful merchant banking technique I had picked up mostly from Jack Hambro – pointed out that Palmerston House was a very valuable property and, like the best of City properties, should not be sold without considerable thought, but, getting round to my point, if any space in the building was to become available, we might like to have a first refusal, before it went on the market. 'Would you like that?' Mr Rodocanachi asked Sir Charles. The chairman of Hambros Bank nodded. The old boy also nodded and said, 'Yes of course'. He kept his word. There was never any correspondence.

That is how the Palmerston restaurant was transformed into the Hambros staff canteen, and how, with the purchase of the old M. Samuel building – made possible when the Bearsted's moved out after its merger with Philip Hill – it was possible for the whole area to be razed for the Hong Kong and Shanghai, and why my suite of offices in Hambros was in Palmerston House, three steps lower than 41 Bishopsgate, through which we made a passage to the partners' room, and why Jack and Michael Morrison and I were seated there that day for our discussion.

We were concentrating on the aspects of respectability and the problems of the moneylenders' Acts. Michael said that he and his father agreed with Walton that sooner rather than later there must be legislation in respect of all the fledgling second mortgage businesses and hire purchase businesses. Meanwhile solid hard work was necessary to obtain a good name; the merest hint of recognition could never be possible unless there was total dedication. Michael said it was worth enduring the uphill struggle, no matter how long it took. Then we got on to financing. I explained that I had worked something out for their consideration and gave them a general idea, but said I wanted to discuss it first in detail with Walton. If they concurred, I suggested that Jack, Michael and I could get together again, see how we should proceed, if at all, and discuss what role Walton and I would play, if any, and on what terms.

By this time we had left Hambros for the Savoy Grill and had begun our lunch. The Savoy Grill, before they destroyed the old grill room, was the finest restaurant in the world – bar none. One could enjoy better food at Taillevent, have better service at Le Voile D'Or, be surrounded by finer furnishings at Grand Vefour, but for sheer champagne quality, whether lunch or dinner, the Savoy Grill was in a class of its own. Within that magnificent room one was always aware that what was happening was happening there, at that moment, whether an important business lunch or a family celebration or dinner, or the applause greeting a ballerina or a tenor after a memorable Opera House performance. The Savoy Grill was peerless in every respect down to showing you the unopened chilled bottle of milk, clothed in its white napkin, to assure you that it was fresh and pristine. It had immense self-assurance and competence and a *maitre d'* of genius, Luigi, who invented the 'placement' stakes and who taught his successor, Vercelli, the difficult art of that game, so that whether you were even given a table or not was as problematic as to where you were to sit – Luigi, who went to Claridges in semi-retirement to impose his same nervy-making placement policy there, who loved shooting, and who at the Fenston/Radziwill Yorkshire shoot looked more ducal than the genuine article, never letting on when on duty, except by a quizzical arch of an eyebrow, that some of his patrons were personal friends. The Savoy Grill was glamorous in the best possible sense, in that, like a truly beautiful woman, each feature was in perfect unison with every other, glowing with an understated and mysterious harmony. We were often there after the ballet. It was very much in its heyday in the 1960s. Lord Goodman, the president of the lunchtime devotees, would feast there regularly, his clients, the Carrs – owners of the *News of the World* before selling to Murdoch – nearby, on liquids first. Heads of industry, heads of banks, merchant bankers, brokers, senior partners, other regulars, sat at their usual tables. My table was by the window, near the entrance, and it was there that I explained to the Morrisons that though I was interested in Cedar, I was very busy on something to do with Barclays Bank. In any case, didn't they agree that we shouldn't rush the Cedar fences?

*   *   *

Barclays played a leading role in the Cotton/Clore group, they played a leading role in Bentworth at Hambros, in Cedar Holdings and also in the Spey saga. I had originally met one or two of their senior people through my father, who had always banked with Barclays, but one man, Darvill, whom I met through Jack Cotton, led to my own later association, starting with the Bentworth/Barclays link. Some few weeks before my lunch with the Morrisons I had arranged to go to 54 Lombard Street, Barclays' head office, to have tea with Darvill, known as Darv. He was the senior general manager of the bank, and would, I suppose, be called the chief executive today. I cogitated upon my forthcoming talk with him, undisturbed by the occasional muffled roar of the Bishopsgate traffic. The question was how far Barclays would like to go in associating with us in Bentworth; the problem we were hoping to overcome was how to combine the strength of an enormous high street bank like Barclays with the strength of a big merchant bank like Hambros. The clearers engrossed in their branch banking operation, were not engaged in any of the core activities of a merchant bank – new issues, mergers and amalgamation, corporate finance, investment advice, portfolio management.

The great strengths of the clearers were their huge tangible resources in money and in customers; what the merchant banks relied upon was the opposite – it was their huge intangible resources, their mystique, their aura; the merchant banking aura of power was very real because it was something which was believed to be true, even though the underlying balance sheet strengths were suspect.

I was captivated on frequent occasions when talking with one or other of the Hambros, or one or other of the merchant banking princes, by an expression, a phrase, a sentiment, a flash of comprehension and judgement which derived from generations-old bankers' instincts, and I sometimes marvelled at the results of the fine tuning of the generations-old genetic engineering. It was less to do with money power or brain power and more to do with wisdom and shrewdness and personal connections; in other words the merchant banking mystique did not arise so much from any technical financial capacity but from its capacity to assess the merits and evaluate the risk in backing, or not backing, a situation or a character. This is why some of the best minds are attracted to merchant banking and also why some of these, including outstanding Whitehall mandarins, have proved to be unexpected failures.

Bentworth was already establishing itself rather nicely at Hambros, and fairly early on in its progress, Jack Hambro (by then chairman of the bank, the great Sir Charles died in 1961) and I had reached the conclusion that it would be sensible to have a large outside share-holder, one which not only had abundant financial resources but abundant potential for new business. On both counts we could not do better than Barclays, the largest clearer at the time. In preliminary discussions, Darvill had already proved amenable to form such an association. The attraction to us of Barclays was the huge reservoir of business lying around (it still is) unexplored, untouched and waiting to be plucked by the more opportunistic and the more innovative merchant banker who recognised, as we certainly did, that in excavating the goodies, our major loading problem was to make clearing banking bureaucracy work for us instead of hindering us. Money and lots of it, and long-term at that, we could negotiate with pension funds. In Bentworth we had already brought in the Unilever Pension Fund on two or three specific venture capital transactions. But we could not – did not – expect any business from our pension fund partner. A high street clearer was a different associate altogether. The attraction to Barclays was to have the means of imbibing the culture and expertise of a merchant bank. Jack Hambro had been extremely shrewd on all of this and, after he died, when Jocelyn became chairman of Hambros and of Bentworth, he was even shrewder.

The initial concept was very simple. Barclays would take up a 50% stake in Bentworth, the balance owned virtually by Hambros and myself. Barclays would put up a certain amount of money, but the real objective was the dialogue, commencing with an impetus from Barclays' head office to the regional and area level, which would directly encourage the manager level to come up with what we wanted – new issue and corporate finance situations. Portfolio advice and management would come later.

The then head office of Barclays in Lombard Street had high-ceilinged lobbies, marbled corridors, hushed anterooms, butlers and messengers, all in livery, all of a style and quality which befitted the country's leading clearing bank. The inception of this great institution is unique: within a decade or so before the First World War, twenty-two separate family banks decided to amalgamate. Being mostly Quakers there was little or no acrimony, on the contrary, there was much gentility and the famous family banking names, Barclays, Bevans, Buxtons, Seebohms, Goodenoughs, Trittons, Thomsons, Tukes, all got together. The story is told that in the very proper Quaker way the new bank would take as its new name the first one in alphabetical order. In charge of the operations was a Barclay, a very shrewd Barclay (there were not many who weren't) who was already able to look past his consonants at the Bevans, and Buxtons and the others and somehow, as the apocryphal goes – it is difficult to prove – it turned out that the terms offered to the family bank whose illustrious name of course started with 'A', were unacceptable. I myself would have preferred a name other than Barclays, because one never knew whether a Barclay was a brewer or a banker, or a bishop, or a nocturnal venue for nightingales; some spelt it as if they were up the wrong family tree, others as if they were in the wrong London square. Bevan would have been next, a healthy Ely name, not sufficiently ex cathedra. After that would have come Buxton, a watering place, perhaps too liquid. The unnamed prima alphabetic inter pares may have suited nicely, being redolent of long summer days at Madingley or Hemingford Gray, punting under weeping willows, girls in white smiling becomingly beneath their parasols, a name without hard consonants, so no hard feelings when refused an overdraft, but Barclays it became, and Barclays it was, and Barclays it is.

The Barclays' butler met me at the lift and took me to Darv's room. We had tea and a desultory conversation which we both knew could have mildly historic City overtones. He was a large man with bright blue eyes and, like all the top men outside the founding families at Barclays, was very conscious of the two-tier management system, each tier more than a step upstairs or downstairs. Darv was before his time. He deplored the lack of expertise on merchant banking matters in his own bank. He also thought there was a real affinity between the young bloods of the Barclays' founding families and their opposite numbers at Hambros. He thought that the association would be of considerable benefit to both sides. He had discussed it with his colleagues.

We all, of course, appreciated that the big obstacle was the Bank of

England: the Old Lady would certainly frown upon a link, unheard of in those days, between a member of the accepting houses, the true élite – from which the Bank of England nearly always derived its Governor – and a clearing bank. It would not do. Darv and his colleagues were ahead of us; they had already come to the conclusion that the Bank's pension fund might instead take up the stake, there was no point in causing the Old Lady to frown, and in those days even a single furrow in the brow was enough to send one down. He wished to give it more thought, and soon after it all happened. There were some further discussions at various lunches, in the directors' dining room of Barclays, at Hambros with Sir John Thomson, the then chairman of Barclays, several meetings with Frank Sherborne, the head of the Barclay Bank pension fund, with various members of the Barclays' founding families. A deal was struck, fifty-fifty, as originally envisaged except that the Barclays Bank pension fund took up its fifty, not the bank. Everyone, it seemed at 41 Bishopsgate and at 54 Lombard Street, was pleased.

As it turned out, our own opposite numbers the founding family stars, the local directors, were not upstairs at their head office; they had their large room, very much like the partners' room of a merchant bank, on the ground floor at 54 Lombard Street. There was Richard Barclay, later a director of Spey, Tim Bevan, later a chairman of Barclays, Alan Tritton and other luminaries. The one I liked most was not one of these, but my new friend, Frank Sherborne, the head of the bank's pension fund who was also in charge of the bank's gilts book. He had a delightful mordant wit and our friendship took off immediately. Each alternate Wednesday the joint Bentworth meeting took place at the headquarters either of Barclays or Hambros, with Peter Eve, a rising star of Barclays, seconded to assist me and in fact moving over to join me in my office at Hambros. The historic association never really gelled. After a year we all came to the same conclusion: it could not work. Superficially each side said it was a question of different cultures. Actually it was my own bungling at the Hambros end. Bentworth at Hambros was in effect a cuckoo in the nest. What we should have done was to have merged Bentworth into the mainstream of Hambros with the actual operation run by one of the Hambros directors.*

---

* Ray Wheeler, who played an important part in the Cedar rescue, would for one have made an excellent job of it.

Nevertheless there had been explicit insight and knowledge into how a clearing bank worked right at the top, how a bank's personality was almost imperceptibly altered by the ever changing elements of business, how a great bank the size of Barclays tended to react to events rather than to shape them, how the signals from the shop floor from branch level filtered laboriously upwards through ever delaying levels of management, how the head office really was the brain with all thinking coming from it and all the commands, how even the large regional offices, the arms and the legs, were severely restricted in having to seek approvals on ludicrously small matters, and how the body, the corpus itself, comprising the thousands of branches, was virtually frozen by old rules and customs. There was very little innovation or desire to make changes, except at the top, and even at that pinnacle, at Barclays at any rate, the awareness and tensions between the two top tiers, between the family members and senior general managers, between Darvill, the Vander Weyers, the Wildes and the Bevans, Buxtons, Tukes and Thomsons were always prevalent. There were various indications of these sensitive interrelated tensions, some bizarre, some illogical, some charming, some pathetic. The first time anyone from downstairs became a director was in 1975 when Derek Vander Weyer was appointed. For example of the board members of Barclays Bank in 1965, the year I formally joined the Cedar Board, there were twenty non-executives, and of the executive directors, all except two were from the family tier. It was a family preserve which didn't exist at any of the other clearers except at Coutts, where you had the Sandons, the Egertons, the Robarts and naturally the Money-Coutts and where, although it was a daughter company of NatWest, it regarded its own parent as unparented.

At the merchant banks, at Hambros, if you were the sort of person who fitted in, you got to the top of the staircase and you were pals with the dynasty, which almost always retained for itself the chair and the deputy chair. If you didn't, you would find that there was a hard landing at the bottom of the staircase, though you would reach the well without knowing how you got there, and when you pulled yourself up, you would find the polite ever-present bank butler already there, ready to brush down your jacket and bowler, opening the door just a little wider than usual, to note his own personal acknowledgement of your final exit. As a general rule, however, for those interested in City lore, the best insight into the personality of a bank is reflected in its luncheon arrangements, indicating who was in or up and who was down or out. At Barclays the custom of the Edwardian fish forks, two of them every Friday in the directors' luncheon room, was a relic of the origins of the bank, a custom worth noting as an *outré* reflection of the effect an abrupt change in a social custom can have on senior bankers who are rather set in their ways.

Fish knives, a Victorian invention, were designed to deal with a new delicacy added to the already heavily laden, indeed the groaning richness of tables of the day. I had always imagined that fish knives and forks came into use because of the lingering fish aroma. This was misguided. The new delicacy was whitebait and the specially crafted fish knives made it that much easier to land. To the staid, anti-new-fangled upper-class Quakers from East Anglia, fish knives could never be faced; so two fish forks it was, at home, and at the bank, until very recently. At the top dining table of Barclays, old man Theodore Barclay, Richard's uncle, was a stickler for traditional customs, and old man Bevan, Tim's uncle, was another stickler; both were stern traditionalists resisting any changes. Richard Barclay must have had somewhere in him, a courageous spirit. A head office local director destined for great things in the bank, brought up with all the rigid dedicated aims of his family and, like each of the younger local directors, expected to take his turn as 'canteen manager'. This meant being in charge for a period of the Directors' luncheon room. During this August, on his rota, the unblemished Barclay, a young married man with several young children, on his way to the very top and the man undoubtedly who was also destined to sign the travellers cheques (then all important) so that Barclays were one up on the other clearers and on cheque level with Hambros, Barings, Schroders, decided that he had had enough of two fish forks, so indeed had some of the others. But he had the guts to do something about it and I think it cost him dear.

When the two old boys came back from their holiday and saw fish knives on the first Friday, they exploded. When I too returned from Beaulieu that summer, I recall my thunderstruck lunch with Richard, when he told me that he had been asked to see them at short notice, and had been offered the choice of two posts, one in Australia, the other in Barbados. I doubt if any director from any of the founding families had ever before, except for short bursts in a regional office, served further afield than EC3, or had ever been given an appointment of such a kind before. A year or two later, when Nadia and I were cruising with friends in the Grenadines, Richard joined us for lunch at Mill Reef in Antigua. Charles Clore was just leaving our party for the airport and when I mentioned Richard's *faux main*, his immediate response was: 'They got it wrong, they should have made him chairman'.

*   *   *

Being a strong opponent of the banks' usual method of advancing loans on a yearly basis, in framing the financing strategy of Cedar I started from that vantage point. The banks' loans, invariably short-term, were subject to an annual review; term loans, borrowing for a fixed period of three, five or seven years, were an exception. British industry had been starved of new investment during the critical post-War decade, not only because of a lack of tax incentives, but also because the clearing banks, with their psychological block on term loans, suffocated forward planning by insisting almost entirely on their prescription of annually renewable overdrafts. They were, of course, mostly renewed, but an insidious motive was that as far as the banks' balance sheets were concerned the technical right to review annually, qualified these loans as twelve-month loans, although renewed year after year, they were more akin to medium- or long-term loans. Even Jack's clever initial overdraft for £500,000 was subject to Cedar's own bank having the right to demand repayment at the end of each year. The rug could be pulled and there would be no argument. It was a dubious practice which created incalculable harm.

As second mortgage loans were essentially term loans for one, two, three or more years, it was obvious that Cedar should borrow money for at least three years in order to establish a stable matching strategy. In all forms of financing, the longer the term the more sure is the stability and survival of the borrower, the shorter the period of a loan, the more geometric is the increase of danger. In property, yearly renewable loans were habitually made to developers for specific developments on the supposition that the property developer would be able to re-finance into long-term money once construction had been completed. The intention to re-finance is all very well, but if it cannot be fulfilled then both the borrower and his bank have been on a gamble. Who was deluding whom? No bank should make a short-term loan on property, unless the borrower has a pre-commitment of take-out funds, or the ability to repay from another source, or unless the bank itself has the right to purchase the property – at cost or valuation, whichever is the lower, and with the junior debt, quite properly at the sharp end of *caveat emptor* – if interest is in arrears or if the loan has not been repaid.*

Jack Cotton's genius was to initiate the concept of applying long-term money to property development; no risks, no refinancing: one-stop financing. I had worked closely with him and indeed had widened his concept, particularly in the application of pension fund monies. In framing the structure of Cedar's borrowings, on seven-year or ten-year money, it was inevitable that I would base the borrowing policy on pension fund money rather than on bank finance. Pension fund money is essentially medium- to long-term money, therefore ideal for any form of property financing, including financing second mortgages. If Cedar borrowed seven-year money from a pension fund then in matching terms, Cedar, taking into account generous turn round time, could lend one six-year loan once, two three-year loans twice, three two-year loans three times and five one-year loans five or six times during that seven-year period; all with little or no risks.

From the point of view of a conservative pension fund putting money into a company like Cedar, it was security at its best and the returns of the best.† As long as there is an adequate margin between the forced sale price of the house, and the total of first and second mortgages outstanding, the security is as safe as H——s.

Cedar, therefore, could satisfy even the most stringent demands of a pension fund on the safety of its loan and the strength of its security. It could go further: it could satisfy the most stringent scrutiny by any outside body that its loan was probably safer than most high street bank advances. Whilst the commercial risk was less than conventional bank lending, the interest charged, the rate of return, was much higher than it needed to be, taking into account the low risk factor. I appreciated why Izzy's father had very few, if any, bad debts, and why Izzy, the most cautious of men, was so enthusiastic about the second mortgage business.

---

* Old fashioned foreclosure rights have long since served their purpose.
† If a borrower has a house with a forced sale value of £100,000 and a first mortgage of £70,000 (forced sale value is usually 90% of normal value) he has an equity of £30,000. If he borrows £6,000 on his second mortgage, it is at least five times covered by his equity value. If the forced sale value is £110,000, the first mortgage does not alter but the owner's equity has increased by more than 30%, the £6,000 second mortgage loan now being covered nearly seven times. The security also improves from day one, because disregarding any increase in the value of the house, the £6,000 loan plus interest decreases with each monthly repayment.

The strategy and form of the financing was, however, only half of the problem. There were two disquieting ghosts which had to be exorcised: the first was the ominous spectre of repossession, the second was, if anything, the more ominous spectre of respectability. And both ghosts had to be exorcised before any pension fund could even be approached. The ghost of repossession was solved for me by a Hambros man, and the ghost of respectability was solved by a Barclays man: the Hambros man was Jack Hambro and the Barclays man was Frank Sherborne.

Repossession of someone's house is to my mind monstrous. I had made up my mind that no one to whom I was responsible could be involved in Cedar if repossession was applied, unless the householder was a proven villain. If the debt was in doubt for valid reasons, i.e. unemployment, it should be rescheduled on a generous basis and not treated as a bad debt, and in certain cases written down to remove some pressure from the borrower.* Not to repossess was well advised from another point of view. A pension fund, say Unilever, could be seriously embarrassed if a householder obtained the support of a tabloid with a screaming headline such as 'soap giant throws family into the street'. How did Jack Hambro kill this repossession ogre? By simply pointing out to me with his usual sapience that there was no compulsion on a lender to disclose to the borrower that he did not intend to enforce his legal rights. Neat and simple, not entirely dissimilar, although it would not be wise to take the analogy too far in logic, to Don Quixote's helmet, which Sancho explained would be all right as long as no one knew it was made of paper. I was grateful to Sancho Hambro for his innate wisdom.

Respectability was something else. Respectability is not technical, it

---

* In 1991 there began a wave of repossessions in Britain which caused great human misery and a political scandal. Attempts were made by the Major government, in consultation with the building societies, to lessen the dire effects on the wretched home owners. I felt strongly that the government should have penalised the building societies for having done something quite reprehensible. The real scandal was that the building societies, encouraged by certain insurance companies, contracted a series of mortgage indemnity policies whereby the building societies were insured against nonpayment by the lender for the percentage over the normal level of 70% to 80%. This encouraged the building societies to lend 90% to 100% (even higher) to borrowers, who like their lenders, were banking on ever-increasing house values. What made it worse was that on repossession, the legal obligation was merely to sell 'at best', which meant that the borrowers were at the open-ended shute of a bottomless market.

is impalpable, it is normally conspicuous only by its absence. Of all the intangible attributes, respectability is the most precious which, when compromised, is lost in a twinkling, only regained, if at all, after unblemished activity. Respectability? I first got around to it one day at lunch with Sherborne. He knew all about respectability. Barclays could walk on water. Would his own august institution embark on a financial undertaking if the activity were generally considered unrespectable? His response? Banks embark on new business on merit whether respectable or not, as long as it was legal: in the finance area what was not respectable yesterday could easily be respectable tomorrow: the question was not what is respectable, but *who* is respectable. Not so simple and not so neat, but I thought an acceptable form of *QED*. What I read in his observation and in subsequent asides was that if a financial company conducted itself in the most proper manner and had the most respectable shareholders, it would be considered respectable. To a material extent, a share holder and loan holder like Unilever pension fund would answer the problem.

So as long as it was perfectly legal, it was who, not what. Sherborne had defined the City's own central ethos with stunning simplicity and in ironical vindication it was his own Barclays Bank Trust Company which later handled the Cedar public quotation, when, as it happened, we only won the day in spite of the derogation by the press because it was who, not what, because it was the impeccable quality of the people involved which neutralised the criticism and which brought victory. Since then to a formidable extent, the fact that, for many years now, second mortgage lending has been considered a respectable activity can be laid at the door of Cedar and the respectability of its supporting institutions.

I spoke to Walton, as promised, before speaking to the Morrisons. This was the gist: 'I have in mind approaching a pension fund, very probably Unilever, for a smallish loan to begin with, say £250,000. The period will be seven years. They would not have a normal debenture but something more secure, the actual security, the actual documentation which Cedar itself possessed as security. This documentation comprising signed forms, searches, deeds etc., could be kept in special cabinets and if the pension fund wished they could have an auditor's certificate every three months on the precise status of their specific security, their specific cabinets. This would be cumbersome and might not be required but must be offered. Unilever would receive an above average rate of interest on their loan and the right to purchase an agreed number of new shares in Cedar at a low valuation, as near to par as possible. Cedar would make further borrowings, preferably long-term, from Unilever and later other institutional supporters, each of whom would have the right to purchase further newly-issued shares at their rising value rather than at near par. Financing would continue on this basis until the institutions would be in the majority, with the original owners, the Morrisons, in the minority.

'From the beginning, Cedar had to conduct its affairs as a wholly respectable establishment financial entity. The calibre of the board was all important. Unilever would have a representative on the board and I would insist on this as part of the arrangement. It was who, not what, and Unilever's evident support, not so much as a loan holder but as a shareholder with its own man on the Board, which would proclaim support to the world at large. Cedar would be provided with instant credibility. It would be ultra-conservative, always lending short and borrowing long. You, Izzy, and I will go on the board. We would have an option to acquire 10% each of the equity at the same price as Unilever, our equity to come directly from the Morrisons and not to be by way of new shares. There would be no special shares with special voting rights. All shares would rank equally. I would be responsible for all financing. As to repossession, if it were envisaged at all, it had to be specifically approved by the board and if any director said no, it was to be no!'

I waited for Walton's response. He took it all in at once. It was the blueprint of Cedar's financing, the reason for its particular glamour, the reason for its particular growth. But inside that strategy was a poison pill. From the outset the Morrisons' controlling shareholding would dilute until in due course they would become minority shareholders, and much of their later manoeuvres to regain control, could be said to have derived from this early stratagem. To most people having a decreasing part of a more than rapidly increasing cake would more than suffice any greed. Neither Izzy nor I took into account Jack's pathological suspicions, especially of people with whom he was in business, and I now believe that, as this original financial concept materialised, it hardened his determination not to remain in a minority position and to regain control in his own way and in his own time. The pill was a slow poison and Jack's counter-measures, as we were to learn, were numbingly lethal in effect. Apart from misjudging the intensity of Jack's paranoia, Walton and I made another funda-mental mistake. It was an appalling omission from the outset. We should have insisted that a top-ranking banker be appointed as a joint managing director along with Michael. At that moment the Morrisons would have assented with reluctance, but they would have assented. Cedar required a full-time banking expert at the highest level of its management, and the fact that the person who was eventually appointed to this position was David Fischer indicates how appalling a misjudgement it was.

Walton listened to me quietly with as little nasal interruption as possible, then he nodded. 'It's good. But you are going to have problems with Jack on the 10%. Don't let him beat you down, and I don't want to go on the Board and I don't want 10%'. The Morrisons did beat me down but not by much. Izzy did not go on the Board and was genuinely annoyed with me over his own participation upon which I insisted, though he was somewhat appeased when he later sold out at a princely profit.

We had, however, both utterly missed two crucial points. Jack's paranoia on control could not, I think, have been foreseen. The one pertaining to top management most certainly should have been. It taught me a lesson: if there is something amiss in a commercial cake, the cause is almost certainly due to a missing or unbalanced ingredient in the original recipe; here, the missing ingredient, the lack of professional banking management, should have been apparent to Izzy and I from the very beginning, and it was inexcusable not to have insisted upon it.

*   *   *

Cedar had moved from its Woods Mews office by Park Street to Stratton Street, near Devonshire House by Green Park. Walton did not attend the subsequent discussion with the Morrisons which took place in Stratton Street, the first of a large number of discussions with the Morrisons over the following years held there and in Pall Mall until the violent break with them in the middle of 1971. Some of these discussions were amiable and pleasant, others less so; very much less so.

This one on the basic financing strategy was what my mother would have called 'so-so', meaning it could have been better, it could have been worse, but that it should have been better. Walton had already briefed the Morrisons, and I had deliberately not put anything on paper. Michael disliked the no-repossession policy but Jack talked him down, giving Michael a sidelong knowing glance, which I later learnt was his overt coded signal of – agree now, we will talk about it after he has gone. I had not seen this peculiar form of neck turning before, but was to see much of it over the years in the frequent peregrinations between us. Unexpectedly, Jack lasered directly on to the dilution aspect. The principle once set in motion was inherently irreversible and though he was seriously concerned, it was noticeable that he was deciding to put it in the background, presumably, to be dealt with in due course in his own way. Until the transaction with Unilever was actually completed, it was all so much talk. 'Will Unilever do it?' was what he wanted to know. We chatted generally about credibility and of the new Cedar with the advent of an institution like Unilever. We talked about respectability; we talked especially about the Bank of England.

I could discern at this early juncture that Jack and Michael already had ideas above their lending station. They were clearly impatient for the time when Cedar would issue cheque books, paying-in books and bankers' slips; when press announcements would be made by Cedar as a bank. Jack would be showing the world. He had moved from dress shops to property, now he and Michael were moving into banking. Possibly in the near future they would be having a major institution as a partner and then they would stress more forcibly that they were in the banking business, not in the second mortgage business. I could see how the wind was blowing and gently urged that when they met Jasper Knight they concentrated upon the mechanics of the actual business and not on their aspirations. When the meeting was duly held they were both absolutely superb, even to sending Fischer away.

The offices in Stratton Street, situated at the farthest end of Mayfair from the Woods Mews end, meant that Jack had a twenty-minute walk, so he was sometimes driven, in his new Rolls by his chauffeur or picked up by Michael on his way in from St John's Wood. Stratton Street had a narrow though sedate air and not unexpectedly Jack's own room was a replica of his former office. As you entered the building, you turned to the right into the lobby on the ground floor. It was part of the reception area, it had a counter with a secretary and typist sitting behind it. Fischer called it the bank counter, and on it was a sign, a small one, which he'd had specially designed, with the word 'Cashier' emblazoned on it in gold. I did not think Jasper was going to be very impressed by that, nor was he. His first comment when we left after that first presentation was, 'I like Jack Morrison, I like his son. But do ask them to get rid of that cashier sign. It's not the Bank of England.'

The visit by Jasper Knight to the Stratton Street offices had, as it turned out, a slight tinge of financial epoch making. A major UK institution was for the first time investing in a privately-held lending company. Cedar, until the association with Unilever, was just one of many third- or fourth-ranking lending set-ups proliferating throughout the country. There were many scandals, many went bust, some had strange pedigrees. The daddy of them all, First National, started by Pat Matthews with Hambros' support, was originally an offshoot of an East End furniture shop. The antecedents of many of the other companies were unhealthy, their operational activities and methods of financing obscure.

The Morrisons, however, had a good name. They came from a family known for philanthropy and good works, they were rich, they were a definite cut above the others. But their first commercial experience had been in ladies' dress shops, then in property, now in lending, and not in a month of Sundays could one claim that a Morrison was the sort of ilk who had a natural background in finance. Until its association with Unilever, its first institutional shareholder, the main difference between Cedar and most of the others in the fringe banking sector was that, unless Jack lost all his money overnight which was, of course, impossible, Cedar in being owned by the wealthy Morrisons had formidable outside financial resources. In addition Michael had certain undeniable gifts; he had had no training or experience in banking, but he was an outstanding salesman and administrator. During all the time I was involved in Cedar, its paperwork and administration were impeccable, due entirely to Michael Morrison. What Michael had achieved was impressive and he was by no means a daddy's boy; behind his excitable enthusiasm was a real endeavour to make Cedar different from the others, behind that was his great passion to be a banker and to be considered as a banker. Behind all of this was the ruminating influence of his father, to whom he listened attentively; Michael admired his father quite genuinely, it was not put on, it was a pure unabashed admiration.

During all Michael's life, notwithstanding the divorce between his parents, life had been comparatively easy for him. He was lucky, too, in the girl he married; Angela was not only a loving partner, she was a person of character endowed with tact and diplomacy, who knew how to deal with a difficult and complex father-in-law. Her own family, the Ross's, were a fairly affluent business-oriented middle-class Jewish family living in the St John's Wood/Hampstead belt. Their daughter marrying into the Morrison family was a solid, conventional and near-equal alliance. But in his career, in his business, Michael, apart from a brief period with the Wolfson organisation, had never been in an independent job having to work for others. He had never been stretched, his qualities of leadership had not yet been put to the test and there was always the query as to how he would cope under severe pressure.

Jasper Knight was to arrive at Stratton Street mid-morning on his own, and he and I were to leave in his car before lunch, taking me on to Hambros, after dropping him at the Unilever building at Blackfriars. I had already sent him memoranda and relevant Cedar data, and we had discussed the possible association over a period of several months. He had decided that William Broadfield, who was my liaison in Bentworth, would also be the liaison on Cedar. At Bentworth, together with our new Barclays partners, we were working closely with Unilever on several venture capital investments, including a new television rental company which we later sold to Thorn; a joint company with J. Lyons called Wimpey International; a joint company with the Unilever parent, not the pension fund, Commercial Plastics, the company which we had purchased from Isaac. The friendship between Jasper and myself had matured, he had been a guest at home for dinner and Nadia and I had been to his place near Henley.

Jasper had followed his father into Unilever and had been there most of his working life. At Eton he had made a name for himself as an oarsman, indeed we had a joint rowing interest. He was the big burly heavyweight who would always be number four or five in the middle of the boat; I was the indolent passenger with an unexpected gift for watermanship who coxed his college boat three years running. One year at Henley, a great delight for Nadia was when she sat with Jasper amongst all the pink ties in the umpire's launch, and, although at the height of summer, she wore my college rowing scarf – navy blue with white tassels – for the occasion, unperturbed by the raising of pink eyebrows; it was my first present to her when I was an undergraduate and is still worn with pride on special occasions.

Jasper and I saw each other often during those Cotton/Clore and Hambros days. The Thames valley still had lingering Edwardian overtones, happily evident each year at the Regatta, at Phyllis Court, at the Leander Club, where lunch was always poached salmon and tea was always cucumber sandwiches and dinners were always indescribable, and there were dewy-eyed girls and convivial weekends in Thameside houses with Cecil Beaton decor and Bertie Wooster blazers and pre-war Burgundy, and gliding on the clear unruffled water, with few other boats in sight, the only sound being the swishing of the punt pole and the rustling of the willow trees. And then there came that ineffably dismal time, when Jasper saw fit to act against me during the Spey days, when he became the direct cause of a proposed change in the shareholdings of Cedar much to the consternation and alarm of the Morrisons, and when he tried to sink Spey much to my consternation and alarm.

On the way back to Blackfriars from Stratton Street, hurrying because we were late for lunch, he said, 'You can take it you're on'. When I told the Morrisons, they were ecstatic. I could almost hear Jack's tears of joy plopping on the telephone receiver. I was his second son, he burbled with instant fatherly love, we were a close happy family. Cedar was now truly in business. Here he was right. It really was a fresh new era and in a funny way it was quite exciting. Izzy was more than pleased. Jack went off to celebrate on one of his trips – without Fischer. I know because when I invited Michael for a champagne lunch, he asked whether Fischer could join us. The reader will not be surprised to learn that we were just two to crack the bottle.

THREE

The Heavyweight Links

Cedar had been bursting at the seams at Stratton Street, the problem being that some of the Amal people were also working from there. It was necessary to persuade the Morrisons and the institutions that Cedar should be geographically detached from Amal. We were nourishing an embryonic bank specialising in the business of second mortgages, endeavouring to stamp it with its own identity, and what had to be avoided was any form of association with a property company. What had impinged from the beginning on the minds of the institutions was that the Morrisons had a controlling shareholding in a quoted property company, Amalgamated Securities, which was an entirely separate Morrison activity, a separate nest-egg, if one wished to express it that way, which I certainly did.

But as the heavyweight links were being forged I was frequently under pressure from Jack and Michael on this Amal front. Why couldn't Amal have an association with one or other of the institutions who were now part of Cedar? Why was I being so adamant that there could be no cross-over? Having set the institutional ball rolling for Izzy and the Unilever Pension Fund, why did I not do the same for Amal?

The pressures, particularly from Jack, were not easy to withstand, but my rebuttals were consistent: we had agreed from the beginning that Amal was not only a separate entity, it had to be seen as such. Any association between Amal and any of Cedar's institutions would be breaking faith; I had always stressed to the institutions, supported by Michael in this particular aspect of our association with them, that the only link between Cedar and Amal was the personal Morrison link; that the two businesses were and would always remain separate; that if

Cedar was to be taken as seriously as everyone wished, that is as a fledgling bank, it had to be perceived as an independent entity, standing four-square on its own. The separation between these two companies, especially as Amal was already listed on the stock exchange, had to be unambiguous, particularly in the eyes of the Bank of England and particularly in the eyes of Jim Keogh, their man who was at the head of the Discount Office – the dreaded Discount Office – which could say nay to Cedar's aspirations or nay to any aspiring bank for that matter, without giving the slightest reason.

So in striving for Cedar's distinct detachment it was entirely fortuitous that its splendid Pall Mall offices were acquired in a chance opportunity through Bishopsgate Property. This latter company, sponsored by Hambros and its accepting house neighbour M. Samuel, had been conceived by me as a means of supporting budding young property entrepreneurs whilst holding a sizeable portfolio of shares in the larger property companies. Amongst this roster of quoted candidates we had wanted to include Scottish Metropolitan, which would have fitted in comfortably, but Walton was reluctant. He had for a longish period preferred the idea of associating with a pension fund, Unilever being his first choice, so I duly introduced him to Jasper Knight over breakfast one morning in his suite at Grosvenor House. And so began another romance between a quoted property company and an institution, and so unwittingly was started, a train of miscarried thoughts in the minds of the Morrisons.

One of the budding Jack Cottons, supported by Bishopsgate, was a tiny wasp-like property man called Ian Hart. A 25% equity interest in his company was purchased at par in return for a secured loan for £1 million. I went on the board and wanted to get off as soon as I could, so that my new colleague, John Spink, who had just joined the bank could take my place.

To introduce John Spink, a chartered surveyor, into Hambros, had been surprisingly arduous. Jack Hambro, chairman of the bank (Jocelyn was then deputy chairman) and chairman of Bishopsgate, had retained a strong belief that specialists like chartered surveyors had no place being employed in a family merchant bank. You'll want to have engineers and computer operators next, he grumbled. Yes, I said, if they were able to read balance sheets. He was by no means alone in his attitude, for it was the prevalent merchant banking (and also stock-broking) wisdom of the time to take on mostly graduates with no specific qualifications other than personal or family connections and good manners. However, Jack Hambro had a particular regard for the Prudential and we hit on the then other prevalent City practice of reaching a decision by means of sounding out a third party. It was a method, in this instance also a ruse, which worked admirably. What it came to was that Hambro persuaded himself that it must be all right if the chartered surveyor came from the Prudential.

One morning we set out together from 41 Bishopsgate to see the very powerful Leslie Brown, the head of the Prudential, at their vast gothic-tiled headquarters at High Holborn. Tiles everywhere, but probably not in the lavatories, mused Jack.

Let's go and have a look, I said, but at this point Brown came down to greet us and to take us up to his office; it was not every day that the chairman of Hambros came round to see him. Brown had an engaging trick which I have applied myself from time to time with total success. In talking to people who wanted something, a loan, an advance, a request of some sort, he would drop his voice, so one could not hear what he was saying. The person importuning him (commercially, of course) was always thrown and occasionally disoriented, his nerves so shattered by mishearing, that he could not pursue his goal. On this occasion Brown was hearty and decipherable, and there was no need for us to crane our necks or to lose our nerves. After Jack Hambro explained our need he diffidently asked whether Brown would recommend one of his own men. He did. He also did us very proud by coming up with one of his best chaps, such was the ingenuous goodwill of the City in those days. So Spink became the first ever chartered surveyor wholly employed by a merchant bank, and very soon afterwards he became a director of Ian Hart's company.

Hart was clever and if he had not died in his early thirties I believe he may well have ranked amongst today's property leaders. After his death the company and its portfolio had to be reorganised. Agents had been appointed to sell off several buildings, one of which, in that evil property agents' jargon which has seeped like a sewer into the language, was in 'desirable' Pall Mall. It was number 60, opposite St James's Park, almost facing our own Hambros' West End office and Marlborough Gate. The building had a staid individual personality, reticent in character like every other building in Pall Mall, except for the misplaced oversized and over-membered RAC Club. Number 60 had multi-paned windows set in a pleasing stone façade. Its one serious drawback was that the ground floor had two separate front entrances cleaved by Crown Passage. This ancient alley commenced its somewhat meandering journey from Pall Mall, filtering up to King Street and Bury Street at the far end; from the back of number 60 one could look down upon an intriguing collection of hidden village shops (many are still there) with much friendly thronging and jostling during the lunch hour. The Crown Passage archway certainly added an amiable if disjointed dimension to the character of the building.

Pall Mall, until the implementation of the crass one-way system, was one of the most noble thoroughfares in Europe; it was also my favourite, just a length ahead of St James's Street and Piccadilly. I learned the derivation of its name quite by chance one evening from Patrick Plunket, the Queen's equerry. We had picked him up at Buckingham Palace on our way to the Opera House. It was a Gala night and making up the party was Alicia Markova. Driving along the Mall, the evening still bright, the trees in full leaf, London's loveliest boulevard at its soft-shadowed best in the waning sun, Nadia wondered if the word Mall had been taken up by the Americans for their shopping malls. 'Oh yes,' said Patrick. 'And Pall Mall?' 'That,' he explained with the unaffected modesty of the well-bred man of culture, 'came from an ancient French game, played with a mallet. The players had to drive a ball through a suspended iron ring. The game was called Peille Meille.' Patrick spelt it out for us, without a trace of pedantry, his pronunciation having a captivating old-world cadence; then, ending with a smile, he said, 'It was not as difficult a game as croquet,' and it has bothered me ever since how he was able to evince such a comparison, or had we all been so wooden headed as to miss the sly tap of a gentle tease.

I suggested to Michael that he looked in on peille meille, number 60, before it came on the market. It was love at first sight. In due course the move took place and Jack's office on the first floor, his new office in St James's of which he was inordinately proud, was again replicated from previous incarnations, still interchangeable with his drawing room at home. Cedar was no longer 'West End', nor was it 'City': it was St James's.

St James's, the stewards enclosure of old clubland, was famed for its purveyors, who never sold as such – which meant sending an account before obtaining permission to do so – or took cash (not the done thing here as it was around the way in the new street named after the Regent). No, in St James's they only purveyed, which meant that the purveyor was proud of his customer, not the other way around, and the purveying was for gentlemen's perquisites only. For that reason, the very masculine St James's still retains some frock-coated white-spatted old-fashioned appeal despite its near desecration by the men of the Greater London Council. These unknown mindless bureaucrats, without troubling to engage in any public discussion, coldly punctured the lung of St James's when they made Pall Mall and St James's Street one-way, linking it with an equally murderous operation, the force-fed one-way Piccadilly from the Ritz to the Circus.

St James's housed Christies, more art dealers, more arcane specialists in jade, ivory, erotica, Stubbs, Hogarth, first editions, than the rest of London put together, and also silversmiths, barbers, jewellery – for gentlemen only, diamond dress studs, pearl tiepins, lapis lazuli cufflinks, and shirt-makers, always silk (cotton was by special order), and hunting gear, shooting accoutrements and fishing tackle, and hat-makers headed by Locks, shoes cobbled by Lobbs, humidors and cigars and hand-made Turkish cigarettes from Lewis's, snuff tinctured with peppermint or elephant musk, claret and port from Justerini and Brooks and their special initialled J&B rare, and the indefatigable Mrs Rosa Lewis who understood so well, like all old retainers, that not only should one always talk down to the aristocracy but that gentlemen also needed further perquisites, for whom she lavishly and erratically attended at her Cavendish rooms. There were other hostelries and eating and meeting places, there were numerous spacious serviced flats for upper-class American and French collectors, and many more pieds-à-terre, mostly hidden behind obscure doors and bannisters for other sorts of collectors. Through this modish male enclave, the traffic of Pall Mall and St James's Street, now clumsy and fearsome because it cannot make up its mind (nor ever will) on which side of the street it ought to travel, lurches along as an important part of the main exodus from the City, back home to Belgravia, Knightsbridge, South Kensington, Chelsea and beyond. The merchant bankers, insurance and stockbrokers, lawyers, very few accountants – they mostly seemed to live in Kent or Essex – driving or being driven via Buckingham Palace if going straight home, or via Pall Mall if going to Mayfair or onto the wrong side of the Park, or if 'dropping in on the way'. Dropping in on the way meant going to one's club.

My St James's club was not Brooks's, nor White's, nor Boodles, but a small fish restaurant called Wilton's which was a favourite personal stop-over for well over a decade. Some *pâté en croûte* or six of the best washed down by a chilled glass of Bollinger, alone or with a friend, seemed a modest enough nourishment to keep one going until dinner.

Wilton's was a veritable club. The original oysterman, wily old Marks, was now, after an expatriot session at Bucks club, its top man and if he did not like the look of you, even if there were numerous empty tables, they were instantly 'reserved' and you were shown the door. There was no membership committee, only the rapid infallible oyster eye of Mr Marks nodding approval or rejection. Of his pre-war regulars was Olaf Hambro, Jocelyn's father, who had his dozen, some said even more, dropping in on his way. Early in the war, so the story goes, a winter's evening during the Blitz, the owner Mrs Liel unnerved by the bombing, told Hambro that she had had enough of London and the air raids. It was not to Olaf Hambro's taste to be done out of anything he savoured, even if it meant buying the place, and one should not deprive Mrs Liel of her native cunning in choosing the right moment and the right man for a change of ownership.

Marks was brought in from Bucks. Never having been seen to actually walk, always shuffling, he continued his purveying, nothing changed, not even after Jocelyn inherited Wilton's from his father.

The investment never showed a dividend but old Marks seemed to prosper. By the sixties the lease in King Street had run out, and Spink found new premises around the corner in Bury Street. One day the first nerves from Marks I had ever seen were revealed. 'Is Spink your man?' he asked, hovering by my table. 'Yes.' 'Well let me say, your whippersnappers can look at the books any way they like, but they will never find any profits.' I sensed that this may have been his unspoken arrangement with Olaf. 'Mr Marks,' I said, recycling a quip of Jack Cotton's, 'profits are in the eye of the beholder. Now will you do something for me?' 'What?' 'When I visit can I have a better table than Jocelyn?' Marks roared with laughter. 'Anything, young man, as long as you bring madam.' 'It's a deal.'

The next day when I strolled in to see Jocelyn at his desk in the partners' room I told him I had done a smashing deal with Marks. 'Yes?' he said warily, he knew Marks from of old. 'I have arranged for you to have the second-best table.' I don't believe he was particularly amused. When the opening party was held in the new premises, properly decorated in the Mrs Keppel *belle époque* period of Belgravian cads and bounders with real moustaches and false promises, of saucy Gaiety Girls and private banquettes, it was very well organised by

Jocelyn's wife, Sylvia, a most beautiful woman of witty composure, and it was extremely lively, made up only of friends, all members of the Club. It was curious, I told Nadia later, who could not make the opening, I had not noticed anyone else there from the bank.

It was at Wilton's, where Jocelyn and I had a special lunch before I left Hambros to start Spey Investments, sitting in one of the enclosed banquettes, known as horse boxes, with Marks, noting this rare *à deux* by shuffling around more frequently than usual, but still wearing his permanent look of benign hostility; it was at Wilton's where, at dinner with William Walton and his wife, seeing how anguished he was that I might have a bitter row with her over our villa in Ischia, that I decided there and then to assign the lease back to her as a gift, his letter of affectionate thanks asking that I should not tell her that he had written; and it was at Wilton's where Nadia and I sat quietly one evening in the summer of 1971, immediately after I had a cold and bitter session with Jack Morrison, comforted by the intimacy of the horse box.

After Cedar's move to Pall Mall from Stratton Street, with my club around the corner, I had taken to seeing the Morrisons late in the afternoon for any discussion. It was very convenient. I would leave the City slightly early and, as I now recall, when passing by the Athenaeum would habitually mutter about the one-way system; if I didn't, my driver would know that I had other less exacting problems on my mind. I would be set down at number 60, opposite Marlborough Gate, looking forward more to the short walk afterwards to Marks's emporium than to the impending conversations on Cedar matters, although I found to my surprise that I was enjoying my growing relationship with Michael, preferring the occasions when he and I were on our own, when Jack would be away on one of his trips and before Fischer was admitted as of right.

Amongst those frequent meetings was one I shall not forget. It was in autumn 1970, five years after the advent of Unilever. We were in Jack's room to discuss the plans for Cedar's public quotation. He was in his winged chair, quite still, his back straight, his legs crossed, the sitting image of an original Graham Sutherland portrait. Michael was bristling with energy as usual, and it was evident that he was putting on weight; we were all getting older, even Fischer. The nephew himself, having won his spurs from his family could no longer be excluded. Two years earlier he had been appointed a director of the 'bank', which was how he and now also the Morrisons always insisted on calling Cedar. Uplifted in his new stature, he was now a permanent fixture in their lives. This particular afternoon, the Morrison family of Cedar Holdings, was fully on parade.

Through the windows, I could see the corner of Hambros West End and the distant trees in the park beyond St James's Palace. The afternoon sun was flickering through intermittently. It was already three years since I had departed with very amiable good wishes from three quarters of my colleagues at Hambros Bank to start Spey Investments – not too far down the road, just past the Bank of England and Poultry on to Old Jewry, number 10, almost opposite Grocer's Hall.

Since leaving, many diverse events had occurred at Cedar and at Spey. One of these – less significant in money terms but very much more so in respect of the subsequent relationships – was that Spey now owned the greater part of my original holdings in Cedar. That we were able to discuss Cedar's public quotation at all meant that it had made solid progress. My vivid recollection, however, of that afternoon, was not due to the content of our discussion, though very meaningful, it was something dimensionally different, something unsettling and ominous; it was an expression I had seen on Jack's face, directed straight at me – a naked fleeting expression of unbridled animosity. A sudden flicker, an unexpected shaft of light, had revealed a brutality in the chairman of Cedar I had not perceived before; perhaps unnoticed, it had always been there; perhaps, on early occasions, out of sight, it had been directed at my shoulderblades, perhaps Jack even examining the exact point of insertion. Why this animosity? I sat up sharply against my chair with a momentary shudder. It was not something to shrug off and to forget. Nor did I.

Yes, Cedar's progress had been solid. By 1970, when serious consideration was being given to a public quotation, as we were doing at this never to be forgotten meeting, its profits had jumped from virtually nothing, to nearly £500,000. In fact Cedar's progress had been more than solid: it had been spectacular.

Of course, the turning point was Unilever. Its first loan, inherently symbolic, of £250,000, was signed, sealed and delivered in September 1965. In October, William Broadfield was appointed to the board (I also joined on the same day, very fitting, as Jasper Knight remarked). Broadfield was Cedar's first institutional director, the first overt indication of Cedar's financing strategy, the first institutional link, the first heavyweight.

After Unilever, the second institution was the Electricity Supply pension fund. By its rules, members could not take up board positions, so the head of its fund, Sidney Cowtan attended every board meeting and was a director in everything but name. The National Coal Board pension fund was the third institution, and Reginald Edward, who had just retired as its head, joined the board of Cedar. Phoenix Assurance was the fourth and final institution, and its investment manager, Charles Knight, came on to the board in October 1968.

On joining, each of the four put up substantial loan money and took up an equity stake, either directly or by way of converting part of the loans. The loans ranged from medium- to long-term; the matching of borrowing to lending was securely calibrated. As each institution came in, the Morrisons were delighted, and as their delight increased with the advent of a further institution, their majority holding in Cedar decreased. With the entry of Phoenix, taking into account shares held by Spey, Walton, myself, and also the institutions including their convertible rights, the Morrisons' majority turned into a minority. In 1970 when we started discussing the timing for the public quotation it was apparent that, taking into account further dilution arising from the shares to be taken up by the public, the Morrisons would soon own little more than 25%, as against the institutions holding over 30%.

When would the delight of the Morrisons turn sour? Surely they must have a plan? Jack had accepted the slide from majority to minority without producing anything more than his usual aspersions of all and sundry. He was otherwise too equable, too untroubled, far too much so for a man of his paranoid suspicions. He must have made his calculations. They were, of course, interrelated with Amal; if Amal were taken over by Cedar for shares he could then slide back into majority. This was surely his answer. But when would he make his move? And how? I pondered the situation at some length.

With each heavyweight link it was left to me to select the institution, to discuss the association, and to negotiate the transactions. I settled the basic terms with Michael and Jack. The procedure with each was identical; general discussions on the broad aspects of second mortgage lending, specific discussions on the way Cedar worked, a massive amount of paperwork covering every aspect of these inner workings, then finally detailed projections before the formal presentation. What impressed but did not surprise any of us was that all of the paperwork was read, studied and checked; this was evident from the detailed questions which were raised. Once the basic agreement and principle was reached, it was then the moment for the important ceremony of the presentation.

This began with a general chat in Jack's office, the chairman embarking upon his performance, in his own pronounced individual style, immaculate in his own corporate sorcery. He was a master, making all the right noises – and as usual never, except by a sidelong glance, looking in the eye the person or persons he was addressing – making general irrelevancies to demonstrate his increasing social and business lustre, and proceeding with brotherhood comments about Michael and myself, Michael always looking at his father, nodding in agreement and murmuring in assent, and, although not feeling such adoration, I still marvelled at the way Jack made just the right impression by flavour and vagueness rather than by taste and precision. Eventually he would conclude with his valedictory remarks, which were, in effect, that he very much welcomed the institutions to the widening Cedar family of which he was lucky to be the head, each member of the family dedicated to making Cedar not the biggest, that was left to others perhaps less dedicated, but the best – in quality, he would stress.

Jack would then rise from his chair as if waiting for the cheers to subside and would refer with a spontaneous, oft-repeated anecdote to one or another of the photographs on a side table, or to one of the *objets* in the vitrine, apologising for having to take his leave as he had an unbreakable appointment, the merest hint here that his next assignation might have something to do with the solution of an unspecified problem at number 10. Then standing by the door, there would be a fluttering wave of the hand, a grand adieu followed by a curt nod of command to Michael and myself to carry on.

And carry on we did. What followed thereafter clinched matters, although it must be emphasised that Jack's florid performance was a definite part of that clinching. After Jack's departure Michael was at his best, his enthusiasm dynamic and infectious, yet under full control, his clear knowledge and intelligence and expertise in vivid display. If Jack had been present, Michael, paternally inhibited, would have been far less effective, but Jack was clever enough to know when he and his son were more effective by his well chosen absences.

Michael, unleashed but well restrained, would stress the main points of Cedar, the care with which applicants and brokers were screened, the careful matching – borrowing long, lending short – the exact control systems, the very beginnings of a dialogue (of which he was especially proud) with the Discount Office of the Bank of England, the strict application of the Cedar rules and guidelines, the repossession policy subject to board approval with a right of veto by any single director, the separateness and financial strength of the Morrison-controlled public property company Amalgamated Securities, which Michael was always careful to point out, had nothing to do with Cedar. Yes, Michael in these encounters was extremely effective in his own right; he was not only a young counterpoint to the elder-statesman overview of his father, he was the well-liked first-rate operational son who might one day show that he had within him the capability of taking over, this continuity strongly appealing, and rightly so, to the institutions.

Cedar's renowned credibility derived solely from these institutional links. With Jack Cotton and his associations with the institutions, it was the financial link which was pre-eminent, credibility was already there, though enhanced; with Bentworth likewise; but with Cedar exposed to the public, albeit through its brokers, the financial advantages though crucial, were of less importance than this factor of credibility. The perception from outside, particularly in the City, was not only of increasing respect but also of some amazement. These institutional links were comparatively new to the City and indeed to the financial world at large. There was an element of wonder from influential City bodies why such heavyweights, representing some of the greatest industries in the country, would make this type of association and with such a relatively small outfit.

Izzy Walton was also impressed, although characteristically he struck a warning note. It will go to Jack's head, he said, Jack does not know when to consolidate nor when to stop; he says he wants to be the best, not the biggest – that's nonsense, he wants to be both. Michael, too. No matter what the level of advances, Michael wants to lend more and more, which means that Cedar will always want more and more money. Which means that you, Charles, will be under persistent pressure from them. Believe me you're going to have great difficulties. You will never get them to retrench. They are on a roller-coaster; I will do what I can to calm them. Izzy was right as usual; I told him so. We both wondered whether a public quotation would moderate Jack and Michael's volatile ebullience. He recommended that we should continue urging upon them the appointment of a professional banker, an experienced outsider as a managing director. He said this in a desultory fashion for we both now doubted if the Morrisons would

77

ever accept an outsider at such a high level and at such a late stage. Between Walton and myself there was a frequent and wistful harking back to our original misjudgement and to our subsequent lack of success in our attempts to persuade him. What was increasingly evident was that both Jack and Michael regarded Cedar as their 'own' family company.

The strength of Cedar's reputation in those years of the late 1960s, in its run up to a public quotation, when it started issuing cheque books and paying-in books – one of Michael's earliest ambitions – should not be clouded by its later sensational collapse. During those years, when it was forging its golden links, it enjoyed an unblemished character and record. Much of its special quality emanated from the individual contributions made by the representatives of the institutions, either at the formal board meeting or at the more frequent informal contacts. A Cedar *esprit* was certainly apparent, much of it due to Michael's infectious enthusiasm, and what I found particularly satisfying was that the intellectual and commercial camaraderie extolled a central point: that when the representatives of institutions and entrepreneurs work well together, when their different backgrounds are properly ignored, as they should be, it is one of the most formidable unions possible in business. The two cultures, when smoothly enmeshed, could create enormous stengths and produce spectacular results. The relationship had, of course, to be worked at on both sides and, as I and others have discovered, when they do not work out, the reason for discord or failure lay outside the original contractual basis of the association.

The institutions which formed the bedrock of Cedar's *réclame* were themselves varied in many fundamental respects. At Unilever, the forerunner, Jasper Knight, was the supreme delegator; his simple stance was that as long as his boys did all the work and he got all the credit, he was content. And he delegated to two exceptional boys. One was William Broadfield, the head of the pension fund. He was always known as William by me, Bill by everyone else. I have an allergy to the one syllable diminution of people's christian names; I abhor Mikes, Freds, Dons, Berts, and Joes, and have often thought that the oceanic Russian novels would be infinitely less beguiling if the evocative, patronymic names of those wonderfully tormented characters had been truncated to a single syllable. Bill, I mean William, was a Thomas Hardyan man of integrity, a man with a dogged sense of loyalty; he was one of the more intelligent and more sensible of the fund managers, and certainly the nicest, and it is to his everlasting credit that when he was first aware of the proposed acquisition of Amal by Cedar, he made it a resignation issue, only postponing his decision out of loyalty to the Morrisons.

The other Unilever man was Rafe Langham, now the head of its pensions department. Jasper Knight, realising that Cedar required a broad actuarial approach, wisely suggested that we tapped his company's then deputy actuary's experience; it was an inspired suggestion. Langham's knowledge was deep and far ranging, and I couldn't have prepared Cedar's detailed projections, focused on all the financial implications of a fast-growing lending business, with anything like the same confidence and knowledge, without the benefit of his expertise and thinking. Certainly he was of enduring help to me in all the plans to raise new finance and new shares, and Michael and I soon made a practice of going over the various permutations and projections exhaustively with him. Langham had the attribute of a brilliant actuary allied to the judgement of a merchant banker, and it is to his credit, too, particularly after Cedar started using the money market, that he entreated the Morrisons to take on an experienced banker, particularly one skilled in financial disciplines.

At Electricity the top men were Clifford French and Burton Johnson, whose appointees were Sidney Cowtan and George Cumming, both experienced on general market matters and both surprisingly alive to the wider aspects of the second mortgage business. At the Coal Board it was Reg Edward, a shadowy figure, the opposite of the immensely capable Hugh Jenkins who came in later, much too late, for he would have raised hell around the board table over the Cedar excesses of 1973. At Phoenix there was Charles Knight. He was shrewd, but timidly so. He was a kindly man who had a rare understanding of the mortgage business from the insurance and investment point of view, and educated us generally on the potential and the benefits. With the involvement of Phoenix there was a complex irony in that his chairman, Lord De L'Isle, was also chairman in his personal capacity, of First National – the other leading horse in the second mortgage stakes – whose founder Pat Matthews was a director of Phoenix in his personal capacity. Knight retired in 1972 in favour of his colleague Brian Oram. If Knight had stayed on, he, too, like Jenkins, would have been an additional restraining or braking influence, especially as both Morrisons had a special respect for his judgement.

The 1960s were Jack's and Michael's feast, a delicious decade, always delectable and ready for picking, and they ate it all up. One of their plums was the Bahamas. They discovered the wintry sun and far away palm trees, or rather Fischer discovered it for them, having had an early propensity for Florida and its Cuban boys and its easy step to the Out Islands. So they sailed into Bahamian developments with Angela's brother David Ross in charge, and, with Michael and Angela and Juliet and cousin David, visited Freeport with increasing frequency, the only ugly island in the Bahamas, frolicking on the dappled sands, sustained by a guilt-free business rationale derived from the newly-built nearby blocks of air-conditioned balconied apartments, the burgeoning lotus investments of Amal. In those days the Bahamas were still carefree, the Mafia-ridden casinos had not yet fully taken over Paradise Island – then known as the quaint Hog Island.

It was a causeway from Nassau where the Oakes family were still resplendent in pre-dynasty glamour, whilst Lady Baillie, owner of Leeds Castle, gave Gatsby-type romantic sepia parties, where Christie, in the very singular, retained an antique Roman look of papal daggery – was he or was he not the killer of Shirley Oakes's father? Shirley herself, the gorgeous and brainy blonde who died in a coma years after a motor car accident, was married to a man called Butler, who named his own Nassau bank Butler's bank and who made us crease with laughter because of its rotten domestic service, and Charlie Hambro, son of the brave Sir Charles who, in losing one night at the tables of the Bahamian Club, signed and paid with a Hambros cheque and was told by the owner that he too could also print his own cheques, a possibly ugly situation sorted out by my dear friend Peter Follis, Hambros' man in New York, who whispered in the owner's ear what was what, the owner turning the sort of purple hue which possibly only pertains to casino personnel who get their customers' credit rating wrong.

There were candlelit parties in black tie, white jackets and orange tans, when the alcoholics were nearly always very well behaved holding their drinks in frozen fear of breaking down, whilst novices, the author included, tried to blow out the candles, and there was Nadia, swimming at Lyford Cay with a dolphin, a real boy, who sought her company each morning and kept on reappearing, the first fishy balletomane, I offered weakly, which she treated with the disdain it deserved. And during the 1960s, not in Nassau as it used to be in its nubile prime, but out in Freeport – free for all, particularly the demimondanes – the respectable younger Morrisons cavorted, with Jack making an occasional entry, although more happy on a cruise, preferably with a girlfriend, or occasionally with nephew David in attendance, whose social signature, his wide fixed grin, was requiring less effort as the years wore on. David's resolve to get on to equal terms with Uncle Jack and cousin Michael was already showing positive signs of success.

This decade was engaging to many people in different ways. It was not swinging teenage adolescence, as much as England coming of age after the War. To the Morrisons, it was a wonderfully exuberant time; Michael was in his element, idyllically married – he and Angela were always holding hands – a doting father, a successful new-type banker, admired by like-minded ambitious neighbours in the affluent St John's Wood Jewish ghetto, with their similar houses, leafy gardens, young children, au pairs, nannies, the occasional butler, and all of them vying with each other, all of them breathing the competitive but still innocent air of young marrieds on the make, on the way up, planning their bright futures, not as yet tainted by any of their past.

And Jack puffed up, more confident, his penguin chest linen-white and tidy, he, too, was in his element. At last, he was able to prove to those who had doubts about his character and ability (not that he would ever admit that he was bothered) how wrong they were, especially those in his immediate family, his ex-wife, his ex-brother-in-law, his brothers Hymie and Peter. He was now, in his own fashion, teaching them all a lesson or two. He was a success story, and the father of another success story. More, he was the chairman of a bank, a family bank, he always emphasised, stressing in particular its institutional links. Think of my powerful and influential institutions, he would declaim to his family, friends and acquaintances; and, to those closer in business, he would stress amid his very sincere acknowledgements of his friend Charles's contribution in bringing them in, that the Morrisons were the real magnets, that these heavyweights needed massaging, which he and Michael were doing and which they enjoyed doing. But in no circumstances would he ever allow them, or anyone else for that matter, to control him or his son; no, not at any time would he ever allow that to happen.

Jack would also now seek the odd honour, a justice of the peace here, a honorary doctor of literature there, requesting on the receipt of the latter, from Dublin, that he be called Dr Morrison. A knighthood he felt would very soon be in order; perhaps one day even a peerage.

The fantasies which lie within all people, particularly within successful businessmen, are mostly concealed by them in the time-honoured way of surrounding themselves with overtly expensive, sometimes stately material possessions, but they usually remain dormant with only rare outbreaks. In Jack's case the fantasies were alive and real and unceasing. This was readily conspicuous in his more jaunty step and lofty manner, more discernible in his increasing interest in publicity, in his more frequent references to the bi-annual honours list. At home, when in a particularly relaxed and affable mood, he would take out his fiddle to remind a guest modestly of his undoubted skill; sometimes the Stradivarius itself would be brought out with genuine affection. No more than a few bow movements were needed for Jack Morrison's fantasies to float, his chin resting comfortably on the hallowed instrument, his eyes half-closed as he played, his body swaying in unison with the music.

In Jack's office, Marlborough Gate in the distance, the sun in abeyance, sitting further back in my chair, I looked levelly at the Sutherland portrait. I found myself considering what sort of adversary Jack might be in a contest. Not now perhaps, but later. How much later? It could not be too far away. His inner feelings had now been made evident. Certainly we had never been sure of each other; there was admittedly a form of friendship, also some definite respect, but not what one could with truth describe as a genuine bond. Close relationships based on business are strange bonds, in that despite daily or weekly contact, continuing over years, two colleagues or associates or partners, outwardly amenable to the other's foibles or humour or quirks, can develop subsurface feelings of loathing or hostility, without realising how intense they are. Jack and I had always been aware of a strong undertow of wariness; it had never been overtly expressed, it had never become a surface issue, but each of us anticipated that he might be sidestepped or pushed over by the other. Something more than distrust, more akin to enmity was grinding incessantly in his mind. It would be safer, I decided, to take guard, or rather to take more guard. Seeing him in this light, one could no longer afford to merely shudder.

Seeking the public quotation was in our minds, yet enthusiasm varied as did motivation. The one advantage of going public, which appealed to Izzy, was that the constraints applied to a public company might help to stabilise and modulate Jack's turbulent ambitions. This may have been in Walton's mind but it was very far from Jack's. To the Morrisons a public quotation would not only be a public manifestation of Cedar's credibility and success, it would help to further the dialogue with the Old Lady; and enhance along the way Jack's own glory. There were additional advantages. Jack, after all, was getting on and, though he had generally given proper consideration to matters of his estate, there would be more flexibility if the family trusts owned quoted rather than unquoted shares. The quotation would also provide an alternative source of loan money, not necessarily attached to equity, as was the case with the institutions. Furthermore a quoted lending company would have easier access to the money markets. Finally of course, a quoted Cedar would not merely make it easier to acquire the already quoted Amal, but would make it possible. For any one of these reasons, but particularly the last, they were in tune to pushing ahead.

What was behind that brutal look from the chairman of Cedar, from that Sutherland portrait? As ever, Jack was suspicious about what he thought were my undeclared motives; also he was as ever suspicious of the institutions. Perhaps he had decided that the institutions and I would gang up against him, or that I might persuade them to do so. His evaluation of my motives, certainly at this time, was not wide of the mark in the sense that he and Michael knew that if they made any attempt to acquire Amal I would make equal attempts to persuade the institutions against it. Whenever Jack and Michael raised the Amal equation, I had been consistent in expressing my opposition, stressing that Cedar was trying to be a bank, that it should steadfastly stick to that aim. Jack's evaluation of the institutions' ulterior motives was not only wide of the mark, but wholly inaccurate – until their loyalties were tested at the Bank of England marathon. Then they had very little love for the Morrisons, and it showed.

Then the institutions did exactly what Jack feared most. They took actual control. His long-held anxieties, his suspicions, disquiet, qualms and misgivings blew up in his face. The horrors were finally happening and Jack's worst torments of what might occur actually did occur. What he never understood was that it was this very lack of trust in his heavyweight associates, transmitted to his son and to his nephew, which presaged the events at the Bank.

For if the Morrisons had trusted the institutions, Amal may well have been kept as a separate and independent entity. It was a successful and trouble-free quoted company, unassailably controlled and managed by the Morrisons. Instead of retaining Amal as a separate family investment, Jack, in his misguided troubled insecurity, decided to use Amal as a sort of Trojan card, held close to his chest, waiting for the best moment to introduce it. The reason for the merger would be advanced as a means of enlarging the Cedar balance sheet, of strengthening the equity base and borrowing powers. There was never going to be as much as a murmur that it had anything to do with increasing the family shareholding in Cedar. Oh no. Nor was he ever going to admit that a side advantage and a very substantial one was that, after the merger, Amal would have the benefit of a ready source of funds for property development directly from its own new parent.

This would particularly benefit the cash-hungry Buckingham Gate development, the beautifully designed office project between the Palace of Westminster and the Royal Palace, the apple of Jack's property eye of which he wanted as full an ownership as possible. He, Michael and David were emotionally involved in Buckingham Gate, and there were even embryonic plans to use part of it as Cedar's new head office. Jack would want to finance it in-house, whether it became the largest single recipient of Cedar's resources or not.

Ill-founded feverish suspicions based on emotion are bound to corrupt logical conclusions, and the Morrisons inevitably reached the worst possible of all conclusions. Amal was well run and well regarded, with an established market presence. There was no commercial logic for a merger, the opportunity for a merger being possible only, for the most illogical of reasons, that of common shareholding. Banks which own properties for asset reasons, for balance sheet reasons, are inherently verging towards the quicksands of performance in a different terrain. Banks should make their assets sweat in order to earn revenue in the same way as any other well-managed commercial or industrial company. They should not hide behind property assets, whose values in any case could be suspect and which, when sold, could frighten depositors and investors, as was almost certainly the case when the Bank of America sold its well-known headquarters building in San Francisco at a figure well below expectations.*

There have always been and always will be dangers, when bankers want to own property and property men want to own banks. The art of banking is matching well and lending well; the art of property is leasing

---

* It will be interesting to see how Barclays Bank will treat its new expensive building at 54 Lombard Street in its accounts. Its estimated cost and the percentage it represents of its net shareholder funds have not yet been disclosed.

well and borrowing well. Each ethos has its own established coventions, validities and rules; each ethos is wholly different in its derivation and application of funds. So different are they, in fact, and so educative in practice, that amongst the best bankers are those who make it their business to understand property financing, which is essentially long-term, and amongst the best property men are those who genuinely understand the dangers of bank lending, which is (alas) essentially short-term.

If Amal had been a separate public company there would have been no terror at the Bank of England on Wednesday, 19 December. Indeed with the Morrisons having access to personal funds via Amal, they would have been in an entirely different stance. On any disaster day, if an entrepreneur is unable to contribute, his standing drops vertiginously. On the Cedar disaster day, the entrepreneurs, the Morrisons, could have been part of the support scheme; they could have been sitting upstairs, not downstairs, they could have been first-class citizens, the entrepreneurs on a proper level with the institutions. It would have been the Fabulous Five. But Jack had put all his eggs into one basket, he had convinced himself that he was outwitting the institutions who did not even know they were in a contest. He had committed an act of commercial suicide.

Listening over the years to Jack's comments about Amal, ranging from allusions to positive proposals, he never seemed to grasp that a merger would impair the essential integrity of Cedar, of its distinctive name as an expert single-minded lender of second mortgages; that it might possibly do more than impair, it might even destroy Cedar's peerless reputation. It was during these sessions, on the run-up to the quotation, when I began to wonder whether a possible method of avoiding an Amal merger might be a takeover of Cedar by Spey. Spey Finance, Spey's banking arm, was already a formidable financial entity, already larger than Cedar. Was it possible that Jack interpreted my own thoughts before I was aware of them myself? Had I, at the back of my mind, or not so far back, come to some sort of conclusion that if the Morrisons persisted in going down this Amal track, a possible finesse might be a takeover of Cedar by Spey Finance? Was I myself being entirely altruistic?

Michael, who was incapable of being devious, gave some of the game away when he inadvertently disclosed the family worry about its minority share holding. During one particular discussion, just the two of us, he referred to the amount of loan stock which might be issued at the same time as the quotation of the ordinary shares. Why have a public quotation without using the opportunity of obtaining further finance? Why not indeed? It was good commercial sense and was something that had already been aired and mooted. But, he added that what he liked most about deposits was that, unlike loan stock with conversion rights, there was no dilution. Whose? I asked ingenuously.

Once, he blurted out to my astonishment, that he liked the money markets, and that if Cedar were larger, it could tap them much more successfully. He had recently met a man called Gerald Caplan at a party in St John's Wood who had told him that it was money for old rope. One could still be hanged on old rope, I said. Michael reacted quickly, saying that we must not of course do anything to harm Cedar. I then said in no uncertain terms, and perhaps intemperately, that if he or his father or his cousin ever did, it would be over my dead body, and that as far as I was concerned the money markets were definitely out. This somewhat proprietorial feeling about Cedar annoyed him, and we both had good cause to be exercised. We had not before had a conversation as lopsided as this. Until then, I was under the impression that Michael loathed short-term deposits as much as I; the Caplan reference with the carefree irresponsible syndrome of hectic wheeling and dealing and St John's Wood chatter had obviously set my teeth on edge.

There was a further very important element which stirred the emotions of both Morrisons. This was the growing association between Spey and Barclays Bank. I see now that it was a crucial factor in increasing Jack's anxiety about my role and status in Cedar, and was possibly the beginnings of the rift between us, only becoming apparent to me at a later date that there was a distinct correlation in the Morrisons' concern over the growth of Spey's own banking interests and the growth of Cedar.

*   *   *

It was a great feather in Spey's cap that it had the pension fund of a great clearing bank as a shareholder, a feather pinned more firmly in that a Barclay, Richard, was also on its board. The Barclays relationship was set in Bentworth, the Hambros association being the fixing mixture. Spey was new in fact, and new in concept. A financial creature of this character had not been seen before in the City, and at that time the pension fund of a major bank was not a mere heavyweight link – it was the forge of Debrett, a Royal Standard. In these constant mental manoeuvrings of Jack's never serene mind, he may well have

86

imagined that following Spey's association with the Barclay's pension fund, myriad intrigues were being woven around him. Spey was in the Square Mile; Cedar, though in St James's, was still considered to be in the West End, and Jack may have feared that Spey's increasing financial activities in the heart of the financial sector were militating against his own interests. Were the powerful institutions in his own Cedar camp as sincere as they appeared? Were they possibly part of a secret Gordon plot? Phoenix, for example, although not associated with Spey, had in its deputy chairman, Jocelyn Hambro, a friend of Gordon; the Unilever pension fund had always been one of his well-known supporters, so was Electricity; there were also very strong connections with the Coal Board which had originated from the Jack Cotton days. And now the Brighton Marina, controlled by one of Spey's companies, had another bank pension fund, NatWest, as a financial supporter.

In whichever direction Jack looked in the financial institutional sector there would seem to be a Spey tentacle. Of the other Spey institutional shareholders, the Royal Insurance and the ICI pension fund, he had sparse or no knowledge. Where would the machinations of Spey lead? Was it possible that they would lead to 60 Pall Mall? With this terrible thought, Jack's hand may well have clutched his waistcoat, an endearing give-away foible to which he was prone when under pressure. The poison of jealousy was curdling the neurosis of suspicion. What was really going on at Old Jewry? He would watch everything with care and he would warn Michael to regard me with a less friendly disposition.

Jack decided to make a point of becoming more friendly with Nadia and I. Invitations of several varieties poured out, two or three were accepted. It was during one of these outpourings, a notable and enjoyable evening, when he took out the Stradivarius and played it for us quite beautifully. A further gambit was his expressed wish to become friendly with Spey's own institutions and more friendly with Cedar's. Would we and Sir Paul and Lady Chambers (Chambers was now a director of Spey as well as chairman of the Royal Insurance, a Spey shareholder, and had previously been chairman of ICI) like to have dinner with him at Michael and Angela's? Would I introduce them to Cob Stenham, Broadfield's new boss? At Electricity they only knew Cowtan and Cumming, would I introduce them to Clifford French and Burton Johnson? They seemed to have suddenly become aware that Michael and he only knew the institutions' representatives on the Cedar board, not their top men. Was this a deliberate Gordon ploy? They intended now to discover for themselves. Would Sir Joseph Lockwood, the chairman of EMI and a deputy chairman of Spey Finance, like to come round for lunch? These reactions, these overt gambits, were the more exterior drifts in their minds, the commercial warpath embedded one layer down was to be followed by the personal warpath, this being Jack's normal agenda. Questions were fermenting in his mind. Was I being straightforward? What did Izzy Walton think, and whose side was he on? What did I really feel about Cedar going public? Jack eventually decided on his tactics: let's become more friendly with Charles, let's push him on the quotation, let's cool down on Amal, let's keep all of that in the background, let's get closer to Barclays as they are the big Spey supporters. Why can't they be our lead bank? For the present make do with Charles, but as soon as we can, we will find some reason to push him out. Above all, we must not let him know what we are planning.

So when the possibility arose, of having Barclays Bank trust company as Cedar's issue house for the public quotation, there was an ardent response from the Morrisons. It was not merely the enormous attraction and great prestige of Cedar being the trust company's first new issue baby – the Morrison family bank being delivered to the public by one of the country's banking giants – it was not the Morrison exchange of a rook for a bishop, nor the Morrison strengthening defence of their king; it was the Morrison move towards toppling me, their move towards my checkmate.

Perhaps Jack was a better chess player than I had calculated, perhaps he had a better brain than I had thought. Perhaps that brutal javelin look he had just thrown at me, was part of a larger armoury. Perhaps there were weapons which were even more lethal. Perhaps his vagueness and waywardness were a mask, the festering animosity cleverly concealed until now. He was looking at someone whose business star was rising more rapidly than his own, whose ambitions were outstripping his, whose friendships and associations in the City were themselves a talking point. When Paul Chambers, for whom Jack had a feeling of awe, had joined Spey as a director, the story was on the front page of the *Financial Times*. Jack had made a point of remarking upon it, not once or twice but several times. He was now looking at me as if I were more of a rival than an associate, as if my role in Cedar, was ambivalent to say the least. And he was particularly disturbed by my friendship with his son; the brotherhood he had proclaimed for years was now not such a good idea and he would start briefing Michael accordingly. The javelin unleashed by his innermost feelings was now being directed at the closest associate he had ever had outside his family.

Jack decided that my loyalties were not with him, that they never had been, and that they had only been with the institutions. What was I conspiring against his and Michael's interests in my offices in Old Jewry, with the Gerling furniture from Cologne and those strange paintings by Stella and Morris Louis and Rothko on the walls? He was perceiving an adversary, not a friend; no, not an adversary but an enemy; and not only an enemy of his, but also of his son's. The quotation was not possible without Gordon's support, so he would give this a lot more thought after Cedar became a quoted company and, once the quotation was out of the way, every consideration would be given to a merger with Amal, whether Gordon liked it or not. So from now on it would be all smiles; he would conceal his true motives.

And so it was in the conversation we were having that afternoon in his office on the forthcoming birth of Cedar as a publicly-quoted company, on the choice of its midwives and the midwives' attendants. It was all smiles; Spey's brokers were Cazenove; it was agreed that the brokers to the issue would be Cazenove; Spey's solicitors were Slaughter and May, it was agreed that the solicitors to the issue would be Slaughter and May; Spey's auditors were Coopers, it was agreed that Coopers would be the reporting accountants to the issue. There were no neck-turning glances from father to son, no second guesses, no second thoughts. It was yes to everything. It was all too easy.*

When I left number 60, the sun had not yet set. I walked under the arch and looked idly at the shops in Crown Passage, now in its evening siesta. I crossed King Street by Christies and strolled up Bury Street to Wilton's in contemplation, occasionally stopping to look at a shop window, a painting on an easel, a silver tea set, an antique atlas. My driver was waiting patiently outside Wilton's. I greeted Marks, but felt

---

* As to the brokers, the Morrisons knew that they had to be Cazenove. Amal's brokers were Sebags and the Morrisons had initially been pushing them and their senior partner David Eastham for whom in any event I had a mild antipathy. I had known Sebags from of old, and apart from Derek Moore, their analyst (in those early days, for a broker to have an analyst was exceptional) the only other person I knew there and liked was Robin Muir, Jocelyn Hambro's brother-in-law and my friendly feelings towards these two would not have altered my own choice.

oddly ill at ease and disturbed and did not realise how disturbed until I found myself asking him for a large malt instead of a Bollinger.

The key appointment was Cazenove, and the key role, far more crucial than envisaged by anyone, was the one played by its new issue partner, Godfrey Chandler. I had met Chandler some years earlier, through a friend of mine, his partner, Michael Belmont, and had soon discovered that Chandler, known as the best new issue man in the City, was unquestionably worthy of his legendary reputation. Cazenove was riddled with talent. Antony Hornby had recently retired, Luke Meinertzhagen, the new senior partner presided, his judgement rarely out of tune with his celebrated pedigree and his partners; Michael Belmont pitchforked the City almost singlehandedly into the financing of oil exploration in the North Sea, arguing successfully against formidable City apathy at the time that this was no bubble in the South Sea; Michael Richardson, later at Rothschilds, now chairman of Smith New Court, was the best corporate finance negotiator of his generation. There were many other first-rate thinkers and doers in this most elegant of money tanks; Johnny Henderson, Peter Smith, Anthony Forbes, Rae Lyster, all of them swanning around with not so much as a ripple, ever so quietly and ever so competently and ever so Caz-like.

Yet Cedar's public issue was by no means an easy birth. There were unanticipated problems, and one of them, the press reaction, was quite severe; derogatory press comments expressing dislike of the second mortgage business were expected, but what was not expected was the virulence. What saved Cedar were its impressive institutional links, its impressive board, and its impressive midwife, Godfrey Chandler.

It is more normal today for a broker to act as the issue house to a quotation; it would have been unusual then for Cedar not to have had a separate issue house. Nor was it an error of judgement to appoint the Barclays' trust company with its lack of expertise. The trust company was formed after Barclays took over the great Martin's bank of Liverpool, now all but totally erased from people's memory, its well-known grasshopper sign, originally young Gresham's, long since gobbled up by Barclays' spreadeagled bird of prey. One of Martin's stars, Derrick Hanson, appointed a general manager of Martin's at the early age of thirty-five, had been responsible for making its trust company a leader in this field. (He has since written a standard work on banking and on personal finance.) He was sent south to do the same for the new Barclays Trust Company. The remit, vague to begin with and quickly redefined by its new chief, was not only to reorganise the normal trust activities, but to get involved in the more traditional activities of a merchant bank. It was the kernel of what we know today as Barclays de Zoete Bevan, the investment banking arm of the Barclays group. I had, of course, no part in the trust's proposed new directions, but some of the thinking behind it before the Martin's takeover, certainly derived from Barclays' experience with us at Hambros through the Bentworth association. Rightly or wrongly I had a conceit of interest. So rightly or wrongly, as part of its remit was to be involved in the new-issue business, I explored the territory (with the Morrisons' enthusiastic support, they were wholly convinced that this would impress Keogh) to see whether its first new issue baby could be Cedar.

That the trust company had virtually no experience did not worry me or anyone else very much after we got to know Derrick Hanson, for Cazenove could when necessary hold Barclays hand, and because it was Cazenove, Barclays were perfectly relaxed: and that in effect was the prescribed arrangement. What was not foreseen was that the sub-underwriters, following the initial negative press reactions, would indicate strongly that they would be happier if Barclays supported the issue not only as the main underwriter, but also as an investor. Here Hanson dug in his toes on the grounds that the issue had to stand on its own feet without extra support from Barclays. He was justified in his view but it was not helpful, when, at a particularly critical and sensitive juncture, this sub-underwriting problem arose quite alarmingly. When it did we very nearly foundered.

Some months before this, however, during Cedar's pregnancy, in September 1970, an important meeting took place between Frank Sherborne, Godfrey Chandler and myself, at 54 Lombard Street.

As the decades have receded, I find that I hold Frank Sherborne in rising esteem. He once casually told me how he and a fellow officer had escaped from a prisoner of war camp in northern Italy and, in constant peril, had been on the run for weeks before they were able to find sanctuary and eventual freedom. Neither of them spoke Italian and they had to live fully on their wits. If Sherborne was able to survive that, I surmised he was more than able to run Barclays' gilts book and its pension fund. He had played an active role in the Bentworth Barclays association and his rather droll manner was liked by all who encountered it. He had, too, the bemused, quizzical, questioning eyes of a man who already knew the answers and was judging you on yours.

He was always relaxed and unflappable, an expert on money who had no belief in money values – only human values, and consequently had that irredeemable poise and conviction of the true commercial agnostic. He had been helpful in many ways, particularly when he had put me right years earlier on the problem of how to deal with Cedar's respectability.

Our friendship was later put to the test in the Spey confrontation when, in a very delicate situation, he finessed it without a vestige of disloyalty to Barclays and to me. Through his pension fund respon-sibilities he knew the world of underwriting, of new issues and stocks and shares at first hand, and could assimilate the problems of company flotations with ease. He was also a director of the trust company, and was the best man at Barclays to consult on whether the trust company could or indeed should handle Cedar. From Barclays' standpoint, if the trust company was going to engage in the new issue business, what more appropriate first-born could there be than a lending company, a near bank, itself well supported by four of the nation's largest investment institutions?

Sherborne and I had discussed the subject *en passant* on several occasions. It was decided that Chandler and I should meet him to explore the possibility in more detail. At the end of our discussion Sherborne said that he would talk it in with colleagues. He sent Chandler and I a copy of his note of our meeting, which itself was a superb example of lucid unambiguity.

Chandler and I subsequently met Derrick Hanson, the ex-Martin's whiz-kid. He was no innocent novice but a tough-minded cultured northerner who certainly knew his stuff, and what he did not know he soon picked up. He had a superior clear and reflective brain. He asked for the Cedar data to be sent to him, and he and his small staff studied the papers and 60 Pall Mall from top to bottom. Then he asked for, and with his assistant David Moss, was given a formal presentation. Jack and Michael were superb, and even Fischer was effective by remaining silent throughout. What most impressed Hanson was the efficient administration and the fact that the bad debt experience was virtually nil. What he found especially interesting was that here, as he recorded, 'was no classic error' of a bank borrowing short and lending long. He was also interested to learn that I had given Chandler a personal undertaking that this classic error would not be made whilst I was part of Cedar.

We then encountered a very emotional problem as far as the

Morrisons were concerned. It was how Cedar should be described in the prospectus. The Morrisons, despite interventions and advice from Izzy Walton, were adamant that Cedar should be described as bankers. Neither Hanson nor Chandler were disposed to agree. In fact it got to the point where Hanson had to tell the Morrisons point-blank that if they persisted, the trust company would withdraw. Michael took particular umbrage, even more than his father, and I happened to mention this to Jasper Knight. He was wryly amused, recalling his comment after his first meeting at Cedar's offices about the cashier sign on the counter in Stratton Street, and he said that Hanson was absolutely right to dig in his toes. Eventually the Morrisons agreed with Hanson that the Bank of England's guidance should be sought. The Morrisons were fully confident of the outcome; it also appealed to them that a special meeting would be taking place in the Bank just to discuss the status of Cedar. Hanson had a meeting with Rodney Galpin, Keogh's Deputy at the Discount Office. Galpin made it clear that the Bank would not look favourably on the public issue if Cedar were described as bankers. Having persuaded themselves that the Bank would say yes, that it was all right to call themselves bankers, the Morrisons found it exceptionally galling to learn from Hanson that Cedar could not be so described. They felt personally affronted. It was a highly emotional moment, it hurt to the quick and they showed it. I now believe that Galpin's negative verdict was the spur to their later bout of advertising and publicity during Cedar's final years, and a further spur to Michael and David's near obsession to get in touch thereafter with Keogh and Galpin on the slightest pretext.

On any public quotation there are numerous meetings. I recall one which occurred just before the actual issue in the majestic boardroom of Barclays, a large, stolidly Quakerish room with a high ceiling, furnished in the restrained yet imperious post-War style of the 1960s. It was the sort of revered space in which one would expect the directors of one of the world's largest banks to deliberate and where visitors were expected to be overwhelmed by the slightly oversized enlargement of the chunky furniture and feel very privileged to be seated there. We were there as privileged visitors, and every person I feel sure was suitably overwhelmed.

Hanson took the meeting, but asked Chandler to take us through the agenda. The essence of what has made the City of London pre-eminent is that over the centuries it has become the repository of the most diverse expert financial and trading skills and disciplines ranging from options on coffee futures, to oil rig financing, to the endowment of a pension, to the trading of every type of commodity, to insuring against floods, to financing a railway in Bogota, to drafting a fifty-page agreement in as many minutes. Around the huge Barclays board table that day, were the Morrisons, one or more from each of the four institutions, all the midwives, the lawyers, the accountants, the legal secretaries and all their various assistants; we were around thirty to forty persons. Chandler went over the reason for the meeting, why each separate person was in attendance, and then, looking at the checklist, said that he would go over each item on the agenda explaining who had to sign which document and when and why. We went quietly and methodically through the small print of the prospectus. It was an example of archtypal City lore, one of the more fascinating manifestations of City expertise – the delivery of a new issue, especially when handled as it was that particular afternoon, by the senior new issue partner of Cazenove, the chandler of chandlers.

As feared, we hit a rock of Barclays' bureaucracy, not in the middle of the process, but at the end of the afternoon before the day of delivery. The press comments had been mixed and the more adverse observations had affected the sub-underwriters, who became increasingly nervous. To comfort them we had asked Barclays to take up shares in one of their managed funds to be held as an investment. There was a gap of £500,000 in that part of the underwriting which, the underwriters felt, should remain in secure investment hands; we made a further request to Barclays waiting all day for the trust company's decision. I received a somewhat desperate call from Hanson's assistant, David Moss late in the afternoon. The answer was no. Chandler was not yet in the picture, he was out. Hence the call from Moss.

The gap had to be closed before opening business hours next morning. If not, the Stock Exchange would have to be informed and the issue likely to be pulled. The Morrisons were aghast. Any support from them would not have satisfied the sub-underwriters, rather the reverse. The Spey institutional shareholders were contacted immediately and agreement was quickly obtained that if it were found necessary, Spey had the authority to close the gap from its own resources, and also if found necessary, the institutions would take up the shares as an investment at a later date: it was a very good example of how institutions and entrepreneurs can work well together in an emergency. The two mutual institutions of Spey and Cedar were

Unilever and Electricity, and the consensus was that their representatives Broadfield and Cumming should come to old Jewry as soon as they could. They arrived soon after 5 pm.

They sat opposite me. Spey's butler, Manuel, poured tea, not needing to ask the guests' preferences. The three of us were apprehensive; time was very short, logistics were difficult. The trust company had to be informed before the end of business hours whether (or not) the gap was closed. As Hanson was en route to Liverpool, what plainly had to be done was to pin down the trust company's chairman, Hanson's superior, a man I never cared for, who in my view was superior to Hanson only in rank. He had the authority to approve that extra £500,000. We telephoned. He had gone home and it would be at least an hour or two before he would reach his front door. My secretary, Pamela Walton, and her assistant Judith Bowen, knew their opposite numbers at Barclays well; but to no avail. No one at Lombard Street knew his home number. In those days leaving at 5.30 pm and keeping one's personal number private was perfectly normal. Time was passing and the mild-mannered even-tempered Broadfield was rubbing his hands; nerves from William were very unusual. As he said afterwards in his calm fashion, he was sure that the matter would be sorted out, but not finding our man was more than trying.

A remaining Barclays' girl was asked by Pamela Walton whether there was any other general manager in the building. Yes there was – Derek Wilde. We knew each other. I asked to be put through. I started off by letting him know that two others were listening to the conversation, who they were and why they were there. He listened attentively to the details of the predicament. I explained the facts stressing the urgency, the lack of time. He then said it was purely a trust matter and he would not wish to bind them. He would not be able to help. I said, 'I'm terribly sorry to hear that. Do I take it you cannot do anything?' At which Cumming and Broadfield sat straight up. There was a pause as we all looked at each other across the desk. They knew what I was going to say next. 'If you cannot,' I said, 'I will have to request you to do so as Spey's bankers.' There was no response. 'We will take up the half a million pounds worth of shares ourselves to close the gap and with our institutions will hold them as an investment if necessary.' Cumming and Broadfield looked at each other whilst Wilde waited at the other end of the line for me to complete what I was saying, a wait which by no means implied any sympathy, it was the customary Barclays good breeding. I took a deep breath. 'The amount required is less than Spey's standing overdraft facilities. I have my colleagues' authority to apply it and I am now formally asking that it be applied for the purpose by the trust company.'

There was a long silence. The longer it went on the more I liked it; Wilde was a thinker. Broadfield and Cumming were visibly agitated. Eventually Wilde said, 'You won't have to do that. I will see that they have the authority required to take up the £500,000 themselves,' adding with the courtesy I had always encountered at Barclays, that as it was so urgent, he would immediately telephone the trust company himself. 'Thank you very much,' I said. Unsaid by Mr Wilde was, I am not thanking you, Mr Gordon, for anything. I put down the receiver. My companions smiled with relief. 'You deserve a drink,' said George. 'More than you think,' I replied. 'I have just made my first enemy at Barclays.'

Chandler's comment afterwards was typically laconic; he hoped that the Morrisons would not forget what had been done. I learned later that he had made up his mind that they were not going to be given the chance. In the confrontation several months later at Spey between myself and the institutions, Barclays sent in a new man (not known to me) to sit in. Sherborne, as I have already remarked, was too sincere a friend to take part: the new man was clearly under marching orders.

The issue was a success. The price opened at a small premium and it never set back, other than reacting to market fluctuations, until the Amal merger over two years later. Yet buffeted by the mixed press, it was almost stillborn; without the authority of Cazenove, without the institutions and without, it must be added, the good fortune that Derek Wilde was found at his desk working late that crucial evening, it might not have recovered. Years later Derrick Hanson told me how he was overruled by Derek Wilde, 'at the eleventh hour', as he put it. To Broadfield, Cumming and myself it felt more like the final few seconds of the last minute of the eleventh hour.

*   *   *

A hundred years ago, at the time of the penny post, a letter could be placed in a post box in central London in the morning, knowing it would be delivered in London before lunch. Writing once a day, sometimes twice or three times, was for many, not an obsession, but a natural way of life. Letter writing of quality, the description of one's activities or thoughts or feelings conveyed with sensitive care to another, was certainly an art. Happily some old habits die hard and today, always very welcome and heartening are long personal letters received from friends, and also bread-and-butter letters of two or three pages or more – not today's single formal paragraph – and letters of condolence, letters to mark an honour received, an appointment to a post, a family event, letters from fellow artistes.* Happily it is still the custom in the City and other dwindling pockets of resistance to these unpoised over-hurried times, to write personal letters mostly delivered by hand when the occasion arises. The occasion is usually an innovative or successful transaction when not only friends but also acquaintances or even competitors wish to express and record in candid and refreshing sincerity, their respect or admiration. One of the nicest I ever received, the day after the Cedar quotation, was from Malcolm Bates, Weinstock's deputy at GEC, who had joined Spey some weeks earlier. His office down the corridor was less than a minute's walk away. I still retain his note.

The day after the quotation, there was a curious silence from 60 Pall Mall. No handwritten letters from the Morrisons; nor the next day, nor the day after. There was no phone call either. It was as if the Morrisons had been numbed, as if they had gone into their own version of commercial purdah. I am not sure which friend it was, but I can venture a shrewd guess who took it upon himself to nudge Jack or Michael. At any rate it had the effect of a handwritten note arriving from Michael Morrison delivered by hand, not to the office, but to Thurloe Lodge, our house in South Kensington. I have kept this note, too, the only hand-written note I ever received from Michael. In it he thanked me profusely 'on our behalf'. This phrase rather stuck. I had imagined we were all supposed to be on the same team; the expression was probably more eloquent to me than to anyone else, as a long-term student of Morrison behaviour, its inference being that no other parties were concerned, particularly not the heavyweights, who had made it all possible. I found this curiously irritating and I telephoned Michael to assure him, in as friendly a manner as possible, that my efforts had not been done on behalf of the Morrisons but on behalf of Cedar and all of its shareholders. He did not exactly take enthusiastically to my comment and instead of forgetting the gaffe, father and son

---

* One most treasured by Nadia is a letter received from the playwright Peter Shaffer, a friend and next-door neighbour, who wrote of his joy in seeing her *Giselle* and who dropped his letter into our letter box the morning after when he could so easily have just spoken to her.

compounded the solecism in a way which started bordering on comedy.

Some weeks later a package was delivered to Thurloe Lodge*; it contained a small Henry Moore, one of the seated family sequence. There was no note, but presumably as evidence of contrite provenance, there were two separate business cards, one from Jack and one from Michael. As already mentioned, Fischer was a person with all too few attributes, but one of them was his influence in improving his uncle's taste in art. Under Fischer's guidance, Jack had become familiar with some good English artists and with one great one, Henry Moore. That evening Charles Clore was round for drinks with Janet Milford Haven, the four of us then due to go on to the Harmsworths in Eaton Square. The unpacked bronze was on the table. The ladies were elsewhere, probably discussing world affairs with the Siamese cats. Clore looked at the sculpture. It was from the Morrisons I told him. Clore's antipathy to Jack Morrison was not unknown; it was also mutual. For what you did? he asked. I said more or less. Moore is less, he replied. I laughed, he joined in, both of us enjoying the humour, the sudden sparkle of wit, particularly because it had not been intended.

A formal letter of thanks was later sent by me to the Morrisons, in this instance a single paragraph. Normal relations were resumed, as normal as they could ever have been. Curiously I was never attracted by Moore's bronze groups as much as to his wonderful war-time drawings of London families sheltering in the Underground: in his more formal family groups it seems as if mother, father and child never talked to each other; in the Underground sketches there is a poignant impression that they would die for each other.

The bronze, not being in what one could describe as sympathetic ownership, was put away. Several months later, the day after I came off the board of Cedar it was sent back to the gallery. It was one piece of sculpture I never missed, not even more or less.

* Situated off a private road opposite the V&A it was once the home of Lilly Langtry and is now owned by Mark Birley, the proprietor of Annabel's and Mark's.

FOUR

The Break with the Morrisons

The first half of 1971, commencing with the Cedar quotation in January, was a period of intense activity, much of it very depressing. The rumblings towards the foreground were the upheavals at Spey, with one of the prime troublemakers being Jasper Knight, his machinations implicating Cedar and the Morrisons, directly and indirectly. By late June of that year I sold my controlling stake in Spey, and it was to take a decade or two before I was to recover from the shockwaves of that parting. The other parting, the break with the Morrisons, created shockwaves of a different sort, affecting some of the same and some entirely different people and ultimately the Morrisons themselves. Nor did I find any great pleasure in hearing from Michael after his own holocaust, that it might never have occurred if they had not abruptly terminated their association with me. After my break with Spey, one of the more disturbing events of my life, Jack acted with immediate opportunism, moving in as swiftly as a black adder, though he was made to recoil some months later from an unexpected quarter.

How the break with Spey had come about was an enigma, the first cryptic inklings, the first peeling of the onion skins, the first uncovering of the layers of intrigues leading to the core of the mystery, becoming apparent in February of that eventful year. Firstly there was the odd way Jasper Knight, of all people, was starting to behave. This top financial man of the world of commerce, this stalwart Henley oarsman, recently ravaged by major illness, started exposing a sour malevolence which had either not been in existence before, or had not been displayed before. It made itself apparent in small ways – an ugly passing remark or an aside, a glancing cut to the boundary at the end of what had been until then a friendly conversation either at a meeting or on the telephone or when leaving a room; then, as if under starters orders, he unleashed it indiscriminately, recklessly, without restraint, without any regard for the consequences, as if he had not a moment to lose. He was impelled by more than a desire to wound others, a not infrequent and understandable reaction in a person who had enjoyed good health all his life, now suffering from the painful wounds caused by a major operation. He seemed, moreover, to be driven by external pressures. Not to mince words, I became convinced he had been got at, but, at that juncture, I did not know, for sure, by whom.

His illness coincided with the edgy expiring period of his Unilever career when the need arose to find his successor, a task he had deliberately left late in the day. Jasper's tardiness had been accepted with some equanimity and good humour by his colleagues who had become used to his quirks, and who recognised that he was the sort of man who could not bear the thought of one of his underlings taking over his job and moving into his office. Jasper found the procedure of formalising his succession profoundly irksome, frequently saying to people when referring to his impending retirement that it was very difficult to find the right person, implying that if he were not quite indispensable, he was certainly somewhere at the top end of that pecking order. So being slow to make up his mind as to which candidate he might recommend, there was a trickling impression that he was hoping the uncertainty would cause his colleagues to break the rules of retirement and grant him a special reprieve of say a year or two. His chairman, Sir Ernest Woodroofe, having a wry appreciation of his colleague, gave him short shrift that reprieves were not in order and that he should get on with it.

Jasper then decided to concentrate on seeking a successor from outside, someone who would supersede the aspiring lesser lights in head office, and (a novel departure for Unilever which he initiated with some relish, finding this satisfyingly different) someone who would go straight on to the main board of the huge Anglo-Dutch colossus. This top position which in his own mind (and to his growing surprise, not in many others') he felt he had held with distinction, would, he decided, be held by an outsider, someone of such prodigious talent it would reflect credit upon him for making such an admirable choice of successor. Eventually as a result of a fortuitous suggestion from Lord

Poole, Jasper was pleased to be able to recommend his favoured successor. The candidate Cob Stenham appealed to him even before they had actually met; here was not only an outsider and another old Etonian, but also Lord Poole's son-in-law. Lord Poole, the chairman of Lazards, Unilever's merchant bankers, made his recommendation with characteristic integrity as he firmly believed that son-in-law or not, Stenham was suitable for the job. The source of the recommendation suited Knight's social predilections exactly, and Stenham suited Unilever's commercial predilections in the same measure; it was a stroke of luck for all concerned except for the internal hopefuls who had been vainly praying for promotion. They ought to have known Knight better.

In the meantime, as Knight's retirement day approached, his casual optimism and highhandedness in looking around for outside directorships, turned into an anxious scurry. One day during his clearing-out-his-desk period he confessed to me that I was the only friend who had come through. It has occurred to me since, that it was possible his other friends knew more than I, or were better judges of character, or were generally more perceptive.

From being agreeably tetchy and cantankerous, Jasper became unpredictably wilful and destructive. Despite warnings about him from friends in Unilever, particularly from William Broadfield, it undoubtedly took me longer than it should have done to appreciate that dear hulking awkward loyal Jasper of old, was, since his illness, a thoroughly changed person. Certainly I should have taken note when he came up with his quite surprising contention that he should replace Broadfield as a director of Cedar. I told him that this was unfair and that he was out of court to even suggest it. The specific post-retirement invitation he received from our camp at Spey, embossed with the warm support of Richard Fleming and his partners, was to become chairman of Warwick Securities, a joint venture of Flemings and Spey, set up for share-dealing and special market-oriented situations. Jasper accepted with spiky thanks, but within weeks he was back again on his favourite subject. It was an affront, he declared, that he was not on the main board of Spey, or on Cedar's main board. 'Good God, Broadfield used to report to me.' Knight's protestations were loud, frequent, and erratic. It was not what one would have thought was compatible with the standards expected of a man who had been the financial director of one of the world's greatest corporations. His illness was one cause, another may have been an innate lack of fulfilment. But something was sparking off his intermittent spurts of dissatisfaction, of protest and of malevolence.

As the onion skins continued to peel, other figures, some directly connected to Spey and to Jasper, some not, emerged with more prominence. Jasper was manoeuvring clumsily yet effectively; there were indications, I came to the conclusion, that he was knowingly being manipulated. As the signals accumulated, a pattern was emerging that he had been talking to colleagues outside the confines of Warwick, that he had been talking to other Spey associates. He had also talked to Richard Fleming, and here he had grossly misunderstood his man. The Flemings are a celebrated Scottish family, one of them had revolutionised the investment industry by inventing the investment trust movement; Richard himself was chairman of his family investment banking house; brother Peter was a distinguished traveller in Tartary and brother Ian was the creator of 007. Richard Fleming invited me to tea at Crosby Square by the new P&O building. It was here that he told me Jasper Knight was making odd if not reckless statements and that he needed watching. I watched. There was no longer any need for guesswork.

A thorny feature of the problem was that Jasper had retained, for a further year, his position as chairman of the Unilever pension fund; it was thought that Stenham should take over from Jasper a year or so later. It was thought also that Jasper had actively connived in seeking this arrangement, because it was a considerable power base and he obviously intended to enjoy applying it. On separate occasions he muttered to me that I should not forget that he was still chairman – as if one ever could – the threats were as unseemly as they were unnecessary. After my tea with Fleming, I wrote to Jasper to suggest that we should part company on Warwick. He wrote back very apologetically. His reply was a simple letter of apology which I had to accept. It bought him more time as he had fully intended. The Warwick board meetings settled down, but only for a short while, soon they became as strained as before.

Easter that year, Nadia and I went to Israel for the first time. Charles Clore had invited us to be his guests and he had arranged a special programme for Nadia who was especially keen to see the old Biblical sites. On my return Jasper Knight dropped his bombshell. He informed me baldly one morning that he wanted Unilever out of Spey. The reason? 'None. It's my decision.' He could see that I was shocked; I could see that he was pleased, but not as pleased as he would have been if I had not been forewarned by Fleming. I wasted no time. I went to see his old chairman, Ernest Woodroofe, at Unilever and requested him to intervene. It was unheard of, I said, for an investment decision to be made on such an arbitrary and capricious basis. I got nowhere. Woodroofe, pre-echoing the Hollom/Stenham altercation nearly three years later, told me he would not intervene, for Jasper was still chairman of the pension fund. Unilever, he explained, had its own well-laid-down procedures. There was no alternative: Jasper and I had to have our own set-to. The encounter was arranged with careful preparation. He and I sat down at the meeting table with no one else in the room. The other Spey shareholders had been consulted. The only outsider apart from Richard Fleming to whom I had confided was Izzy Walton. His own association with Knight and the Unilever pension fund was working extremely well; the irony was that Broadfield represented Unilever on the board of his company. Jasper had not nobbled Walton; going to Glasgow for a monthly board meeting was obviously not his idea of fun.

Jasper and I regarded each other across the table and the atmosphere was extremely tense. In front of each of us was one sheet of paper. It was our own Spey proposal for the terms of the Unilever withdrawal, approved not without difficulty, by the other shareholders, who were themselves now worried and saddened or irritated by this spiralling turn of events, and unsettled by a swarm of whispers. It had been decided that as the situation had been caused by a personal Jasper Knight caprice, he should no longer be allowed to enjoy the initiative. It was a most delicate situation, if not fraught: Jasper was hell-bent on maximum destruction; I was hell-bent on maximum damage limitation. It was a time for hard business.

Jasper picked up the sheet of paper, read it very carefully, and then put it down. He peered at me over his half-glasses. 'I said we only wanted out of Spey. I didn't say anything about getting out of Cedar.' We had been friends for years, we had disagreements, rumbles yes, but never a cross word between us. He had never before seen me in an obdurate mood. 'Jasper, you are on a wrecking campaign, I don't know why. Spey can look after itself but you are not going to wreck Cedar in the process. It's a public company. I invited you in. I am now inviting you out.' He looked at me firmly without any reaction. I went on, 'The terms for Cedar are reasonable as you can see.' 'Yes, I can see that,' he said. He removed his glasses and snapped them into his spectacle case. 'Have your other people approved this?' I nodded. He said, 'I see no reason why we shouldn't accept these terms.' He got up from his seat. So did I. I looked straight up at him. 'Jasper, I am going to add one more thing. You've been ill. It has been a worry for you and for Betty and for all your friends. Whatever happens I will still forgive you.' He said nothing, looked quickly down at the carpet and shuffled on his feet, and then mumbled goodbye. The tough, shambling, awkward ex-financial director of Unilever was on the verge of tears.

Several months later after my painful severance from Spey, during the autumn of that awful year, he telephoned me at home and asked whether Nadia and I would have dinner at his house in Henley on a not-too-distant Sunday. I said yes. In his own way, gawky but yet sincere, he was in need of some sort of affirmation. The dinner was normal enough. His health had visibly deteriorated. We talked of Ischia, of William Walton, of rowing and of gardening. The Knights had lived in the house nearly all their married life. It had previously belonged to Betty Knight's parents. Betty, a lively and forthcoming person, was born there and on this particular evening her wifely attributes were even more pleasantly accentuated than usual.

We made our adieus in front of the house on the gravel drive. In the Thames Valley the winter nights are cold and somewhat sinister, the trees have shrivelled, the lush green chirping verdure has disappeared, replaced by a black mantle of silence. We sat in the back of the car and were driven off. The dinner had not been easy. Jasper knew why I had immediately accepted his invitation; I had told him that whatever happened he was forgiven. The traumas thereafter had been extremely unpleasant; he was not only making his own gesture of recompense, he was also telling me that he had been manipulated and that he was now very sorry. The congealed decency of the man had oozed out. In the car, Nadia and I were silent. To forgive was one thing, to forget was another. We had almost reached Thurloe Lodge, when I said that it was unlikely that we would ever see him again. 'I know,' Nadia replied. He died soon after.

The sheet of paper on the Unilever withdrawal, as agreed between Jasper and I, was transformed into an agreement and was signed. I left Spey in June, only a few weeks later; the agreement was then unravelled and never implemented. The Unilever Pension Fund remained as shareholders in Spey and they remained as shareholders in Cedar.

Whilst the Unilever withdrawal disagreements were erupting in the months before my departure, Spey's banking arm, Spey Finance, seen by the Morrisons as a thorn in their sides, continued to gather in strength. A year earlier its first banking acquisition had been the purchase of Twentieth Century Banking from its parent company, Hallmark Securities, itself through a recent takeover, now owned by Spey's own property affiliate. The opportunity for this profitable transaction arose because of a bizarre transgression by Hallmark's chairman. This errant bearded ex-solicitor, called Sidney Bloch, had resigned from Hallmark because he had been served with a summons for the alleged smuggling of a fur coat at London airport. His recent spouse was a Royal Ballet dancer (a very good one) called Merle Park, an acquaintance of Nadia.

After his resignation and our takeover of his company, Bloch, wanting to restore his confidence particularly in the waiting period before the trial, asked me whether we would consider taking him on as a consultant. He explained in great detail that the smuggling was a sudden lunacy, a mental block, and this explanation supported by Merle Park, was accepted without question. At his subsequent trial he pleaded guilty; it transpired that the whole thing, involving a third person in the plot, was planned in advance. Bloch later told custom officials: 'the whole scheme was my fault'. Coverage in the newspapers was more than enough to provoke immediate reactions from my colleagues on the Spey board who were angry. Most of them wanted him dismissed. Occurring around the time when Knight was beginning to stalk through the corridors with his machete, the timing could not have been more sensitive. It was a difficult situation; in the final analysis it was the Royal Ballet connection which saved him. The smuggling plot may have had its elements of farce and he was later dubbed Mr Mental Block, but the backwash caused at Old Jewry by this 'nothing to declare' was not funny.

Another even more serious misadventure also arising from the acquisition of Hallmark, involved Boris Marmor, a particular friend of Charles Knight of Phoenix, who through his company Westmoreland, was a substantial shareholder of the Spey property group. As Hallmark was a public company, the stock exchange had to be informed that Marmor was to be appointed as a new director and our stockbrokers were told there was a question mark. Jasper Knight now found something else to hack at with his machete.

In addition to Twentieth Century Banking, Spey Finance acquired two other secondary banks from an associate of NatWest. The need to appoint the head of Spey Finance, already pressing, had become even more so with the proposed purchase of Unilever's holding in Cedar. We had been trying to persuade Peter Eve, my Barclays friend seconded to me at Bentworth, to take up this appointment. He was an ideal candidate, a strong forceful first-rate banker, but he was also a revolving door, constantly circling around the pivot of decision. We had already considered achieving our overall objectives by another route altogether by way of merging Spey Finance with an accepting house with expert banking management. Very confidential discussions had already taken place with Brown Shipley, Montagu Norman's distinguished old family bank. A joint company was mooted and it was whilst these talks were proceeding that I first met Hollom at the Bank of England in his capacity as Deputy Governor.* Despite goodwill all round, we did not proceed. It was a major error of judgement. The Brown Shipley people were not only very nice but also very competent. Instead, moving from the gold standard to tin tacks, we took on a rather sickly humourless French banker. Montagu Norman would have stroked his elegant Van Dyke in total disbelief.

The point had now been reached when the proposed Unilever arrangement had to be disclosed to the relevant associates, above all to the Morrisons. I had already informed Michael of what was transpiring with Unilever. Father and son came to Old Jewry for lunch. I retailed the facts. Jack was intense and engrossed, he did not look at Michael once; I had not seen him in such concentration since I had first discussed the financing strategy of Cedar with him years earlier. His mind was racing and whenever Michael interrupted he waved him into silence. His fears would have been natural even for the least paranoid of men. His conflagration of suspicion already burning for years was now a seething inferno. At the end of my account, I said, and it may have sounded unduly prim and smug, 'To allay any other worries you may have, Jack, I can tell you formally that Spey is prepared to vote its shares with you and Michael'. 'And any further shares you buy?' he asked quickly. 'We haven't considered buying any

---

* At a party in Spring 1971 which I hosted to celebrate Spey's partnership with the US Trust Company, amongst the guests were Hollom and his wife who both graced the occasion with exceptional charm and during that evening Jasper Hollom showed, notwithstanding a lifetime spent within the confines of central banking, that he was very much a three-dimensional man.

further shares, Jack, but, if we did, we would only do so by prior arrangement with you.' Oh yes, he was thinking, you did not exactly do that on this occasion. He had already set a trap and was searching for others we ourselves may have set.

The unasked question, the Damocles sword, was of course Amal. Jack was too shrewd to ask it, Michael wanted to and was starting to do so, but father put a restraining hand on son's arm. To Jack any understanding on voting was worthless unless he had a commitment to approve the acquisition of Amal. But he could not bring it up. He was in a bind. He knew that with a new large shareholder, who might be as much a foe as a friend, an Amal acquisition was dead, that is if the Spey/Unilever deal went through. I could see that he was thinking that I had played a clever move, I could also see that he did not believe it was clever enough. He was thinking hard and furiously, and he was thinking well. He asked the important subsidiary questions. What did Broadfield know? Who from Unilever would talk to him, Broadfield or Knight? Would someone else come on the Cedar Board from Spey to join me? Thank you. We must go now. He stood up to leave.

Father and son left Old Jewry for Pall Mall. They were both in a state of extreme anxiety. Arm in arm, hardly saying goodbye they whispered furiously to each other on the way to the lift. The prospect of having Spey as a dominant shareholder was repugnant. Up to the time of that lunch, they were convinced that my position at Spey was pretty nearly impregnable. I was not so sure. I knew that I was on a highwire. The tensions by and through Jasper and by and through others, mostly unknown to the Morrisons, made for a difficult balance. In June, during Ascot week, I lost my balance, and toppled over, mainly through following very reluctantly the advice of Leonard Sainer, my own solicitor, and I signed my withdrawal agreement with Spey, the severance from my own company a few days after. Later I was told that when Jack Morrison was informed the same night, he was delighted. I myself was shattered.

*   *   *

During those long tremulous summer days, Spey was being torn apart at the seams. There had been endless white-hot confrontations with my fellow shareholders flanked by their emotionless stony Frink-faced lawyers, and led like sheep by Norman Freeman, the not very far from frenetic fund manager of ICI pension fund, who seemed to be constantly yapping at my throat. Before the final settlement, during those endless days and nights, like a flickering flashback, I seemed to see Elliott Kastner at every corner. No one had the heart to tell him to go away.

Kastner was a highly successful but a chronically impecunious Hollywood film producer, hardened by dire straits and with a winning desire to survive at all costs. Uninvited, but with access provided by the Spey staff accustomed to his ingratiating blandishments, he had been stalking the offices – by no means deterred by the heavyweight names and contests – a genial interloper stopping outside the various meeting rooms, waiting forlornly after whispering appeals to one or other of the secretaries for an opportunity to speak to me, his buddy, so that I could fill his palm and ease his financial plight.

Elliott was my friend who would never do me any harm, but if a ship was foundering or seemed in danger then his old Hollywood instincts would surface with determination to survive against all odds and against all others. Elliott, who on early Sunday mornings when he was in London, would personally deliver unsolicited packets of smoked salmon to a wide range of lucky recipients, was extremely short of what he called the readies. I was his final salvation and in his epic survival he had decided to cast me in the starring role. Knowing what I was enduring, sincerely upset because he had a great affection for me, and aware that I had neither the time nor the will to listen to him, he had nevertheless been offering me sincere pugilistic advice: do not get up from the floor, regain your strength before you hit back, take stock whilst you are lying down, and, in the meantime, can you please help me out with a small advance, say £100,000? Or £50,000?

He was like a spruce, clean, pastel-bleached Groucho prowling the Spey corridors, greeting those of the colleagues he had not met before with a beatific grin, the film-maker's passport to instant frienship, not expecting any specific answers, but still asking how things were going in the larger set pieces in the main and subsidiary boardrooms; pursuing Lord Chalfont whom he knew best, and who had a particular liking for him, for the latest briefing, exhorting him, I noticed on one brief emergence, with a comforting Beverly Hills arm on his shoulder telling him, I was sure, that Charles should bear up and that he, Elliott, would always stand behind him, a true friend; he would, too. My true friend on these prowls was shadowed by his Harpo, a far-from-dumb Hollywood lawyer, whose expression whenever I caught him in the distance, had that mad, slightly hysterical lawyer's look of 'who is going to pay my fees?' Harpo, not of course concerned about my concerns except as to how they impinged upon his own, was clearly worried sick whether I, as his client's last funding resort, would please God enable him to fly back home, TWA first-class, clutching his sweaty fee.

Kastner wanted me to save him by having the privilege of paying his dangerously overdue bills. His problem, and mine for that matter, was that he could not have chosen a worse moment. He was a person for whom I had a great affection. He had tremendous courage, particularly in adversity, and I always helped out, and would do so today, if necessary. A company I controlled, set up as a specialist merchant bank to finance scriptwriters, producers and directors, had made him a substantial loan to produce a film located in Cambridge, starring Marlon Brando. He picked his location and his man carefully because he knew Nadia and I had met in Cambridge. I knew my man because I had early on discerned that, not so deep inside Kastner, who affected a toughish Hollywood exterior, was an extremely honourable man fighting to get out. There would, I decided, be no paperwork, being sure that Elliott would make every effort to keep his side of a gentleman's understanding as a moral justification of his *raison d'être*, rather than being tied to a strictly legal contract which would cause him to rebel against the written word and to regard me, the party to the other side, as his enemy. I had learned that most film people tended to bite the contractual hand that fed them. Kastner had kept his word on the Brando film. He now urgently needed money for general purposes.

Having the night before finally and wearily signed with the institutional shareholders, selling my entire controlling stake in Spey, and buying back certain of its minor interests, with the agreement sealed not only by me but also by Nadia and by our trustees, the Bank of Butterfield, I decided to take Kastner's advice: I would pick myself up slowly from the floor. So the next morning I was not going to see anyone, nor would I take any calls, other than a very puzzling call I had already had from Charles Clore. I rested upstairs in our large cream bedroom. From the windows on the left facing our private driveway the stubby round tower of the Victoria and Albert could just be glimpsed, on the other side one could look down over the balcony on to a rural London garden festooned with roses which climbed riotously in all directions. I was restless and unsettled, racking my brain trying to think things through, listening to one cello sonata after another. I was at a complete loss to understand what on earth had made me accept the very determined advice given to me by Leonard Sainer.

The lawyer, as he was sometimes called by Clore, was my lawyer now, was now acting for me in the Spey saga. His advice has been ambivalent, if not downright bad. So why had I taken it? The previous Friday on my own, without lawyers, I had agreed a very sensible deal with my co-shareholders, selling a proportion of my holdings, selling control, but leaving me with a net equity of 25%. The next day, Saturday, Sainer insisted on seeing me at home. He stayed for hours; his pressure was unremitting. On no account must you sign this agreement, you should sell out altogether, he kept insisting. He finally prevailed. He left. On Sunday I phoned him to say stet. Leave it, I said. He responded by saying that he had spent most of the day drafting a long letter which he would send round to the other side first thing in the morning. He got his way. This lack of stamina on my part has appalled me ever since. On Monday morning the lawyers on the other side received his letter undoing the deal. Constant non-stop negotiations then took place until Tuesday night. I then agreed and signed a new second agreement which was manifestly worse than the first, the one Sainer had forced me to discard. Why had he been so insistent? And why had I succumbed? It was now Wednesday morning and the only call I had taken was this very puzzling one from Sainer's master.

I was mulling over this, not giving much thought to Spey nor to the abysmal contract which I had signed, but every thought to Sainer and Clore. What *was* Sainer up to? And Clore? My closest friend, was he trying to trip me up? If he was, what was behind it?

The refreshing smooth Casals' tones were interrupted. Our butler, Brown, was at the door: 'I have put Mr Kastner and a colleague in the dining room. Mr Kastner said they needed a large table for all their papers, and madam said it was perfectly all right. I have already served them coffee'. From Brown's delivery I knew that he had exposed both men to his considerable put-down skills, for he was a man who practised his own style of irony with polished supremacy, so that, on hearing Brown call them sir, they would have tended to feel that it ought to have been the other way around. I played the Brown game with unstated pleasure: he was a man of subtlety and dignity, had been with us for many years and we were to see him frequently when he later retired to Oxford.* 'Brown, did you give them milk or cream?' I asked.

---

* Brown died of cancer in 1988, not before he had performed a special service for his sister Rosalie. She had a remarkable talent as a painter of illuminated manuscripts. In his last months, Brown spent much of his time discussing with the Ashmoleum whether they would accept her work as a gift. They agreed to do so just before he died.

'Cream, of course, sir, they are Americans,' sounding the last syllable as though the visitors were metal containers. 'Good,' I said, 'but when they have finished please tell Mr Kastner I am thankful for his advice and that I am getting up from the floor very slowly. He will understand. If it suits him I can see him the same time tomorrow morning.' Soon afterwards I could hear from the drive the tense, not too well subdued West Coast tones of Groucho and Harpo emasculating the new turn of events, Elliott probably explaining that it was all right, not to worry, that his buddy would come through.

Around midday Brown returned. He said there had been a minor scene. Mr Jack Morrison had arrived and had insisted on seeing me. Madam had not been too pleased and was talking to Mr Morrison in the study. She asked whether I wanted to see him. I knew exactly what madam's message meant: Jack was being extremely difficult and unless I came down to receive him she would have no hesitation in asking him to leave. His chauffeur-driven Rolls was in the drive. I did not have to be told that sitting in the back was David Fischer, along for the ride, not able to wait a second, before gloating over the anticipated outcome of Uncle Jack's visit.

*   *   *

'Of course I had to see you, Charles, and you had to see me. Friends are for help. You are like another son, your mother such a great lady, she would agree with me. Your late father – so sadly no longer with us – would be very proud of you. I too am very proud of you. Michael regards you as a brother. You are like a member of my family. We have built Cedar together. The credit goes to you and to Michael – without you there would be no Cedar today, Cedar is bigger than all of us. Our public shareholders – how well we have done for them. I have played a small part in guiding you and Michael – I am not looking for any credit. I did it for you, the young ones. Between us we did it all for Cedar. Cedar is now so much more important than any of us. More important than any one person.'

I could see it all coming, the ringing discursiveness before the bell tolled, his elusive thoughts forming a vague rambling logic, his *non sequiturs* and half-finished sentences wingeing and swooping and spiralling towards his chosen target. I watched him whilst he was talking, his moon-faced innocent eyes looking around the panelled study, fully away from me when he was launching a more flagrant high-flyer, alighting past me on a large portrait of Nadia in Pavlova's *Dragonfly*, glancing askance at a Morris Louis with its brilliant, pristine honest-coloured stripes, gazing fixedly at the ceiling when searching for divine inspiration for just the right word, the prelude to summoning up the tears which would display the intensity of his overwrought feelings, and then leaving, until last, his deliberate meditative look through the French windows, not registering the green lawn and the clusters of roses, but concentrating on his last ventriloquist throw of, it's not me talking to you, my boy, but your father, and I know what's good for you, and then, finally, the thrust, the *coup de grace*.

I lay back in my armchair, muffled in my dressing gown and in furious silence, aware of what he was going to say, anticipating the moment when the blade would glisten, waiting for the moment when he would lunge to insert his final point. 'So Charles, after hours of talk, all night, between Michael and I, you can imagine how much we are really against it – we sympathise with what happened last night – we really are very sorry. But we think from Cedar's point of view, not mine, not Michael's – we shall always remain close friends, always together – we have come to the very sad conclusion . . . er . . . that you . . . er . . . should resign.' At which, overcome with emotion and fumbling to remove his spectacles, he sagged exhausted, dabbing one eye with his large white handkerchief, forgetting in his overwhelming grief and suffering to dab the other.

What was most fascinating in his more-in-sorrow, trust-your-father soliloquy was not his grandiloquent acting and superb performance, but that whilst he was projecting his feelings with such emotion, he knew perfectly well that I did not believe a word he was saying – other than that he wanted my resignation.

He was applying his well-tried technique, his most favoured business and social gambit – undiluted flattery, which he had always hedged with flowery rhetoric and which was underpinned and nourished by his own sense of loyalty, which though carefully concealed, made sudden appearances on chosen occasions, flashed out Mackintosh-style for immediate impact and under wraps thereafter, until the next exposure. So in speaking to me as he did, providing me with the full portfolio of his remarkable talents, he was utterly sincere in his own disbelief in what he was saying. He was not put off his stroke by one jot. Indeed it was his devout faith in what he judged to be the feelings he wished to display, which gave him the confidence to overcome the obvious falsehoods which might otherwise have repelled, even him. In his personal life, it was an old ploy, exercised over the years on his various girlfriends, and perhaps it was its successful application in this personal part of his life, which spurred on his confidence to pursue his ends and increase his gratification.

He invariably mentioned my father, with whom he was hardly acquainted, a plump, cheerful and friendly, rather shrewd and intelligent man who had died some six years earlier in 1965, whose own word for Morrison was 'bluffer', a term my father, greatly respected for his probity, applied to anyone who had a hazy sense of accuracy. It was one of those appellations which stuck like a bad smell, and indeed it had helped to make me that much more cautious in my earliest dealings with Jack, something my father probably intended. Jack's references to my mother had been increasing of late because of her growing lustre as a painter. He did not refer to Nadia as there had been been, as reported by Brown, a minor scene that morning. It was part of Jack's adhesive synergy to combine flattery with snobbery. He would drop names with inimitable ease, that is if dropped could adequately describe the cascading profusion, for, Jack, a dedicated evangelist of reflected glory, was ever-active in seeking the most vicarious of relationships. But his references to Michael were always heart-felt and rock-solid. Although dredged up for effect, Michael was definitely his Absalom: Michael my son, my son Michael, was a constant litany reflecting his deep all-abiding affection. The bond between them had passed all tests, except during a brief period just before the Cedar collapse when Fischer temporarily succeeded in getting between them.

Jack's performance over, his lines played to perfection, fidgeting nervously with his white handkerchief, mopping his brow, waiting for the response, he looked specifically in my direction for the first time, peering at me quizzically, his short pug-like button nose cocked and sniffing like a terrier for signs of any possible danger. He was wondering if, when, and how, I was going to surrender. I looked back at him closely, wondering whether he or I would have to raise a white flag. I had clearly underestimated his strength of purpose. I had also seriously underestimated his tactics and his timing. I was down on the floor, it was only a few hours after the Spey settlement. He had not wasted a minute. He had managed for years to get away with his own-brand well-contained toxic sense of solidarity. But not any more. If he wanted a fight, he would have one.

'Jack,' I started, 'you shouldn't be here, and you should only have come here at a time like this to offer me your full support. Not this.' My own spleen and nerves spilled out when I next found myself referring to Fischer's vigil in the driveway outside. 'And you were absolutely right to keep David outside. He would never be allowed in here.' Jack feigned indifference to his nephew, there were more important things to sort out than a defence of Fischer, but it was not difficult to detect his glint of pleasure that I had let down my guard.

I went on, 'The real trouble, Jack, is that you don't trust anyone. You don't trust me and you don't even trust the institutions. You feel that one day they will push you and Michael out and that I will be behind them. Last night I did a deal with the institutions – they did not push me out. It was, to be frank, far more complicated than that. You have always been nervous of me, and now at the first opportunity you have come round here to have me out of the way. When was it? Only last Tuesday? The party at the Gavroche for Sidney Cowtan? You were asked to make the main speech. You said that you were extremely honoured and your remarks about me were extravagant.' Jack's head now started nodding in all directions, immensely bored at what I was saying and at such length too. 'What you really want is to strengthen your shareholding. What you really want is to get Amal into Cedar. With me out of the way there will be no one to stop you bringing in Amal.'

Jack jerked in his armchair and hissed at me. 'You can't stop me doing anything. Nor are you in that position.' Already the Spey sell-out of the night before had taken effect. 'I may not now be in that position, Jack. I don't know. But what I do know is that you're a bloody lousy friend.' There were no protests. 'And Jack, don't you ever forget that Cedar is a financial company, not a property company. If you ever succeeded in getting Amal into Cedar then I would most certainly resign as a director.'

At the word resign Jack suddenly sat still, he perked up, cocking his ear, no more fiddling with his handkerchief. This is what he had come for. I looked at him coolly. 'Jack, my father was right about you –' But before I could finish he reacted with an incoherent mumble, the habitual Jack Morrison preamble before venting anger, before lashing out, the suggestion that my own father had warned me about him loosened all his restraints. References to close friendship, to family ties, were not only forgotten but rejected. 'Now look here Charles, don't you –' But I'd had enough: 'Jack, it's time for you to go.'

We walked out through the marble lobby, through the front door, through the paved Italian courtyard, to the white lodge gate. I opened it to let him out. Not a word between us. His chauffeur was waiting by the door to let him into his car. He got in beside his nephew. I stood watching until the car disappeared through the wrought-iron gates. My hands were tightly clenched in the deep pockets of my dressing gown. Both of us had been shaking with anger. But I was not only angry with him, but also with myself. I had read him incorrectly, despite all the warning signs and despite that brutal Sutherland look. He would not only kick if someone was down, he would kill.

The next day Pamela Walton, a particular fan of Elliott's, was delighted to deal with him and with his Harpo; TWA first-class no doubt had a happy and relieved passenger. I picked myself off the floor and commenced dealing with the various letters which had to be written in respect of my withdrawal and in connection with the various Spey companies; Twentieth Century Banking, the Brighton Marina Company, National Car Parks, Warwick Securities and the rest. Letters also had to be written and phonecalls made on the Cedar situation. A message was left with the relevant persons amongst the institutions, at Coal, Electricity, and Phoenix, to let each of them know that I had received a personal request from the chairman to resign: I wanted them to hear this directly from me. To William Broadfield I spoke personally and at some length. He knew the Morrisons best. I suggested he took a firm stand and opposed any move by the Morrisons to bring Amal into Cedar; but I had the impression that he was too upset over my own future to take in what I was saying to him about Cedar's future.

About a fortnight later, Godfrey Chandler came to see me. We sat at the white round travertine table in my meeting room. I had not yet moved out of the Spey offices; I had made arrangements to take the floor above which had recently been vacated by Kuhn Loeb. Chandler, with his wide calm forehead, his hair unruffled, with the slightly triste appearance of one of King Charles's cavaliers, was saying how sorry he was to learn that Morrison had asked me to resign. Chandler observed that as I had been responsible for his firm being involved in Cedar, he thought he should inform me that he was happy to recommend to his partners that if I were to resign, Cazenove would consider resigning as brokers. This was the refined Cazenove mechanism working at its best, a beautifully-crafted handmade engine, the distillation of years of experience, elegant in its precision, always reliable, never a false move, never a false note, Mozartian in its seamless perfection.

I expected no less from Cazenove and no less from Godfrey. There was no question in the Cazenove consensus whether there would be a gain or loss in their possible resignation, no concern whether one or other of the institutions in Cedar who were major Cazenove clients, might take umbrage. Cazenove's objective as usual was to do the right and proper thing; the financial cost was immaterial. In switching my own mechanism into gear, a machine nowhere near such purring levels, I told Godfrey how much I appreciated what he had said, that I saw no reason why Cazenove should consider resigning, and that any decision either way would, of course, have to be the sole decision of the partners. Godfrey, I believe, expected no less from me; over a longish period we had enjoyed a rare understanding of each other's intelligence and judgement. He said he would toddle back to his office and speak to his partners. I thanked him for coming.

Nadia and I spent most of that summer, apart from two or three miserable trips to London, at La Reserve in Beaulieu. Friends came to visit and stayed either on our boat berthed nearby in the marina, or at the hotel. If one is in a state of shock, then, as one companion remarked to me whilst we were looking over the indigo bay towards St Jean Cap Ferrat, there are worse places then Hotel La Reserve from which to recover. To Nadia and I, for nearly twenty years, it was almost home from home. The house we were building in Mustique would never take its place and it never did. Without a word, Nadia had asked Alain who looked after the boat, to disconnect the telephone, and at La Reserve she requested that no calls be put through, except from Pamela Walton or Judith Bowen from Old Jewry, or from Brown or Mrs Blackwell from Thurloe Lodge.

Much appeared in the press, going on for weeks. Most of it was unpleasant. On one of the wretched visits to London, during lunch with Alec Dibbs, the weighty chief executive of National Westminster Bank, I commented about the undue fuss. He expostulated as always in his bluff manner. He was a man large in every way, physique, presence, opinions, support, and when addressing himself to a person or to an argument, both were prone to being pulverised by his massive physical and intellectual bulk. 'You are being too naive,' he said, 'don't you realise that in the City you were talked about and written about more than anyone else during the whole of the last year or so.' Gulping his food, 'Mind you, it was generally positive stuff. Spey's demise is a disappointment; it was a terrific venture.'

If anything, his comments were sending me into worse shock. Dibbs had been an intelligent supporter of Spey and the thinking that went behind it. He liked its ethos, frequently saying it was what the City needed, in fact not just one Spey but many of them. I looked at my plate with no appetite. He took another mouthful. 'You failed hopelessly in the task of managing.' This remark, too, rankled for years, mainly because he had, as usual, put his finger on it. 'You bungled it all badly.' Then trying to make amends, 'Don't worry. Spey is not just your loss but also the City's. Both will recover.' And with a smile, 'Why aren't you eating?'

I knew the entanglement and disentanglement had been handled badly. I knew that Paul Chambers had also, like Jasper Knight, behaved curiously. My City banker friend, the one with the aphorisms, Johnny Speyer, once said to me, beware of old men. Why? Because they are at the end of their careers with little or nothing to lose by being difficult. I thought of Chambers and of Knight, both old men. But there were others. Younger men whose careers were nowhere near their end. People were manipulating and being manipulated. I analysed words and actions of the parties concerned, the institutions, the merchant banks, the directors, full-time or otherwise, the numerous people connected with the major or minor subsidiaries of Spey. Many of these people were formidable or distinguished in their own right. In particular, the most jangling part of my anguish was my inability, at the time, to decipher how and why it had happened. There were unknown forces involved, other personalities; there was a definite mystery and there was a definite Brutus syndrome; not just one Brutus, but several.

I went over certain events, one in particular which occurred within days after I withdrew from Spey, when Spey Finance was so very smoothly sold to First National on whose board Sainer had only just been appointed. Here was something peculiar, if not sinister. I scratched around mentally until my mind ached. The most recurrent question was the role played by Leonard Sainer. What had he been up to? And if my suspicions were well-founded, what role had my ever-so-close friend, Charles Clore, played? Was he playing a labyrinthine game?

More of the onion skins were peeling off. I sought the advice of Martin Lampard, a clever lawyer and, like Leonard Sainer, senior partner of a large City law firm. I then decided to write to Sainer. My letter questioned his motives, particularly his involvement in the purchase by First National of Spey Finance. The letter was deadly. Sainer telephoned me, affronted. The facts speak for themselves, I told him. What are you going to do? he asked. For a man of his enormous manipulative skill, to ask such an unskilfull question was an indication of how rattled he was. He normally gave nothing away. I felt more poised. I told him he would have to wait and see. The letter became a timebomb and in effect remained so, till he died. After I departed from Spey, immediately after this conversation, I was disinclined to see Clore and I stopped answering his telephone calls.

Our friendship was resumed some months later after Stash Radziwill invited me to have lunch with him at the Savoy Grill. How far Clore was behind it I was not able to find out, Stash parrying my archly-angled questions with deft ease; he was an excellent swordsman. But he urged me to see Clore, who, Stash said, was most upset, and then suddenly switching, told me that Charles thought that the Morrisons were also behind the Spey 'nonsense' as he called it. This shook me. It had not fully occurred to me until then that Jack would have been up to his usual tricks, stirring the pot in my territory. I had of course realised from the moment father and son whispered together after our lunch, on their way to the lift, that they would meddle and stir, but I had not taken any counter-measures. I must have been far more tired than I realised. As Kastner had advised, I should take more time to get off from the floor.

Radziwill was one of London's most attractive, raffish, social landmarks. He was married to Jackie Kennedy's sister and would refer with gusto to President Kennedy who was known to have had a special liking for him, not by name, but as 'my dear brother-in-law'. When in New York, he would stay in the President's suite at the Carlyle, photographs of the first family prominently displayed, and Stash would say, in unaffected candour, useful for business when he held meetings in the suite. A naturally urbane figure, he was the quintessential European aristocrat.

Nadia and I had first met him through Felix Fenston, his charismatic bearded one-legged partner, their teasing interplay and badinage and chaffing having the Kitchener flavour of testing brothers-in-arms, anti-four-feathers talk, men's talk. 'I can tear the London telephone directory in half with my bare hands, can you?' 'Let's have more of the 1892 brandy, and turn the pages for me, Stash, whilst I play your favourite prelude before we indulge the girls.' My own affectionate goodwill towards Stash did not extend to his wife Lee, the proverbial younger sister who, in any event, irritated me because of her manifest liking for Nureyev, a person who irritated me even more; she was another unsuspecting moth scorched by the fierce searchlight of Russia's most illustrious egomaniac.

I heard Stash out carefully, his large watery Polish eyes slightly bulging, his friendly frame comfortably crumpled in his chair, a natural aristocrat even if he had not been born a Radziwill prince. Shrewd on people, but sadly not in business situations, savouring his cigar like a true cigar smoker, husbanding each draw as if he were sipping a beautifully-balanced claret, we conversed with easy pleasure. I had always been attracted to his ancient worldliness, his weary good-natured acceptance that life was but a comedy designed to make one laugh as well as to cry before that final curtain. So laugh he did, amiably prepared for the worst to happen, but determined to find amusement in the one-way trundle trip to the final exit. He would say that as long as there was love, only a little bit, then one would be forgiven any transgressions in this life or the next. 'Charles loves you,' he said without any sentimentality but with enough intriguing emphasis to suggest that Clore was showing particular keenness for a rapprochement. 'Why don't you see him?'

Dear Stash, who once said to me that everything you think may go wrong will go wrong; who said one must never give up, because it can only get worse; who went out of his way, without fuss, to help friends in need, financial or emotional; who made life enhancing for all around him; dear Stash, who died, almost bust, at Moynes a year later, the house of his great friend Ivor Bryce, a man of astonishing good looks, the man believed to be the inspiration of Ian Fleming's 007 and the uncle of Lady Milford Haven.

By the autumn of 1971, Clore and I resumed our friendship. We were grateful to Radziwill for intervening, and we spoke of him frequently and warmly, which is, I suppose, the most unaffected testimonial one can pay to a friend who has passed away. But Clore and I both knew that sooner or later we would have to have our serious tussle about Sainer, First National and Spey. When it did occur in Paris, one tempestuous night several years later, we went for each other with no holds barred. By the end both of us were utterly drained. It was a turning point in my relationship with him; a man who rarely felt or showed sympathy to another, he began to display signs of genuine affection, he became less captious, there was less carping, there was more laughter. It was also a turning point in his relations with Sainer, and it was after this I believe that he rearranged some of his estate matters, where Sainer was excluded from an official role.

As Stash said, everything you think may go wrong, will go wrong. Spey had gone wrong, so things could only get worse. But at the Savoy, with a comforting shoulder hug at the table as we were about to depart, Stash said in his non-pareil accent, a wonderful *mélange* of Warsaw, Park Avenue and Park Lane, 'Don't vorry my boy, Nadia will help to pull you through. Vot a girl'.

In between islands of clear recollection, that summer was a blur. We saw many of our friends who had places on the coast: Princess Antoinette, Prince Rainier's sister, in the family enclave in Eze, Arpad Plesch, the mysterious Hungarian financier, in the Villa Leonina facing the Beaulieu marina; Antony and Anne Norman at the Chateau de la Garoupe at Cap d'Antibes, which he had inherited from his grandmother, the wife of the founder of Boots. John Schlesinger, the South African industrialist, telephoned to ask what he could do to help; one of our best friends particularly in foul weather, he had originally introduced us decades earlier to the charms of La Reserve. Meg Stenham stayed for a while on our boat. Her marriage to Cob was breaking up, I suggested she should visit Mustique to recover – she did and stayed for years. Arnold Haskell and his wife were staying with friends in Monte Carlo. Her sister, Alicia Markova, had made her name dancing around the world with Anton Dolin. He had become one of our closest friends. The Diaghilev nostalgia still wistfully pervades this scented section of the Côte d'Azur. It was the Princesse de Polignac, mother of Rainier and Antoinette, who had provided home and security to Diaghilev in Monte Carlo. Dolin had given ballet classes to Princess Antoinette when she was hardly out of knicker-bockers. Markova and Dolin and Ninette de Valois were among the few Anglo-Saxons in the Diaghilev company, spending much of their early professional life in the most perfect opera house in the world, Garnier's real masterpiece. Every day, even now, 'Le Train Bleu' speeds to Paris and back; the ballet with costumes by Chanel, curtain by Picasso and music by Milhaud was Dolin's greatest Diaghilev triumph. Sometimes impishly, at nine in the evening, pretending to hear the train from La Reserve, he would raise a glass in memory.

We used to give Dolin a birthday party each year in July, sometimes there, sometimes at Le Voile D'Or, and this year was no exception. On one occasion Efraim Kurtz and his lovely Texan wife joined us and this was one occasion when Dolin did not take the floor, for Effy Kurtz had a long baton going back to his conducting days with Pavlova. Haskell was our most distinguished ballet critic, this hallowed seat now occupied by another close friend, Clement Crisp of the *Financial Times*, and Nadia's first-ever bouquet was from Haskell's mother.

The days went by, lunch on the boat, at friends, dinner on the terrace of the Hotel de Paris, in perfumed gardens of private villas, at the Roquebrune owned and run by balletomanes. There is no laughter like ballet laughter, for no one in the ballet is ever old; rivalries and triumphs of yesteryear are constantly recalled with an enthusiasm and energy, a bubbling invective and humour engendered uniquely by the everlastingly young. All this helped to restore a rhythm of stability. Underneath, there was a raging turbulence and at moments I would notice Nadia, her deep turquoise eyes, as cool and luminous as the Mediterranean dawn, looking in my direction. As Stash had said, 'vot a girl'.

Arnold Haskell, in his nice, semi-academic manner, took me aside; think in years, he said, not in weeks or months. Arpad Plesch, knowing that I was in no mood to talk about business and who had bizarre family relationships of his own, asked me about my relationship with my three brothers, shaking with mirth, and sadly also with his increasing Parkinson's disease, when I told him that I was always forgetting the name of one brother I hardly knew. A second, Max, an architect well known for his acerbic wit, had all the limp selfishness of someone incapable of love; the third, David, at the *Economist*, now running it, then writing for it, who had just telephoned me, but as I confided to Arpad, I suspected, and still do, that he was really after an exclusive story. Arpad, a born journalist, shook even more. 'Why not? I would do the same myself!'

In July I arranged to see Jack Morrison at his office very late in the afternoon, the date fixed as a result of various messages between the secretaries. He was the chairman and I was a member of the board. There was a clear protocol. It was also one of those encounters which was doomed to failure before it started, but which had to take place so that the end game could proceed to its conclusion.

When I entered his room Jack was already in his chair, pretending to read a newspaper. He put it down and got up. He greeted me with icy politeness. I could see that he was determined not to uncap his pent-up feelings. We had known each other well for years: we had been closely associated for most of that time; undoubtedly there had always been an underlying uneasiness, but equally there had always been a mutual respect. Now there was a vehement mutual distaste. The collision at Thurloe Lodge had broken any relationship, but it had not shattered the modicum of politeness between us.

'I've asked Rose to let us have some tea.' 'Splendid,' I said. She entered, greeted me, left the tray and departed. Jack poured, a little too carefully, otherwise his nerves were fully disguised. He said, 'I still want you to resign'. 'I know,' I replied. 'If you don't resign we shall be in for a fight.' 'So be it,' I said. 'I am sorry it has come to this,' he added. 'You are not sorry,' I said. We looked at each other with intense barely-contained animosity. 'I propose to be away for most of the summer, and I will drop you a note in the morning,' I told him with icy politeness. We got up to say goodbye. We shook hands, something I do not recall we had ever done before. It was a joint nervous reaction, perhaps we both wanted to grapple with each other. Afterwards in the banquette at Wilton's, talking to Nadia, I described the five-minute tea party. 'Jack said how sorry he was it had come to this.' Nadia's comment was that perhaps one day he might discover what the word sorry meant.

Next day, I wrote him a note. I referred to our meeting and stated that I would, as I put it, be away on a short sabbatical, and that I would not be able to attend any boards of Cedar until October. On any further communication he could get in touch with Pamela Walton. I telephoned Izzy in Glasgow. I told him about my encounter with Jack, and added that whereas before I had found it hard to believe the family gossip that Jack's ex-wife and ex-brother-in-law had been brought together because of their mutual dislike for him, I was now convinced that it was authentic, that the Jack Morrison hate club must have had a larger membership than I had suspected. Izzy said that when he next came down to London we should have lunch together, by which time I might have calmed down. I declined, saying I would be away all summer and I would rather we left things for a while. 'Fine, let's do that,' Izzy said, and then gently added an observation which he thought might placate me, 'Don't forget that Jack's a funny man'. I replied that he was a funny man in more respects than even Izzy guessed. Some years later Izzy received a call from the funny man just before he died. It was a *cri de coeur*, a cry of desperation and despair, and Izzy wept. Although Jack and he had drifted apart, a thread had remained, sufficiently strong for Izzy to be the one person with whom Jack wished to confide at that particular moment.

During August I came over to London for another brief visit. Michael must have known. I had hardly arrived in my office in Old

Jewry when Pamela Walton told me that Michael Morrison and David Fischer were in reception. Could they possibly see me? It would not have been considered unreasonable nor intractable if I had sent both away, but my resignation from Cedar had to be resolved and I had already made arrangements to do it my way.

When I came into the meeting room they were both already seated. Fischer was visibly throbbing with nerves. I ignored him. Michael was also in an excitable state but, strictly speaking, this was not an unusual state for him to be in. He greeted me and apologised for the intrusion. He said we would always be friends, he knew that his father had upset me deeply, and with a nervous giggle, 'We all know my father'. Fischer then shot in saying that Jack was not only upset but angry. I turned to Fischer and told him that if he uttered another sound I would personally eject him. 'You're only here because I would never send Michael away.' I turned to Michael. 'I have already decided not to stay on.' 'Thank you,' said Michael, not concealing a feeling of immense relief. I took them to the lift and on the way I said to Michael, 'Yes, we all do know your father'.

Cedar had its AGM on Thursday 8 October at noon. As usual it would be held at the Dorchester, followed by a private lunch to which the directors, the institutional shareholders, the banks, solicitors and auditors, the financial advisers and other special friends of Cedar and the Morrisons were invited. This AGM was the first since Cedar had become a public company. It was a prime occasion for Jack to stand up as its chairman, to act the titular role of the head of a newly-quoted bank, resplendent and full of pride with his always well-cut waistcoat lending a dignified façade to his proud and newly acquired magisterial bearing. I had seen it before at meetings and celebrations, like the recent one a few months earlier at Sidney Cowtan's retirement party. He was very good at this sort of thing, as his own brothers would be the first to admit, fufilling these tasks with the same persuasive *élan* he had shown in their Morrisons shops business, and I had no doubt he would put himself over superbly at this first public AGM of Cedar. He would certainly be puffed up looking forward to it.

The exact date of the AGM had slipped my mind, memory playing one of its tricks, switching off when it is more then usually needed. One evening there was a telephone call at home from Michael Belmont, my special friend at Cazenove. 'I thought you would like to know that there was a vote of thanks for you today at the Cedar AGM.' I was speechless. Belmont went on, 'Godfrey asked Jack Morrison if

Cazenove could second the vote of thanks at the meeting. He was there today with Rae Lyster. It was actually a vote of thanks to you and for everything you had done for Cedar. The institutions and the others were delighted, but I gather that Morrison went puce.' I laughed. Michael continued, 'You know, we have a rule at Cazenove, that no matter how important the client, we decline invitations to give the vote of thanks at an AGM. This is only the second time in our history that we have broken our rule'. Cazenove's breaking one of its own rules was virtually unheard of; but that I should have been told after the event was very much in character.

I was touched and told Michael I would phone his partner next day. When I did, Godfrey Chandler explained how he had gone to the AGM with Rae Lyster and that, due to a State visit, there was a frightful traffic jam and they had just made it in the nick of time. In his droll way Godfrey said that his remarks went down well particularly with the institutions, although it was possible 'Jack was not wholly pleased'. Puce, I recalled Michael Belmont telling me. It was only later that I learnt that Godfrey never saw the Morrisons again.

My severance from Cedar was settled with the unobtrusive help of Godfrey Chandler in a manner which fitted in with a finely judged act of propriety. Each year at the AGM by way of a rota directors came up for re-election. This year it was the turn of Broadfield and myself. I did not offer myself for re-election. That was all. There was no resignation, forced or otherwise. The cord was unravelled simply and neatly. The man responsible for originally attaching the cord some ten years earlier, was down from Glasgow on one of his London visits. In his suite at Grosvenor House we shared some strongly-brewed tea followed by a wee dram. We talked until the trees in the Park started to disappear in the dusk. When I emerged into Park Lane, the air was fresh but inviting. I sent the driver home and decided to walk through the Park to Kensington Gore and then down to Thurloe Lodge. The trees were in their autumn silhouette, most of their leaves had been shed and were thick on the ground, swishing comfortingly around one's ankles. There was very little sound other than the occasional country yelp of a dog and the soft rumble in the distance of the far away London traffic.

It had been a long summer.

FIVE

The Evergreen Lady

'The Old Lady of Threadneedle Street' was a sobriquet from the cartoonist Gilray, emanating from a sly remark by Sheridan during a debate in the House of Commons. In view however of her longstanding constancy and decorum, she deserves perhaps the more gallant description of 'The Evergreen Lady'. The following brief account of the City and the Bank provides what I hope is a helpful background to the evergreen Lady's significance in the growth of the City in which she played and still plays such a dominating role.

Since well before Roman days, when it was a tiny habitation by the Thames, with the River Fleet flowing from the west and the Walbrook coursing through its centre, London, with extraordinary consistency, has been based upon trade. Although it is still considered one of the world's financial centres, its trading pedigree can be traced back to the mystic legends of ancient pre-Roman Britain. The Romans themselves had a wonderfully well endowed sense of location – London was the hub of their remarkable road system – and as early as 61 AD Tacitus said that Londinium was 'greatly celebrated by the number of its markets and the abundance of its supplies'. Nevertheless the Romans left Britain in 410 AD, also seemingly leaving half their coins behind.

The Jews arrived soon after, and because it was an irreligious act for a Christian to lend money on interest, the Jews, without any such religious scruple, cornered the lending market protected by the monarchs, who, in return for huge fines, allowed their progeny to carry on these very essential financial services. In the City of London the Jews congregated in and around Old Jewry, a stone's throw from where the Bank of England is now situated and close to Cheapside, the busiest market of all – ceape was the Saxon word for bartering – where prolific shops and stalls straggled along both sides, with specialists selling their particular wares in the narrow adjoining thoroughfares, in Milk Street, Wood Street, Bread Street, Friday Street (for fish), in Ironmonger Lane, Poultry, and Corn Hill, and for money at Change Alley.

When the Jews were pushed out in 1290, the Italians returned, not this time along the Roman road seeking conquests, but along the Lombard plains seeking fortunes. The Lombards, uninhibited like the Jews by religious scruples, were in every way as clever at money-lending, indeed even cleverer and more usurious. They perfected the use of bills of exchange and started their own bancos like their Venetian and Florentine forebears, who, trading originally from alfresco benches, were made bankrupt when in default by angry depositors who axed – 'ruptus' in graphic old Italian – their wooden bancos. But the Italians, generous as always in spreading their gifts, not only gave to the lending industry their overpotent sign – the three golden balls of Lombardy – but also their genius for style and good manners, which has since permeated all the respectable, and some not so respectable, banking parlours throughout the world.

Very early on, the craft Guilds emerged, the creative innovators of the City of London. Initially religious fraternities, several had Charters with monopoly rights dating from well before the Black Death of 1348. These early tradesmen instituted the City Corporation and defined the voting wards of the City, they strengthened the mayorality, they established their Hall of Guilds, and, wearing their own liveries, proudly attended the frequent ceremonial gatherings in the distinctive halls they had founded. Many of these are still in the same location; like the Grocers, which started in 1180 as the Pepperers, like the Barbers, started in 1308 by the dual-disciplined Richard le Barber – barbers not only cut hair but bones – like the Brewers, the Clock-makers, the Musicians (minstrels), and many others representing fascinating occupations long since discontinued, such as the Fletchers (arrow makers), the Girdlers (a giralle or girdle is still presented to the monarch and worn on coronation day), the Coopers (barrel makers), the Upholders (upholstery not faith), the Borderers (embroidery), and also the Cooks, dating from 1311 – the art of English cooking having a distinguished pedigree, but now alas not much else besides.

The Guilds were the first exponents of sustained quality control through the brilliantly conceived apprenticeship system, and because wool was the country's largest and most staple item of manufacture and export, the richest guild was the Mercers', whose apprentices, after serving seven years in order to qualify as a Master, had to produce their master pieces. Also very rich were the Goldsmiths, who even today provide a mark of quality, which refers literally to their own Hall mark for gold and silver, whilst the Fishmongers, chartered in 1272, continue to have statutory powers to inspect fish under three Acts of Parliament, the most recent in 1967.

All the hustle and bustle took place within and around the City walls, whose gates were securely closed at night. The oldest gate, the Bishop's goes back to 675; the Moor gate leading to the vast moor fields was finally taken down in 1762; the Alders gate, one of the earliest openings of the old City wall, was in existence in 1243; Lud gate had a flap or lid instead of an upright door post; Cripple gate, erected fifty years before the Battle of Hastings, was part of a tunnel (crepel) used by Roman soldiers to crawl surreptitiously from the London wall to the barbican – a barbican was a high watchtower or a loophole in a fortification, the present manifestation gloomily demonstrating very little improvement.

Situated in the centre of the City with some aplomb, almost exactly where the present banking hall of the Bank of England is today, at the corner of Threadneedle and Princes Streets, was one of England's earliest churches, the popular St Christopher. It was later known as St Christopher-le-Stocks because it was opposite the livestock market and also because the City's other form of stocks (wooden leg and hand cuffs) designed to punish wrongdoers and to deter others, was always placed in the most conspicuous position; stockbrokers taking their name from these beginnings should perhaps also take note how the City's earliest proven miscreants were punished publicly as guilty outsiders. All around in this teeming section, in Bishopsgate, Lothbury, Cornhill, the rich merchants had their mansions; their chosen leader, the Lord Mayor, selected – the first in 1191 – by an elaborate procedure laid down by Royal Charter, and reigning for a year at a time at the Mansion House. Business, not only trade but also the new business of insuring against risk, was conducted anywhere and everywhere; from private mansions and dwellings, from pavements, alleys, stalls and markets, from inns and taverns, and – after the exotic aroma of coffee aroused the Englishman's taste and fancy – from coffeehouses, the most famous of which was owned by a Mr Lloyd, who, though underwritten for posterity, has nevertheless been truly abused by Rogers' gigantic espresso machine masquerading as the headquarters of the world's most celebrated insurance centre.

The kings lived on their dues and on their fees. The Royal Office, run by the Royal Exchanger, used chequered cloth borrowed from a checkboard or chessboard for counting purposes, so the office was called the Exchequer, the Royal Exchanger later becoming known as the Chancellor. With the enormous surge of trade in the fifteenth and sixteenth centuries, trade routes were opened in the East and the West by Chartered Corporations which had exclusive rights, like the East India Company, the Turkey Company, the Levant Company, the Hudson Bay Company, whilst the Port of London kept on expanding till it became by far the largest in the world. Today though transformed and somewhat disfigured by the New Docklands, it still retains much of the compelling allure of its great mercantile history.

The insatiable and extortionate financial needs of the Tudors – of the numerous Henrys – of the singular Elizabeth until our present monarch, of the Stuarts, Charles I and II and James I and II – were a bitter part of the long and unsettled background to the growing demand for more parliamentary control. Taxes were imposed *ad hoc* by the monarch, who relied on ad hoc borrowings from the Jews and from the City merchants; during prosperous times the system creaked along, but during depressions or worse it broke down with lamentable repercussions.

Fortunately for the Tudors the Greshams arrived, and with them some order. Richard Gresham was King Henry VIII's Exchanger. His prodigy of a son, Thomas, becoming Queen Elizabeth's Royal Merchant, had a tremendous capacity for work and a superb innovative mind which he exercised with an uncanny sense of judgement and management. He reorganised the entire marketing of all types of commodities, he enunciated his Law – the economists' first but by no means last cliché – and he founded, at his own expense, the Royal Exchange (1571), which became a central money market attracting traders from all over the world. He operated his own business from his mansion at 68 Lombard Street, his Gresham sign the Grasshopper, which was later arrogated by Martin's Bank, and he was as usual more far-sighted than most in encouraging the crucial if not desperate need for a 'national' bank. There were constant protests that financial equilibrium between the monarch and the State had to be engendered.

Indeed, by 1581, a Mr Hagenbach had a signed and sealed agreement with Queen Elizabeth for a more formal arrangement, but their haggling ended in nought. Hagenbach asked for an interest rate of 6%, the Queen offered 2%, they agreed at 4%. Her second thoughts were as usual more stingy and she lost interest.

Though by far the most important trading centre in the world, London was still lagging well behind its competitors in having its own bank: Amsterdam had its bank in 1609, Hamburg in 1619, Rotterdam in 1635, Stockholm in 1656; and if one ignores the Chinese who had banknotes more than a thousand years earlier, the Swedes, who were the first to have a true National Bank, were also the first in the Western world to have banknotes, invented by a countryman with the exquisite name of Palmstruck.

The English, as usual, were jolted into action by scandal. The merchants had taken to keeping their money in the Royal Mint at the Tower of London, but the temptation proved too much for Charles I. Particularly short of money, he stole it all like a true cavalier. It amounted to £130,000 and, though he finally repaid a goodly portion, his flagrant dishonesty galvanised the betrayed and angry merchants into using the Goldsmiths as their bankers. This gave banking just the impetus it needed. When Charles lost his head in 1649 (by one vote) and was followed by Cromwell, it was soon apparent that the great Protector not only had a head for governing but also for rounding up business. He supported the return of the Jews, he reopened the East Indies, and he challenged the Dutch monopoly on their trading routes.

After the Cromwells, the Monarchy in the attractive and witty form of Charles II was restored in 1660. The new King though generally under-rated was shrewd, but the goldsmiths were even shrewder. The term banker was by now synonymous with that of goldsmith and many amongst them were to germinate the earliest family banks, such as Childs and Hoares and Martins, but it was to be well over a century or more before the mainstream family merchant banks, the Barings, Rothschilds, Hambros, Schroders and Kleinworts, emerged. Charles II also attacked the Dutch, who, bitterly furious at losing their trade routes, swept up the Thames; fortunately they were swept back, but enormous debts were incurred which couldn't be repaid. Panic ensued: this was the first bank 'run'.

Then, on the second night of September 1666, inadvertently set alight by the Royal Baker, the Great Fire of London raged through the centre of the City. Though this disaster was incalculable, rebuilding started immediately. Amongst the guilds, many, including the halls of the Mercers' and the Goldsmith's, were burnt to the ground. The ancient Guildhall itself was severely damaged though intact, but hundreds of buildings which had survived for centuries were destroyed. Mercifully Christopher Wren, the young Professor of Mathematics now starting his great career as an architect, rose like a human phoenix from the ashes in all his genius; he planned and built over fifty churches and in creating St Paul's came up with the most elegant of all valedictions which, enstoned in his great edifice, simply states in Latin, 'If you seek my memorial look around you'.

Charles II, more profligate than any other Stuart, which was no mean achievement, could no longer hold out. He defaulted on all his loans, closed the Exchequer and suspended payments. It was the worst crisis the City had yet endured, the second royal robbery in so many years, the monarch, this time, stealing nearly ten times more than his father, a majestic case of rampant inflation. There was wide outrage and it became abundantly clear that the country had to have a 'central' or 'national' bank able to sustain these dangerous predations by the Crown.

The English, having tired of the Tudors, were now thoroughly fed up with the Stuarts, and with James II banished, someone new was sought. The nation's traditional enemy produced the answer, his son-in-law King William III of Holland, husband of the rather lively Mary, both now better known as related pieces of fairly gloomy furniture. There was also definite commercial self-interest between the new king waging his trade wars and the City providing him with financial support. However, there was still not enough money, so William used every penny he could lay his hands on – he even pawned his personal jewellery – to finance the army against his long time enemy Louis XIV. He embraced any method of taxing, old or new; he got rid of the hated chimney tax but substituted a window tax, and a poll tax, a peddlers tax, a birth tax, a stamp tax – still an irritant – a bachelor's tax, a marriage tax, even a death tax: the taxes were wholly ineffective. An effective solution had to be implemented – and quickly. At long last it was.

In 1694, the Bank of England, the Lady of Threadneedle Street, came to life. A bill was introduced incorporating 'The Governor and the Company of the Bank of England'. It was as much political expediency as financial. The new institution was permitted to raise a permanent loan of £1.2 million by public subscription, the subscribers receiving a return of 4%. The £1.2 million would be lent at 8% to its first customer, the penurious and gasping Government, which in turn with the consent of Parliament, could service the monarch. The Corporation also received £4,000 as a management fee, an early example of one of the City's greatest financial inventions. The successful subscription took place on 21 June inside the new Mercers Hall, situated between Old Jewry and Ironmonger Lane, restored since the great fire with a Wren-designed doorway. There was a strong Huguenot involvement and it was not widely proclaimed that a large minority of the subscribers were shrewd Dutch investors, wishing (of course) to follow their king – and their commercial instincts.

The Board of Managers consisted of a Governor, a Deputy Governor and a Court of Directors. A national bank was in business. The mastermind behind the neat concept, indeed a dealmaker of brilliant imagination, was a Scot named William Paterson. The first deputy Governor was Sir Michael Godfrey who, after a year with the Bank and with the prescience of nearly half a millennium, wrote a short history of the Bank of England specifically defending the Bank from criticism that in attracting money it was diverting resources from the fostering of commerce. The first Governor was Sir John Houblon, descended from a Huguenot family and as Pepys's closest friend, is frequently referred to in that ubiquitous diary. Sir John was a marvellously fortunate first choice, for he was wise and temperate, an outstanding administrator who never made as much as a single false step during his entire tenure as Governor.

England was now acknowledged as the greatest mercantile nation and was to remain so for over two centuries, and the City as its financial and trading centre was acknowledged to be more formidable and powerful than any other. It had finally and completely eclipsed Amsterdam, and, with its trading and financing hooks grasping onto every part of the globe, it became the bankers to the world. The Bank of England, also growing from strength to strength, moved from its birthplace at the Mercers' Hall to the Grocers' Hall, and was an impeccable guest there for forty years. Then, in January 1735, it made its historic move to Threadneedle Street, where it has been in resplendent, but not entirely uncritical, authority ever since.

A year before the move the bank had acquired Sir John Houblon's mansion in Threadneedle Street, together, it is thought, with his livery, the now famous pink and red. It thanked the Grocers for their generous hospitality and settled alongside St Christopher-le-Stocks.

In 1780 Lord George Gordon, a virulent Protestant who later converted to Judaism, roused the rabble against a pro-Catholic Act of Parliament: he was clearly very mixed up, but the Gordon riots, though sparked off in Westminster, quickly moved to the City where the mob attacked the Bank. As a result a Guards detachment thereafter marched each evening from St James's barracks to the Bank to spend the night, a ceremonial protection which only ceased in 1973.

It was evident, however, that the bank had to seek maximum security. Soon after the riots, for this purpose and also for reasons of expansion, it purchased adjoining properties. St Christopher was also acquired and was then demolished with genuine condolences, though its large garden was retained. It was at this time, too, that a stone moulding of Britannia sitting on a mound was erected over the entrance to the banking hall; the mound was so amorphously designed it could have represented anything, the sea or even banknotes, but at any rate the gender was established in the public eye – the Lady of indeterminate age had now started on her great financial saga, sitting, it was decided, on her money. With the onset of the French Revolution the Old Lady suspended payments and over a hundred banks collapsed, but with the hand of Pitt on the tiller, aided by the eye of Nelson and the boot of Wellington, stability was restored. Napoleon was exiled and became better known to the English as a man who had made his rendezvous with destiny at a mainline railway station; to the French who disliked Corsicans as they did everyone else, including themselves, he became a national obsession, which explains why, though imbued with peerless intellectual courage and reason and great culture, they were such easy prey to the Germans for the next hundred years or more.

England, benefiting from the demise of Napoleon, was also benefiting from the enormous wealth engendered by the Industrial Revolution. The City banks proliferated, so did financial scandals and so did bank runs. In 1838 the Royal Exchange was destroyed by a fire which very nearly engulfed the Old Lady. An early Black Friday, 11 May 1866, was when the powerful Overend Gurney banking partnership collapsed folowing the cotton crisis caused by the American Civil War; but that run was not as severe as the Baring Crisis in 1891. The Barings were saved by the Bank of England together with the concerted efforts of their rivals, the other dynastic family merchant banks, and also by the new joint stock banks. As an indication that some of the family later extended their talents from banking into public service, the Barings can boast no less than four peerages, three more than any other banking family.

Dickens mentions a visit to the Bank of England in *The Pickwick Papers*. Old Sam Weller asks why the clerks are eating ham sandwiches behind the counter and his son tells him 'It's their dooty, it's part o' the system'. One wonders what young Weller would have said about duty and the system if he had known that before 1830 the ham-eating clerks had forty-seven bank holidays per year.

Gradually the custom grew of having the sons of the ham-eating clerks, the doormen, the messengers, the managers, coming into the bank: indeed positions were reserved for them. Though not persisting there are still many second- and third-generation members of the same family continuing a family tradition; one family, the Bowers, serving in the Bank uninterruptedly from 1780 until almost the present day.

An early architect to the Bank was the great Sir John Soane. From the beginning Soane designed the bank perfectly, with a stunning mixture of styles, no where more evident than in the Court Room where he installed three chimneypieces designed by Robert Taylor, two of which, installed with beautiful effect in the directors' court room, are amongst the most magnificent chimneypieces in the country. Construction of the Bank started in 1788; the most prominent feature then, as it is today, was Soane's monumental stone curtain-wall, hiding even now much of the Bank building which overlooks the rampart in stately but benign assurance. The present building was designed by Sir Herbert Baker in the 1920s and finally completed in 1939. He was no Soane, but he had a lot more ground to work upon, the Bank having acquired its existing near-four-acre site a century earlier. But, above all, Baker's best decision was to retain and re-position in its entirety, the Soane splendour of the 'Governor's House', as he called that rich and magnificent segment.

From the outside, the Bank of England building is an intrusion, the building that is; it is a prison in reverse, designed not to keep people in but to keep people out. Of its four surrounds, Prince's Street is a cold canyon, avoided, even though quicker, by the bank messengers; Lothbury, opposite Tokenhouse – Cazenove's landed seat and the National Westminster Bank headquarters, is where the second entrance is positioned, for Governors, gold and groceries; by Bartholomew Lane there are taxis in rank, the previous sombre aspect now brightened by the entrance to the new Bank museum; by

Threadneedle, flanking the main entrance, there are ten sturdy Soane Corinthian Greek pillars on either side of Baker's new massive bronze doors, each eighteen feet high with two additional smaller doors of burnished bronze. City folk seen scurrying by this most impressive façade and on the surrounding Bank of England pavements, tend to hurry, their heads veering away from the continuous wall towards the kerb as if it was designed to discourage contact with the outside world. This stone bulwark, a full thirty feet high and nearly half a mile in length, is a veritable rampart, ribbed by horizontal lintels, no windows, the odd setback and occasional pillar, little statuary, no foliage, not quite a fort, but, at ground level, with true hauteur, rejecting any gestures of sociability.

Rising decorously behind and high above this stony countenance are the rectangular hillocks of the offices with more windows than one would suppose, not quite friendly but still beckoning. The stronghold of the country's banking system, our financial citadel, the bastion of its integrity, is in the epicentre of the City. Yet it lends an impression of being out of scale with its surroundings, whereas St Paul's, a few hundred yards west and a few hundred years earlier, is a wonderful counterpoint to its surviving lanes and alleys. The Bank of England, like nearly all stately homes, has always been too large for its neighbours.

Inside, it is a Protestant Florentine palace as envisaged by a Chippendale-minded English architect; clean lines, a court, lawns, trees, staircases, passages, mosaics, cornices, mouldings, vistas, and high ceilings. Every visitor to the Bank always feels slightly cowed, slightly discomposed, yet also slightly uplifted, like visiting a Royal House. Members of the staff, even after decades of service still feel they are entering an uncommon world. The Bank has a special atmosphere of its own; not the overpowering vulgarity of material possessions, not the awesome omniscience of power, not the hushed erudition of scholarship, but the special atmosphere of distilled authority which derives from the spiritual essence of money – the unique atmosphere of a great Central Bank.

Yet the true wonder is the Governor's House, hidden within this vast fortress, a calm oasis, a rectangular segment on two floors, the inner sanctum of the Governor and the Deputy Governor, designed to welcome guests including Directors of the Court, not for the weekend, or overnight, but for an hour or two, or for a morning, or an afternoon, or for lunch, or for the very occasional grand dinner. This marvellously encapsulated segment has all the serene appurtenances of a beautiful country house, surrounded, not by the friendly green undulations of leafy Wiltshire nor the hidden rural paths of secretive Norfolk, but by the throbbing restless pulse and beat, the never-ending trading activity of the most vital electronic flashing financial market in the world.

Looking inside each of these room, at their beautifully-crafted contents, one is constantly reminded that the early Governors and directors were men who had rolling country estates, who had inherited land and artifacts, who felt at home under glittering chandeliers, with gleaming carved highly polished wood, with flunkies and retainers in family liveries, who had always used heavily crested silver cutlery and specially made services of family china, who had been brought up to be surveilled by watchful ancestors immortalised by Reynolds and Gainsborough, and to be reminded by the ever-present ticking and chiming that the clocks were there not merely to tell the time, but that its effluxion was the root of their family tree. These were men who not only wanted to feel at home in the Bank, but also wanted their guests to feel at home.

The Bank of England not only has the monopoly in England and Wales to issue notes, it also holds the gold reserves in its own underground vaults and does all the banking of the State, keeping all the accounts of the various Government departments, including the Treasury and the Inland Revenue. It manages the National Debt, which has crept up from the original £1.2 million to nearly £200 billion. It borrows on behalf of the Government by issuing gilt-edged securities, and regulates that market. It acts as adviser and financial agent to the Government and fixes the rate pattern. It holds the accounts of the clearing banks. It exercises control over the proper running of the City. It supervises the banks. It also maintains very carefully its crucial relationship with the Treasury which, in the time-honoured ambiguity of the English, relies upon the personal relationships between its own top officials and those at the Treasury. This has now moved to the political stage where the personal relationship between the Governor and the Prime Minister has become increasingly sensitive in the jockeying for position as to who should be the true guardian of the country's monetary policy. The Governor's tenure is five years. The Chancellor used to have the first and last say on appointments or re-appointments. Now the Prime Minister has the last say – which provides no better proof of the capriciously continuing strength of the Bank.

The Governors came and went. Almost every one of them was a family member of a merchant bank. In the early part of the century standing out amongst the others, is the elegant bearded figure of Montagu Norman, mainly because of the unprecedented length of his tenure – around a quarter of a century. His City lineage, like his banking knowledge, was impeccable; both his grandfathers were directors of the Bank of England, and he was himself appointed a director in 1918 and Governor in 1920. In 1944 at the age of seventy-three he was finally replaced and, though he received fulsome praise, he resented till his end having to take what he considered was exceedingly premature retirement.

He was followed by Lord Catto, sensible and old-fashioned, who served during the Attlee administration with Sir Stafford Cripps and Hugh Dalton as Chancellors. He also served through what was thought to be the ignominy of the 1946 Act of Parliament which nationalised the Bank of England. This was one public takeover which at the time made hardly a jot of difference. The Old Lady never blinked an eyelid: one cannot nationalise integrity. Next until 1961 was Lord Cobbold, more sensible than his predecessor and still as nicely old-fashioned, who served with notable distinction under Attlee, Churchill, Eden and Macmillan, the latter with Butler being the formative Chancellors during his period of office. Next was Lord Cromer until 1966, Governor during the Profumo era and for two years under Harold Wilson; Cromer was a man of good if not excellent judgement, a holder of one of the Barings' peerages, who quite rightly found George Brown's rumbustious interference from the new Department of Economic Affairs more than he should bear.

Next, until 1973, was Lord O'Brien, who, starting his career in the Bank straight from school, was the lucky recipient of the anti-patrician pro-egalitarian state of mind of a Labour government in office after nearly fourteen years of opposition: he was the first Governor of the Bank to rise from the ranks. Lord O'Brien served under Wilson and Callaghan and under Roy Jenkins, most economists' favourite chancellor, and for a further two-year tenure from 1971 until just before the banking crisis under Heath and Barber. Not too many would share his disappointment that he had not originally been asked to serve a full second term.

In July 1973 Gordon (now Lord) Richardson, appointed by Edward Heath, commenced his period as Governor. He well may turn out to be amongst the great Governors of the Bank. He was succeeded by

Robin Leigh-Pemberton, a gentleman farmer, who is a born gentle-man and a born farmer and who, in his second term, also showed signs of being a born central banker.

The Old Lady has been criticised, cajoled, disparaged, attacked, condemned and excoriated, but she has never been degraded. In her dignity and in her monetary grace, she is evergreen; the hem of Britannia may occasionally have been splattered but it has never so much as been raised to the ankle. She is the conscience of the City and she is wedded, as she always will be, to her two great loves – Money and Confidence – secure over the three hundred years of her existence in her profound and justifiable conviction that her periodically changing guardians, the Governors, the Deputy Governors, the high officials and the directors, would do everything in their powers never to let her down.

Her domain has increased its borders ten-fold and its electronic links a million-fold, and she is now wistfully casting her eyes over the Channel at the wider European scene, at the other member states of the EC, each of which has its own central bank. There is treasonable talk in certain quarters that she may lose some independence, and there is speculation in other quarters that she may be granted more. Sitting on her money high up on the front façade of the Bank in Threadneedle Street, there could be a hint, a suggestion, of a smile, and it is quite possible that she may have something far more to smile about than the Mona Lisa.

SIX

Borrow Short, Lend Long, and Go Bust

Until the Banking Act 1979, a UK bank had not in any legal sense been defined. What then was a bank? Very simple. A bank was a bank if the Bank of England thought it was a bank. Here a certain old definition of a Jew is apposite, which was that a Jew was a person who thought he was a Jew. This did not apply to banks. A bank was not a bank if its directors thought it was a bank, only if the Bank of England thought it was. How did the aspiring directors know what the Bank of England thought? Very simple. They would scrutinise the Bank's facial gestures because the Old Lady's method of conveying recognition, was by way of a nod and a wink. This may sound frivolous – far from it, for in the absence of a legal definition of a bank, there was a perverse logic in these mannerisms, bearing in mind that banking recognition is, after all, one of the more serious prudential safeguards in a well-conducted commercial society, and what better countenance was there than the country's central bank, to decide how and to whom it should face with its discretionary signals of recognition?

The Act which nationalised the Bank of England in 1946 did not attempt to define a bank, but it did have a try at defining a banker, described in exquisite circular mandarinese, as 'any person carrying on a banking undertaking as declared by order of the Treasury to be a banker for the purposes of this section'. These 'bankers', if still breathing after being sectionalised by Treasury order, were also deemed to be worthy of being subjected to directives, which the Bank, under this Act, was now empowered to apply when it thought fit.

The next piece of relevant legislation, in 1947, was the Exchange Control Act which required the Treasury and the Bank of England to establish a list of banks authorised to deal in foreign exchange. Those included in this list became known as 'authorised banks'.

Next, was the Companies Act of 1948, which required not the Treasury but the Board of Trade – as the Department of Trade and Industry was then called – and the Bank to establish another list of banks which would be allowed certain privileges, under its Section 8, relating to the maintenance of inner reserves. The main criterion for qualifying under this list was that the banking undertaking concerned should be acceptable to the Bank. Having been nationalised a little abruptly two years earlier, the Labour government in its oblique way was acknowledging the Old Lady's traditional prerogatives. Under-takings in this list became known as 'recognised' or 'Section 8' banks.

Next, was the Protection of Depositors Act of 1963 which came under the aegis of the Board of Trade. Its object was to restrict the freedom of companies from advertising for deposits. It was aimed at the numerous hire-purchase companies, the finance companies in consumer credit and also, of course, at those lenders outside con-sumer credit, like the second mortgage lenders. These could no longer advertise for deposits unless they applied for and were granted exemption under this Act; in practice only the large finance houses applied for the accolade. They became known as 'exempt' banks. However, despite the 1963 Act, any company which had not been exempted, could still use the words 'Bankers' or 'Banking' on its letterhead and indeed on any of its material, as long as such material was not used for advertising purposes. How this afforded the depositors with protection it is difficult to deduce.

We now come to the villain of these pieces of legislation – the famous Section 123 of the Companies Act 1967, the springboard behind the rise of the secondary banks, the cause of the baffling contradictions surrounding secondary bank status and their recog-nition, the reason for one of the most confusing periods in the history of the lending industry. And to cap it all, it resulted from an observation by an English judge, Lord Denning no less, who should be saluted as the honorary president of the secondary banking fraternity for providing them – it must have been wittingly, for during his long dicta-ridden life, Lord Denning is not known to have done anything unwittingly – with a legal credential to negotiate the fraught road to banking recognition.

This astonishing situation arose from a specific clause in one of the moneylending Acts, passed in the early part of the century, which highlighted deeply-felt snobbish semantics whereby people in the business of consumer credit and second mortgages were assertively proud to be in the business of lending money, but apoplectic if they were called moneylenders. So, in making loans to their customers, they ran a mile from ever seeking a moneylender's licence – relying instead, upon the protection of this clause. The possession of the moneylender's licence would have given them the inalienable legal right to sue for non-repayment of their debts, and, though the soul of lending is the redemption of the debt, aloof and in disdain, they relied devoutly upon this one particular clause which stated that a moneylender's licence was not required 'if the person was *bona fide* carrying on the business of banking'. They confidently regarded themselves as such *bona fide* persons in the business of banking, and in good faith they made loans to their customers on this integral assumption. They were bankers, not moneylenders or pawnbrokers, and they unquestionably assumed that they could sue for the repayment of debts without requiring a licence. Until that is, a Mr Kirkwood decided that it was not unquestionable and took the most sizeable finance house to court, claiming that it had no legal right to sue him for the repayment of his debt as they did not have a moneylender's licence.

Lord Denning's judgment in 1966 on this notorious Kirkwood case was: 'If any concern should wish to be regarded by the courts as a banker, it ought to ask the Board of Trade for a certificate that it should be treated as a banker'. The lenders' assumption that they did not require a licence was subvented; a huge number of loans were at risk, a situation too serious not to be rectified at an early opportunity. The Board of Trade, taking heed of what Lord Denning had said, as did most people or bodies confronted by this tough nutcracker of hard pragmatic judgment, got down to it swiftly. And so, in the Companies Act 1967, the notorious Section 123 appeared, even down to courteously accommodating those applicants of poorer memories with its convenient numeration.

Section 123 did not define a bank – no one was yet brave enough to do that – but it did formulate that if anyone were in possession of a 123 Certificate 'it could be treated for the purposes of the moneylenders' Acts 1900–1927 as being a person *bona fide* carrying on the business of banking'. The sole purpose of the certificate was to allow the possessor of that certificate to enforce a debt. It had no other purpose. That was the theory and that was how the Bank saw it. The entrepreneurs building up their fledgling lending companies did not see it that way:

they saw a fabulous opportunity. If they were not moneylenders they were indubitably bankers. To them this was not theory, this was practice, the practice of banking; they saw it as a visa stamped upon their passport. It would, they believed, force the Bank to scrutinise their credentials and nod them through the banking borders, and to a fatal extent they succeeded, not as they or anyone else intended or expected, but by default.

The applicants for 123 certificates had to complete a detailed questionnaire. It was subsequently examined by the Department of Trade 'in consultation with the Bank of England'. This was the crux. The Bank was the consultant, not the authority. The criterion used by the Bank in this consultative capacity, was to inspect the application for the 'functional' characteristics of a banking business. It was not expected to be drawn into making judgemental tests of quality or repute – its most sanctified and most sensitive responsibility. The certificate was merely an isolated document to allow the holder to enforce a debt; it was in no way the first rung of banking status; it was in no way a wink of approval. The Bank of England had no legal responsibility for the granting of the certificate, it was merely being consulted by a government department to determine whether the applicants were *bona fide* undertakings in the 'functional' business of banking, in order to determine whether they should be exempted from requiring a moneylender's licence. That was all. The Department would issue a certificate if the applicant was declared by its consultant as having functional appurtenances. The Bank, having been consulted, took the view that if a concern 'had the functional characteristics of a banking business' its technical verdict conveyed to its client was all that it was required to do. The Act did not require it to make, 'judgemental tests of quality or repute'. It was a very dangerous fudge.

Sooner or later the Bank would have to explain why and how it had condoned such a muddle, and it did so many years later by way of its background papers, subscribed in 1978 to the Wilson Committee. They are revealing, not least because the Bank's interpretations and admissions are beautifully exact in their eloquence, by which I mean that when the Bank seeks to be clear, it is crystal clear, and when it seeks to defend itself, knowing it is on weak ground, it does so in language which is wondrously effective in its deliberate intent not to be clear. The Bank makes the artful explanation that the causes were 'to be found in a complex skein of macro- and micro-economic factors which combined and interacted in a way that even in retrospect it is

difficult to unravel'. I do not believe that the Bank found such
intellectual difficulty in unravelling those causes four years after the
crisis, and it could be gently underlined and with some compassion
that it was not truly difficult to unravel at any time; nor do I believe that
the Bank can avoid criticism that its resistance, during Governor
O'Brien's regime, to be drawn into making judgemental appraisals,
actually helped to germinate the secondary banking crisis.

What the Bank did impute carefully and confusingly was that 'in
more general and unanticipated ways' the possession of the 123
certificate 'allowed the impression to be created that the companies
concerned were recognised by the responsible government department as carrying on a banking business without drawing attention to
the fact that they were only so recognised for one narrow purpose'. If
the government department were being arraigned for not drawing
attention, it should not have been, because it could not have gone
beyond the strict letter of the law; and if the companies were being
censured for not drawing attention, it stretches credulity to suppose
that they would have done so. No one should have been surprised that
the secondary banking companies with unflagging enthusiasm, gobbled up the opportunity offered to them, on this plate of fudge. The
party which should have been arraigned was, of course, the Bank itself,
for not drawing attention to the fact that in being consulted it was
'recognising', even if limited only to the functional characteristics,
these very same companies.

Before one could say Jack Robinson O'Brien, the Board of Trade
had issued over one hundred and thirty certificates. A lending sector
called any number of names – 'a sort of culture and a lifestyle which
was totally alien to the tradition of the City' by Lord Griffiths,* the
'fringe' by the Bank, the 'secondary banking sector' by the money
brokers, 'family banks' by the controlling directors – may have been in
no-mans land, but the territory now had a name, or rather a codename:
it was a 123 bank. The applicants had passed muster with the Bank
and it was surely splitting hairs to refuse them membership to the Old
Lady's club whose members numbered over three hundred as against
one hundred and thirty thumping 123s. The successful applicants had
been issued with a legal certificate, this was their statutory member-

* Head of number 10's think tank in the late 80's; before that a Director of the
Bank of England 1984–86; before that Professor of Banking at the City University
Business School.

ship form and why should they not use their new status with unbridled enthusiasm? They were certainly not going to draw attention to the fact that the certificate had only one narrow purpose; on the contrary, they would put the description 'bankers' or 'banking' on their letterhead and on their 'non-advertising' brochures and they would not stop there, they would issue their own cheque books, paying-in books and deposit books.

They were in from the cold, they were no longer frozen out, they were in the banking stakes – they would advance an unsecured loan to Lord Denning at any time – they were no longer illegitimate, no longer waifs, they had squatters' rights, and so, not unsurprisingly, they would allow the impression, rather they would enhance the impression, that they were officially considered to be in the banking business. So the agile little secondaries tried to scale the thirty-feet high stone curtain wall; to little avail. For, though still guarded by the Praetorian Discount Office with the same number of eyes and ears, all intrusions were repelled.

When it came to Cedar's public quotation, Rodney Galpin of the Bank, the then Deputy Principal of the Discount Office, told Derrick Hanson that Cedar could not describe itself as 'Bankers' in its prospectus. That was Galpin's verdict, that was the Bank's statement: a bank was not a bank if the directors, with or without a government certificate, thought it was; only if the Bank thought it was. Was it back to square one? Only as far as the Bank was concerned. Not for the 123s; they went along their merry unrestricted expansionist way – until crisis time and then they had to be recognised. Their existence could no longer be officially ignored, they had become a horrible danger to the entire banking system, and, lo and behold, in order to avoid the domino effect, the directors of an untouchable, Cedar Holdings, the well-known possessor of a 123 certificate amongst its other distinctions, were all actually ensconced in the Bank's holy quarters. It was recognition at last, if only by default.

To appreciate why the Bank was so sensitive about its exact role as consultant on the 123 certificate, it is illuminating to see how, in its own words, as expressed below, it perceived its wider more central roles regarding its process of recognition, its supervisory responsibility, and indeed its general role in the City. On the latter, it divides the powers which govern the manner in which financial institutions in the City are conducted, into statutory and non-statutory. The problem with statutory powers, the Bank explains with justification, particularly in the light of recent mishaps, is that they do not impose ideal standards, they provide sanctions for failure to adhere to minimum standards, they tend to the letter and not the spirit. The Bank's main contention was that systems that relied on law and specific regulation as the sole guide to behaviour in commercial affairs could lead to any conduct being regarded as permissible if it merely satisfied the legal requirement.

The non-statutory regulations on the other hand, the nub of the Bank's own authority, are another matter, and here, with its authentic power traditionally embedded in these non-statutory regulations, it could and did prescribe certain rules and a quality of ethical behaviour, which statute law could not sufficiently embrace. Moreover non-statutory processes were quicker to introduce and to modify than legal processes, and speedier in execution.

The Bank saw the non-statutory regulations as divided into two categories. The first concerned the Bank's exercise as the central bank, in controlling and supervising generally the banking system and money markets, by means of recommendations and requests which despite their informality were treated by the markets (on the whole) as effectively mandatory. The second type of non-statutory regulation can be defined as self-regulation where members, in a common business or profession, subscribe by common assent to appropriate standards of professional conduct and competence. The success of self-regulation depends upon believing that the rules or regulations are in their best mutual interests and upon scrupulous observance of the rules. The spirit of the City grew out of the wish to conform to generally accepted and prescribed standards of behaviour. This is how self-regulation in the City developed. Governors were able to play the role of confidant and arbiter of the City, and guardian of its standards. In some cases the Bank would take an active role, in others a more passive role. Here is the authentic Richardson voice: 'In appearance the style is in all cases, one of government by consensus, because this has proved over many years to produce the most satisfactory results'.

Regarding the Bank's perception of its process of recognition, it must be stressed that this process, extremely arduous from any point of view, was made more so for the Bank in the absence of an overall legal definition of a bank. It evolved its own evaluation in what it has described as a status ladder with a series of rungs represented by individual recognitions: the companies could progress up these rungs as their reputation and expertise developed. Only those banks which acquired the highest recognition would be regarded by the Bank as banks in the fullest sense of the word. This is back to the nod and the wink, for, until the 1979 Banking Act, the Bank could only take on informally the task of gathering intelligence on the rung climbers. In fact, it stated to the Wilson Committee that its practice was not to maintain 'formal or regular contact with companies which did not fall within the banking sector proper', so with non-banks such as Cedar, it maintained informal and non-regular contact.

In other words, until 1979 the Bank operated its signals of recognition in a twilight world, illuminated by its nods and winks. In order, therefore, to have a grasp of the astonishing rise of the secondary banks we have to go back to the O'Brien years, at the turn of the decade, when the Bank formulated a measure called Competition and Credit Control.

It was a cataclysmic Bank of England measure; City-oriented, not Westminster inspired, introduced in September 1971 through some curious alchemy of time, events, moods, personalities and even psychology. The edict, which became infamous under its better known appellation of C&CC, was, in the view of many, one of the more catastrophic single initiatives made by the Bank of England in this century. It was also one of the fundamental causes of the financial crisis and it is beyond belief that Lord O'Brien, its well-intentioned sponsor, did not appreciate that though it included some extremely welcome and important measures it was nevertheless bound to cause serious problems, particularly in the way it was implemented. Designed to solve a number of problems at the same time, planned to embrace a number of disparate matters, mixing domestic banking requirements with monetary and fiscal policies, C&CC was a lethal example of how an originator or sponsor, in this case the Bank of England, ventured without hindrance on to another's preserve, in this case the Treasury's, which in Treasury terms means that whilst it did not approve, it did not stand in the Bank's way.

What Lord O'Brien had in mind and in execution, was that the clearing banks should respond more effectively to the needs of their customers, especially those in the manufacturing sector, and, in order that they should compete for business, the long-established cartel on interest rates and on deposit rates should be abolished together with bank ceilings. Moreover, the government broker would be more market minded, there would be no more free rides on his coat-tails, gilt-edged markets would be more responsive to changes in interest rates, there would be reliance on interest rates for monetary control (long overdue and not applied early enough after its introduction) rather than on loan ceilings. On cash ratios, the conservative requirement that the banks had to retain 28% of their assets in cash or near cash would be discarded; instead, 12.5% of cash and near cash would be required. So not only would the abolition of the cartel stimulate competition, the declamping of the cash ratios would also push hundreds of millions of pounds of additional liquidity towards the sluice gates. After decades of tight control, after generations of an officially-blessed inflexible rigorous cartel on interest rates and on deposit rates, these gates to total freedom were opened to their full extension, not gradually and carefully over months, but all in one go, creating a torrent of unrestrained liquidity.

What O'Brien also had in mind and in real execution was to kill off the secondaries. Remarkably, the intention to do so was not at all widely known and only admitted years later, and then almost in parenthesis. The Bank considered that once the primary banks had powers to compete freely for business, the secondaries would not get a look in. The Bank did however admit that it might have had another possible response for the secondaries, which would have been 'to seek to bring them within the credit control system without classifying them as banks'. This seemingly practical response was resisted. So, what was the alternative plan? Out it comes: to drive the fringe element out of business, or as the Bank more elegantly put it to the Wilson Committee: 'The expectation was that perhaps, not immediately, but in a short while, the fringe would contract to a level of comparative unimportance.' In Bankspeak comparative unimportance means the unimportance of a drop compared to an ocean.

What is baffling is that it was not obvious to the Bank that the one lending sector which would thrive most from the introduction of C&CC was the very sector it wished to eradicate. The secondaries were the ideal recipients of loans from newly competing primaries desperately looking for new customers. It is an extraordinary irony that the bank crisis was in large part caused by C&CC. It is a double-irony that the envisaged endangered species, instead of contracting to comparative unimportance, enlarged into being the fat cats of lending and it is a treble-irony that the primary bankers, endeavouring later through the Lifeboat to save the banking system, had to rescue the secondaries whose very existence they deprecated.

146

When C&CC was introduced, bank lending in the private sector, much of it from non-clearing banks (it is difficult to break it down accurately), was £1.9 billion. Yet, within a year it jumped to £6.4 billion. The dangers of the virtually unrestrained lending was apparent to everyone: a crisis was inevitable unless checked. It was not checked. The Bank of England looked on. One might well ask why? One might well ask a number of whys. Why when the dangers were not only apparent but real, did the Bank continue to manage its supervisory role in virtually the same manner and with the same number of staff as before the introduction of C&CC? Why did it not realise that major cultural changes should not take place without controls nor all at once? Why was it not more severe in seeing that its restrictions on property lending were adhered to? Why did it still regard the secondaries as untouchables, even after it knew that C&CC, designed in part to destroy them, had signally failed in this aim? Why did it not insist upon using higher interest rates as a deterrent in the year of 1972? Above all, why did it not institute measures to bar the fringe from having access to the money market?

The Bank explains. 'After the introduction of Competition and Credit Control, the nature of the borrowing demand in this period was such as to encourage the fringe to extend their position in property lending, particularly at the speculative end of the market.' Quite. 'This was greatly facilitated by the relative ease with which the fringe was able to obtain deposits. Individual depositors accounted for only a small part, despite energetic use of advertising. The bulk of the fringe's deposit requirements was met by the money market.' Quite. 'In the new more competitive conditions, the banks were keen to increase their loan books in order to maximise their market shares. But with the slow pick-up in loan demand from the manufacturing sector, the banks generally had more lendable funds than they were finding traditional opportunities to lend. They were therefore increasingly prepared to on-lend surplus resources through the medium of the money markets.' Quite. And who took up this on-lending? The answer: 'the fringe institutions' who found 'they were able to attract wholesale deposits, in substantial volume but mostly at short-term.' Quite. Then progressing towards their dénouement, the Bank explains that because of the attractions of the property market 'a large proportion of the funds flowing into the fringe, was employed in that market,' the apparent ability to renew the deposits at maturity, leaving the fringe to disregard the risk of being locked-in. 'Accordingly when the renewal of deposits became difficult, liquidity problems rapidly arose.' Quite.*

Finally the Bank stabs itself in a far from ironical reference to the untouchables, who had 'the opportunity because they were not banks, to establish and expand in the business of lending. These opportunities were sufficiently exploited, that by the end of the decade, the effectiveness of the credit control technique was being appreciably affected'. Quite. And this self-criticism, made several years after the crisis, was it seemed as far as any successor was prepared to go in reproving a former regime.

So the former regime allowed the credit control technique to be appreciably affected. With what result? Well there is no more reckless financial animal, than a bank competing for borrowers and depositors; it is a creature bent on a jungle rampage, aware yet curiously disdainful of the dangers of hidden ravines. Banking is a jungle which requires surefootedness, training and experience; it is an environment which needs extreme survival tactics. But when bankers have not before trodden through this tough escarpment, when they have been firmly instructed to pursue borrowers wherever they can be found, it is courting disaster, no worse, it is (and was) the actual engagement of disaster. Two avalanches of dangerously unknown forces were released simultaneously, both part of the central nervous system of banking: competition to attract deposits and competition to seek borrowers, each of which was virtually uncontrolled. At the best of times it is fiendishly difficult to match incoming deposits with outgoing lendings; the best of times being within the pre-C&CC placid non-competitive cartel. But to do so when the shackles are freed overnight, not in stages, all at once, and when senior and middle management had no previous experience of a free market, was asking for unbounded trouble, and we got it in spades.

Industrial companies also went into this deposit free-for-all. Why should they deposit with their own clearing bank when they could receive more through the money market or from a large finance house, or from a fringe bank? Better still, why not use old-established large undrawn facilities arranged at old keen rates, and put it in the money market or with fringe banks at higher rates, their own bank powerless

* Background papers to the Wilson Committee. B.E.Q.B. June and September 1978.

to stop them, furious that these long established facilities arranged for use for normal business requirements were being used for a purpose never intended, and even more furious that they could not themselves rescind the unused facilities until the annual review date, when they could apply the extra liquidity for their own benefit. Lord Griffiths was unequivocal. 'The Bank of England was fundamentally responsible. It blew the whistle for a free-for-all in banking, without having the controls necessary to prevent fly-by-night operators getting in and taking people for a ride.'

These immediate years after C&CC were wonderful shovelling times. The main thrust of the banks (there were a number of honorable exceptions) was to apply the shovel with gusto not with discretion, lip-service was mouthed to the authorities, consequences were ignored, and pious condemnations were made of those who were found out in patently overdoing it. Old-established lending practices were contaminated, most of the lending industry was embroiled – from the newly liberated primary banks to the reeking sewage level of the tertiary lenders. O'Brien had wanted market forces to operate, but he had neglected to remember that market forces, especially if released after a cartel, are dynamic unstoppable forces if not dyked or dammed. He should have explicitly defined the exact areas of competition and of control, he should have imposed prudent safeguards and guidelines, and he should, as an experienced banker, have foreseen that provision had to be made for the inexperienced and untrained corpus of banking personnel to learn how to cope with these new unknown forces.

Denis Healey, Labour's Chancellor of the Exchequer after Heath's defeat in February 1974, made a characteristically bruising comment in his inimical combination of a luxuriant high-brow intellect and a low, yet above the belt, pommelling, when questioned about this: 'The Bank of England before Gordon Richardson took over, under its previous Governor was extremely imprudent in agreeing to the introduction of unregulated competition in banking, under the famous white paper Competition and Credit Control, without making any effort to control the consequences'.

It was decreed by C&CC that a free market would prevail; so market forces did prevail. The banks embarked for the first time on advertising their own strengths, as they saw them, to entice more business. The money market already booming took a quantum leap forward. The brokers were ecstatic. The clearers, the primaries, could not only top up or top down their now volatile day-to-day fluctuations of supply and demand; they made loans, more specifically they shovelled them out directly to the gluttonous borrowers, and indirectly by on-lending to the money markets.

The borrowers, mostly the property customers, had the use of far more easy money than they had projects, so they put their money into property sites, in many cases sites they had never even seen, sites without planning consent; they had the sites valued for them for borrowing purposes on the basis that the entire development had already been built and completed, that these buildings which had not yet been started, which may not even have had the benefit of planning consent, were already fully let to a tenant. And there wasn't even a hole in the ground. They went further. These 'valuations' showed great surpluses over cost and the auditors allowed the property companies to treat the surpluses as reserves which could be capitalised and issued as new shares to the shareholders, or to purchase other companies. The auditors allowed this to be done even though interest costs incurred on current developments, instead of being charged as an expense in the profit and loss account, had been capitalised. They went even further. The financial houses and the fringe banks took front-end fees and front-end shares of profits on property projects, not yet even commenced, never mind not completed and not sold. And the ever-growing declared profits, meant that the quoted shares of these fringe entities, swelled up, and with their over-crested shares being liberally issued to purchase other businesses, whose own shares were at similar frothy levels for the same reasons.

So the primaries lent directly to their own finance subsidiaries and to those secondaries with whom they had a special link. They also lent to their own property customers. The secondaries avidly borrowed from them, and as they got into the swing, they got on to the roundabout by borrowing from the money markets; they then lent to their own subsidiaries, to their property clients or to their own associated property companies. The property fraternity, with money hurled at them by primaries and secondaries, borrowed up to the hilt on valuations which were spurious or false, with interest not payable, but rolled over and deferred. And the borrowings were not advanced on a prudent 65% of a true valuation, but at 100% of a false valuation. Those who sold sites, uncompleted developments or investment properties, whether they were individual dealers or sizeable banks, made enormous profits which, as they were gleefully disclosed, inevitably became a rancorous and bitter element of the political scene.

The profits were huge and easy and these most succulent unique money-making opportunities were available, thanks to C&CC, thanks to the unregulated money markets, and thanks to the government's monetary and economic policy.

*　　　　　*　　　　　*

It was an economic and social era, when the mood of the warriors was to forget the War, when the mood of their children (the notable baby bulge) was to seek pleasure and irresponsibility, when a vast range of new consumer products were created, when many existing industries were transformed out of all recognition. In the lending industry, the ethos was market share, and the primary banks stumbled over each other to get bigger. Thousands of new branches were opened, tens of thousands of credit balances were created and the banks enjoyed enormous revenues. The secondaries, instead of contracting to comparative unimportance spawned as never before, and, as in any trawl, the big fish rarely escape while the small ones have little or no difficulty; so the big fish, the primary banks, had to accept, at any rate most of the time, the fiscal restrictions emanating from the Government in the form of the mostly annual budget measures, and directives emanating from the Bank of England in the form of official letters, whilst the little fish, the secondary banks, wriggling through the net, laughed all the way to the Stock Exchange.

The secondaries' main customers who made them so happy were of course the egregious property developers and traders, whose appetite for money has never had any equal, their intake making any other kind of borrower seem anorexic. Yet the property sector's voracious demand for money, and indeed the demand of the second mortgage borrowers, of the personal borrowers, of the equipment hirers, of the share and commodity speculators, could never have been accommodated by the secondaries, unless they had an ever-ready source. Indeed, an *embarras de richesses*, they had two. One, already referred to, was C&CC, the other fabulous in its limitless supply, fabulous in the ease in which it could be tapped, were the phenomenal money markets.

The sterling money market, known as the wholesale market, and the way it operated was a perfect companion in arms for the unrestrained cash-hungry secondary banks. Also emerging at the same time as the sterling market was the wholesale market in foreign currency deposits, the Euro-dollar, the Euro-currency markets. The colonial expansion of overseas banks into London in the 1960s and 1970s created a near ring-fenced on-shore unregulated lending activity, which was simply mind-boggling in its enormous size. It arose not only because of the City's *laissez faire* tradition and ingrained expertise, not only because of the liberal tax aspects, not only because one or two brilliant merchant bankers, notably Siegmund Warburg, saw the fabulous possibilities early on (most merchant bankers, not Jocelyn Hambro, I might add, woke up too late), but because the US authorities designed their internal bank regulations almost as if they wanted to create a rival financial centre outside their own shores. The City embraced its main chance with open tills and an international tax haven was created in the City of London, with many totally unaware of the exotic giant money-making markets growing under their very noses, and many of the practitioners unaware that they were the earliest operators of what has now become the casino-minded international foreign exchange markets.

A money market is a comparatively simple mechanism. It is like an hydraulic tank, never the same size, but with clean perimeters, because what goes in simultaneously goes out. The mechanics are the money brokers, the dealers who place the lender's (increasingly their parent company's) money for specific periods with the borrower. The contracts, amounting in London to billions of pounds a day, are verbally binding agreements, only confirmed on paper after the transaction has been completed. Any amnesia would be a veritable disaster.

Borrowing from the sterling wholesale money markets is unsecured borrowing: once a lender deals in this inter-bank money market, it loses control over its deposit until the renewal date. The money goes in and out, back to back, the broker takes a tiny fee and engineers the renewal, or the non-renewal, of the incoming and outgoing deposits. Although the percentage fee is tiny, cumulatively it represents tens of millions of pounds of profit. Anyone had access to the money market; the money brokers took what ever business they could get hold of. They were in no way licensed nor regulated.

Even to the less strong, the less exalted, the less respectable, the money markets were an extraordinary boon allowing the fringe to lend on with partial or nil security to its own customers, who were even less strong, even less exalted and even less respectable. So at the taking end, the secondaries, big and small, borrowed overnight, overweek, overmonth, having their borrowings renewed by the lenders, virtually automatically and, at the giving end, lending it on, not overnight, not overweek, not overmonth, but for a year, for two years, for three years, for five years or even for twenty years. This dangerous mismatching, channelling, slurring and waterfalling, had no brake.

A Bank of England survey of unsecured loans made through the inter-bank market including the amount in issue of sterling certificates of deposits (CDs) was conducted in April 1973 and was published in the Bank's Quarterly Bulletin in September 1973. It disclosed startling facts, the most startling, that the average life of the borrowings was under 20 days. These enormous outpourings of monies comprising unsecured lendings and borrowings had increased from nearly £4 billion at the commencement of C&CC in September 1973 to nearly £14 billion by December 1973.

Few in the City asked what would happen if the fringe banks locked into such grisly mismatching were not able to renew their short-term deposits. Most in the City, not only the experts, knew that indiscriminate easy borrowings and lendings always led to aberrations and they knew that here was uncorrected mismatching of deadly proportions. But few questioned why such a demonstrable free-for-all should be permitted and why the powers-that-be should be looking on with such quiescence.

The ingredients leading to a forthcoming financial crisis had been apparent to any official watchdog. The Bank by its own claim had considerable non-statutory powers and influence. However it seemed that it was only prepared to make little more than the occasional muffled bark. What prompted Lord O'Brien to be so keen to introduce C&CC in the way he did, was I believe that as the first Governor to have risen from within the ranks, he may have had a special desire to make his mark as an ultra-effective Governor. I also believe that if Lord O'Brien had not had his term extended by the two crucial years from summer 1971 to summer 1973, if Lord Richardson had been appointed two years earlier and if the Chancellor had been of the calibre of Healey, Jenkins or McLeod the country might well have avoided its worse-ever banking crisis.

*   *   *

The nature and personality of the various secondary banks were very similar in their endeavours to increase their incoming deposits and outgoing advances, all of them convinced, as Hollom put it, in thinking, 'they could always get deposits if their rates were better than the clearers'. They were however dissimilar in style, for they invariably reflected, for good or ill, the personality of the entrepreneurial guiding spirit or spirits behind them.* The fertile ebullience and opportunism of these various new-style entrepreneurial bankers created, broadly speaking, four categories of secondaries. These were specialists in consumer credit like United Dominions Trust; specialists in second mortgages like Cedar or Twentieth Century Banking; specialists in share transactions like Slater Walker; and specialists in property deals like First National.

Amongst the first category, were the larger consumer credit houses who liked to think of themselves, with some justification, as primary banks. A selected few indeed became fully recognised by the Bank, their exhaustion after pulling themselves from the undergrowth of the twilight zone to the top rung, being manifested in weary misjudgements soon after they received recognition. The finance houses had made their money mostly out of consumer credit, financing retailers (especially motor dealers) before diversifying into leasing, contract hire and personal loans, and, during the secondary boom, into property loans and second mortgages. United Dominions Trust (later part of T.S.B.), Mercantile Credit (later part of Barclays), Bowmaker (later part of Lloyds), Lombard (later part of NatWest) were each certainly of a size to dwarf many of the established merchant banks. But, like the fringe banks, not being subject to the Bank's controls, they too, during the boom, provided a convenient receptacle for the primaries seeking higher rates of interest without seeming to circumvent the Bank's restrictions.

United Dominions Trust finally became a fully recognised bank at the end of 1973. It was not only the largest finance house, it also subsequently had the distinction of being the largest beneficiary – at £500 million – of the Lifeboat. It had suffered substantial losses not

---

* Fringe and near fringe banks, some of which weathered the crisis satisfactorily, included: Audley Holdings (receiver appointed 1975), Beverly Bentinck (taken over 1978), British Bank of Commerce (taken over 1974), Cannon Street Investments (reconstructed), Cornhill Consolidated Group (liquidation 1974), Cripps Warburg (taken over 1975), David Samuel Trust (liquidation 1976), Edward Bates and Sons (reconstructed), First Maryland (receiver appointed 1975), Gresham Trust (weathered the crisis satisfactorily), Hawtin and Partners (taken over 1975), Jacobs Kroll (receiver appointed 1975), Jessel Securities (liquidation), Keyser Ullman (taken over 1980), Manson Finance (weathered the crisis satisfactorily), Maurice Wigram (taken over 1974), Sterling Industrial Securities (controlled running down by the Crown Agents), Triumph Investment Trust (receiver appointed 1974), J H Vavasseur (absorbed 1978), Wallace Brothers (taken over 1976), Wintrust (weathered the crisis satisfactorily).

from its traditional consumer business, but from new diversions – loans to residential housing and commercial property developers. UDT found itself in trouble because it borrowed short and lent long; but for the Lifeboat, it would have gone bust.

In the second category, a specialist on second mortgages, similar to Cedar in some respects, was Twentieth Century Banking. It had an excellent reputation for making medium-term loans on property, on first mortages – not only second mortgages – and, unlike Cedar, it also made loans on commercial property. In the early 1970s it had four owners in almost as many months: from Spey to First National, to Bovis, to P&O. Until this parental shuffle, Twentieth Century's loan book was sound, so was its matching policy. By October 1973, just before the crisis, at which time its loan book had increased threefold, Bovis, a very cock-a-hoop owner, was making noises about taking Twentieth Century public – at a value of £20 million – as against its purchase cost from First National of £7 million. By this stage, however, Twentieth Century had borrowed short from the money markets and had lent long; it was locked into serious mismatching. With the advent of the deposit run it caused Bovis's share price to slump – indeed the Bovis price plummeted to a level which gave it a value including Twentieth Century of £20 million, the same value it had accorded to Twentieth Century on its own, only a few weeks earlier. Such are the vagaries of fortune which present themselves in sudden dramatic swoops: earlier in the year Bovis spurned an offer of £135 million from P&O. Now, to avoid going bust, it grabbed P&O's offer – at a humiliating 15% of the price it had only recently spurned.

In the third category Slater Walker, the specialist in share transactions, was a City beehive of activity remorselessly in search of honey. Slater was Jim Slater, the chairman and dominant personality. Walker was Peter Walker. An inventive financier in his earliest days in the City, he not only founded Slater Walker but, with Edward Du Cann, introduced single premium payments for Unit Trusts. Later he became the longest serving Thatcher Cabinet member who had also served under Heath, and for this as much as for lending his name to Slater, he deserves a double-barrelled honour. Jim Slater, his erstwhile partner, originally a successful financial executive at British Leyland, was an extremely enterprising investment brain. He discovered that if he exercised sufficient instant rationalisation in the method and manner of shuffling his resources, he could establish a financial strategy acceptable to investors, and his adept generalship was admired to such good effect that most of the City establishment and its analysts accepted his ad hoc campaigns as if Clausewicz and Standard and Poor were on his board as non-executive directors.

What Slater did, not only with panache but with real public relations flair and investment capability, was to engage in share dealing on a massive scale, buying, selling, bundling, unbundling,* rebundling the shares of companies with which he had close associations, to increase performance and keep the share price surging forward. He was so skilful in marshalling his forces, that three venerable merchant bankers considered a merger; that great master Warburgs on an off day, Lazards on an off month and Hill Samuel going as far as the starting gate, on an off season.

As it later transpired, the mismatching at Slater Walker was pretty horrendous. It not only borrowed short, it not only lent long, but it lent something like two thirds of its total loan book to its own subsidiaries or associates. Slater Walker would have gone bust but for the direct support of what was considered one of the Bank's most controversial decisions during the whole of the crisis.†

In the fourth and final category, the property specialist in the fringe fraternity, First National, chaired by Lord De L'Isle with Jocelyn Hambro and Leonard Sainer on its board, was Pat Matthew's baby. This company, which had a curious relationship with the Crown Agents, could be described as a property bank, because, although it had considerable lendings in second mortgages, share dealing and consumer credit, its main thrust was in lending on property itself and to property companies. It nevertheless borrowed short, lent long, and

---

* Sir James Goldsmith was the person who made a notorious use of the term unbundling, in the context of what he would have done with B.A.T. if he had taken it over. Some of his ideas derive from Jim Slater, who in turn, must have been extremely grateful to Goldsmith who accepted the chair of Slater Walker after he felt compelled to resign in 1975. Goldsmith, a larger than life yet most attractive personality, is described in Ivan Fallon's book *Billionaire*. Slater has written a book on his investment ideas in *The Zulu Principle*.

† The Bank eventually took over Slater Walker's secondary bank to protect, so it claimed, the City's reputation in the Eurobond market. Many thought the Bank should have let Slater Walker go under. Its rump, later named Britannia Arrow, played a minor walk-on part in the Cedar story, well after the curtain had dropped after its rescue.

but for the support of some £350 million which it received with difficulty from the Lifeboat, it would have gone bust.

Many of these secondaries were similar in an especial area – the breezy share incentives, available to top managers, which later caused many of these wretched second and third car and home owners to be sucked under by the whirlpool of collapsed share prices. Executives who took up incentive shares as options were fully taxable, either by taking up a loan or by borrowing on partly-paid shares with payment deferred for the balance at reduced prices; some banks arranged or guaranteed borrowings from other banks to lend to their own executives on their own shares.

The most blatant of them all, London and County, did not bother to go this route; it lent freely to its own executives on the security of its own shares eventually holding 10% of its own equity as security. This must be something of a world record in secondary or tertiary banking. A bank could of course make loans to its own executives and directors if it was 'in the ordinary course of banking business'. As far as several of the secondary banks were concerned, the ordinary course of banking business was what suited them from one hour to the next: evidently London and County considered that holding 10% of its entire equity, as security on loans made to its own executives, was in the ordinary course of its banking business. Amal itself had originally arranged loans from Samuel Montagu for its executive directors and subsequently Cedar took them over, on the basis that these loans to the executives were considered to have been made in the ordinary course of banking business.*

The scramble by the fringe to lend out as fast as possible was reflected in the upsurge of profits of the different categories of lenders. United Dominions Trust made £11 million in 1971 and £24.3 million in 1973; Slater Walker made £16.25 million in 1971 and £24 million in 1973; First National made £7.5 million in 1971 and £18.4 million in 1973. Some entities were far more avidly into this greedy scramble than others and of course some shovellers were more ambitious than others; amongst the clearers the leader was NatWest; amongst the merchant banks nearly all kept their heads; amongst the finance houses, three of the largest, United Dominions Trust, Mercantile and Bowmaker vied with each other as to who could outdo the others; amongst the fringe banks, almost without exception, all were shov-

* See page 291.

ellers of Olympic gold medal standard.* Nor should it be forgotten that not only the fringe banks were jeopardised by the profligacy; many of their own commercial and industrial associates were also affected. Some were more lucky than others. Amongst the mini-conglomerates the luckiest to be alive was Hanson Trust, a minor limpet attached to its big brother – a laughable thought today, Hanson being one of the largest companies in Europe – as a satellite of the rich magnanimous dominating Slater Walker.

Whilst the entrepreneurs behind the secondary banks grasped every advantage offered by the fudge, the growth of their companies coincided with a seminal change in the Englishman's approach to borrowing and spending. Behind this shift were a number of factors. The most potent, because it erased his guilt, derived from the phenomenon of television advertising, which spurred the viewer, far more effectively than press advertising, to buy and to buy again and again. People were no longer members of a community but members of a consumer society – a strictly categorised hierarchy whereby a person was either A or B or C depending on demography and spending power, but, in whichever category, the message of the ceaseless advertising was clear: spending is good for you. It was no longer immoral nor sinful to spend. Better yet, it was no longer immoral to spend money you didn't have, you were encouraged to borrow freely with no security. Even old Pinstripes was waving you on, flashing funny little plastic cards at you, unaware that he was pushing himself out of a job, unaware that his inner sanctum would become a relic of former splendour to be replaced by the Cashpoint and the Freephone. Victorian thrift and old family values were out; modern day unsecured credit and permissive values were in.

Borrowing as a concept, as well as a practice, became a consumer product to be advertised like any other product. Higher remuneration provided more opportunities for savings and as house prices increased in value, owners – post-war first-time buyers, young-married beneficiaries, retired couples – found themselves comparatively well-off, and could either swap into more expensive houses, or could take

---

* The upsurge in lending is also reflected in the increase in gross assets. In 1971, gross assets of NatWest were £6,680 million, in 1973 they were £11,850 million; in 1971 the gross assets of Slater Walker were £280 million, in 1973 they were £588 million; in 1971 the gross assets of First National were £182 million, in 1973 they were £543 million; and in 1971 the gross assets of Cedar were £18 million, in 1973 they were £128 million.

up second mortgages from the secondary banks on their rising equity. Thoroughly brain-washed, they spent the money borrowed on what they had been screened to regard as absolute essentials, such as Hi-Fi or house improvements or cocktail cabinets or Spanish holidays. Another factor was that, with private savings in overall surplus, wonderful new saving schemes were sprouting with ever more shorter shelf lives as newer schemes were produced.

This, too, was the beginning of the splurge of TV advertising by financial services companies, Cedar itself being in the foreground of this thrust, so savings too became a consumer product to be advertised like any other product. The pre-war, hard-working, non-hedonist, family-oriented, anti-spendthrift, was becoming the guilt-free, pleasure-seeking, not-so-hard-working, avid consumer. In Jonesing his way upwards, he found no lack of friends, counsellors, advisers, to help him on his increasingly addictive, restless, materialist spending trip. At work, you could now discuss with your colleagues not only your favourite television programmes and favourite consumer products, but your building society mortgage rates, and the various saving schemes being offered. The financial services companies were seeking you out, you did not know, nor did you care, how they financed themselves. Deposits were always safe. You did not know that many lenders were borrowing short and lending long, that, in conducting their business in this manner, they would inevitably go under.

It was not known till much later what Alec Dibbs of NatWest thought of most of these financial services companies and the people behind them: 'They were not bankers by my standards. We chaps who are career bankers get a bit snobbish about them, perhaps, but the late 1960s and the early 1970s seemed to produce a lot of financial entrepreneurs without any knowledge of liability or risk, but with major desire to build up their assets on the basis of speculative things', then adding, 'and the big banks, I must say, facilitated some of this, perhaps too much'.

Alec Dibbs, though contrite, certainly felt snobbish, but it did not deter his own bank from becoming more heavily involved with these unknowledgeable entrepeneurs than any other primary bank. However, to comprehend more fully the banking moves of the time, one has to take a brief look at the political and economic background.

SEVEN

The Great Leader

Economics and Prime Ministers go together, in more senses than one. There is a masterly historical account of the UK economy in the report of the Wilson Committee published in 1980, masterly in the context that the chairman, a recent Prime Minister, is commenting in part on his own performance. Harold Wilson had been appointed three years earlier by James Callaghan, his successor as Prime Minister, to head this committee. It was instigated to review the functioning of the financial institutions – the first such review since Radcliffe in 1959 – and the pleasing fluency of the report provokes the thought that a greater loss may have been suffered by the UK world of academic economists after Wilson's entry into politics, than by the Labour party when he retired. It must however also be observed with (almost) complete impartiality that the calibre of Labour leaders, possibly because their election process passed out of the unique domain of the parliamentary Labour party, has declined markedly since Callaghan.

By way of an historical perspective, Wilson observed that towards the end of the nineteenth century, after nearly two hundred years of dominance as the leading trading nation of the world, Britain's productivity was already rearing its sluggish head; there had been little alteration in Britain's uncompetitiveness with the other industrialised nations, the decline had never halted, if anything it had accelerated. The balance of payments as a long-term recurrent source of difficulty was not a new headache, but originated from before the First World War, and whilst productivity between the wars continued to fall, British manufacturing prices consistently rose more than those of its competitors. It was a miserable long-term deteriorating shrinkage of wealth; it was as if the country was too tired to do anything except to live on its declining capital and reputation.

There was then the Second World War, the horrors of which are unknown to most of today's younger grandparents, and its subsequent political and social after-effects. The inflexible policy of full employment, paramount with both the Conservatives and Labour post-war governments, triggered off green light expansionary measures designed to reduce unemployment, and red light contractionary measures designed to counterbalance payments deficits and increased demand. This period was aptly labelled 'Stop Go' and, whilst it was stopping and going, inflation was uncontrolled during most of the relevant years. Those attempts which were made were by way of cutting capital investment rather than by cutting current expenditure, and wages therefore rose more rapidly than productivity, and the economy continued to degenerate into even greater uncompetitiveness. During Macmillan's five-year tenure from 1959 to 1964 Germany's economy grew by twice, and Japan's by more than four times as much as ours, although admittedly they started from a lower base. In 1950 our share in the value of the world's export of manufactured goods had been a resplendent 25%; by 1965 it was down to 12·6%. Today it is 7·8%. The abysmal proportion of GNP devoted to new investment was always calamitously low and it was a national tragedy that succeeding Tory and Labour governments, in the 1950s and 1960s, failed to introduce positive fiscal and economic measures in order to get the country out of its depressing inertia.

Britain could not continue year after year lagging behind other industrialised nations without serious economic and social repercussions. One underlying problem was that the Conservatives during the immediate post-War period were mostly gentlemen of the shires, if not in actual wealth, at any rate in temperament; they were more concerned with conserving wealth than creating it. There was, too, an unexpected gap of understanding between the old Tories of the political establishment and the new Tories of the CBI-ridden industrial establishment, who were far from being in sympathy with the wistful Edwardian nostalgia which permeated pre-Heath Toryism. Harold Macmillan, the arch-Edwardian and the de Gaulle *manqué* in his exercise of superiority, was sentimental and backward looking. Recalling his golden youth, layered in memory with more gilt than accuracy, he wrote, 'Talleyrand once said that no one who had known France before the Revolution could understand in its true sense *la douceur de la* *vie*. The same is true of anyone who did not know England before the First World War'. Macmillan had his great qualities but he was no Talleyrand,* nor was he a de Gaulle, who though venerating *La Gloire* was nonetheless astringent on economic matters.

The French were immensely fortunate in having their de Gaulle during and after the War; the British, fortunate in having their Churchill during the war, were immensely unfortunate during the post-War period in not having a great peace leader. Heath, in his entrenched pursuit of reasonableness in a period which now seems to have resembled a state of siege, had the potential but not the timing; Macmillan had the opportunity and missed it by a generation. With a great peace leader, Britain could have taken over the leadership of Europe with ease and assurance, not only politically and economically (the feather-bedding Commonwealth trading ties should have been cut years earlier), but also bureaucratically. This powerful sovereigncy of administration being all too easily overlooked and belittled, and Brussels, instead of being established upon the rigidities of French bureaucracy – a system very good for the French but infuriatingly inappropriate for anyone else, particularly not for the English bureaucrat with his own sense of file play – would have been based upon the infinitely more flexible British bureaucracy. This, though not overly perfect, would have been more easily assimilable by our continental cousins.

There has been very little *douceur de la vie* in the economic life of the UK since the war. The frequent balance of payments crises were one reason, another was the misguided policies of both parties in being committed to full employment instead of to greater productivity. It was also exiguous ill-luck that monetarism was not wholly respectable in Heath's day. Monetarists believe that any attempt to control unemployment directly is pointless and mistaken, their cardinal principle is to control inflation even if that means temporary but sharp increased unemployment. If Heath had extolled monetarism fully; if he had concentrated upon productivity rather than full employment; if he had fought against the union bosses for the democratic rights of its

* Who could ever be? That most pragmatic of men, Talleyrand, who bestrode generations, was a colossus, a giant of manipulation, a man who could judge what was going to be, by sheer intellectual prescience, a man who could play both ends to the middle with such overwhelming and elegant skill that he made first-rate practitioners in the field of government, of diplomacy, of trade and speculation, of love-making and gambling, and even of religion, seem like amateurs.

members, so forcing the bosses to be more reasonable, he may well
have succeeded in an important aspect of Thatcherism before it was
created. But, as in all things in life, one has to have luck, the Arabs call
it *baraka*; Heath had nearly everything except *baraka*, just as Margaret
Thatcher enjoyed a great period of *baraka* until, it would seem, we
were a grandmother.

But when an administration exercises an economic policy, whose is
it essentially? The party in power whose political philosophy helped to
win the election? The Government's? The Cabinet's? The Chancellor's? Or the Prime Minister's? In the final analysis, of course, it is the
character, nature and calibre of the Prime Minister which counts
most, and the awful corollary is that, in politics, his or her appointment
(even though the Tory party, like the Labour Party, changed the
method of electing its leader) has come about more by luck or intrigue
– or the lack of it – than by intrinsic merit. In the Cedar Story, the
Prime Minister who is most concerned is Heath, and his route to the
prime ministerial pinnacle, is worth a brief study.

One of the better cards held by the Tory party, after the Attlee
administration, was the feeling of voters that its members had the
patrician aura, that they were natural rulers. Of the post-War conservative Prime Ministers, Churchill, Eden and Douglas-Home were
more or less patrician by birth, Macmillan was alongside by marriage and
certainly there by osmosis; Edward Heath, the first leader to emerge
from the solid lower-middle-class, ascended sharply up-market at
Oxford and in the army, developing his patrician flavour by sheer
application. Churchill indubitably was the Great Saviour, irrepressible
and heroic with a deep sense of history, Eden was the Great Disaster
with his double-breasted prejudices and peevish intelligence, Douglas-
Home was the Great Aristocrat with his insouciant brain and
overpowering goodness, Harold Macmillan was the Great Entertainer
with his intellectual mantle displayed like a liberated conjuror; Heath
was the Great Leader with his strong character and willpower.*

---

* In the patrician stakes, Margaret Thatcher determined to go further up the
ladder than anyone else, created her own entirely new class, called One of Us,
which has now not-so-gradually wittled down to its singular originator. She is
surely the Great Missionary with her zeal in caring for objectives rather than for
people. John Major is anti-patrician, but this will not stop him changing his tailor
and barber and accent. He is the Great Manager with his talent for administration
and tidiness, not obsessed as yet by any deep political philosophy.

The pivotal Tory Prime Minister was, of course, Macmillan because of the way he manipulated his succession. A man of exceptional intelligence, which earned him well-deserved respect, he had a dangerous streak of mischief which has not yet earned him the calumny he deserves. As a genuine player of roles, living a lie in the reality of life, he pursued the actor's most sincere relationship, an unceasing devotion to the self-reflection in the mirror of his mind, and he clothed himself ever more forcibly each succeeding year in the attire of the well-read nobleman from the Palace of Westminster, his performance improving as he improved the make-up of his image. Yet his inner life was a fraud, for his outer urbanity, exuding an air of detached indifference to the affairs of wife and State, was his attempt to conceal the humiliation caused by his Devonshire wife's passionate love for somebody else. This alien body was a brilliant gregarious Scottish MP, Robert Boothby, whom he later ennobled, probably the first adulterer knowingly made a peer by his own cuckold. If his wife's illicit romance had ever become public knowledge, Macmillan's political career would have ended in ignominy there and then.

And then the Profumo scandal came along. When this otherwise honorable man's public duplicity revealed him as an adulterer, it struck Macmillan, quite literally, below the belt and led directly to his remarkably muddled resignation and departure. It explained how, in leaving the central political scene, he caused his country the worst possible service, for motivated by deep jealousy of Rab Butler's joyous first and second marriages, he denied his detested rival the succession; emotionally shattered and a politician down to his stiletto fountain pen, he scratched Butler's name out of number 10, and in so doing he changed the course of history.

The Prime Minister who was truly unflappable, who achieved office after Douglas-Home and Harold Wilson, by way of Macmillan's cruel conjuring tricks, was Ted Heath, inappropriately bowdlerised from Edward and now appropriately restored by way of the Queen's Garter. Like many of those privileged to know him, I admire him not only for his solid virtues but for one or two of his more solid faults. His administration, marred inescapably by sheer bad luck, was marred escapably by his high-profile relationship with one man, not with an MP or a member of the Government or a Tory official, but with a civil servant – William Armstrong. A less explored aspect of the Heath premiership but one which requires a closer study, as does the overall nature of Downing Street advisers, was this unusual and intriguing relationship – between Heath, then aged fifty, and Armstrong, then sixty-five. It was a relationship of great significance because Armstrong's influence was exercised in the political area, which he never understood, and because he detached Heath from being closer to one or other of his own Cabinet colleagues who had immense political judgement, such as Whitelaw, Rippon or Prior, each of whom at a crucial time could have had an important beneficial influence, each of whom could have helped Heath to steer the economy with winning results. But it was not to be.*

Heath's cabinet was extremely well-conducted; he had no need for a kitchen cabinet, nor for any cronies to help with the washing up. Yet somehow this relationship of the nephew-uncle grew to the extent whereby Heath lost some of his sense of proportion, the Government lost some of its equilibrium and the economy lost most of its way.

Heath came to office in June 1970 with high hopes, and it was during his tenure, which came to such a dismal end in February 1974, that his economic and fiscal policy, aided and abetted by C&CC, sowed the seeds for the banking crisis. During his politically affluent leadership in opposition, Tory policy had been re-examined and redefined in thorough detail. In office, economic policy was to be set fair with his first Chancellor of Exchequer, Iain McLeod. This man, a heavyweight Tory philosopher, an orator of distinction, as tough-minded as Heath and widely tipped to be his successor, a chancellor of great potential who would have smacked down the secondary banking jamboree with one phone call to Threadneedle, died just a month after his appointment. To everyone's astonishment, including his own, Anthony Barber was appointed. His tenure, running for three and a half years and for three and a half budgets was known as the Barber-Dash-For-Growth, remembered as a sensational but intelligent gamble. If it had come off, Anthony Barber would have been considered a miracle man, and Ted Heath may have been the longest-ever serving Prime Minister, instead of his erstwhile enemy Margaret Thatcher.

The gamble was a race for a win, not for a place, but it never stood a chance because the gamble relied on having the support of the union bosses. The descendants of the old affiliated societies, of the Tol-puddle martyrs no less, were now dressed-up brothers with ties and

---

*Very soon after he retired Armstrong suffered a mental breakdown.

jackets, but very much up the social ladder; they had nothing to doff because they had snipped off their forelocks, but doff they did – to their own union leaders. Diehard sincere martyrdom had been replaced by diehard sincere power seeking. The progeny of Victorian self-help were now in a modern guise, ruled by militant men who were concerned with political power, who created mighty oligarchies of monumental bureaucratic strength, tempered only occasionally by attempts to recapture their earliest traditions of truly helping their now meek and unballoted members.

So, Ted ran for growth, hoping that the employers, especially the manufacturers, would run with him, and he ran for that win, arms flaying, knees splayed, chest out, head forward to break the tape – which was always out of reach – because the union bosses coolly moved it forward. If it was not an official strike, it was a go-slow; if it was not a go-slow, it was an unofficial strike; if it was not an unofficial strike, it was a shop-floor outburst; the so-called tough obdurate employers in the private sector joined with Heath in opposing labour demands, but buckled at the first sight of such demands, their opposition as paper-thin as their press releases proclaiming their concern over spiralling wage costs. It was only after the Heath administration, when the CBI, the employers' own trade union, began to emerge with a strong voice on behalf of its own members, that the employers started practising what they had preached.

In Barber's first budget of 1971, it was all go. He expanded the economy, increased spending, reduced taxation and abolished hire purchase control. A huge liquidity was created, money availability was easy and with the introduction of C&CC, in September of that year, availability became even more easy. Heath stolidly tackled the unions by attempting to engage their leaders in reasonable discussion. When that failed he introduced what was considered a reasonable voluntary incomes policy. The union leaders sniffed around before acting. The first reaction in the early part of 1972 was a power workers go-slow, they decided to switch off in the middle of a bitter winter. The miners, never wanting to be in shade, also went on strike, only returning after the Wilberforce award, the beginning of their determined long-standing fight against the Government, ending only with Heath's downfall in February 1974.

In 1972, in Barber's second budget there were large tax cuts plus further expansionary measures resulting in a public sector deficit of £1.6 billion, which rose in the following year to the then unprecedented level of £2.7 billion. Only then, and too late, was essential thought applied to curbing the huge surge of monetary expansion – in 1972 an increase of 20% over 1971 and in 1973 a further increase of 20% over 1972.

Around this time Nadia and I were seeing a lot of Esmond Rothermere (then chairman of his family-controlled *Daily Mail* newspaper group) and his third wife, Mary, a Southern beauty with brains, a mother of six small sons from a previous marriage, now with her seventh, young Ez, as we came to call him. One weekend at Daylesford, their place in the country, the house guests included the *Daily Mail*'s celebrated foreign correspondent, Noel Barber, and Tina, his strikingly attractive Italian wife. Noel Barber and Esmond Rothermere were firm friends and passionately competitive tennis players who never had to settle any of their differences out of court. I asked Noel if he thought his younger brother knew what he was doing. 'You know we are part Danish' he responded, 'and we are pretty athletic. I hope he makes his dash for all our sakes.' It was Noel Barber who made it, subsequently in a new career, as a bestselling novelist. 'Your own dash for monetary growth?' I asked him at a party years later. He laughed at the fraternal allusion and patted his wallet vigorously.

By May 1972, there was a railway dispute; in June the dockworkers went on strike and did not return till August. Also in June there was the chronic British whooping cough, another sterling crisis, and bank rate was raised from 5% to 6%, but the stock of money increased to what should have been alarming levels, helping to fuel the Stock Exchange boom, the exports boom, the commodity boom and the property boom. Any boom adds to an increase in the price of housing and of commercial property. From early 1971 to the end of 1973, house prices doubled – a record – and commercial property prices trebled – another record.

In the early summer, the Bretton Woods concordat on currency in existence since the War was abolished, the pound was floated and immediately depreciated by 6.5%. Inflation increased whilst company profitability and investment declined. The inflationary boom continued. Heath's voluntary incomes policy having moved into a political cul-de-sac, led in autumn 1972 to one of his famous U-turns, the imposition of statutory incomes and dividends. The net result was to seriously exacerbate the conflict with the unions, despite the sop of imposing a rent freeze on commercial rents. This rent freeze had no effect whatsoever on the union leaders nor on the surging boom.* Company profits continued to be depressed mainly due to the rapid increase in wage costs, followed by a further famous U-turn, the enacting of wide ranging powers to assist industry under the Industry Act. Then, what no Tory ever thought would occur – price control from a Tory Government was announced.

Each of the U-turns was seen for what it was by the union bosses who, far from being allayed and comforted, started smelling blood and became more assertive, demanding and strike-addicted: more man-hours were lost than at any time since the General Strike of 1929. Heath wanted the union bosses to be reasonable, but they were behaving as politicians not as trade unionists, and the Government never seemed to fully appreciate that the wage demands, strikes and union belligerency were politically motivated, first, second and third. Whitelaw, an ideal minister of employment, an ideal man to deal with the unions – his velvet glove could have shaken the hand of any union leader till it withered without any pain being felt – was still busy in Northern Ireland and lamentably could not be released from there until it was too late.

In October 1972, as edicted by C&CC, the bank rate was superseded by MLR, the minimum lending rate; no more artificial wait at noon on Thursday; no more would the top-hatted Government broker ceremonially cross the street from Mullens just before noon, to await outside the Court Room for the bank rate verdict. These Government brokers, all Mullens men, were without exception, inordinately decent people with immense pride in their duties and with immense attachment to an unusually high level of integrity. I knew two or three of them, and recall one in particular, Peter Daniell. I met him through a mutual friend, Rupert Raw, an adviser to the Governor, with whom I would occasionally take tea in his small corner office in the

---

* A rent freeze means that a building is under-rented, which only marginally affects its value, because value is based on the true rent. Many post-war 21 year leases fell in at ridiculously low levels. Forward estimates of cash flow were severely adrift, which was far from helpful in the subsequent crash two years later. One effect of the rent freeze was that interest was rolled over and added to the loan, which is how 'rolled up' interest flowered from the ever enterprising brains of the secondary bankers, a lending device subsequently and eagerly taken up by the primaries. Commercial rents were unfrozen by the Labour government in February 1975, some cynics observing that it was because the trade union leaders did not like to suffer the effects of the restriction on their pension fund investments.

Bank. Raw was a man who with engaging eccentricity, had the energetic habit of walking rapidly each morning from Sloane to Soane, in very erect military bearing, his swooping brigadier's nose able to sniff out any problems before breakfast, and, occasionally hailing him as I drove past, I knew that by the time he reached Threadneedle, cool as a cucumber, sterling was safe.

The weekly Thursday bank-rate ritual was banished; MLR was now to be announced when and as required. The Government broker was interred; no more Mullens men, the Bank was to have its own dealing room and would conduct its own gilts operation. I wonder what has happened to the stove-black top hat, the perquisite of the Mullens partner who had the weekly noon ritual. I remember lunching at Mullens one day, where hats, umbrellas, walking sticks, were piled haphazardly as if it were the entrance to a country house, and pondering why it was that somehow at City lunches, the more refined the manners of one's hosts, the less discriminating the food. I remember, too, an evening in the summer of 1972, when the Daniells and the Raws joined Nadia and I for dinner at La Reserve. It was during the days of exchange control. We talked about a number of things that evening, and to my immense relief, and perhaps to theirs too, the topic of foreign spending never came up.

The last months of 1972 brought very little respite for Heath. The summer dock strike left a bitter taste when several dockers were imprisoned under the Industrial Relations Act. The TUC declared it would expel any union which registered under the Act, a clear call to open warfare. Not surprisingly, Douglas Hurd wrote in his book on this era that wage disputes in the public sector took more of the Cabinet's time than any other issue. Parliament became so heated there was talk of a constitutional crisis.

It seemed like years, not months, before 1973 finally commenced; it was to prove a year of important events, mostly negative; the most positive and the most momentous was Britain's formal entry into the Common Market in January. It was an awesome step, part of the process of the merging of cultures and of boundaries, merging villages, boroughs, districts, counties, regions, nations, all following an inexorable historical march forward to a single Europe, and, who knows, a single continent, a single globe? The Six became the Nine. Mr Heath was lauded as a great European and will go down in history for his efforts; his minister in charge, Geoffrey Rippon, who conducted the negotiations with great skill, and was lauded as Mr Europe, should be twinned with Heath for his efforts. As a strong European, I had a great sense of joy, as did many others over our entry, and a tiny bit of satisfaction in that I had quietly helped to finance the European League for Economic Co-operation – a non-party pressure group brilliantly led by Geoffrey Rippon, Roy Jenkins and Geoffrey Tucker – which played a material, deliberately unsung role in our entry. As a personal bonus, which has given me enormous pleasure, Rippon and Tucker have become long-standing personal friends.

On entering the EEC, in order not to allow our new economic partners to forget our national disease, we coughed up yet another sterling crisis, and MLR was increased from 6% to 7.5%. In the spring, as a foretaste of things to come, the Scottish Co-operative Bank got itself into a technical mess with its certificates of deposit and had to be bailed out by the Bank and the Scottish clearers.

In the months before the budget of 1973, there was increasing anxiety in the property and secondary banking industry that Barber would impose penal tax restraints. It was not a question of whether they would be imposed, but the degree of their severity and speed. Would surpluses arising from revaluations be taxed? Would the secondaries be prohibited from using the money markets? Would there be a special property development tax? Would it be a combination of these horrors? Worse, would it be retroactive? There was intense speculation, not as to whether it would happen – that had already been taken for granted – but as to the degree of pain to be suffered.

When Barber's 1973 Budget was proclaimed, his third, another clarion call for expansion, this time for a 5% growth – there was no reference at all to property. The entire real estate industry, and its lenders, mainly the secondaries, escaped unscathed. There was a gasp of disbelief then immediate relief followed by frantic activity. The phones went white-hot. The buzz was at fever pitch. No tax measures? Extraordinary. What was the rationale?

It appeared the Treasury thought, that, like the hoary man who owes the bank so much that he has to be treated with kid gloves, any measures causing the deterioration or collapse of the property market would bring with it a disrupting effect on the Government's overall policy of expansion. It was, I believe, an absurd miscalculation, for not only had everyone braced themselves for the 'inevitable' severe enactments, the market had already discounted it; at this particular moment there was a psychological equilibrium well in tune to receiving punishment, to making a fundamental and necessary and hurtful readjustment.

Interest rates rose sharply after the budget. The punitive application of interest rates as a direct monetary measure now came very much into its own. Interest rates since C&CC, applied as a prime measure of monetary control was new to Westminster, were still abhorrent to many in the Treasury. When introduced eighteen months earlier, interest rates had been as low as 5% and the possibility of increasing rates, to restrain an inflationary boom, seemed remote. Now with these high rates, it looked as if the building societies would break through the politically nightmarish level of charging double digit rates. It was too much for Heath and, in his guise as King Canute and in a measure now forgotten, his Government made an outright grant to the building societies to keep their rates below 10%.

A furious controversy both in and out of Parliament, aggravated by the elementary budget miscalculation, ensued over the profits being made by property developers. Attention lasered upon the mythology of Centre Point, a thin thirty-two storey pencil building at the corner of Tottenham Court Road and Oxford Street. It was owned by the well-known multi-millionaire recluse Harry Hyams, another early partner of Felix Fenston. Libel-free MPs wildly accused Hyams of deliberately keeping Centre Point empty in order to demand a maximum rent, an absurd accusation from any commercial point of view; but the central point of Centre Point was missed not only by Westminster, but also by Whitehall and Fleet Street. It was not so much that Hyams did not want to rent the building, he could not. For designed as it was as a resonance, in a different form, of the Banque Lambert in Brussels, the building was seriously under-lifted. Few surveyors could advise their clients to rent a building with so few lifts and with such a large number of smallish single floors. Hyams, an attractive, combative personality, who loathed any form of criticism, particularly unfair criticism, tackled Westminster head on with the successful assistance of Lord Goodman.* The furore against property developers increased in acrimony as a direct result of this particular tussle. The Government took note

* Goodman's uncle, Morrie Mauerberger (known, in the post-war era, as South Africa's third richest man after Harry Oppenheimer and John Schlesinger) was a friend of my father. Through him we met Arnold Goodman who was always known to us as Abie. When my mother and I once saw Goodman on a legal point arising from my father's will, she said to me in front of the great lawyer: 'Don't argue with Abie. If he says it's all right, it's all right.' I did not argue with Abie.

by later proposing a payment of rates on empty buildings, an inequitable measure, which hard-pressed owners of office buildings twenty years later remember with justifiable distaste.

Then industry also took note. For in June, the most important figure in the property industry, Lord Samuel, the head of Land Securities, the most regal property investment company in the country, indeed in the whole of Europe, the owner of more property crown jewels, of more illustrious tenants than any other, revalued the portfolio of his company. The resultant surplus was £370 million, an increase of over 30%. The figure thrown up was a sensation. The surplus alone was considerably more than the total market valuation of British Leyland, the UK's largest indigenous motor manufacturer. Its chairman, Lord Stokes saw red and exploded his views to the press and to everyone around. The furore against the property world intensified.

By 20 July 1973 MLR itself finally broke into double figures, Canute got his feet wet, and, with a further increase to 11.5% only a week later, the water reached up to his knees. This second increase in seven days was to my mind the exact turning point of the share, property and commodity booms.

In the period since the introduction of C&CC nearly two years earlier, the property market, devouring as much as it could borrow, had not been overly unstable because interest rates were still at a comparatively low level. But borrowing at these new high levels was deadly. Most borrowers didn't seem to care, particularly as many had been rolling up the interest, their apparent unconcern propped up by profit sharing arrangements with their lenders, these sweetheart deals having proliferated since the rent freeze. High interest rates are the worst possible abomination to the well-being and stability of property investment and development: at the first portent of increasing rates, property companies should delay borrowing from banks, and banks should delay lending to property companies: unstructured borrowing and lending during a period of high interest rates is administering easy credit to a gambler – it must inevitably end in disaster, to the borrower or lender, or both.

And then, in early November, Harold Samuel dropped another, more unexpected bombshell; he revalued his portfolio once again; it showed a further increased surplus of 25%, but what staggered the market was that he had revalued a second time in a year. In the majestic history of his great company he had never done this before: nor had any other property company. At one time, Samuel revalued occasionally, every few years or so; then every three years; then it became once a year. Now he had revalued twice in the same year and in property terms, during a critical year, when property should have been in his and everyone else's intensive care. No one could have known better than he, that what he had done could only cause serious damage, not only to the industry, but to his own reputation. For the first time in his career Samuel did something which was inherently discreditable.

The City as a whole was perplexed and worried, but the more nefarious fringe bankers and property dealers were delighted. Here was solid proof from an unimpeachable source that values were not over the top, on the contrary, they were still rising, and the brazen opportunistic view taken by many of the property pack, whether lenders or borrowers, was that loans were over-secured. So as values were increasing, why not top up the loans? Which is exactly what many of the secondary lenders did; they immediately topped up and lent out more, on the same security. Why not? They argued that the money market was still, after all, gushing it out, and now the godfather of property himself had descended Mount Sinai with a second valuation in a year. The property shovellers could not have had more reassurance; it was a tablet of health writ in stone. It was also one of the most subversive actions in the history of commercial property valuation; with interest rates rising sharply it undermined stability and confidence at a most sensitive time, and I believe that Samuel's ghastly blunder had, like a late nasty squall, a direct effect on the increasingly unsettled financial climate.

But overshadowing everything else, an event unpredicted, except by a few lone disparaged Cassandras, was the rocket-like oil price explosion after the Yom Kippur war, the direct cause of the country's energy crisis and the reason for the unparalleled emergency measures imposed by the Government at the beginning of December.

*   *   *

I have occasionally speculated on how Richardson, as the new Governor, regarded the financial and economic situation, after he took office in July of that ominous year: day after day, week after week sitting at his large square desk, he must have wondered how it had come about that the fates had engineered such a fearsome set of circumstances. What went on in that formidable mind during his baptism?

Never a man to jump to conclusions, he had always preferred being there in advance of others, then moving back to gather support of those behind him. What even some of his closer colleagues never appreciated, was that, having already reached a conclusion, the entire cast of his mind and judgement was formed within a profound disposition towards reaching a consensus, towards bringing the colleagues into the focus of his own vision of what in his own mind should be done. The success of the Schroder bank today is due in no small part to this Richardson ethos, this concept of consensus built carefully on solid foundations, the building blocks always securely bound together; delays there certainly were in putting it all into place, but there were rarely, if ever, any misjoints or cracks. It was tiresome to some of his colleagues but eventually when the judgement was uttered, the decision made, it was very nearly always the best one, the right one, nearly always perfectly structured, and firmly cemented with and by the agreement of those consulted. This slow process in building firm blocks of consensus, irritated some, and it has invariably bemused me, amongst others, how his old colleagues at Schroders and even at the Bank of England have abjured and sniped at what they perceived was his indecision. They did not seem to appreciate, and many still do not, that it was not so much indecision, as his active decision to take everyone with him, slowly perhaps, but surely. He had in most instances already made up his mind where to go and how to get there, but in aiming for an overall consensus, he wanted his colleagues to be in one mind in supporting the proposal or decision, and if one or two were slower than others, Richardson would wait for them to catch up. Having surveyed from the front, having perceived the problems, having decided upon the solutions, he then led from the midst of his cohorts. This was the way Richardson worked.

In the summer of 1973, when he first took on his great office, the dangerous developments in the banking sector were taking place against a seriously deteriorating economic background. Confronting him was a heaving sea of disturbing white horses. Richardson lost no time in dealing with the easy credit situation. In August central bankers go on holiday; not for Gordon Richardson, it was a time to think and to decide. In September, he wrote his first Governor's letter to the clearers expressing in strong terms his wish that they restrain lendings on financial transactions and on property companies. His concept of the 'Corset' was commencing, the big banks now took heed.

There was talk of a possible half budget in the winter. In October, the trebling of the prices of oil shook the foundations of the world economy. By the end of November, MLR, at 8% in July, had risen to 13%. The run on deposits commenced its fearful outflow during the last week of November. In early December the horizon darkened, with the energy crisis, a state of emergency was imposed, the working week was limited to three days, street lighting was extinguished, the speed limit was restricted to 50 mph including motorways. On Monday 17 December Barber announced his final budget, a half-budget: the measures were not a Christmas present. The outflow of deposits became a torrent. The urgent problem was to avoid a widening circle of collapse 'through the contagion of fear'. On Wednesday, 19 December, the storm was ready to burst.

*   *   *

How had Cedar been faring during the previous two years? How had it been faring during the months since the merger with Amal? What had been happening, especially during the last weeks and days, before its directors, and its institutional shareholders and its advisers, found themselves summoned to the Bank of England on the day the storm was ready to burst?

EIGHT

The Deadly Merger

In assessing Cedar's activities, or indeed any commercial enterprise, there are two sources of information, the external, the public information available to all, and the internal, the private, sometimes privileged information, available only to directors, specialist advisers and management. Externally there are invariably events which enable the outside observer to discern that things are not in balance; to such an external observer, the investor or the competitor, the analyst or journalist, it could be the resignation of a director, the hurried sale of a headquarters building, the change of an accounting date or a problematic acquisition. Internally to the executive or non-executive directors, the senior and middle managers, the signs that things are going wrong are buttressed by personal contacts and relationships, daily or monthly meetings, interleaved by the normal continuous vital interchange of views and ideas, ranging from high-level discussions to office gossip and shop talk. When, as happens all too frequently, the internal pressures detonate, the shrapnel can hurt everyone in all directions, or like a laser can strike at one particular victim. There is little justice in these ugly and unexpected, usually sudden situations, and even if they result from activity which is improper, or unethical, or criminal, the innocent suffer as well as the guilty.

Talks, discussions, rumours and intrigues are all part of the business game, part of the jostling of brains and personalities, of a combative career atmosphere, part of being in the same organisation when individuals say 'we' in talking to third parties and are not even aware of the ambiguous effect the plural representation has on the hearer and on himself. Permeating every level of day-to-day activities, there is that special nervy hum, sometimes intolerable, sometimes fearful, always exciting, whether corporate or individual, a tensioned continuous immanence – the dynamic throb of competition. Rules, regulations and customs have emerged, some formal, others impalpable, which comprise the rhythm of humans in a closed society, its very essence being communication, made up of whispers, drones, shouts, notes, letters, messages, friendly or not so friendly, when a shafted whisper can destroy the career of a single individual or set off an avalanche which can bury an entire organisation. In the case of Cedar, there were a number of portents and warnings during the period leading to the crisis which caused escalating concern to both the external observers and to the insiders.

To an insider, like a non-executive institutional director, myriad events must have tended to sweep him off his feet. To an outsider, such as a banking analyst, a financial journalist, a competitor, a customer, a depositor, or even an ex-director, the impression was of hyperactivity, of there being too many events, some impressive, others less so, still others controversial, if not provocative. Above all else was, of course, the acquisition of Amal, the culmination of the Morrison ambitions, the poisoned sword, which they had themselves carefully arranged and positioned, and upon which they were to fall and come to grief.

First, the board changes. At Unilever there had been no change, William Broadfield was still its representative. At Electricity, Sidney Cowtan, now retired from his post and still in some sort of after-glow from the party at the Gavroche to mark his retirement, was appointed an executive director; he resigned in November 1972, and George Cumming, his successor at Electricity (directorships were now permitted) was then appointed. At Coal, Reg Edward remained on the Board until the appointment of Hugh Jenkins. At Phoenix, Charles Knight resigned in November 1972 and was replaced by his deputy Brian Oram. Of the executive directors, John Eames joined Cedar's board in November 1972; Philip Johnstone in April 1973; Yusuf Ahmed, Michael Grinling and Alan Watt in June 1973 after the Amal merger; and Alan Glass in December 1973.

Next the profit position. It was brilliant. The results for each year, which ended 30 June, were always announced in September, followed by the AGM in October. For the year ending 30 June 1971 the profits were £900,000 against the forecast in the prospectus of £725,000; for the year ending June 1972 the profits increased to £1,270,000; for the year ending June 1973, ignoring the contribution from Amal, the profits increased to £1,820,000.

Next the share price.* On the public quotation in January 1971, the price was 65p per share, valuing the company at £10 million; by September it moved up to just over 100p, valuing the company at £20 million; by September 1972, the high point for the secondary sector, the price zoomed up to its highest-ever level to 144 pence, valuing the company at £30 million. From then it was downhill. In January 1973 the price had dropped to 90 pence. In February 1973 the price came down to 65 pence, which on a price-earnings ratio of 23.3 was still more than double that of the bank sector of 10.7. In July, this remarkable premium rating was only to disappear after the Amal merger, when the price dropped to 30 pence.

As to the deposits, when Cedar became a public company because of the nature of its financing strategy with the institutions, it had no need for deposits, except as existential proof that it was in the business of banking to impress its authenticity to the Bank of England. The character of any lender lies in its deposit taking policy and the source of its funds, and it was this aspect of Cedar, its reliance on its heavyweight partners for finance, which was what, from the beginning, had impressed Cazenove most. Cedar, until well after its public quotation, had never taken deposits from the money market and virtually none from the general public; as a 123, Cedar was unique in this respect. On prospectus day, in January 1971, the deposit figure was £2.8 million, of which £1 million represented a deposit from Electricity pending conversion into a medium term loan, most of the balance being friendly deposits from its other institutional share-holders and Spey.

Although deposits were at a derisory level in relation to its size, they were not required because of the institutional funding: this was Cedar's unique strength. The question still remained as to whether and what sort of deposits Cedar should take in after the public quotation and after it had reached a stage in its growth when it could or should no longer rely upon such institutional funding. In the late

---

* Adjusting for the issue of new shares, in October 1972 the capital was doubled by a scrip issue of one for one. Generally on these 1972/73 figures one should multiply by 6-7 times to relate to today's pound.

autumn of 1970, in the run up to the quotation, Michael and I concentrating on this question, were learning most from the example set by Twentieth Century Banking. Earlier that year, Twentieth Century had launched an income plan with enormous success. Its concept was to take in one- two- three-year deposits, the depositors being paid a fixed sum each month at a fixed rate of interest. This had tremendous appeal for the elderly and those living on regular incomes in the lower income brackets, who could budget with more precision, something they could not do with the building societies which paid a composite rate of tax.

It was a most adroit form of deposit taking, with no element of the short-term about it; one could match one's loans to advances with extraordinary accuracy. At Spey Finance it was appreciated that if there were concentration if not exclusive stress on long-term deposits, matching would be easy, risks would diminish – but not profit margins. This was one of the paramount attractions to Spey of Twentieth Century Banking, and when Spey later acquired Goulston Finance and Graham Finance, both of which relied almost entirely on short-term deposits, the set plan was to rebalance the deposits into medium and long-term only. The irony was that when these Spey secondaries were sold off to First National, the rebalancing had hardly begun, and the post hoc owners who had purchased them unchanged from First National were faced with terminal problems, as has already been noted, in the case of Bovis and Twentieth Century.

From the exact time I withdrew from Cedar, there was no holding Michael and David from the money market. For the year ending June 1971, deposits were at the very low level of £3.9 million. The money market tap had not yet been turned. Cedar was still inviolate, but not for much longer. By June 1972 deposits soared to £21 million. Cedar was insatiable in its wanton turning of the tap. By June 1973, deposits had nearly trebled to £61.3 million, of which more than two thirds was for less than three months – nearly all of this from the money markets. By December 1973, deposits had risen to £74.1 million, of which over £67 million was for less than three months – nearly all of this from the money market. Not differentiating whether the directors were institutional or not, evident to them or to any external observer, was that these deposits were dangerously short-term.

The Morrisons had rumbustiously hit Cedar's lending heritage on the head; they had also exterpated, not that it worried them, my original personal committment to Godfrey Chandler, that Cedar would not deviate from borrowing long and lending short. The ghastly way in which they did deviate, appears gruesomely below.*

In March 1973 there occurred Cedar's largest ever issue of loan stock, it amounted to £10 million 7.5% unsecured convertibles. It was neat impressive financing. The Morrisons used all their resources to take up as much of the convertibles as they could. It was the old dilution ogre again, and this time they borrowed in order to take up more: three months before the Amal merger, it was the first lethal appearance of the Samurai sword.

Now the advances to customers: by June 1971 the advances were £14 million; by June 1972 they had risen to £26 million; by June 1973 they had risen to £54 million; by December 1973 they had risen to just over £70 million. Advances had increased five-fold in two and a half years. Cedar not only actively competed for deposits with the best of them, it had actively competed for borrowers. This had always been the task of its mortgage brokers with whom Cedar continued having close ties and they were urged to advertise for new business,

---

* The breakdown of the deposits and the depositors are as follows:

30 June 1971. Deposit accounts £3.9 million: within one month £2.78 million comprising 118 customers of which 5 customers (mostly the four institutions and the Morrisons) contributed 90%; within three months £0.49 million comprising 39 customers of which one customer (again a friendly shareholder) contributed 80%; within twelve months but after three months £0.24 million comprising 5 customers; over twelve months £0.39 million comprising 41 customers of which one customer contributed 70%. Total number of depositors 193.

30 June 1972. Deposit accounts of £21.1 million: within one month £9.08 million comprising 33,809 customers of which two customers contributed £2.32 million; within three months £3.43 million comprising 167 customers of which one customer contributed £1.01 million; within twelve months but after three months £3.91 million comprising 71 customers of which one customer contributed £0.5 million; after twelve months £4.64 million comprising 2,253 customers. Total number of depositors 36,300.

30 June 1973. Deposit accounts of £61.3 million; within one month £36.49 million comprising 52,997 customers: within three months £11.15 million comprising 746 customers; within twelve months but after three months £11.65 million comprising 1783 customers; after twelve months £1.98 million comprising 1433 customers. Total number of depositors 56959.

30 June 1974. Deposit accounts of £8.40 million comprising 49,553 customers; within one month £2.96 million; within three months £2.30 million; within twelve months £2.40 million; after twelve months £0.75 million. In addition £54.62 million. Part of the rescue funds, £50 million from the four institutions; the balance part of the Barclays' £22 million.

encouraged by an incentive scheme on their results. Few applicants were turned down. One broker who had worked with Cedar from its earliest days told me recently that he was amazed at the sudden change in the spring of 1973, how standards had been dropped, how applications had been readily accepted. In his rich Northern accent, which still echoes in my mind as I write because of the intensity of his feelings nearly twenty years later, he said that it was mayhem. There was constant pressure to obtain fresh business from John Eames and his assistants, exuberant business pushers with their expensive cars. There was also pressure from David Fischer, frequently telephoning the larger brokers, such as himself, putting on pressure to find new borrowers, to send in more applications. He said that he and others became distinctly worried over the pressure to find new business and hoped that the Morrisons knew what they were doing and that they had enough money to cope with the new applications. He was, in fact, sufficiently perturbed to insist on a meeting with Michael and David, but whereas in the early days of their association he was able to pop in and see them at any time, now he had great difficulty in obtaining an appointment. Eventually it was granted and he found a solid front of breezy optimism. Michael told him: 'You just get the business, that's all you have to worry about. We can raise all the money to meet any new business you bring in'.

The safeguard which had originally impressed Jasper Knight that a loan would be limited to not more than 80% of the forced sale value of the house became lax; the institutional representatives on the Board were not informed of the laxity, nor were they informed that in some instances the brokers were not only allowed to vet and approve applications themselves but were able to sign cheques on a special Cedar bank account. Getting it in and getting it out, was the name of the game. Getting it in was easy. The issue of the £10 million convertible in spring (and the spur to the brokers to get it out) had been a smooth negotiation with the four institutions; moreover the effects of advertising for deposits were showing some results. But overriding institutional money and deposits from the general public, there was always the facile open tap of the money market.

Getting it out was the problem. The brokers redoubled their efforts, but borrowers were not coming in quickly enough. The Morrisons looked around. When Amal became a subsidiary it became a big in-house borrower. The Morrisons looked for other outlets: they purchased 10% of Manson Finance, another secondary lender; they

purchased 100% of Alexanders Stores; they made an agreed bid for
50% of Chester National Bank of New York, subject only to approval
of the Federal Reserve; all of these were long-term investments
financed or to be financed on short-term money market deposits.
These were approved at the board meetings. No questions were
asked.

In the area of advertising and publicity, which put Cedar onto the
national map, Fischer was in his element. In 1971, before almost
anyone else, Cedar went for current accounts, and it did so with real
imagination. 'Have we any answers to your current account charges?'
Yes. 'We at Cedar make no charges and we guarantee to pay you 3%
on current accounts.' That was not all, there were further goodies. 'Do
you accept the charges for standing orders lying down? We make no
charge for this service.' A banking first. Then another banking first.
'We have a free postal service. You pay us by post wherever you are,
with fully stamped and addressed envelopes supplied free by the bank.
Why not write and ask about the advantages of banking at Cedar? It
will cost you just this once a few pence. It could save you pounds.'

Then came the real blockbuster, the one aimed at Jim Keogh, the
one which would cause Fischer (a habit from his earliest days on
anything to do with printing and design) to rush into Jack's office with
great pride and show him the proofs. 'Don't compare us with other
banks.' Why not? 'Because at other banks, charges are the rule; every
entry is charged; at Cedar – no charge on current accounts whilst they
are maintained in credit. Standing orders – other banks charge every
time it is executed; at Cedar no charge. Deposit accounts – at other
banks interest is below bank rate, at Cedar our rate is 0.5% above bank
rate. Post – not catered for by most banks; at Cedar post is free.
Service – at other banks it is mechanical, at most other banks the
customer is just another account number; at Cedar, you have warm
friendly relationships. All our customers are important to us. Find out
for yourselves how we compare.'

By the middle of 1972 the new customers were finding out how they
compared. The campaign was working, and one or two of the non-
executive directors of Cedar were regarding Fischer with growing
respect, one or two others were raising eyebrows. Fischer was not
deterred. The romance between Cedar and the general public was
warming up: 'People give us their dearest love. We return it with
interest.' With this one, there would certainly have been cluckings
from Michael and David, hovering impatiently for Jack's reaction

Lord Richardson: the Governor of the Bank of England He could, like any genuine patrician, take centre stage without moving from the wings.

Sir Jasper Hollom: the Deputy Governor of the Bank of England This cool, central banker displayed a fixity of purpose as hard as the coinage it was his job to protect.

The Court Room, the Bank of England
This hallowed and famous room, though large and spacious,
retains a wonderful sense of intimacy with a strong aroma of history.

The Governor's Room, the Bank of England If this is the reckoning room of Heaven, then so be it, you say to yourself. You start praying.

The Parlour Corridor, the Bank of England One of the Parlour rooms housed the executive directors of Cedar. By midnight, Wednesday 19 December, it was dubbed by those upstairs as the 'Nether Regions'.

James Keogh: the Head of the Discount Office of the Bank of England Mixed memories of him linger on.

Sir Kenneth Cork: the liquidator Cork surveyed the table. At last he could talk; at last he could express his views.

Lord De L'Isle: Phoenix Assurance
Probably the only hereditary peer
qualified to read a balance sheet.

Cob Stenham: Unilever A one-off, a
sort of loner, a passionate and genuine
workaholic.

Hugh Jenkins: the Coal Board
Favoured with dark, celtic good looks
and the thrusting presence of a colonel
soon to be a general, he had a certain
star quality.

**Burton Johnson: the Electricity
Supply Industry** A model adjutant
with quiet good manners.

Jack Morrison
His short, pug-like button-nose, cocked and sniffing like a terrier for signs of any possible danger.

Jack Morrison and his mother, Edith Morrison Possessing a quiet but firm propriety, Edith Morrison raised standards of behaviour without so much as raising an eyebrow.

Jack Morrison, Nadia Nerina and Charles Gordon on board the *Queen Mary*
On the boat, Jack, in true character, lost no time
in leap-frogging cousinhood to brotherhood.

The Hawker Siddeley 125/600B
Someone said that the jet would have to be sold. What do you mean,
the jet would have to be sold? We didn't even know the jet existed.

**Isadore Walton: the progenitor of
Cedar** A man who never ventured to
take one step forward when half a step
would suffice.

**Arnold Ziff: Jack Morrison's son-
in-law** He liked to keep his feet where
every Yorkshireman likes to keep his
feet: firmly on the ground.

Sir Timothy Bevan: Barclays Bank
He was a man of high intelligence
and low boiling-point.

**Deryk Vander Weyer: Barclays
Bank** One of the best, if not the best,
general managers produced by Barclays
in recent history.

Godfrey Chandler: Cazenove
Unquestionably worthy of
his legendary reputation.

Sir Michael Richardson: Cazenove
The consummate negotiator.

Jasper Knight: Unilever
He said, 'I didn't say anything
about coming out of Cedar'.

William Broadfield: Unilever
It is to his everlasting credit that
he made the acquisition by Cedar of
Amal a resignation issue.

Derrick Hanson: Barclays Bank
He was no innocent novice, but a
tough-minded, cultured northerner.

Donald Bardsley:
London and County Bank
The button-presser of
the financial avalanche.

John Gillum: Samuel Montagu
He elected to stay upstairs with the
institutions and their advisers.

Ray Wheeler: Hambros The clear
advice from Wheeler marked the
beginning of the estrangement between
the Morrisons and the institutions.

Alan Glass: Cedar executive
director 'Without that plucky young
accountant standing up in that room,
we may have been there forever.'

Yusuf Ahmed Of the executive
directors, he, with Alan Watt, was the
most liked and trusted by the
Morrisons.

Leonard Sainer: the solicitor
Standing by a portrait of his master, Sir Charles Clore.

Buckingham Gate
A Rolls Royce building, let to a Rolls
Royce tenant. The painful property
bone of contention between the
Morrisons and the institutions.

The 'Marie Hall'
Created by Stradivari in 1709. Purchased
at Sotheby's in 1968 by an ecstatic
Jack Morrison; later sold in one of
his darkest hours.

whilst he perused the copy from his winged armchair. Many times in the past I had experienced at first-hand their exultations when success was rampant; Michael and David were prone to screeching with glee, and the pitch of their frenzy could almost be heard down the entire stretch of Pall Mall: it was not a pleasant sound.

This new romance between Cedar and the public also inspired a pandering to Jack's musical interest, but not I feel to his taste. Tens of thousands of copies of a plastic record, the first floppy disc of its kind, were circulated by direct mailshot. This was clearly the manifestation of comparative unimportance which O'Brien had in mind in his plan to drive the secondaries out of business through C&CC; it had, too, a title which would have brought tears of joy to course down O'Brien's cheeks: 'Don't pay us, we'll pay you'. The lyrics were in the same strain, the reprise was 'I'm with Cedar because they know what money is all about'. If the institutional directors who ostensibly knew what money was all about had the temerity to play the record to their wives, they may have been met with stupefication, for it is a commercial truism that the wives of non-executive directors, even if they had broad musical tastes, are noted for being considerably more down to earth and more realistic than their husbands in their assessment of his new board friends and acquaintances.

The TV advertising campaign was distinctly competent and innovative. Today financial advertising is a mainstay of TV advertising. In the early 1970s very few financial companies advertised on television, none of the banks, and only one or two building societies; but this did not stop Cedar. Fischer declared at board meetings that in the US the banks and savings institutions were major advertisers and that it was bound to happen here. He was right. He said that other banks would follow Cedar. He was right. Cedar and its television advertising programme became a major talking point within the media and the square mile. It spent what was a great amount in those days; the campaign was professional and effective, and it achieved its purposes as the public at large became increasingly aware of Cedar.

Sooner or later, however, Fischer, being Fischer, was going to overdo it. He did so when he persuaded Michael and Jack that they ought to launch a gifts campaign, specifically to attract deposits. It was April 1973, and *The Times* hooked it, caught it and threw it back beautifully. 'Premium offers have hit the big time. Who wants a plastic daffodil for buying a packet of detergent if you can get a free colour television, a free freezer, for depositing £5,000 with Cedar Holdings?'

Yes, this really is an extract from *The Times*. It goes on, 'Free offers have been the backbone of bank pushing in America for many years, but Cedar has the honour of being the first to introduce the scheme into this country. Surprise, surprise, one of the company's managing directors, David Fischer is an American. There are many more gifts in the £300 deposit section of the Cedar catalogue. Roll up and take your pick from branded blenders, from silver-plated Georgian candelabra *à la* Liberace and the usual range of pots, pans, kettles, power drills. In the £750 range the emphasis is more sporting with a pair of water skis, a climbing frame and a golf trolley.' The gifts catalogue was later inserted in a Sunday supplement and the down-to-earth *Yorkshire Post* took up another point: 'Having long believed that the law prescribed terrible penalties for those offering gifts for inducement to buy shares, I was astonished when a glossy leaflet with scores of inviting colour photographs dropped from my copy of the *Telegraph* colour magazine last week'.

There was much more of this elsewhere. The American-style gifts offer tied to the return from sacred deposits smacked of shady inducement; it was legal, but was this the spirit of British banking? The murmur was that we did not want this sort of thing here. But it was not only the banking community and the commentators who had their hackles raised, for in that mysterious way in which the public responds to overtures, including the symphonic blasts from politicians, it gave its own verdict: not for us. By early summer 1973 the campaign was dropped; the candelabras and the power drills rusted in the warehouse and although it was known that the Morrisons were not waterskiers nor mountain climbers, there were rumours which proved to be unfounded that they were taking up golf.

However, Jack and Michael Morrison and David Fischer, glowing over Cedar's national prominence, had something much closer to their hearts to think about, something about which they were truly emotional – the acquisition of Amal by Cedar.

*   *   *

One of the most overpowering openings of a chapter in any novel is the commencing rolling Tolstoyan sentence, surging on to the reader's mind with overwhelming intensity, that what Vronsky and Anna Karenina most feared, the consummation of their love affair, had at long last happened. Other writers have spent volumes trying to describe this most tremulous of human situations. Made aware that the profound event has taken place, the reader is moved by its passionate inevitability, nothing more needs to be expressed, its awful implications conveyed in full by that great master in one thought, in one great sentence. It would be banal to suggest by even the most tenuous stretch of the imagination, that there is a resonance between Vronsky and Anna and the corporate union between Cedar and Amal – except in one respect. Anna was doomed from that event, from that consummation, from that sentence. And, when on 29 June 1973 Cedar finally merged with Amalgamated Securities Limited, so were the Morrisons.

At long last, the Morrisons had made it. They had achieved their most relentlessly pursued objective; what they had wanted to happen for a long time had happened; what some had feared would happen, had happened. Anna's heart-rending decision to hurl herself under the wheels of that merciless train, is, for me, one of the most moving accounts in literature of a fatal doom-laden end. The aftermath for the Morrisons of this deadly consummation, was also in its own way moving, but in the world of business, of commerce, in the competitiveness of money making, in fighting not to lose it, the least romantic feelings come to the fore and the least romantic means of expression. On the fate of the Morrisons, when Cedar finally got Amal, an institutional friend said to me in terms which were no less exact for being so brutal, 'They have not only shot themselves in the foot, they have put a noose round their necks'.

So Cedar took over Amal. So the merger took place, and the arithmetical terms gave no immediate foreboding of the deadly consequences. Cedar was valued at £20 million, nearly the same as Amal. It issued £23 million worth of its shares and convertibles, and it acquired all of Amal. Cedar issued its shares at a price of 53 pence per share, earlier in the year they had been as high as 100 pence: Amal was taken over at a price of 220 pence per share, but earlier in the year they had stood at less than half that price. So the Morrisons' dearest objective Amal, standing at the highest price in its history, was being acquired by Cedar, its price at the lowest in its history. So the Morrisons, in accepting new Cedar shares and new Cedar convertibles in already owning half of Amal, had now decisively increased their stake in Cedar, just as they always planned to do. They now owned as much of the enlarged Cedar as the institutions. Now they were happy. But not for long.

On the announcement of the merger, the *Financial Times*, as usual, hit the nail on the head. 'Cedar's merger with Amalgamated Securities was a signal for the former premium rating to come to an end, and this year Cedar's price has dropped from 90 pence to 30 pence'. It was no longer a well-known innovative bank with its own clear identity and with its own premium rating, based on the secured borrowings of 60,000 plus customers on second mortgages; it was a hybrid second mortgage lending company or a hybrid property investment and development company, whichever way you looked at it. A second mortgage lending company was engaged in the business of providing financial services to the public and there was a clear method of valuing such a company. A property investment and development company was engaged in the business of increasing the value of its assets; there was a clear (though, in respect of developments, a thoroughly imperfect) method of valuing such a company. The shares of each type of undertaking were valued on completely different criteria. Merging both companies meant that two and two equalled less than four. How much less was horribly apparent within days.

The Morrisons had put their two valuable separate golden eggs, all they possessed, into one basket. They had committed an act of irreversible investment folly. But this was not all. In wanting to redress the contingent diminution from the £6 million convertible stock taken up by the Amal shareholders on the merger terms, they arranged for their family trusts, already stuffed up to the gills with Cedar shares, Cedar loan stock and Amal loan stock, to purchase these further Cedar convertibles. In order to take them up, the Morrison trusts borrowed £1 million from Williams and Glynn (The Royal Bank of Scotland) for this very purpose. In creating this substantial liability, the trustees would have had to take into account that if anything catastrophic ever happened to Cedar, the Morrisons would not only lose everything they had owned personally, but their trusts would be in serious debt. It is against all rules of prudence for a trust to have only one single asset; it is wholly irresponsible if it goes into debt in order to add to that single asset; it is in a very grey area, if this single asset should also be the only asset comprising the security for that debt.

From the date of the merger, everything started to go wrong, externally and internally. The Morrisons thought that the consummation would be an end to their problems; it was in fact a beginning. The price of Cedar having already dropped with the market, plummeted for the simple reason that its long-standing premium rating based on well-esteemed single-minded specialism had been erased. There were also a lot of shares floating around seeking a home in the market. As the price fell, in addition to the £1 million borrowed by the trusts, the Morrisons began borrowing personally to purchase more shares in Cedar to bolster up the price, sincerely convinced that the business was materially undervalued. They recommended the shares to their family, to friends, to acquaintances, to brokers. They were not in any mood to listen to advice, to be told that it is always a futile exercise at any time to purchase in a falling market, that it was rash if not bordering on financial lunacy to do so, when there was a good market reason for that fall. Cedar had lost its premium rating for good reason, the market knew it, the market was adjusting the price, and by the very nature of the market, always over-sensitive upwards or downwards, adjustments were excessive.

But in market terms, what is excessive on Monday is over-cautious on Tuesday. So prices are marked up or down. The market is in a constant state of flux. It reacts to the slightest whisper or shout, and when it reacts to actual facts, it is already reflecting the signs of the hotline, the communications between the more alert to the more intelligent to the more frightened. There are many men with a nose for claret, but there are not so many with a nose for the market. These men are worth more than their weight in carats. They rely on their noses not on facts. They are the necromancers, the olifactory experts, the witch-doctors of the market, and the last thing they need for their nose is privileged information. Despite global investment and electronic precision the market nose is as essential as ever. If it smells right, buy it: if it smells wrong, sell it. The nose always wins. In the case of Cedar, the nose led the way.

The Morrisons thought the price was based on earnings, on asset values, on merit. But no amount of purchases in the market, whatever the stream of press releases of new ventures could increase the price; nothing could restore Cedar's traditional premium rating. Cedar had lost its special charm, it was no longer the blue chip amongst the secondaries. It may have been criticised, and justifiably, for some of its activities, for being brash, for being impetuous and cocky, but it had been respected for having one of the most powerful board of directors in the City. It also was admired for its financial strength and its concentrated specialism. It had deserved, to a large extent, the market's assessment. Now it was a hybrid. The premium rating had gone for ever. And the price kept on dropping.

A director who knew this was going to happen and who severely opposed the acquisition of Amal was William Broadfield. In this he was not so much influenced by the views I had imparted to him when I had left Spey, but more so by Izzy Walton's, which were simple: Cedar was in the lending business; Amal was in the property business. Broadfield also harked back to the original Unilever entry when the Morrisons had made it clear that the two companies were separate and would remain separate. William tried to dissuade the Morrisons and finding he was unable to do so, said he would have to resign. They were quite alarmed and rightly so. A resignation by an institutional representative would have scuttled merger plans there and then. Desperate calls were made to Blackfriars at higher levels and Broadfield very reluctantly agreed to stay on, the understanding being that he was doing so for reasons of loyalty and solidarity but he was nevertheless vigorously opposed to the merger and that he would be replaced quietly some months later. In the light of the Morrisons' final anguish, William Broadfield's resignation issue has an unforgettable echo.

I knew Jack was obsessed about control but I had not thought he would ever go to the lengths of putting Michael and himself and his family trusts in such jeopardy. The Morrisons had believed that the share price, after the merger, was bound to go upwards. They had believed there was never going to be a rainy day, that Cedar was gilt-edged, that nothing could ever go wrong. They were astounded, when post-merger, when post-consummation, the price fell. It had never occurred to Jack and Michael that their personal financial strength lay not so much in Cedar, but in the separate conservative affluent Amal. They never realised that they were particularly respected by the institutions and by the various advisers for being independently rich; it had never impinged upon them that the quality of their standing, as the bankers they strove so hard to be and the respect in which they were held, was at a high level for this very reason.

In his chairman's statement in the 30 June 1973 accounts Jack said: 'The merger with Amalgamated enlarges the group and provides an asset strength that will enable full advantage to be taken of the opportunities for expanding the Group's activities. The Group's bank premises and properties as valued now amount to £39.9 million. At the present time the major development in hand is Buckingham Gate SW1 which is expected to be completed in June 1975.' The small print, Izzy Walton's particular *épicerie*, contained as usual more interesting delicacies than the large print. The most succulent morsel was the note referring to Amal's property valuation. The figure of £39.9 million included Buckingham Gate, a development comprising over a quarter in value of the total portfolio properties, of which not even a quarter was completed. This building had been valued as if it had been fully completed and also as if it had been fully let – although it would be a further two years before the front entrance of the building could be opened for the tenants.

Buckingham Gate was the apple of the Morrisons' eye. It was also to be the new head office of the Bank, another small print morsel, the first time it being disclosed that Cedar planned to move from one side of St James's Park to the other. As a single venture, more time was spent on Buckingham Gate by the Morrisons than on any other. Originally Amal acquired two short leaseholds in Chandos Court, a key building on the Buckingham Gate site. The site and building costs were estimated in 30 June 1973 at £5.3 million and provisions were made for a total figure in the accounts of nearly £10 million. The difference represented the valuation surplus of around £4.5 million. This amount was given full value in arriving at the net assets of Amal; it was a substantial part of the revaluation surplus, paid for in full by the Cedar shareholders, yet it was not much more than a hole in the ground, nor did it have full planning consent. Moreover it was going to be two years before any tenant, including the owner, could move in. Yet, astoundingly it was valued as if it was already completed and already fully let.

The October AGM, held as usual at the Dorchester was cheerless. Jack never one to give any sign of gloom, never bearish, was nonetheless cautious. 'There appears to be a growing demand for The Bank's services, but market conditions, which have arisen since the balance sheet date, must be viewed with caution. Although current high levels of interest rates could have the effect of reducing profit margins and result in a temporary diminution in the value of long-term investments, the directors continue to have confidence in the future progress of the enlarged group'.

A month later, in early November, a month after the less than exhilarating AGM, Cedar launched its ambitious investment programme, by way of unit trusts – three in all. This was Philip Johnstone's baby or babies. He had never represented Coal on the Cedar board as this post had been filled by Reg Edward, but, having left the Coal Board in April, he had become the full-time managing director of Cedar's fund management subsidiary, with a seat on the main board. The three unit trusts were called Cedar British, Cedar European and Cedar Overseas. It covered the globe. Not even the Morrisons could go further.

There was an interesting innovation, typical of Michael and David's fertile minds. For every £100 invested, a loan facility of four times was made available. *The Times* commented: 'A life assurance subsidiary at this stage, would have been more useful, without a life assurance subsidiary Cedar would not be able to market the really popular items in the investment and saving industrys' present repertoire'. Michael and David had been watching the growth of Abbey Life and the beginnings of Hambro Life, and Charles Knight of Phoenix had been gently pushing an association on these lines between his own group and Cedar. Plans for a joint venture with Phoenix's New Zealand offshoot had already been concluded. Jack, especially keen, had entered these discussions with enthusiasm; he had made plans to be in New Zealand in December, to consolidate the association, although it was known that the chief executive of Phoenix's New Zealand insurance company did not share Charles Knight's strong support for this association.

Philip Johnstone had a first-rate market reputation. He was a chartist; what was more, he even drew his own charts. The Johnstone charts indicated that the share markets were at their lowest point and that markets were at the top of a fifty-four-year interest rate cycle. His charts, like all charts, always prove what they want to prove on a long view; they are a seismic geological history of the past. They cannot take into account sudden acts of God, acts of legislation, acts of cataclysmic events. Patrick Hutber of the *Sunday Telegraph* expressed his view in no uncertain manner: 'This is an offer you can refuse from Cedar Holdings'.

But the advertising campaign was well conceived; full-page advertisements in the papers, two-thirds of the page splashed with a striking photograph of three youngish, bowler-hatted, pin-striped, black-brollied ecstatic City gents jumping and laughing with joy on the steps of the Royal Exchange, an outline of the Bank of England suggesting association and security in the background. Their unbounded joy was because they were the lucky ones who had invested or were going to invest in these three new Cedar trusts. But there was a jarring commercial-climbing element inherent in the metabolism of all the secondaries eager for recognition; a bank higher up the status ladder would not have used the Old Lady as a backdrop, nor would it have allowed one of the 'gents' in the photograph to wear what no City gentleman wore in those days – slip-on shoes. This particular advertisement, a sad last laugh, was to be Cedar's last declamation of its corporate vibrancy.

The Cedar price had dropped to 30 pence. Still shouting in the wind, Michael and David kept on issuing press releases. One blown straight into waste-paper oblivion, stated that with the absorption of Amal, the net underlying value of the shares was 50–60 pence per share. The price kept moving downwards. The Morrisons were obsessed with the dropping share price. They could not believe what was happening. The share price should have gone up, not down; how was it possible that the value of Cedar combined with Amal could now have fallen to well below the value before it had even acquired Amal? They watched with horror as the price kept on falling, and by the time the deposit run began its inexorable lap of death, they were so locked onto the downward swoop of the share price, so transfixed by the dramatic erosion of Cedar's market capitalisation, so aghast at the tumbling of their net worth, that they were incapable of squaring up to the deposit run and incapable of providing the qualities of leadership which were desperately required.

*   *   *

During the summer Cedar had first produced its own newsletter: there were two issues only, the first in July, the second in November. There were now over 250 people employed; a decade earlier in Park Street the staff numbered three, including Rose the tea lady. The newsletter was A4 in size and the contents were a model for any company morale booster; it was first-rate in concept and design.

It had of course the inevitable wooden title, 'The Cedar Log'. The November issue makes uneasy reading in view of the ensuing events. The headline on the front page was 'Records all the way for Cedar'. It stated that the previous year's profits as at 30 June had been made during a period of rapid growth due to the benefit of the efforts of a hardworking staff. Bank customers were up from 60,000 to 100,000. There was a large photograph of Buckingham Gate and the caption: 'Now under construction, a tower block comprising flats and offices and a 10,000 square foot roof garden, a novel and exciting departure in central London'. There were stories of acquisitions, and of members of the staff. Amongst the latter, was a feature about Mr Bates, in charge of stationery, who worked from Cedar's new storage depot in Old Street. He explained: 'We have to carry some 100,000 envelopes. It sounds a lot. But 20,000 window envelopes and about 10,000 of the conventional type are used every week'. This was a lot of envelopes for a so-called secondary bank. The profile also stated that Mr Bates was the husband of Rose; she had been promoted from being the tea lady and was now 'responsible for directors and management catering at Pall Mall'. Perusing this so many years later, I found the story of dear old Rose's promotion oddly touching. Jack had always treated her with special consideration since the Park Street days and then, of all things, I suddenly found my heart racing at the thought that she and her husband may have invested their life's savings in Cedar shares.

In late November 1973, the forerunner of nasty months to come in the lives of many, the underground tremors of liquidity had risen to the surface. The dam was full. At any moment it would burst; the moment when it did, can be fixed precisely. It was late on Monday afternoon November 26 1973 when it was announced that Donald Bardsley, a respected City banker, who had recently joined a very unrespectable secondary bank as an executive director, had resigned from the Board. Which secondary bank was it? It was London and County. Who was its head? He was a Mr Gerald Caplan. Who was a celebrated non-executive director? He was Jeremy Thorpe, the Leader of the Liberal Party no less. And who was Donald Bardsley who unsluiced the dam?

NINE

The Tailspin

I always connect Donald Bardsley with our Spey board table. He was, like Derrick Hanson, another ex-Martins Bank stalwart. They had learned at one of the best schools, for Martin's had an excellent reputation especially for administration, and Bardsley deciding not to show Barclays how to improve theirs, favoured joining Hill Samuel where he was given a top operational job which included monitoring the branch expansion programme. The first new branch was to be in St James's Square, by the King Street corner, not far from Wilton's before it moved to Bury Street. The formidable chairman of Hill Samuel was Lord Keith. He had recently been appointed the chairman of Rolls Royce and, by operating from St James's, he could allow Robert Clarke, his Hill Samuel deputy, the luxury of a little less of his elbow at Wood Street, whilst he was getting the aero engine business into flight; which he did subsequently with enormous success, to some people's surprise, but not at all to those who knew him well. He was one of the very few merchant bankers who truly understood how an industrial company should be run, *vide* his success as chairman of Beechams, Standard Telephones and Rolls Royce.

My brother Max was Hill Samuel's architect and he worked with Bardsley on the specifications for this new branch, splendid even for a City merchant bank. The ground-floor banking hall had a capacious slowly-rising spiral staircase leading to the first-floor offices, and to Kenneth Keith's resplendent West End suite. It included a superb dining room and board room, whose centrepiece was a specially-designed beige oak board table, easily and comfortably seating more than two dozen directors. Max could not solve the means of getting the more notable occupants and guests entering the banking hall from the St James's Street entrance up to the first floor, the King Street entrance being considered overly modest, and it was Nadia who suggested the spiral staircase. Max, uplifted, designed it quite beautifully.

I once had a confidential lunch with Kenneth Keith in his new office suite. It was autumn 1971, each of us testing out the other; he was sounding out, it was hardly audible, whether I might possibly be interested after my withdrawal from Spey in associating with Hill Samuel; I was wondering how I could possibly ally myself to someone who was so outrageously tall and clever, surrounded by equally outrageously tall and clever acolytes. One of these, Harry Moore, now alas the forgotten man of Hill Samuel, I had especially admired for many years, though from a somewhat lower physical (and intellectual) standpoint. At lunch, Keith, whose sense of humour is less limited than his patience, was amused to learn that I had acquired his board table after he had decreed that the St James's boardroom should be used for other purposes. I had much earlier acquired the old M. Samuel board table when Dick Bearsted agreed to merge his family bank with Keith's Philip Hill Higginson. This merger had been pushed by Bearsted's number two, the hugely talented Julian Melchett, who regretted it (quite rightly) before he himself saw a door marked exit. Keith, as always from any tussle, emerged victorious, and with Clarke, went on to make Hill Samuel one of the most enterprising merchant banks in the City. Melchett left to run British Steel, which was child's play after being evened out by Keith's mettle. It was after this, and after Keith's aggrandisement diversions, a merger with MEPC, a large property group (believable), and a merger with Slater Walker (unbelievable), that a well-known Episcopalian Wall Street banker coined the name Hill Schlemiel. I do not know what he would call it today now that it is part of (and the sore thumb of) the Trustee Savings Bank group. M. Samuel and Co, the Bearsted family bank, started by Marcus Samuel, the East End Jewish business genius, the peddler of shells who founded Shell Oil, seems to have reached a contorted and tortuous destination very far removed from its original exotic heritage.

It was around this time that I met Donald Bardsley. I probably struck him as his architect's rather odd brother, who had an arcane partiality for discarded bank board tables (I do); he on the other hand struck me as a fine old terror, getting the results he wanted, certainly terrifying Max with the tight budgets and precisely maintained timetables. Just the man of character and experience to put London and County into order. If he could not do it, no one could.

There has always been an element of mystery why Bardsley, who as it turned it out was the actual button-presser of the financial avalanche, a man with such a superior banking pedigree, could have been persuaded to leave his well-ordered job at Hill Samuel to join a secondary bank of the quality of London and County. This was, I guess, the nub of his dilemma; he was so clearly the perfect man to solve the London and County problem that, when asked to assuage the Old Lady's acute worries over the cabalistic activities of Gerald Caplan, the man of Martins with a Northern sense of duty felt that he must acquiesce. There was pressure, too, from Sir Brian Mountain, the chairman of the Eagle Star insurance group (also one of Keith's earliest supporters), which had a substantial shareholding in London and County with a representative on the board. The example of institutional associations having been set by Cedar, Caplan, ever desperate for respectability, was not one to desist from imitation with or without the need to resort to flattery.

The Caplan kettle of fish became a matter of serious concern to the Bank of England after the occurrence of three separate events. The first was in May 1971 when the leader of a major political party became a director; the second was in 1972 when London and County suddenly widened its activities into retail banking by way of an arrangement to operate two dozen branches within the department stores of United Drapery Group, also closely associated to Eagle Star; the third event, possibly the most alarming, was in early 1973 when Caplan did something rather strange in City terms. He took a full-page advertisement in the *Financial Times*. The headline was 'The Energy Generation', and his text started with the following words: 'The financial scene is experiencing a transformation inspired by a generation of individuals or, if you like, pioneers'. Guess who? This was too much for the Bank and indeed for many others. Very soon after, Caplan was informed that the Old Lady was not impressed by The Caplan Declaration, and that what London and County needed, and quickly, was a respected banking administrator. Bardsley, for his virtues, became that man. His appointment was warmly received.

Much has been learnt about Caplan since the crash, none of it endearing. The Department of Trade Report was crushing. It disclosed that the demise of London and County was due entirely to business defects rather than banking problems, and that it would have come to grief irrespective of any financial crisis. It also disclosed that Caplan was a liar and that he was flagrantly dishonest. He was in fact a five-feet ex-barrister known for his judo prowess and his fast foot-work who, according to the Report, ran his group 'like a monarch in a medieval court'. His most pronounced talent, it would seem, was to make the respectable unrespectable, though in his early days, when the Eagle Star association commenced, his activities were muted and much less evident. By the time he persuaded Jeremy Thorpe to come on to his board, he was already a controversial figure.

The Thorpe association caused more ripples than he could have intended; it certainly made London and County instantly more respectable, but it also made the Liberal Party and Jeremy Thorpe immediately less so. I had known Thorpe off and on since he was up at Oxford and it should be noted that whatever Thorpe's faults, he was a grown-up politician, far more so than his successor, David Steel, whose name has mostly belied his resolution. Thorpe's serious political principles, though not helpfully addressed by his dandyish appearance, were respected by serious politicians in other parties, not only by thinking Liberals such as Bonham Carter and Tanlaw.

Lord Tanlaw, brother of the Earl of Inchcape, a director of his family company and of other City companies, with whom I shared a passion for innovative clocks, and who had been a Liberal spokesman in the upper House, talked to me at the time about Thorpe's intention to join the London and County Board, and about his own vain endeavours to dissuade him. But Thorpe, like many politicians, was misguided by an exaggerated sympathy for the non-establishment figure and he went ahead, prompted not only because of Caplan's financial support for the Party and its leader, but also because of the link with Eagle Star. There was a blaze of publicity; for Caplan there was prestige, but for Thorpe's party there was embarrassment.

By summer 1973, when Bardsley joined London and County, there had already been several external signs of a curiously managed company in business difficulties whose days were numbered. Bardsley, to his consternation, quickly discovered it was a veritable can of worms. When the 1973 accounts of London and County were published in August, just after Bardsley had joined the group, the *Daily Telegraph* commented: 'Shareholders should find several things in this latest Annual Report to cause them some distress'. Bardsley, the very new boy, was himself in great distress. He was particularly incensed that banking fees, amounting to 20% of the total, were taken in as profits at the time the loans were granted, instead of being spread over their lifetime. He insisted that this should be stopped, and Caplan, in no position to argue with the Bank of England's 'man', had to scramble for profits in time for the interim results due in November. As the Department of Trade Report subsequently disclosed, it was not so much a scramble as a hectic series of fraudulent manoeuvres.

Caplan, in a last-ditch attempt to smokescreen his balance sheet, made a bid for the substantial Inveresk Paper Company. Despite a technical problem which arose on the offer documents, Caplan insisted that Bardsley sign the board minute formally approving the document. Bardsley felt there was undue duress and said he would only do so if Eagle Star had approved the document. Caplan assured him that they had. Bardsley telephoned the Eagle Star board representative at home that evening to discover that Caplan had not received any such approval nor had he even asked for it. First thing next morning, Thursday 22 November, Bardsley promptly resigned. Caplan true to form did not issue a public announcement until the following Monday. The interim results were, however, announced as planned, on the Friday, the day after Bardsley's resignation.

His abrupt surprising resignation caught the financial headlines smack in the middle of the City pages of the morning papers on Tuesday 27th. The press was vitriolic. The *Guardian*'s headline was 'Thorpe's battered bank'. Some of the commentators, particularly those close to the money markets, sensed there was something more ominous, that there were signs of a possible deposit run. On Tuesday the money market brokers knew there was a problem; on Wednesday they knew it was a serious problem; on Thursday they knew it was far more than a serious problem, it was a definite deposit run.

The price of London and County's shares, at a peak level of 303 pence earlier in the year and at 130 pence before the resignation, fell sharply nosediving to less than 60 pence. A month earlier, Keyser Ullman purchased certain loans from London and County for £10 million.* Two of their managing directors, Jack Dellal and Stanley

* Keyser Ullman purchased Dalton Barton in early 1973. Keyser Ullman based in the City and conducting the conventional business of a second line merchant bank was run by two brothers-in-law Roland Franklin and Ian Stoutzker: Dalton Barton based in Knightsbridge and conducting the conventional business of a secondary property bank was owned and run by two inseparable friends Jack Dellal and Stanley Van Gelder. The latter twosome were responsible for a spectacular secondary banking property transaction. In 1972 Keyser Ullmann purchased a

Van Gelder, instantly recognised that the Bardsley resignation had all the ingredients of a terminal disaster.

They took immediate action on Thursday 29 and called an urgent meeting at their Knightsbridge offices; it included Gerald Caplan, Jeremy Thorpe, two *apparatchiks* from London and County, and Sir Brian Mountain. Jim Keogh arrived at 11.30 pm. No one can now remember for sure who telephoned him or who asked him to attend, but it is thought it was Sir Brian Mountain. As soon as Keogh heard the facts, he there and then telephoned Alec Dibbs to agree a meeting at NatWest for first thing next morning. It started at 9.30 am attended not only by Keogh, but also by Pat Matthews of First National Finance who appeared on the scene for the first time. No one can now remember for sure who telephoned him and who asked him to attend, but it is thought that it was Jim Keogh. At the NatWest meeting on Friday morning, it was decided to mount a rescue. That afternoon accountants from the various parties started inspecting the books. They worked at it non stop.

The Saturday press commenting on the general financial situation, took the general line that London and County's difficulties could affect large parts of the banking and property market sectors. A journalist friend told me that he had wanted his Saturday article to have as its heading the motto of London and County. His editor said no. The motto was 'With every step we gather strength'.

Of particular concern that Saturday morning was the situation at London and County's twenty-three retail branches, housed in United Drapery stores all over the country, all of which – their unique marketing feature – would be open as usual on a Saturday. Reporters were sent to discover what was going on at several of the branches: Whiteleys in Queensway, Arding and Hobbs in Clapham, Owen and Owen in Southampton, Ely's in Wimbledon. There were queues at the banking counters, but they were orderly. At Owen and Owen withdrawals were limited to £5 per person, a cashier was quoted as saying 'there were two or three times as many customers as usual'. It

---

property company, Central and District, by way of shares for £69 million, a merger in some respects with similar overtones as Cedar's merger with Amal. In September 1973, just three months before the crisis, Dellal and Van Gelder instigated the sale of Central and District for £97 million realising a cash profit of £28 million, say £200 million in today's value. With so much cash in the till, Keyser Ullmann looked around anxiously for borrowers, one of them was Gerald Caplan.

was this spectre of public queues at branches over the country which had first startled Keogh and prompted him to telephone Dibbs late the previous Thursday night. The accountants continued working on the books throughout Saturday and Sunday.

The Sunday press gave London and County wide coverage. The consensus was that since the Bardsley resignation, confidence was diminishing fast, and the knock-on effect meant that the other secondaries had already been seriously affected. There were also vague comments that a rescue was in progress. As always, Patrick Hutber, an outstanding journalist in the Harold Wincott mould, was to the point: his final comment on the situation, 'Now to Mr Thorpe. I warned him on this page more than a year ago that London and County was not a company of the calibre with which he should be associated'.

On Monday morning, following a hectic weekend and three days of intensive talks and investigations, an announcement was made that London and County had been rescued by a consortium headed by 'Mr Pat Matthew's First National Finance'. Jeremy Thorpe and the Eagle Star representative were to stay on board; the rest of the directors including the Pioneer were to go over. Alec Dibbs was quoted as saying: 'The backing for the project should reassure depositors and the City, that it is a goer. This is a very substantial commitment, about £25 to £30 million'.

During that week when the deposit run at Cedar commenced its scourge, as confidence plummeted throughout the secondary banking sector, and as deposits were just not being renewed, the gorgeous ever-available tap of limitless deposits had been turned off. Now it was not merely a matter of paying higher interest rates. Michael asked Yusuf Ahmed, Amal's financial director, to contact Cedar's money broker. The broker did not mince his words: 'It is not a question of paying half a point or one point or two points, more. They just won't lend at all. No one wants to know you'. Cedar was forced to use its existing facility with the Royal Bank of Scotland. Ahmed wondered anxiously how long it would last. It was not in fact until after the announcement of the London and County rescue, nearly a week after the announcement of the Bardsley resignation, that Michael and David made a truly positive move. Even then, when every hour was crucial, it was in slow motion. Eventually on Monday 3 December Michael and David went to see Gillum at Samuel Montagu. His immediate advice was that an urgent meeting should be held with the institutions. They phoned around to set up such a meeting, and Broadfield, going up to Glasgow for Izzy Walton's AGM, did not even know about it until it was too late.

By the previous Friday morning, roughly when the London and County rescuers were meeting at NatWest with Jim Keogh, a similar full-scale Cedar meeting should have been held as the bank went into free-fall. But at this most crucial moment Michael and David were in shock. Instead of being decisive they were mentally immobile. It could be said that it was excusable; but not for more than a day or two at the most. Izzy Walton would have put the key into the ignition and got the engine running immediately: he was a genuine driving force. He would have assembled the institutional directors plus its merchant bank, plus its clearing bank, plus Keogh by Friday at the latest. Precious time was lost, and, as the days sped by, signs appeared for the first time that Michael and David were beginning to lose credibility, by far the most essential commodity for leaders to retain in any crisis.

A week after the Bardsley resignation, on Tuesday 4 December the Scottish Metropolitan AGM took place in Glasgow. Broadfield went up on Monday evening and stayed at the Central Hotel. As soon as he arrived at the meeting, Izzy Walton took him aside urgently to tell him how alarmed he was about the run on Cedar's deposits, and asked what was being done about it. Broadfield was stunned as this was his first intimation that Cedar even had a problem; he had not heard from anyone at Cedar, not at any time, after the Bardsley resignation. He was not only the longest serving institutional director, he was not only a friend of the Morrisons but, as Izzy would know from past experience, he was the first person whom Michael or David would normally have telephoned if there were any business hitch. Why hadn't they got in touch with him immediately as they had always done in the past? Broadfield was also surprised that Izzy was so well informed, for it was fairly widely known that the Morrisons and Izzy were no longer on the best of terms.

Bad news travels fast, but on this occasion it did not live up to its reputation. At the end of the AGM there was an urgent message from Bert Aylmer, an assistant of Cob Stenham's, for Broadfield to telephone him immediately. 'Bill, there is a crisis at Cedar. A meeting has been called for this afternoon. Can you come down straight away?' Broadfield expostulated as to why he had only now been told about the crisis. How was it that Walton already knew? Why had he not been informed earlier? He would not only have given Glasgow a miss but something could and should have been done about having such a meeting much sooner. He could not get there in time. A colleague, Hans Uewe, who had never met the Morrisons before, went instead. He knew no one there.

As presented by Michael and David, to the institutions that afternoon, the impression made was that yes, the run on deposits was very serious, but not over alarming; that in their estimation they needed £20–£25 million, straight away and for the foreseeable future. Michael was extremely agitated, which he did not attempt to conceal. He also gave the impression that he was more panicky about the dropping share price than the run on deposits. Perhaps he needed his father's guidance. Yet at this moment of crisis Michael avoided telling his father, who was on one of his cruises, *en route* to New Zealand, that anything was amiss. Michael's inclination was to inform Jack only when the crisis was over. His concern for his father was exemplary but dreadfully misjudged, not only from Cedar's point of view but also from his father's. If Jack Morrison had returned immediately his very presence would have immediately galvanised Michael and David, and it is also worth venturing the thought that Jack may not himself have suffered such a deep and irreversible shock.

At this first meeting after the run, when Broadfield was unable to attend and when the pitchforked Hans Uewe listened with amazement, the institutions were not only friendly but fully supportive. Yes, of course, they would help. They would put up £25 million straight away: it could be secured against the properties, documents could be prepared immediately, Barclays might also arrange some sort of standby in case of further need. Here, too, they miscalculated; they were in too low a gear, available cash was going out in torrents, and a decisive rescue could have been achieved there and then if the institutions themselves had provided the standby until it had actually been obtained from Barclays. In effect this meeting was badly structured. It should not have taken place without Barclays, nor should it have taken place without Keogh or one of his colleagues.

But what was most remarkable was that no immediate announcement was made that this very formidable commitment of £25 million had been unequivocally provided. A well-drafted rapidly-announced statement *à la* Alec Dibbs at this time would almost certainly have quelled the deposit run. All that appeared in the press and then days later on Friday 14 December, was confirmation from Brian Oram who had been telephoned by a journalist, that the institutions had made a commitment to provide standby facilities. Michael and David were not exclusively concerned with the deposit run, they were thinking of the shareholders and not enough of the depositors. They clearly believed such an announcement would destroy the price of the shares. What they should have understood, as those at the Bank had always understood, what Keogh would have told them if he had been at the meeting, was that in a deposit run the depositors are given over-riding consideration and shareholders are not considered until after the deposit run has been successfully arrested.

But astonishingly no announcement was made and the deposit run continued unabatedly, and then thereafter instead of polarising on a single concentrated thrust at a single large-scale meeting of everyone concerned to prevent the situation getting worse, the two managing directors talked to everyone individually. Michael and David talked to calm their nerves, talking on the telephone, talking to each other, talking about talks, their own and others, passing messages, then repeating the messages to others: they talked to Gillum at Samuel Montagu, they talked to Higginson at Herbert Smith, they talked to each of the four institutional representatives, then they rehashed what each person had said to each of the others. Cash figures were circulated daily to the institutions, as bulletins, as background information, with no comments. Then, as if there were no other matters to worry about, Michael and David issued a press announcement on the Thursday about Buckingham Gate, stating that detailed plans for its development had been approved. If anything, as a reminder of the further moneys required for its completion, it was setting a match to the tinder box. It was also another indication that the two cousins, obsessed about the share price, simply could not comprehend that the only thing to stop the run was an immediate injection of cash or firm commitments to provide cash.

Michael's actions and misuse of precious time should be compared and underlined with that of London and County. With the latter, an emergency meeting was called within two days of the deposit run, and significantly this meeting included Keogh. Early next morning there was a meeting at NatWest and it virtually continued non-stop through that day, Friday, and on the Saturday and Sunday – the rescuers' experts sifting through the loan book and the assets. On the Monday morning the rescue package was announced. The whole process starting with the emergency meeting on Thursday night had taken three full days – it was quick, tough and effective. The fact that

London and County had dry rot up to its eaves did not in any way deter its successful rescue.

Cedar, by comparison, had an impeccable structure, lavishly and almost extravagantly buttressed by enormously powerful supporters. At the London and County rescue there was a profusion of men with leadership qualities; and they showed their calibre by leading. At Cedar no one came forward. The comparison is cruelly odious. On the other hand, the institutions still regarded Cedar as a 'family bank'; they were over-hesitant and over-tentative and they found it difficult to take charge – this was something against their basic temperament, though if Hugh Jenkins of the Coal Board had been appointed a director months earlier, there is little doubt that things would have been different. The institutions discovered that the more Michael and David displayed their panic, the more their confidence in the family subsided, something that even they were surprised to experience after so many years of unstinting support. A new element crept in, a questioning, a disrespect, from one or two even a contempt, for Michael and David, which had never been there before; the disenchantment gathered momentum by the day.

We now come to the final week before the Bank of England meeting, the last days the Morrison family were in charge of their family bank. With the accumulating pressure, Michael and David had wilted, already perceived as two pitiful co-managing directors who were out of their depth, showing none of their habitual self-confidence. Monday, Tuesday, Wednesday. The week wore on, the deposit run continued, and Michael and David's panic increased. It expressed itself in more frequent and persistent phone calls, in hastily-organised small caucus meetings, in circulating the cash position of the institutions not once a day but twice a day, as if that in itself was a solution. Action was fragmented, there was no coherent plan, instead there was a dither of separate exhortations, mainly directed towards Barclays. The two cousins were totally inseparable, they were always together, if you saw one you saw the other, they fed on each other, ineffectual leaders searching for leadership; under severe pressure, fully stretched for the first time in their lives, they demonstrated during these last days, a pathetic lack of direction. And Michael had his own ghastly personal dilemma; he had still avoided telephoning his father, feeling sure that once he made the call, it would destroy Jack.

Then by an odd twist of timing on Thursday 13 December, Cedar's long-awaited approval from the Federal Reserve Bank came through for its proposed purchase of the Chester National Bank of New York. The bid had originally been made over a year earlier in October 1972 and had clearly had a long rough ride with the US authorities. The purchase cost to Cedar was £1.6 million in cash. Michael insisted on making an announcement; it was not only meaningless but counter-productive, stupefying as it did the institutions. On this day another vacuous press statement was also issued: that early in the New Year Cedar would open a branch in Holland. This caused further conster-nation and made the institutions feel even more nervous. How on earth, they asked each other, could this help the deposit run? Surely the two co-managing directors must realise that information of this nature, rather than bolstering confidence, would have the opposite effect? The institutions became more troubled and wondered what Michael and David were up to. The market, of course, treated the announcements with contempt, the shares kept dropping and were now standing at an all-time low of 21 pence.

By the end of this week, on the Friday, the institutional mood had shifted from that of a week ago. Relationships between the Morrisons and the institutions were still good, but the incessant spate of separate conversations, phone calls and meetings, and now these two slightly hysterical press announcements, had left them with a fuzzy impression, a lack of clarity and a rising anxiety that Michael and David were adrift, that they could not cope. They were all still on the same side, but somehow the goalposts had shifted and the strength of individual members of the team had altered. No on could put their finger on what had changed. It is a situation which can send tremors through the most stout-hearted, when the forwards find themselves on their own, when the team has somehow got itself into a new formation, its shape altered, when the captain suddenly realises that he is not in control, worse, that he is a target. Who, me? Yes. He then finds that he is himself an issue. In Cedar they had all been running around in circles for days, at a most critical time, and somehow the problem had become circular. Would Barclays help? Not really. Not at all. Would the institutions help? Well, yes. But they had already helped. What more was required of them? How much more? What did Samuel Montagu think? Why wasn't Gillum put in full charge by the Morrisons?

Days later than he should have done, on Friday 14 December, Michael decided that he would get the institutions together for a crisis meeting on a more formal basis over the weekend. That Friday evening was not a happy one. David Clement, the financial director of the Coal Board, had an urgent plea from Michael and David to see them. It was another example of fragmentation. Clement, in black tie, arrived cross and impatient in the early evening, on his way to a dinner. The past week had been amongst the most exacting of his life, the intricacies of the coal go-slow were unpleasant and nasty; to deal with it required a cool head. His chairman, Lord Ezra, was an exceptionally formidable man; Clement was known to be a strong financial man. They both had other immense problems with which to contend and, on this Friday evening, after an arduous week and late for his dinner, Clement was in no mood to listen to the emotional overtones of the appeal from the Morrisons. He listened courteously but with rising irritation and, though not unkind, he was distinctly peremptory in making his feelings known. The Coal Board pension fund would, he made clear, have to look at all the facts before committing any further funds. This was the first time the Morrisons heard other than encouraging words from one of the institutions in all the years of the heavyweight links. Michael was visibly winded.

It was arranged to have the weekend crisis meeting on Sunday, and on the surface it seemed a practical way of meeting the problems head on. The institutions were by now reeling, if not punch-drunk from the plethora of phone calls and exhortations; the shrill tones of Michael and David, ever shriller, were scratching at their normal placidity, uncovering deep institutional nerves.

The meeting was held that Sunday in David Fischer's flat in Hertford Street, Mayfair. It was the first time any of the institutional persons had ever visited. It was decorated sumptuously and expensively, after all, this was the personal abode of the joint managing director, a member of the family, no longer on his uppers, who had his impressive Portuguese manservant to serve the guests with a full array of refreshments. The talks went on and on and on and the decision was reached, eventually, to hold a full board meeting on the following Tuesday. But one institutional representative, the mild-mannered calm respectable man from Phoenix, Brian Oram, reached another conclusion. He decided that he had had enough of Michael and David's dithering and lack of leadership. He conveyed his concern immediately to his Phoenix colleagues, and recommended that they seek independent advice. As a result they made an important decision that Sunday night: to bring Hambros in as their advisers. It was the first overt indication of a procedural – possibly more sinister – cleavage between the institutions and the Morrisons. Ray Wheeler of Hambros was telephoned at home. Would he see the Morrisons as early as possible the next morning to acquaint himself with all the details? Yes. Would he please report back as quickly as possible. Yes.

That Sunday, Michael knew he had to inform his father. He could no longer put it off. He dreaded making the call; the most difficult he ever had to make. The effect on his father was exactly what he had feared; the effect on Absalom was still evident when several months later, in describing his ordeal to me, his voice faltered and stammered with emotion.

Early the next morning, Monday 17, Michael and David went over the money book. It was now in such a perilous state, they considered for the first time what assets could be sold quickly. They realised that the Sunday meeting had been a dismal failure, and they blamed the institutions. The Clement encounter of the previous Friday evening had also demoralised Michael, and all his ancient suspicions bred by his father came to the fore. He knew he had not been anywhere near his best on Sunday, and Oram's questioning worried him as he seemed to be taking the same line as Clement. David and he had done all they could to brief everyone, including Keogh and Galpin at the Discount Office. What more could they do? The shares were plunging. Their net assets were disappearing. Why didn't the institutions do something? Well, they had, or rather the Phoenix had, for Ray Wheeler as arranged, arrived for his meeting with them. Alan Glass was in attendance. Wheeler asked a lot of pertinent questions and departed. His advice to Phoenix was unambiguous; the institutions should immediately work together as a separate coherent entity. This clear advice from Wheeler marked the beginning of the estrangement between the Morrisons and the institutions. Talks would now take place without the knowledge of Michael and David.

At lunchtime the company secretary, Ronald Stanley, came into Michael's room. 'Mr Morrison, I have just had a call from the Stock Exchange. They are very concerned about the drop in our share price and are threatening suspension. They want us to make a statement. I said I would speak to you and would telephone them back.' Michael told Stanley to tell the Stock Exchange that a full board meeting was due to be held tomorrow afternoon, on the Tuesday, and that a statement could only be made after that meeting. Stanley passed the message on to the Stock Exchange. He had the impression that they were distinctly unhappy.

That Monday was the day of Barber's tough half-budget. The Chancellor announced his measures to cut expenditure and to reduce demand, to be imposed mostly in the public sector. Barber stated there were 'unprecedented uncertainties'. In the private sector, hire purchase was severely restricted and there was to be a development land tax. Uncertainty increased. Stock exchange prices fell sharply. The contagion of fear spread. The money market was in disarray. The corporate men in charge of their company's deposits switched to the larger banks; they were going for safety first and were uninterested in offers of higher deposit rates.

On Tuesday 18 December the price fell to 10p, valuing the company at £7.5 million. The deposit run continued unabated. The full Cedar board was due to meet in the afternoon at 3 pm. Stanley asked to see Michael and David. The Stock Exchange had telephoned again. With the share prices still dropping, they were very concerned and they now wanted to suspend the quotation. Michael told the flustered company secretary to inform the Stock Exchange that they couldn't make an announcement until after the board meeting scheduled for later that afternoon.

Towards the end of the morning, Alan Glass asked if he could speak to Michael and David. Why? What was the problem? Glass said that the institutions thought it would be an error for the board meeting to take place. He understood from Oram that the institutions were not too happy about it and would prefer it to be postponed; they wanted to have further talks amongst themselves and with Hambros. Michael and David were non-plussed and extremely disturbed. Meeting amongst themselves? The board meeting postponed? And why had they not been informed directly? Why now through Glass? What was this conduit between Glass and the institutions? They felt their positions, as joint managing directors, and as the family in control, had altered ominously. It seemed as if decisions were being made elsewhere. As the institutions did not want the meeting, it was cancelled and, from that moment onwards, Michael knew for certain that he had lost the initiative and the decisions were being made elsewhere. This decision to cancel the board meeting, as he later admitted, was a major blunder on his part. He wished he had stuck to his guns and had told Glass the meeting had to be held as planned.

Michael and David decided to speak to Cazenove to ask them to intercede. The pressure from the Stock Exchange had become intolerable, they would want to know the board decision, and now the board meeting had been cancelled. Cazenove's argument to the Stock Exchange was that any suspension without a simultaneous announcement that a rescue was in place, would not only do irreparable harm to the shareholders, but would cause a serious ripple effect on the other quoted fringe banks. The Stock Exchange people were not impressed by this argument.

However it did impress the Discount Office. Keogh reported to Hollom. There was then a heated altercation between the Bank and the Stock Exchange. The Bank requested that there be no suspension. The Stock Exchange said that they would be prepared to suspend the quotation, but only until first thing Thursday morning, December 20. The Bank then told the Stock Exchange that they should not do anything until they were informed that a rescue had been agreed. This stark confrontation between the Bank of England and the Stock Exchange was unprecedented.

The Bank decided to make its own moves. The Governors had made their decisions. The confidence factor had to be dealt with immediately. As Hollom recalls: 'There was a chance that deposits were moving increasingly to the clearers as the safest haven. It became clear that we had to get hold of those deposits and put them back where they came from. The Bank had to be quick about it and had to devise a suitable piece of machinery'. There was no time to lose, Hollom said. 'You have to move quickly. The first thing was to get hold of the people concerned.' Certain individuals were to be summoned to the Bank to meet them, others were to be asked to stand by. The central scene was now to be at the Bank of England.

Jack was flying back from the other end of the world. Michael dreaded his drive to Heathrow to greet his father.

*   *   *

A few months earlier, unknown to the public, the press, the shareholders, the depositors, unknown also to many of its executive directors and all of the non-executive directors, a luxurious private jet aeroplane, a brand-new twin-engined Hawker Siddeley 125/600B, seating ten in great comfort and able to fly nearly 2000 miles non-stop (excluding the reserve tanks), was purchased by a small London bank. There had been daily discussions on the telephone and almost daily conferences and meetings between the owners and the manufacturers on the design of the interior, on the colour scheme, the texture of the upholstery, and the lighting. The spanking, gleaming, superbly crafted machine had every optional extra available and it was apparent to the manufacturers that only the very best was good enough for the owner and for the passengers. The HS/125 was going to be operated through a specially formed company with its own full-time general manager, an aviation expert, Harry Green, plus a hand-picked full-time crew made up of the chief pilot and a second pilot, all of whom would receive special training from the Hawker Siddeley people. Who was the super-rich owner whose specifications and requirements were so detailed, and who wanted only the best of everything?

Within the entire breadth of Great Britain, very few industrial companies had their own private jet and in the City not a single bank owned one: not Barclays, not National Westminster, nor Midland, nor Lloyds, nor any of the Scottish banks. Cedar had frequently been described as a high-flying bank. Had the Morrisons decided to take this literally? Had Jack and Michael Morrison and David Fischer taken leave of their senses? A private jet? It was bordering on the grotesque.

In keeping with the fabulous jet, the crew was of the very best. As even a tiny error can cause death, flying men have a serious sense of responsibility; they are prudent men and they earn the respect of their passengers because they do not and cannot take their responsibilities lightly. The whole of the airline industry is geared entirely to the passengers' confidence in the pilot; without such confidence there would simply be no industry. Virtually all pilots are men of character who, as part of their necessary talents, are able to read not only into the weakness of machines, but also of human beings. One of this admirable breed was Roger Seymour, Cedar's chief pilot, who, with his chosen co-pilot, Al Thomas, was soon to size up their new employers: they are both still flying today, based at Heathrow, Roger Seymour, then flying for Beechams, was approached by Harry Green, with whom he was acquainted. Green said the owner was unusual – a bank. This disarmed the seasoned airline pilots. But not for long. Disillusion and worse was to follow.

When Fischer first interviewed Green in Spring 1973, he said that he and Michael Morrison, his co-managing director, had recently returned from the States where 'everyone' was going around in private jets. They travelled to the States frequently, he explained, always on business and, although they always travelled first-class, a jet would be more practical, especially for the increasing number of short trips to the continent; Cedar was becoming an international banking business (not counting the international property business), offices were being opened in Holland and New Zealand, and it had purchased half of a New York bank.

It was a formidable litany, but realising that they were obviously taken by the idea of private jet travel, Green pointed out that it was far more practical to hire a jet whenever necessary as ownership was only economic if requirements were to the order of least 400 hours a year. Fischer retorted that Cedar had need of at least 400 hours of business travel, and selective chartering could increase the use way beyond that minimum. Green concluded that perhaps a bank's requirements were even greater than a large industrial company. He took Fischer's word for it. Subsequently it was his impression that the co-managing directors likened the jet to a chauffeur-driven motor car which was used from time to time. They had no idea of the enormous running expenses. After his appointment as manager, Green was patted on the back by the two cousins, instructed to take on a crew, and to run the operation from newly-decorated offices at Heathrow.

From the moment the pilots joined, there was immediate speculation about the 400 hours. Did the bank have customers the size of Beechams who had not yet bought its own jet? Were the shareholders and directors they kept hearing about, representing huge industrial sectors like Coal and Electricity, the parties who were going to use the jet? That seemed more like it. But a bank? And a bank like Cedar? And two managing directors like Morrison and Fischer? Increasingly perplexed, the crew went to Hawker Siddeley's base in Hatfield for their training schedules. The Middle East war started and ended: oil prices tripled. The crew became even more anxious because of the hugely increased fuel costs. The plane was ready for delivery in October 1973. The crew flew it from Hatfield to Heathrow with great pride. It was a champion. A reception was held in the hangar hosted by Michael and David and attended by some of the office staff from Pall Mall. 'Today,' said Fischer, 'is the beginning of the Aviation Division of Cedar.' There were no sniggers, just a little clapping.

Thereafter Green reported directly to a personal assistant of Fischer's at Pall Mall. Communication was haphazard, though there was much toing and froing on the quality of the food to be served, the PA stressing that this was one of Mr Fischer's special interests. No schedules of requirements were forthcoming. Eventually, increasingly perplexed and worried, Green, Seymour and Thomas requested a formal meeting with the owners. After various postponements the meeting was held, and Michael and David were questioned at length. Finally squeezed out of them was what had already been guessed – that Cedar's requirements were not anywhere near 400 hours. What then were they? 300 hours? 200 hours? Less? What? Perhaps 100 hours? They questioned relentlessly. Michael and David squirmed. Eventually David admitted that he thought 100 hours was nearest the requirement. There was dismay. Not even 100 hours, only 'perhaps' – was it nearer 50 hours? Michael and David declined to reply.

Seymour told them they couldn't possibly have realised what the running costs of an aeroplane amounted to. 'You don't understand,' he pointed out, 'that even in the hangar a plane can eat its head off.' The cousins said they knew this. But they were clearly jolted; when the questioning began they had been evasive and sheepish, now they were visibly shaken. The professionals they employed had brought them down to earth with an unambiguous and sickening thump. The two cousins trembling with the enormity of what they had initiated, kept their silence; appreciating that if they said anything at all, the crew might explode. The pilots were aghast. It was a far worse mess than they had feared.

The obvious course, said Green, as a matter of extreme urgency, was to go all out for chartering, the only thing to do was to make the best of it. The cousins perked up and with some fervour agreed that chartering was the order of the day. Thus ended the first and last formal meeting of the aviation division of Cedar Holdings.

Fischer, who was fixated by personal car number plates, had earlier transferred his curious addiction to seeking a special call sign for the jet. He sought 'MD' to represent Michael and David, and unheard of in those days, and even now, he actually obtained 'MD', the international call sign Mike Delta. Normal seating on the Hawker Siddeley was around seven, according to owner's need. Fischer had insisted on a seating arrangment for ten passengers, in case, as he put it, 'all the Cedar directors wanted to travel together'. In fact, because of Fischer's extra seating it subsequently proved an advantage in chartering.

A lavish twelve-page brochure was produced in double-quick time with Fischer's flair for good design appearing on every page. It had full-colour photographs and seating plans and mileage charts, which would have done justice to a scheduled airline. It described the Hawker Siddeley in graphic detail, stressing that it was powered by twin Rolls Royce Bristol engines, that it could cruise at 520 miles per hour, and that, because of its construction, it was less prone to turbulence, operating smoothly up to a height of 40,000 feet.

Pilots derive enormous enjoyment in flying particular aeroplanes, similar to the enthusiasm of motor racing drivers for particular cars. This Hawker Siddeley 125 was one such plane. Seymour and Thomas said that it was a fabulous plane to fly, the best that they had ever come across. And even years later, Seymour's pride has the engaging possessiveness of a school teacher discussing a favourite pupil long after he has left school. The crew, disillusioned by their employers and in the unprofessional situation they found themselves, had one glorious compensation, the sheer joy of flying their wonderful new aeroplane.

The first flight at the end of October, a trial spin, was to Copenhagen, a day trip. The passengers were Fischer, his Portuguese manservant, his chauffeur and Cedar's graphic designer. Caviar and champagne were served. The second flight was to Paris on 5 November. The next outing was to Madeira. This was definitely a holiday trip. There were no second mortgage interests or property interests in Madeira.

In early November there were two trips to Amsterdam. On Thursday 22, Jack and Michael and David Fischer flew to Glasgow. They were jubilant, Jack peacocked in his home town; and when they flew to Aberdeen the next morning, Izzy declined an invitation to join them. On arrival in Aberdeen Fischer said, 'I have never been to the Orkneys, let's go there for lunch'. They flew to the Orkneys. It was the crew's impression during the Orkneys trip, after flying to Glasgow, that Jack was not a very happy passenger.

There were murmurs of forthcoming trips to Zurich, Brussels, Israel and the US. The crew knew that the trips were essentially joyrides aimed at persuading them that Cedar had a need for the plane. Fischer went out of his way to humour the pilots, which they found particularly irksome. Frantic efforts were made to obtain charters, Green, Seymour and Thomas aware that the whole project was seriously underfunded; and for most of the weeks following delivery, the highly-paid crew found themselves sitting around the office at Heathrow or at home awaiting instructions.

On Tuesday, 27 November, on the day Bardsley's resignation was made public, there was a flight to Paris. It was the last trip.

Meanwhile, the expensive beautiful Hawker Siddley 125/600B, the meter ticking away relentlessly by the minute, purred in the hangar like a perfectly-trained athlete, impatient to get out on a run.

Meanwhile, Cedar, its deposit run gathering a horrible momentum, was in a tailspin. The Stock Exchange had made the position clear to the Bank: rescue by opening hours on Thursday morning, 20 December – or suspension. Suspension without a rescue would inevitably lead to a crash. The Bank had made the position clear to the Stock Exchange: there was no question of any suspension before there was a rescue. The Governor and the Deputy Governor moved swiftly.

TEN

The Wrangle

You have been summoned by the Governor to an early morning meeting in the Bank of England. You enter through the central arch past two huge bronze doors into a large lobby. You find yourself in a completely different environment. You are cut off from Threadneedle, from the busy Royal Exchange forecourt, from the buses, taxis, newspaper sellers, messengers and clerks. You look around you. The vaulted ceiling is near heaven. You are two feet high. You can just perceive the underchin of Mr Pointer, the consummately named gatekeeper; mosaics on the floor depict a symbolic scene; you are conscious of stepping on ancient history not on stone. Standing next to Mr Pointer is the deputy gatekeeper. They both look like dressed-up Corinthian pillars, in curved starchy pink frockcoats, black top hats, red waistcoats, white shirt, dark tie, household cavalry trousers neatly flared over bulbous shiny capped boots. 'Yes, sir?' they ask exceedingly politely. You are made to feel slightly apologetic for intruding but still very welcome. You are pointed towards the friendly but forbidding bank messengers. 'Can I help you, sir?' You give your name. Behind the desk are more attendants and three or four security men disguised in bank executive serge. 'My colleague will accompany you. This way, sir.' You are guarded, led, conducted, along a wide stone decorated passageway. You try to keep calm. Through a window as you follow, you see a garden court, a large lawn dotted with a few pieces of statuary. You look down, you are still walking on pictorial scenes grouted in mosaic. Your knees are weak. You reach a corner. 'This way, sir.' Your messenger, your guard, your conductor, opens two thickly-lacquered doors set in a moulded architrave. This is the west entrance. You enter into the parlours.

You are taken aback. You are now in a palatial, hushed and reticent stately house, ivory walls, gilt frames, large paintings, luxurious carpets, gleaming Sheraton furniture, the occasional interloping Chippendale. You are in a large anteroom. You notice a wide corridor through an open arch. This is the parlour corridor. On the right are the doors leading to the private rooms of the Governor and the Deputy Governor, and the offices of directors and secretaries. Along the left side are a number of darkish rooms, little or no windows, elegant high cornices, they are waiting rooms. At the far end, at the east entrance, there are further laquered doors leading to another decorated stone passage. Guests and colleagues can also enter from here. This is where the parlour stewards are enclaved with one or two sitting on occasional seats opposite the Governor's and the Deputy Governor's doors. They can see the movement of any person from one end of the parlour corridor to the other. They are invisible except for a haze of pink and red. You are now in a waiting room. You wait, and you wait. The windows seem more like a grill. You stare at the high cornices. The minutes seem like hours. The door opens. 'Would you? Thank you, sir.' You cross the divide. The opposite door is open. The pink haze disappears. You are now in the Governor's room.

Its creamy-white appearance has an immediate impact of spaciousness. It is more imposing, more unnerving than you ever expected; one superb chimneypiece, not one but two clocks; the French doors leading to the garden are huge and so, too, is the Governor's square desk. If this is the reckoning room of Heaven, so be it, you say to yourself, for you are now mentally genuflecting in the all-powerful presence of a supreme financial emissary. You start praying.

The Governor welcomes you. You nod or bow or click your heels. You greet the others in the room. Your knees are weak. You sit down on your chair which glides into place on its own. You look at the prayer mat which resembles a large square leather-topped desk. You look at the Governor. His eyes are piercing. You are transfixed. You are part of a frozen tableau which now comes to life. The meeting begins. So does the explanation.

The Governor has Sir Jasper Hollom sitting beside him; on their right, along one side, sit the barons of Barclays, Timothy Bevan and Deryk Vander Weyer: opposite them are the heads of the four institutions –

Hugh Jenkins of Coal, Cob Stenham of Unilever, Burton Johnson of Electricity, and, the second time he was seeing the Governor that morning, Lord De L'Isle of Phoenix. Eight men in all.

Head and shoulders above the others, was the Governor, Gordon Richardson, a star in any gathering. With a Nottingham background similar to Lady Thatcher's, he was a Cambridge law graduate, an army staff officer during the Second World War, a barrister acknowledged before he was forty as a leading expert on company law, the chairman of Schroders at the age of forty-six, a director of the Bank of England when he was fifty and Governor when he was fifty-eight. Richardson, tall and imposing, in possession of a distinguished physical appearance, had the rugged intellectual look of an actor, the look of a Henry Irving. He had a natural authority and could, like any genuine patrician, take centrestage without moving from the wings; at any table he would be the centre of gravity, the person to whom other individuals would find themself addressing their remarks. He was the most spectacular success in the City since the war. Newly appointed as the Governor in July he had only been at the helm for a few months.*

His deputy, Jasper Hollom, had spent his entire career in the Bank, entering when he was eighteen years old, becoming a Director in 1966 and Deputy Governor in 1970. He had the prim archdeaconish expression of a Harley Street specialist, one whose second opinion would be no different from his first, whose pointedly good manners and precisely cadenced diagnoses were all the more telling for the firm concealment of a tough interior. Hollom is what is known as a 'nice man' before the word nice also meant weak, a failing which could not, even under these trying circumstances, have been applied to him. Dennis Healey has called him the 'unsung hero' and though Hollom would acknowledge the sincerity of this accolade from a major politician better known for his brickbats than his praise, he is the sort of man who would prefer to remain unsung. He was however, given a

---

* I had myself first met Richardson during my early months as financial adviser to the Cotton/Clore property group when he was chairman of Schroders. He was the main reason and magnet why, when I was at Hambros Bank, I tended to invite Schroders into any appropriate investment situation with which I was involved. The most important of these investments was Intershop AG, which is still thriving today in Zurich as one of Europe's larger quoted property companies. Remarkably it has as its recently appointed chairman and managing director, the same man (Dr Jacques Muller) whom we appointed as the equivalent of managing director some thirty years ago.

richly deserved knighthood in 1975 for his valiant efforts during the crisis.

The bravest of the guests, was Lord De L'Isle of Phoenix Assurance: a VC no less. He had been Secretary of State for Air from 1950 to 1955, thereafter Governor General of Australia, (one of the last Englishmen to hold the office) and for the last seven years the chairman of Phoenix Assurance. His family, the Sidneys, had owned Penshurt in Sussex for centuries and, as the sixth Baron and the first Viscount, he took particular pride and delight in his ancestral possession. Seeking a living, an unexpected pursuit for a Sidney, he qualified as a chartered accountant, probably the only Knight of the Garter who had ever been one, and probably the only hereditary peer qualified to read a balance sheet. He wore his honours and courage and expertise lightly, and it was easy to forget that he had been a successful minister of the Crown (the City has always tended to underrate the peculiar hardships of ministerial office) and a successful Governor General. He had the traditional Tory attribute of not seeming to have any hard edges, and though of more than medium build his physical presence was modest if not bland.

I had met him first through Jocelyn Hambro after his return from Australia, just before he took on the Phoenix. It was lunch at the bank followed by a discussion between the three of us. Jocelyn was another brave soldier who had himself earned an MC. I had never before met a VC and as the litmus test of a coward is to avoid a litmus test, I hardly said a word.

Lord De L'Isle was now a City grandee, and the Governor was fortunate that a man of his stature was the chairman of one of Cedar's institutional supporters, and well-placed too, because of his involvement as chairman of First National in the rescue of London and County. This experience was to have a direct effect on De L'Isle's thinking in respect of Cedar. In having arranged to speak first to De L'Isle amongst the Fabulous Four, Richardson, a master mason, was deftly positioning a solid cornerstone of support.

The second institutional man was Hugh Jenkins, of the Coal Board, formidable, strong-minded, intelligent and endowed with native wisdom; woe betide any person who disagreed with him without having done his homework for he could be very difficult, and woe betide any person who attempted to persuade or dissuade him without solid argument, for he could be very caustic. Jenkins always thought for himself; few would dare to push him in a direction he had not already decided to face. In his early days at the Coal Board, soon after Eric Young left to join Cotton at the Dorchester, it was noticeable that Aubrey Orchard Lyle, the Coal Board's property adviser, and indeed also Jack Cotton's, increasingly went out of his way to bring this young surveyor, hailing from the sturdy coal country of Llanelli, into discussions and meetings.

Favoured with dark celtic good looks and the thrusting presence of a colonel soon to be a general, Jenkins had a certain star quality which I and many others found appealing. He was the first-ever property expert to be in charge of all the investments of a major pension fund, that is, not just the property portfolio but also its equity and fixed interests portfolios. He had a natural feel for investment and was a safe pair of hands. Under the watchful eyes of David Clement, the financial director of the Coal Board, and the benign approval of the chairman, Derek Ezra, he had been put in control of the Coal Board's funds when his predecessor, Philip Johnstone – in charge only of equities and fixed interests – left to join Cedar. I had come to learn that Jenkins was particularly adept at making well-conceived strategic investment decisions. He once decided and obtained approval for a recommendation not to invest in property north of The Wash – this at the Coal Board of all places. Listening to the Governor, he would not only be entirely pragmatic, but also entirely positive, whichever way his judgement led him.

The third institutional man, Burton Johnson of Electricity, was the sort of person frequently found in a high position in a nationalised industry or in local government, who was good at school or college and, by dint of hard work, obtained the qualifications necessary to take on a job of importance. During a lifetime's career in the electricity supply industry he had risen steadily to the top. His predecessor, Clifford French, had appeared more frequently in the various meetings between Electricity and third parties, but Johnson was more of a career politician and, though usually unwilling to appear in the forefront of pension fund affairs, whether it was a problem area or otherwise, he would certainly derive some satisfaction in being a guest of the Governor. Short and pudgy, he was a model adjutant with quiet good manners, with a sincere regard for getting things done in what he considered was the right way.

The fourth, and by no means the least of the Fabulous Four, was Cob Stenham. He had already proved his worth as the financial director of the great Anglo-Dutch colossus, and knew how to flex his muscles. Stenham invariably elicited respect if not admiration for his innate ability. After taking over from Jasper Knight, he had made a successs of his job at Unilever, and in general was known as an abrasive if not a prickly person, who could not suffer fools gladly or otherwise. His own responses to this all too-prevalent cadre in corporate life were generally quick-tempered – for in lacking a sense of diplomacy he was reluctant, if not unwilling, to recognise that on most occasions it was possible to express oneself on some matter or to achieve some objective without treading on toes or kicking shins, or aiming even higher. With his fellow main board directors at Blackfriars or Rotterdam, his sheer competence was a breath of fresh air, particularly after Jasper Knight's exiguous reign. His colleagues, though initially taken aback by his idiosyncrasies, came to like them, and came to accept his Warhol prints displayed prominently almost pugnaciously on the walls of his office, their colours in full harmony with his multi-coloured socks.

Stenham was a one-off, a sort of loner, a passionate and genuine workaholic, packing into one day what most people do in three, pursuing a punishing schedule which his loyal exhausted staff were, mostly, pleased to follow. Of slight build, Danish in complexion, with a baldish bullet head and an occasional roguish smile, he never liked being rushed. But already he felt rushed. Anyone who knew him would have long since read the signs. Sir Jasper Hollom did not know him and later in the day when these two crossed swords, Hollom may well have come to the sanguine conclusion that he and Stenham were perhaps better off in not having the dubious pleasure of a closer acquaintanceship.

Of the two men from Barclays, Tim Bevan was always destined for the top position; a member of one of Barclays' founding families, it was his birthright and his heritage. He was a man of high intelligence and low boiling point, astutely concealing a first-rate mind from his colleagues. One of those taken in was Peter Eve, my Barclays colleague seconded to me at Bentworth and someone not easily fooled: I always thought how clever it was of Bevan to have engineered this impression. But what Bevan could not conceal was his volatile temperament and he had his many critics who did not find the Bevan quick fuse particularly electrifying. He did not seem to care as much about making friends as he did about influencing people. Bevan was Eton, Trinity, the Guards and a sailor, and a man of youthful if not schoolboy appearance. He would have instantly sized up the Cedar situation and, long before anyone else, would have already decided how far his bank would go in support – as little as possible.

His colleague Deryk Vander Weyer was not a member of the founding families but could easily have been considered one. In fact like his distinguished predecessors Darvill and Wilde, he had worked himself up staunchly through the branch system. He was mature and sensible and had a cast of judgement which made him one of the best, if not the best, general manager produced by Barclays in recent history; he was later to become a director of the Bank of England, and was to be the first person from a non-founding family to become chairman of Barclays Bank (UK).

Of the men in the Governor's room, the Governor and the Deputy Governor knew De L'Isle, but were meeting Jenkins, Johnson and Stenham for the first time. They knew Bevan and Vander Weyer, who themselves knew De L'Isle and Jenkins and Stenham only slightly, and Johnson not at all. Curiously and unexpectedly, the four top men of the institutions were meeting each other virtually for the first time.

By dawn of the next morning, they would, whether they wished it or not, know almost every nuance of each other's character.

The six guests waited for the Governor to begin his explanation.

*   *   *

The Governor spoke for the next twenty minutes or so, and if the exact genesis of the Lifeboat had to be pinpointed I would hazard a judgement that it was during this disquisition. To the Governor and the Deputy Governor it was the beginning of what they had quickly appreciated was going to be a military-type campaign. The Cedar rescue, had to be settled and cleared off the field, before the first staff conference with the generals already marshalled for later that afternoon. The Governors had already foreseen that the campaign was going to be long and gruelling, settled in years and not in months. They were digging in. They were doing their spade work.

Lord Richardson and Sir Jasper Hollom have clear memories of the meeting; their guests do not all have the same 20/20 clarity, but each has his own personal fixed recollection. They listened intently to the Governor. What they heard had to be evaluated on its intrinsic meaning and in addition each man had to translate its significance in terms of the implications for his own institution. They had to concentrate their minds, they had to be extremely alert and attentive.

Richardson's explanation was simple and direct. It was good of them, he said, to have come at such short notice. The run on Cedar's deposits was serious. Cedar had to be able to open its doors for business next day. It would only be able to do so if the institutions and Barclays came up with a total support package. The situation was not only serious in respect of Cedar but for the entire banking system. There were wider implications. One had to avoid the domino effect. Cedar could not be allowed to collapse. He would like them to consider all the implications and to discuss amongst themselves the terms of a rescue. He would like them to remain in the Bank until they had reached a solution. He would like to thank them again for coming to see him at such short notice.

Burton Johnson retains a particularly vivid recollection of the Governor. 'He was very impressive in appearance and in delivery. If you had to define what a true English gentleman looked like, he would be someone who looked like the Governor.' Johnson went further: 'Richardson gave us his explanation with a sort of lofty detachment. But of one thing I am absolutely sure. If it was necessary to be ruthless in a righteous cause, Richardson would be as tough as blazes'.

The saving of Cedar was a righteous cause; there was no doubt about that. They had to stay in the Bank until they had come up with a solution for Cedar's rescue; there was no doubt about that. The true English gentleman had placed a steel gauntlet before them; there was no doubt about that.

The explanation at an end, the guests stood up. They departed, or rather they trooped out, one or two with an impression of being in the wrong, like a schoolboy who had transgressed. Attended by a parlour steward, they were taken to the ground-floor anteroom. A Bank official appeared. He said that rooms had been made available upstairs. They then moved to the first floor and this is where the wrangle commenced, and this is where, to their astonishment, which persists to this day, they battled almost continuously until 3 am the next morning.

Upstairs had a flavour of sedate grandeur. Each room, the Court Room, the directors' dining room, the committee room, even the spacious anteroom, was a set piece. The committee room, also known as the octagon room, had four of its walls artfully covered with mirrors and paintings; of the remaining four, two had double doorways, one was taken up almost entirely by the garden window and another housed the chimneypiece. Soundproofing was solid, the doors of rich mahogany were solid, the quiet atmosphere was solid, heated discussions would be cooled by the refined low-temperature aesthetics of an earlier, more confident age. In the Court Room one could not imagine anything but sincere accord between the directors of the Bank. Here they convened as members of the Court Room each Thursday morning. This famous room, though large and spacious, retains a wonderful sense of intimacy with a strong aroma of history, and, though to some extent slightly overpowering, it has a pleasant and unaggressive air. It is as if the room were a setting for an everlasting stage-set, where discreet actors made hushed, hardly audible, financial judgements on the nation's most important commodities – its money and its reputation. The table, long and slender, sits in the middle surrounded by equally slender Sheratons and buttressed by space which seems as tangible as the furniture. The Governor's chair is at the far end of the table facing the Octagon Room. The wall on his left is framed by three garden windows, each seemingly the size of an atrium. The wall on his right has three famous beautifully carved chimneypieces, imposing yet reticent and undemonstrative in their treble features. Above and adjoining the chimneypieces are paintings, mostly of monarchs, and classically-framed mirrors, and completing the perfectly harmonious backdrop are two sets of double doors leading to the outside corridor, itself wide and discreet. Behind the Governor's chair, a further set of double doors lead on to the directors' dining room. Everywhere the heavy carpeting is of a thickness which muffles every footstep.

The two Barclays' barons were shown into the anteroom whilst the other four were shown into the Octagon Room.

The four immediately went into committee. Straight away De L'Isle said that he supported a rescue. Burton Johnson said, 'I agree with Lord De L'Isle'. Stenham and Jenkins both demurred. From the onset there was the locking of horns; half for a rescue, half against.

It was quickly apparent that Stenham was indignant, if not angry. He liked being under the steady pressure of the regular weight of work, not the inorderly lurch of a sudden load. Indeed, as I knew myself, his brain was even more effective under pressure. It became more icy, harder, more precise. This haste was indecent, it was out of control. Why should the institutions foot the bill? They were shareholders and loanholders. All right, if they lost their investment, that was too bad, that was the occupational hazard of making any investment. But wider issues? Why should that be part of the equation? And if there were wider issues, that was surely the specific task of the Bank of England

and the big banks. They should pick up the pieces, not the share-holders. Stenham, a bright corporate finance merchant banker at Hill Samuel earlier in his career, had already sensed that something on these lines would have to emerge. He was not concerned that Cedar should be saved, he was concerned that his fund, having possibly lost its money, should not be exposed to any more risk. It was a technical financial situation which had to be looked at coolly. As he said later, 'I certainly took the view that the rush was indecent and that a better situation would have been for Cedar's quotation to have been suspended. Things done in a hurry tend often to be mistaken'.

De L'Isle's positive view would have been his natural response, even if he had not been involved in the London and County rescue. But he had already made up his mind; Cedar had to be saved at all costs. One had to take the wider view; it was undoubtedly the correct view. As chairman of First National, Cedar's main rival, he recognised the dangers of a contagious deposit run – indeed it might even infect First National if it were not stopped. There might also be some possible indirect benefits to First National, in making his support so positive. De L'Isle was, however, in complete sympathy with the Governor's observation, it was the unequivocal responsibility for any involvement to include the wider interests, in this instance the wider interests of the banking system as a whole, and the wider interests of the country. Ex-minister, ex-Governor General, owner of Penshurst and holder of the Victoria Cross, he was a patriot first and foremost. As one participant later observed, 'The trouble with De L'Isle is that he wears red, white and blue braces'. To which another replied, 'It's a pity more of us don't wear the same colours'.

Johnson, as he made apparent to the other three, did wear the same colours as De L'Isle. He too was convinced by the wider issue; something had to be done, but he was not sure in exactly what form. He did not question whether Cedar had to be saved, that was a foregone conclusion – there was nothing to discuss, only how and how much. It was up to the institutions to put their hands in their pockets. It was not only financially correct to do so, not only morally correct but also in the country's interest. In the forefront of his mind was the fact that the City, the public, the depositors, had known for years that this huge fund, representing all the electricity supply employees of the country, had been financial supporters of Cedar. In no way could they abdicate their distinct responsibilities. Moreover Cedar was in trouble through no fault of its own. Help must be provided in its time of trouble. And without any doubt whatsoever, the wider issues as expressed by the Governor had to be taken fully into account.

Jenkins, as much a patriot as the others including Stenham, did not agree with De L'Isle, nor with Johnson, nor with Stenham. He wanted to look at every aspect, he wanted to judge the viability of every point and every viewpoint and certainly he wanted to give Stenham's views more of an airing. As a trustee of the pension fund of a major nationalised industry, he had to consider the beneficiaries, the country's coalminers, past and present, men who worked hard and dangerously for their pensions. He was not concerned with their current political militancy, nor the reasons behind the crucial national go-slow. That was their business; his business was to safeguard their pensions. Why not walk away from an investment which had been lost and let Cedar go under? It was an option which had to be considered and chewed over. He recognised that the institutions had lent their names to the investment, that his own fund had its own man on the board of Cedar and furthermore his own predecessor had even joined the board of Cedar as its investment director. But when does prudent investment become imprudent charity? He was conscious too, as he recalled, of 'an overwhelming feeling that we should not be putting good money after bad, not going more deeply into a situation not of our making'.

He also had a special responsibility. Jenkins was the only one amongst the four who truly understood property. If there was to be a rescue package, the value of the properties would be the salient and crucial factor. What security would it comprise in this sort of desperate situation? Properties of high quality had shown that they could normally weather temporary buffetings. He was already evaluating in his own mind, what the cost of a rescue package might be, what would be the cost of those risks, and how those costs would be minimised. In his view, too, Barclays' role was critical. Why did it not take a wider view? Why did it not put its own hands into its very deep pockets? Jenkins had not been very happy with Tim Bevans's truculent response when he had taken the trouble to see him the previous week. If and when it came to it, he was prepared for a tough battle with Barclays. But it was still 'if', not yet 'when'.

Two were for a rescue package, one was against, one was neutral to negative. They got up, they phoned their offices, they sought out their colleagues. They asked for a further discussion with Sir Jasper Hollom.

Why, Hollom was asked, should shareholders who had already lost their investment, risk anything more? Hollom said that they had lent their support and their name, and because this was known 'they had incurred at least a moral obligation to assist the Bank to deal with the situation'. In referring to this many years later he said to me, 'At first, they were inclined to rest on the position, an understandable one of course, that their involvement should be limited to the extent of their investment'.

Stenham said that he did not think there was any moral position. Hollom said there most certainly was. Jenkins said afterwards, 'The atmosphere became very tense'. In fact, it became heated. There was an astonishing exchange between Hollom and Stenham; there seemed to be an element of personal animosity. Hollom concealed his anger. No one could recall whether he was drumming his fingers on the table, a sure sign of Hollom reaching the trenchline of exasperation and anger, but they all do recall his suggestion that perhaps he should telephone Sir Ernest Woodroofe, Stenham's chairman at Unilever. Stenham tartly replied that he could do so but it would be of no avail, as Sir Ernest would undoubtedly inform Sir Jasper that he, Stenham, had full authority and responsibility to deal with this situation. 'This is how Unilever works', said Stenham with asperity. Hollom's description of what could have developed as a nasty scene was typical and masterly and pure Hollomism: 'I think it would be fair to say from my point of view, that the case was argued hard on both sides and both of us probably spoke with reasonable conviction'.

At this dangerous juncture, the rescue discussions could have gone off the rails quite irreversibly. The atmosphere was not only strained but jumpy. Later, Stenham choosing his words carefully, said he thought Hollom was very authoritarian, that his tone 'was often counter-productive'. Hollom may have seemed counter-productive to Stenham, but he did produce the desired effect, even if, as is descibed later, Hollom directed his sights, not in so many words, on to Unilever itself.

Years later, Hollom told me that what had been of overriding importance, at this juncture, was that the four institutions should recognise that they had a moral duty to save Cedar. 'There is a specific responsibility,' he emphasised in his nice, deliberate and diagnostic manner, 'that if you are a senior shareholder with a representative on the board, there are implied and implicit responsibilities.' The main theme of Hollom's argument was that the institutions had no choice but to play their proper part in shouldering the burden, that they could not walk away without doing damage to themselves, the wider interests were paramount, and, because of these wider interests, the institutions, whatever Stenham's own beliefs, had to accept full responsibility.

Jenkins recalls that Hollom left them in no doubt as to what was at stake: 'It was being brought home to us time and again that what we were looking at was the wider interest of our investment, not only our investment in Cedar Holdings but our investment in the financial sector, that is the clearing banks, merchant banks, the insurance companies, all of these were considered to be at some substantial financial risk if the dominoes started to fall'. The domino syndrome, the rat-a-tat of cumulative collapse was not merely a verbal expression: it did not strike terror, but it struck home. Jenkins said, 'We were all very conscious at the time that what we might be witnessing was the removal of one domino from the stack.'

From time to time the Deputy Governor, immovable in his posture, deflected suggestions that they depart and reconvene the next day. Stenham insisted, 'We need time to consider.' Hollom said it was not possible: Cedar had to open its doors for business in the morning.

Finally it was the domino argument which swung Jenkins.

There were now three for the rescue, one against. A hardly undisguised feeling of irritation permeated towards Stenham. He was sticking to principles, these were his guns. He still found it incomprehensible that a pension fund should be forced to go outside its basic remit. Trustees had legal obligations, not moral ones. He was still unconvinced by the wider issues. He regarded it, in all logic, as a separate issue, but he was increasingly aware that he had to consider another factor which did not apply to the other three. He was not only chairman of the trustees of the pension fund, he was also the financial director of the parent company: he had to take into account Unilever parent company's relationship with the Bank of England. Unilever was an international company, it traded throughout the world, and it required exchange control permissions on all its relevant trading and investment transactions, on a day to day basis. It had to have a good working relationship with the Bank. This was vital: if the Bank wanted to be difficult it could substantially affect Unilever's international trade. The gauntlet had menacing overtones.

To Stenham, with his wider responsibilities as the finance director of one of the world's largest multinationals, the well-being of which depended upon smooth unmolested trading, the wider issue meant far more than it meant to the others. Of the other three, two represented great industries, but they were home-based, the third was a leading insurance company; only Stenham's company had to seek continuous exchange control permissions from the Bank. The others were not trammelled by Unilever's special considerations, and, though mindful of the need to have good relations with the Bank, were concentrating more specifically upon the wider financial issues as described to them that morning by the Governor and as amplified later by Hollom. Yet irritated as they were by Stenham's recalcitrance, there was no lessening of respect for him. If there had been reactions of this sort, he would have been unperturbed; an essential attribute of any great financial director is not to be interested in popularity contests, only in facts and principles. To Stenham a principle now increasingly endemic to this situation was that the wider issue was not only one related to the pension fund but to the Unilever parent company. Had Hollom something more in mind in suggesting that he would telephone Sir Ernest Woodroofe?

Although Hollom had stressed and restressed the wider issues and the moral obligations, he had not of course revealed anything about the parallel secret meeting with the chairmen of the clearing banks. He had given no sign whatsoever that if the secret meeting was other than an unambiguous success, the entire banking system could collapse; or that the successful rescue of Cedar was a crucial part of the plan to avoid any such collapse. Time and again, in making his points to the Fabulous Four, this cool central banker displayed a fixity of purpose which was as hard as the coinage it was his job to protect. He was in a difficult position: he had exercised pressure even to suggesting that he might telephone the chairman of Unilever, he had gone a little further – one could not call it a threat, that word did not appear in the Hollom vocabulary – he had made intimations that the four institutions should consider their overall relationships with the City and with the Bank, and not risk jeopardising them. 'He was a gentleman throughout,' Jenkins recalled, 'he never put a foot wrong in any way. He gave a marvellous impression of being totally calm and he never showed any reaction, even when the institutions were saying no. He just got on with it very quietly, very firmly and very cautiously.'

*   *   *

The talks went on, lunch went by, time was flowing away and little progress had been made – dangerously little progress.

Tempers were rising. Burton Johnson contemplated Stenham in his understated manner. He was impressed with his intellect but not with his explicit juridical attitude. Johnson believed in moral commitment. He felt a moral commitment was as tangible as any other. The name of his fund, Electricity, had been attached to Cedar for a long time and indeed Unilever's name had been attached to Cedar even longer. He felt strongly that the institutions had to be saviours not only for moral reasons but also for very practical reasons to protect their good name. Why couldn't Stenham see the point?

Eventually Stenham did, and it was over Unilever's relations with the Bank. The turning point occurred inherently during his confrontation with Hollom. Their battle was a classic battle of wills overlaid by differing priorities. Something in Hollom's level looks, the strength of will-power behind the bland courteous countenance, something in his composure, may have unnerved Stenham. But perhaps because Stenham appreciated more finely the realities of the Unilever situation, perhaps his sense of logic brought him to the correct commercial conclusion, perhaps having weighed the Governor's and the Deputy Governor's argument of the wider issue – with which he was not in favour – against the implications concerning wider trading issues of Unilever itself, perhaps weighing all this in his mind, he decided that it would be more pragmatic, more business-like, more secure to support a rescue of Cedar. But Stenham did not stop there: he took the logic to its very proper end. The pension fund was in the firing line; the parent company might suffer if the pension fund did not provide protection and agree to the Cedar rescue; therefore the pension fund had to be protected. He sought and obtained approval from his board that the Unilever parent would guarantee its pension fund against any losses which might arise in its support for Cedar. To a certain extent, Stenham's logic had an admirable element of justice about it.

It was now no longer a question of whether the institutions would help, but how much they would have to put up. Here, Hollom was breathtakingly unambiguous: the whole of the current liabilities, on the left hand-side of the balance sheet, more than £70 million, around £400 million today. Did they hear correctly?

They had – the whole of current liabilities on the left-hand side of the balance sheet. Three weeks earlier a forceful press release from the institutions declaring their unqualified support, without even mentioning any figures, might have sufficed. Two weeks earlier a forceful press release accompanying the £25 million advance might have sufficed. Now not less than £70 million would suffice. It was a shock, and all the more authentic for its chilling simplicity.

Hollom, was quite inflexible; he wanted a clean sweep; he wanted no ambiguities: this meant that all the current liabilities had to be underwritten. The steel gauntlet had shimmered from its first appearance at the early-morning meeting with the Governor. Burton Johnson had said that, if necessary, the Governor could be as tough as blazes. It was apparent that Hollom, too, could be as tough as blazes. Gentlemen, Hollom said to them, the whole of the lefthand-side of the balance sheet: all of the liabilities. One could not be tougher than that, or more inflexible. The shimmering gauntlet was pure steel.

Stenham has never got over his encounter with Hollom. He is still smarting over it. The Deputy Governor has all but forgotten it. Stenham later vented his spleen to my brother David, then writing in the *Economist*. David claims that it was I who suggested that he should contact Stenham. Then, as now, the *Economist* has no by-line. The article was headlined 'How the City was Saved' and was published a fortnight later, early in the New Year. It was a sensational headline, and the article caused a sensation. This was the opening: 'Just before Christmas when Cedar Holdings was saved, the City of London was on the brink of a terrifying collapse of confidence in the banking system'. The Governors were known to be extremely displeased. The source was correctly guessed to be Stenham, and if he ever thought there was the slightest chance of his becoming a director of the Bank of England, his hopes were very possibly dashed on that one article.

More directly, and more distressing to me as a long-time friend of them both, was the way he behaved towards his own colleague William Broadfield. That day at the Bank, Stenham would have preferred anyone from Unilever other than Broadfield to be with him. Of the leading actors in the Cedar story, nearly all of whom were known to me as acquaintances or friends, Stenham was my closest companion. We had enjoyed a friendship, occasionally erratic, occasionally in abeyance, which had survived our many differences of opinion and our rare squabbles; and in that curious convolution of an enduring friendship, these seemed to strengthen rather than diminish our liking for each other. I had admired him for the way he overcame a triple-bypass operation, the way he regarded it as a mere tiresome interruption to getting on with his job. I had a liking, too, for his self-deprecating humour which was invariably more amusing and more winsome for being so accurately observed.

At the Bank of England that day he was undoubtedly sniffing similar resonances of my own confrontation two years earlier with the institutions associated with Spey. Inevitably he was involved then, though less directly than he was now. He was irritated by the whole Cedar situation, it was messy. Stenham was not anti Morrison; if anything, he was anti Broadfield and anti special investment situations, and anti Cedar and Spey situations which involved a close relationship between entrepreneurs and institutions. He vowed that day that, as long as he had any say in the running of the Unilever pension fund, he would never again sanction approval for any special investment situations, or anything remotely similar to a Cedar-type investment association.

At long last the beleaguered institutions were in accord to mount a rescue for Cedar and were aware of the formidable amount of money required. Each one of them would want to inform his colleagues and would want to discuss the level and the terms of the rescue with them, each in his own way.

Stenham went back to Blackfriars and talked first of all to Woodroofe. He then asked Eric Rogers, the head of the pension fund department and Broadfield's immediate superior, to come to his office and told him quite flatly that he wanted him to take charge of the Cedar situation; and also that, for the sake of continuity, Broadfield should still stay on Cedar's board. He still wanted Eric Rogers to call all the shots. Stenham said that though Broadfield was good at his job, he was too nice and too soft and that he should have put a brake on the Morrisons, forgetting that Broadfield had wanted to resign six months earlier on the merger between Cedar and Amal. Stenham's bite was worse than his bark, he utterly destroyed Broadfield's confidence, and dear William, the most pleasant amongst a pleasant Cedar covey of institutional investment managers, and now a retired pensioner for over a decade, has still not completely recovered his composure.

Leaving Blackfriars to return to the Bank, Stenham and Broadfield sat together at the back of the car. It was not an easy ride, Stenham unable to desist from making critical remarks about the other institutions, about Hollom about the Morrisons, and of course about William himself. Stenham made it clear also that in framing the rescue terms, they would, by God, tie up Cedar and the Morrisons as tightly as possible, the knots would be so tight there would be no room for manoeuvre.

There was no problem of this kind with the colleagues in the other three institutions. Hugh Jenkins spoke to David Clement, who said he would join him later in the day, which he did. With the coal industry in chaos because of its national go-slow, he had other more important duties with which to contend. Jenkins decided to stay and to await the arrival of David Clement.

Johnson, of Electricity, sat quietly, saying very little. Nearly three weeks earlier, at the very beginning of the crisis, when at the urgent insistence of his colleague George Cumming, he met Michael Morrison and David Fischer at Pall Mall, Johnson had formed a good impression of them and told Cumming afterwards that he would encourage any support to be provided by the institutions. Michael almost destroyed Johnson's regard by sending him a crate of wine which was promptly returned with many thanks. This reflected Michael's nerves, for over the years he had come to learn, like everyone else, that people from the institutions, except for one rotten apple from a leading fund, were scrupulously correct in all their dealings. On this day, Johnson's most abiding memories were of the strong personality and character of the Governor, of Hollom's stamina and willpower, and of the patent decency of De L'Isle. He didn't think there was any need to go back to his office at Millbank. Instead he called George Cumming over to join him. They sat together thereafter, with identical views on the strength of the support their fund would and should provide.

At Phoenix, it was well known that De L'Isle ran the board as chairman and that Bill Harris ran the company as general manager. They were part of a formidable trio completed by Harris's excellent deputy, Ron Bishop. Harris was in New York on business. De L'Isle went back to Phoenix's headquarters at King William IV Street, a few minutes walk away. He spoke at some length with Harris in New York. He then had a chat with Bishop and the two of them returned together to the Bank.

The Barclays barons went back to 54 Lombard Street. They had internal confabulations endemic to the labyrinthine communication system of a clearing bank. They then returned to the Bank to be joined later by a further baron, Douglas Horner, the head of London region, which, including the City, was by far the most important section of Barclays' UK business.

The nature of the support had to be defined. How was it to be done? It was no longer a matter of whether there would be a basis of agreement, it was more a matter of thorny technical aspects. How would the money be put up? On what security? And the by now perennial question: what was Barclays prepared to do? What did not have to be considered, normally the first consideration, was whether the rescuers had the means; for each one of these wealthy institutions had the means and more to finance the entire rescue from its own internal resources. This had always been Cedar's underlying strength, that its institutional supporters were powerful financial heavyweights of the highest rank, and it was this quality of their financial strength, which was, from the beginning, the unstated received assumption behind the Governor's summons.

The fresh questions required fresh specialist skills and advice. 'It was time,' said Stenham, 'for the professionals to get in on the act.' The four, having conferred with their own colleagues, now needed to confer with their professional advisers. The institutions had already decided on Hambros. Barclays had most of the specialist skills already in-house, except one; this was the specialism of the liquidator. Its man, in this slightly odorous area, was the sibling of a family well-versed in this subfusc skill. A Mr Cork. In due course when he was permitted to do so, he performed his act with such bravura that the ovations he earned were still ringing in his ears decades later.

In each instance, as each head of each of the institutions discussed with colleagues at their respective HQs or over the telephone, and returned with new colleagues or invited others to join them, the identical procedure was enacted by the Bank. The Governor's secretariat would disclose to the messengers the name of the person expected. By the time the new addition arrived the method of induction was established. The room to which he was taken was precisely assigned, and no one, but no one, saw the chairmen of the four clearing banks entering or leaving.

*　　　　*　　　　*

It was time for the professionals to get in on the act.

ELEVEN

The Rescue

The first professional to be asked, a key figure, was John Gillum of Samuel Montagu, Cedar's financial adviser. Arriving at the Bank, he had gone straight up to the Octagon Room on the first floor, and apart from the specific occasions when he went downstairs to have discussions with his clients, he based himself upstairs until the end. It was a controversial decision. As Samuel Montagu represented Cedar, the question raised was why didn't Gillum base himself downstairs with his clients, going upstairs when necessary to negotiate. But he did not do so, he elected to stay upstairs with the institutions and with their advisers. Immediately he arrived, Gillum telephoned for his assistant William Sadleir to join him. Sadleir, then only twenty-eight and now one of the City's leading merchant bankers, is still at the same House. Gillum tracked Sadleir down at Barclays bank where he was with David Higginson, Cedar's lawyer, talking to Douglas Horner, trying to determine the form of help, if any, Barclays might provide. It was during their discussion, that Horner too, received a call from Bevan to join him and Vander Weyer. So, late in the afternoon, Horner, Sadleir and Higginson left Barclays to go to the Bank together.

Entering the Court Room, Sadleir sat next to Gillum. When he saw Lord De L'Isle he got up to greet him warmly, as anyone would expect of a person who had not seen his godfather for some time. Gillum, taken by surprise, was also taken by a reluctantly admitted twinge of pleasure that his own assistant had such grand connections. Ray Wheeler arrived on his own. A large lumbering man, with a good brain and even better judgement, he had an exemplary knack of getting to the core of a problem, of doggedly finding a solution. The lawyers arrived: they usually worked in pairs, one of the first rules laid down by their managing partners who would never confess that any such duplication had the remotest connection with fee-earning. At Coward Chance, acting for the institutions, their man was Paul Boyce. On this momentous occasion he played solo, his assistant, the very competent Richard Coleman participating immediately after the rescue. At Herbert Smith, acting for Cedar, was David Higginson, his assistant was the very competent David Bolton. Perhaps, on further thought, in view of the calibre of the assistants, their managing partners may, in these instances, have had a winning argument.

The professionals were there to exercise their special skills. One of the most professional and most intelligent of them all arrived from Cazenove, Cedar's stockbrockers. He was the silky, seamless, brilliant, immensely likeable Michael Richardson. He had taken over the Cedar account from Chandler. Richardson would offer the very best technical advice on Stock Exchange requirements, and though as skilled as anyone, if not more so on the particular tasks of a merchant banker, on this occasion he would be limited to advising on the Stock Exchange aspects.

There were various representatives from amongst the higher and lower echelons of the Bank of England, the Deputy Governor occasionally; Rodney Galpin, Deputy Principal of the Discount Office frequently; but the most prominent, always in high profile, like a ubiquitous lumbering shaggy dog, was Jim Keogh, the celebrated Principal of the Discount Office, who on banking supervision reported directly to the Governors, whereas on all other matters he reported to the Chief Cashier. Keogh, plus Galpin and assistants, had made the necessary arrangements for the visitors to be called, with Keogh himself seen to be sniffing in every room and corridor, greeting and talking to those with whom he was acquainted. Memories of him linger on with mixed feelings. His main responsibility as head of the Discount Office, apart from casting his eye over the money market, was to liaise with the recognised banks, to listen to the enquiries and appeals of the near banks and even the non-banks, to be the general listening post. That he had fallen short on some of his responsibilities was not in dispute (he still has his friends and they may well disagree), though the nature of the job and of the office was to say the least ill-defined not only as to its scope, but even as to its internal reporting procedures. To my mind, Keogh was an odd person to find in the Bank, and though he was later castigated somewhat excessively as a scapegoat, he must bear much of the responsibility for the Bank's lack of basic, never mind detailed knowledge of the management of the fringe banks, with whom he was the main Bank of England interface. Although in Galpin he had a deputy of real calibre as was proven in his later career, Keogh was not prone to delegating.

On this day, he was very much to the fore, increasingly in evidence, his propensity for indulging in the amber-hued nectar also much in evidence. To many he was irritating, to some he was infuriating, but to all he displayed a sincere, albeit awkward anxiety and a desire to help in any way he could. When I think of the persons who worked for the Bank of England of that era, I reflect particularly on the oddity of finding in the same great institution, two such completely dissimilar men as Jasper Hollom and Jim Keogh: Hollom the model mandarin exuding the smooth granite impression of an all-encompassing financial sage, and Keogh, two or three rungs lower down, the questionable, imperfect head of one of the Bank's most sensitive departments, exuding the impression of a slightly louche winking-and-nudging clubman on the verge of disclosing incredibly indiscreet titbits of gossip and information.

The numbers had swollen. The Court Room was now almost filled. They sat and whispered, they smoked, they tiptoed looking for refreshments. In the octagon room, Gillum, Sadleir and Wheeler bandied the rescue terms backwards and forwards with Higginson plus Bolton and Boyce evaluating the legal implications and starting to work on the first draft of the proposed heads of agreement.

The lawyers, having received their instructions, were getting on with it. The agreement in the process of formulation had one overriding feature: the institutions now committed to a rescue, wanted their pound of flesh. The cleavage between the institutions and the Morrisons, which first appeared at the Sunday meeting in Fischer's flat, resulting in Oram and his colleagues calling in Hambros, was now a complete separation; the institutions now on one side of a widening gap, the Morrisons on the other; the institutions upstairs, the Morrisons downstairs. It was not only a physical separation, a commercial separation, it was as if there were two opposing sides; them and us; years of friendship, years of support, years of pandering to the blandishments of the Morrisons, had been swept aside. This was very evident in the emerging heads of agreement reinforced by the hard drafting of Boyce. The heavyweight links were broken spiritually and physically. The institutions were in a strong position, Barclays was in a stronger position, but those in the weakest position were the executive directors. They were not considered, waiting like sheep in their downstairs pen. It was assumed they would accept, readily if not eagerly, any financial terms. Down on the ground floor they were hardly given a thought by those on the first floor.

There were occasional caucas meetings, the institutions amongst themselves, Barclays amongst themselves, a financial adviser with his clients, a stockbroker with a financial adviser, a lawyer with his principals, a lawyer with another lawyer. The arguments progressed.

Stenham has a fitting description: 'Of course the sheer logistics, the physical background, was highly unusual. I recall only too well that there was a power cut, we were all bitterly cold. The number of people in the various meetings did not know fully what was going on. People were milling from one room to another and the whole time there was this rush to get on with it'.

It was expected that Gillum could soon descend to the nether regions to inform the Cedar executive directors that an agreement had been reached on the rescue, that the parties could sign and then they could all go home. Several telephoned their wives to say that they would be home in time for a late dinner. Burton Johnson told his wife: 'I am going to be damned late.' If he had known how late, he may possibly have used a more forceful expression, but he certainly was not too pleased, though he showed little reaction to find when he returned to the Court Room after speaking to his wife, that sandwiches had not only been served but had been consumed in his absence. The last time he had had anything to eat was at breakfast.

It was mid evening. The main vestiges of the rescue had been settled. The total sum agreed to be underwritten after making necessary adjustments was £72 million, the whole of the left-hand side of the balance sheet just as Hollom had 'requested'. Barclays had finally agreed reluctantly to advance £22 million, but only if it ranked before the institutions and only if the Bank of England would chip in £2 million – a contribution not made public, at least not for several months. There had been fervent bargaining before Barclays' security was defined. Not one pound of their commitment would be at risk, whatever the state of the Cedar loan book and whatever the value of the Cedar properties. The institutions had responded by declaring that, as this was as far as Barclays was prepared to go, they would take control of the company. Be our guest, said Barclays. Control of the company by four of the nation's most formidable financial institutions could only improve Barclays' security.

Bevan did not endear himself. In refusing to budge, he gave the impression, indeed he proffered it, that he did not care about the outcome. At a certain moment an institutional man told him that if he did not budge, Cedar would go under. 'Well, let it go under', he said. His bank did not lose any face, Horner and Vander Weyer saw to that, although it may have lost banking business from one or other of the institutions. If Bevan cared about this, he did not and would not have shown it; he was making it patently clear that his bank was only there because its trust company had been the issue house for Cedar when it went public, not because his bank had been Cedar's bankers. There had never, he declared, been any especially close banking relationship between Barclays and Cedar, and although it was generally supposed that it was the lead bankers, it did not consider itself as ever having that role, or as ever having that responsibility. Barclays was adopting a similar approach towards the institutions' responsibilities as had Hollom earlier, that as being shareholders and loan holders, and with representatives on the board, the institutions had to be in the forefront and they had to take all the risks. At times it looked as if the institutions versus Barclays bank would itself become an issue, and that fact that it never formally turned into one, was probably due to the mollification attempts from Bevan's more ameliorative colleagues, Vander Weyer and Horner.

The institutions, miffed that Barclays did not respond to their suggestion that they could convert loan stock into equity, reacted by closing ranks; they would take full control of the company, and as an indication of their over-reaction to Barclays' intransigence they decided that the Morrisons would have to transfer all their shares to them. The legal implications of such a transfer were appalling, even ignoring the effect which such a demand would have on the Morrisons, and the unpleasantness it would cause. However, the fact that a demand of this nature, was even expressed, was a reflection not only of the institutions' indignation with Barclays, but of their distinctly unfriendly if not hostile attitude towards the Morrisons. It was then that the institutions decided that a special new share would be issued, one for each institution, each share having 10 million votes and, going further in order to show Barclays they meant hard business and that the risks they were being forced to take should have their own rewards, they decided to achieve this by way of a high interest rate and by charging a substantial fee.

Moreover, a nasty twist for those who would have to sign, the institutions wanted undated letters of resignation signed by each executive director of Cedar, including every member of the Morrison family. Barclays was indifferent: perfectly safe with its own security on its advance of £22 million, this was to it disparate legal paraphernalia, something for the institutions and their own lawyers to sort out with Cedar. After this day, Burton Johnson could not be described as a fan of Barclays: 'They were playing the game of brinkmanship, and were not really as helpful as they could or should have been'.

Stenham and Jenkins were extremely skilful negotiators and Wheeler, exploiting to the full the strength of his clients, was squeezing every drop he could on their behalf. He was not making things very easy for Gillum. Gillum too, a man of detail, was being as meticulous as usual. He was a slide rule negotiator and if that meant it took longer to reach agreement, then it meant it would have to take longer. At one point, he was aware of a heated outrage from the institutions, which was really directed at the Morrisons. Someone said that the jet would have to be sold. What do you mean the jet would have to be sold? We didn't even know the jet existed.

Advisers and the lawyers proceeded to work on the different interests, the demands simple or complex, the inevitable counter-demands less simple, more complex, the alterations, the changes of emphases, the different stresses and then, like the phrasing in a complex ballet, when the lines of the choreography become discernable, the structure of the Cedar rescue became visible and conclusive and the professionals could see the first signs of what could be defined as an acceptable financial formula.

It is always at this juncture of a major financing or refinancing or a complicated negotiation, that the participants, weary or exultant or more usually both, pause intellectually if not physically, and enjoy the unstinted exhilaration of knowing that they are within reach of a successful end to the task they have set themselves. At this stage a lawyer will perhaps relax and face his opponents with a thin smile of satisfaction, not so much the smile of having done well for his client as the smug pursed-lip smile of the professional who feels he has won points over his opponent, and is damned if he will let him know it, although he would still like him to know it. The Cedar rescue had reached this stage. The terms were agreed. One or two were not smiling. The institutions sat back. The advisers sat back. Barclays sat back. Gillum was ready to go downstairs to inform the executive directors that the rescue terms were agreed. He was to be accompanied by Michael Richardson, Bill Sadleir, David Higginson and David Bolton.

*   *   *

The butler of the Bank of England used to be known as the first doorkeeper and he answered directly to the secretary of the Bank. His assistant was known as the second doorkeeper and under him was the first parlour steward, the most senior of his rank, very much in keeping with the downstairs hierarchy of a large country house, with each man of whatever rank very proud of his actual and literal position, of his own standing on the well-trodden, precisely bordered paths of service. In 1973, the first parlour steward was Ray Simpson. He had joined the Bank ten years earlier, proud that his father had been a parlour steward before him. His own son, a university graduate, has become a banker himself, and however successful he becomes, he too will be proud that his father had been appointed to the position of the first parlour steward by the time he was thirty years old.

The first and second doorkeepers controlled their realm from the east entrance of the ground floor. They were responsible for stewarding visitors, serving morning coffee, lunch and afternoon teas, lubricating the wheels of the system. Without their services it would grind to a halt, the Governors and the directors would not be able to perform properly, or at any rate not sufficiently near the style and standards which they and their predecessors had been accustomed to and which their guests naturally expected. The great central Bank, like any great country house, relied utterly and completely on the smooth efficiency of the servants, and to a large extent was judged by others on their quality. As always with this cadre they were treated with immense respect, and, just as the lord and master of a stately home might well hesitate over the ineluctable choice of whether he should risk losing his wife or his butler, the top echelon of the Bank of England might well hesitate over the measure of regret that would be felt if a parlour steward as against a top manager were lost to the Bank. It was not that stewards were more important, it was because they were an intrinsic part of the Bank's code of behaviour – based on past precedents, customs and traditions – to provide the best possible service at all times. Excellence was the ingrained rule for the servers and the served, and if a director of the Bank of England asked after the well-being of a steward's son, it was not merely polite curiosity, it was genuine interest and concern. These never servile but always subservient aristocrats, ruled from their bastion at the east entrance behind a high wooden screen, apprising every movement, their tentacles reaching into all corners. They also had their own private room, where they received their official guests, offering them tea, served to them by one of their own colleagues on the same silver tray and with the same bone china as the directors; there was never any question of service being at a lesser level or provided in any other way. This had been laid down in time-worn protocol.

As a rule, a keyholder remained on duty until the Governor or the Deputy Governor or the last executive director or visitor had departed. Only the first and second doorkeepers and the first parlour stewards were keyholders, a privilege of similar cachet to that of a bank signatory in the Chief Cashier's department. It was very rare indeed for the most junior keyholder, the first parlour messenger, to fill this role.

On Wednesday 19 December 1973, an unprecedented day in the annals of the Bank of England, and one not even remotely repeated since, Douglas Drury, the first doorkeeper who had commenced his duties early in the morning, had left at 8.30 pm well after his normal roster. The second doorkeeper was off duty, so Ray Simpson, the first parlour messenger, found himself in charge. He remembers this day as one of the most extraordinary of his entire working life.

He and his colleagues were not aware of anything unusual until after tea, when Simpson sensed without being told that he was going to be late that evening. After Drury had left, well into Wednesday night, Simpson had to consider the need for refreshments at a time when the kitchens would normally have been locked several hours earlier. To make matters worse, the kitchens were on the fourth floor and because of the emergency power cuts, they had not been fully operational. With limited resources, Simpson organised the refreshments: the directors' lunchtime coffee was reheated and served, only sufficient for upstairs, plus smoked salmon and ham sandwiches and biscuits. Downstairs they were served with whisky and beer and left-over ham sandwiches. The Morrisons did not partake: they had never eaten ham in their lives.

At around 10 pm Simpson was asked to escort a small party from the Court Room to the waiting room downstairs, to the room assigned to the Cedar executive directors. It was led by a rather tall slim man, a merchant banker with well sculptured features and a fine head of hair just turning grey. They were escorted downstairs. Not one of them thought they would encounter anything other than a most friendly response of enormous relief from the Morrisons and the executive directors.

Upstairs, as Kenneth Cork recalled, 'We waited and they didn't come back, and they didn't come back and they didn't come back'.

Eventually John Gillum and his party returned. He was ashen. 'They refused to sign.'

*   *   *

An audible gasp reverberated throughout the first floor of the Governor's House.

TWELVE

The Downstairs

The conflict at the Bank of England, as Michael told me weeks later, was the most bewildering, the most shocking and painful day of his life. It started with a dark December morning when he, like the other executive directors, were standing by for the summons from the Bank. They had waited at Cedar's City office in the Commercial Union building, a five-minute walk away from the Bank. This was where they collected in the morning, and this is where they waited. All day. It was cold, not bitterly, but because they knew that the heating could not be increased because of the Government restrictions, it felt colder. Father, son and nephew sat on their own. Dazed and shaken and jet-lagged from the long flight home, Jack Morrison could not take in anything, although his subdued dignified bearing gave the two younger men some confidence.

Ahmed and Watts, the closest and oldest colleagues from the Amal board, were invited to join the Morrisons in their office, the only executive directors so asked. 'This is a family meeting, by that I mean you two are part of the family,' was how Michael put it to them. There was no Alan Glass; his absence was conspicuous and as was noted by David, 'I bet he's with the institutions'. When Glass did arrive later, he was not made aware, nor was he aware that his message-passing postponement of the previous afternoon's board meeting rankled with the Morrisons; they now very much regarded him as an outcast, if not an enemy. During waiting periods, frequent attempts were made to brief Jack, more to find a reason for talking, to pass the time; he listened attentively but he was not hearing a word. Michael would frequently give him an anxious glance. Then, Arnold Ziff, Jack's son-in-law married to Michael's only sister, joined them. It was mid morning. They waited for the call for them to go to the Bank.

Lunchtime. The Morrisons, Ahmed and Watt had cold fish, salad and Perrier. Still no call from Gillum. They were becoming increasingly worried. Why was it taking such a long time? By early afternoon the waiting had induced a stupor. Suddenly Gillum was on the phone: could Michael and David come over at once to the Bank, there were one or two queries, the others were to follow later. Michael left with David, but before departing he told Ahmed to bring Bailey, a figures man, with him to help with the projections and schedules. Cheerfulness immediately pervaded it. Ahmed had been going over the figures again and again from every combination. It was like a nervous tic, but he knew all the numbers by heart and he was confident that a rescue plan could be reasonably secured; the inherent position was strong, all that was required was some temporary help to bolster up the left-hand-side of the balance sheet, the deposit side; the right-hand-side was no problem, its loan book was rock solid, so were the properties.

Soon after 6 pm Gillum called again. Could they all come to the Bank. A slight feeling of cheerfulness prevailed. The executive directors left the City office and emerged into the street. There was no street lighting, very little traffic, the buildings were sombre and dark. There was a feeling once again of gloom, the cheerfulness after Gillum's call evaporated as quickly as it had arisen. One director remembers the walk from Fenchurch to Threadneedle as being even more miserable than the whole day of waiting; he felt as if he were walking to a court of justice to hear a verdict, to receive some sort of sentence. Another remembers how they foregathered before leaving for the Bank, how he was near Jack Morrison in companionable but worried silence, the old boy shuffling towards the lobby, walking seemed an effort.

On arrival at the Bank, and on entering the parlour corridor, they were shown into a small waiting room. Whilst there, they could hear Michael and David almost shouting at each other in an adjoining room, with David repeatedly saying, 'Michael, stop worrying'. They were then conducted into a larger room next door which, though used for meetings, they did not feel was any larger as most of the space was taken up by a meeting table and chairs. The co-managing directors joined them. They were both a little flustered. Michael said Gillum had asked for some figures on the properties. There had been a mix-up and a misunderstanding. Gillum had wanted the net figure of certain properties after gearing, and they had thought he wanted the gross figure. Michael was slightly upset because there was a suggestion that the institutions did not think it was merely a misunderstanding.

Thirteen men in all: Stanley, the company secretary; Bailey, the figures man; Ziff, the son-in-law; and ten executive directors. Upstairs were their fellow directors, the non-executive representatives of the institutions with their top men, upstairs were their finanical advisers, their lawyers, their stockbrokers; downstairs they were unaware who else had been summoned and where they might be in the Bank, but as their ignorance receded, as the significance of the physical demarcation and their isolation dawned upon them, their ignorance turned from bewilderment to resentment. The territorial boundaries also stirred deep personal feelings; they felt socially humiliated and their mood, and certainly the mood of the Morrisons, progressed from resentment to anger. They had waited most of the day in the Cedar offices and now they had to endure further waiting, not as equals, but as inferior beings. Adding to their discomfiture they were overpowered by their surroundings; the Bank of England seemed like a fortress, forbidding, and distinctly unfriendly.

They began pondering their fate, with various shades of fear, anxiety, fury and not a little curiosity. Who else was in the Bank? What had they been discussing all day? Now they had an additional worry: why were they being treated in this off-hand way? The thirteen men sat at the oval table, inactive, waiting for news, waiting for something to happen – at the receiving end. One man though, the only person who was not a director or an officer of Cedar, the son-in-law, Arnold Ziff, was not frightened or worried: he was hopping mad.

Ziff, a North-country Crowther of Bankdom, a stalwart Leeds businessman, proud of his city's reputation and achievements, a prominent member of its enterprising Jewish community whose members had been especially inspired by Montagu Burton, their earliest icon of national business success, was a man who liked to keep his feet where every Yorkshiremen likes to keep them – firmly on the ground. He was a wealthy man in his own right, he was a rich son-in-law of a rich father-in-law, a man of substance, a man who always spoke his mind; he was not only the head of his own family business, he was a Yorkshireman. On no account should they sign anything, was what he was telling them in his Yorkshire manner.

Thirteen men in an airless frigid room. Excluding Stanley the secretary, Bailey the figures man, and the four members of the family, the remaining seven, all executive directors, were easily divisible into two separate groups: the 'Cedar group' and the 'Amal group'. Each group was an uneven cluster, ill assorted and not homogenous; not one of them thought alike as they had always worked as individuals, answering directly to one or other of the Morrisons they had never been part of a team.

In the Cedar group, were Philip Johnstone, in charge of investments; Reg Edward, the original Coal Board representative, now retired but still an executive director without portfolio; John Eames, general manager of mortgage business development; Alan Glass, in charge of financial operations. In the Amal Group, were Alan Watt, responsible for the Scottish property portfolio; Yusuf Ahmed, financial director of Amal before the merger, now encroaching upon Alan Glass's responsibilities; and Michael Grinling, responsible for the UK property portfolio.

Philip Johnstone was sixty-two. Well known in the City and well respected, he was an institutional man, an investment man, through and through. What was he doing in such a situation? His proper level it might have been thought would have been with those on the floor above, where his successor Hugh Jenkins was to be found. A full-time director of Cedar with his definite executive responsibilities, which of course he would stick to, he had no special commitments to the Morrisons, but certainly to the company which now employed him. He would agree to any reasonable proposals for a rescue, but only after taking into full consideration the rights of the shareholders, including the Morrisons for whom he had a liking and respect: if he had not liked them he wouldn't have accepted their offers of association in the first place. He knew Reg Edward and recognised that though Edward only nominally represented the Coal Board, the real power lay with Jenkins (appointed only a fortnight earlier). Johnstone, not one to mince words when it was necessary, would be the first to declare that the Coal Board involvements with Cedar could be considered confusing.

John Eames, the longest-serving Cedar employee amongst them, had risen to the level of general manager and had been appointed a director on the Amal merger. It might have been considered that the general manager of Cedar should have been a trained banker, not someone whose background had been in instalment credit. Eames represented the sort of person more likely to be found in a hire purchase or a mortgage brokerage business, who, though possessing a perfectly legitimate breed of discipline, had just the sort of background which elicited the particular distaste which true bankers felt towards fringe bankers. Eame's job was to maintain the relationships with the brokers and to expand and administer the inflow of loan applications. He had recently taken on two senior assistants to help him, each of them concentrating on visiting the brokers; Eames considered he had become too busy to visit them himself.

Alan Glass, who had been with Coopers and Lybrand as a management consultant, joined Cedar some fifteen months earlier to concentrate upon financial administration and had only joined the board fifteen days earlier. He was to play a crucial role. In his relatively short tenure he had already shown that he was a first-rate executive with possible leadership qualities, though these were kept on a tight rein by Michael and David, particularly in the area of reporting to the board. He had a mild, gentle, polite manner; underneath he was a man of determination with a surprisingly strong character. He was also subtle in his way and was now considered by the enlarged 'family' as part of the 'enemy', as an informant. Michael, having trusted him thoroughly only a fortnight earlier, distrusted him completely now. There was no cause for Michael to do so and it was one of his more foolish misjudgements, for Glass was clearly a person whom the institutions had not only learnt to trust, but upon whom they had decided to rely; they had listened to his reports at the various crisis meetings, he appeared to know his facts and he delivered his information without fuss. It was evident there was a growing respect for him.

Nor did the institutions hide this from Michael, who may not have liked it and who might have considered that it would have been more sensible if he had himself adopted a more overt respect for Glass, even if he did not feel it, which he did not. Michael, however, took no pains to conceal his greater solidarity towards Ahmed in preference to Glass, adding to the institutions' drift away from his family and to the lessening of their confidence in him. So it was not surprising during those fraught crisis days, that the institutions began to regard Glass as a special friend in the Cedar camp, which they could not have made more obvious than by using Glass as their trusted messenger. It was made apparent on the dismal Sunday meeting that the institutions had marked Alan Glass's card. They chose their man well.

In the Amal group, Alan Watt was very much director calibre and, just as Alan Glass was a first-rate chartered accountant, Watt was a first-rate chartered surveyor. A Glaswegian, he had joined Amal early on, recommended by Izzy Walton and by Ian Morrison with whom he was very friendly. He looked after the Scottish portfolio and was the sole person in the room who was a truly professional property man, just as Hugh Jenkins was the sole person upstairs with the same qualified expertise. These two were inevitably to engage in heated exchanges over the value of the properties for many months to come.

Other than Watt, Yusuf Ahmed was the director most liked and trusted by the Morrisons. Following the Amal merger where he had been finance director, Michael had drawn him into many of the functions of the financial director of Cedar, perhaps into a deliberately confusing overlap with Alan Glass, causing inevitable clashes between the two, exacerbated by the institutions' recent leanings towards Glass. Ahmed, a well-educated Pakistani, was an intelligent man with an active sense of humour. From first to last he was bemused to be in the Bank of England and though not worried like the others over the amounts they owed on their incentive shares – he had opted for convertibles – he was very worried for the Morrisons. He had his A4 pad in front of him and spent most of his time, like an artist at his sketch pad, constantly working, juggling and reworking the figures. He had discussed the various permutations with Michael and David, determined to demonstrate to them the strength of the Cedar balance sheet. If any detailed technical backup was required, as Michael had suggested, Bailey, the figures man, had all the compendious schedules at hand.

Michael Grinling was an unexpected person to find within the Morrison orbit. A nervy person, he was an orthodox property man with development expertise, the type of man who might well have been running his own property company. He was particularly wary of the intentions of the institutions upstairs and was sensitive to the personal issues. He had been enduring a rising anger over the whole situation; to him it was a mess which should have been cleared up days or weeks earlier. He wanted none of it and he had already decided that he was going to pack it in and resign.

To Michael Morrison the room was a dungeon; that image of despair and imprisonment never left him, but a dungeon it was not. It was one of the larger parlour rooms on the ground floor, a meeting room or committee room, rather than a waiting room, one of the first on the left, encountered by visitors as they entered the parlour corridor from the west entrance. The room itself was squarish with high walls; at the top of one wall by the ceiling there was a dormer window, it had no view, only the winter darkness filtered through. In addition to the meeting table, there were two side tables; on one there was *Country Life* and the *Banker* – both magazines aptly reflecting the unique personality of their host – on the other was a telephone which was to be used by David Fischer in a grim tragi-comedy which brought Michael to tears of frustration. There were a generous number of chairs around the meeting table. There was the inevitable clock, the pictures on the walls were prints with no merit other than decoration. The walls were off-white, a soft ivory.

It has been recalled by everyone without exception that Jack Morrison made a good impression. By far the oldest (on his birthday a fortnight later he would be seventy-two years old), he was not so much the elder statesman as the oldest relic of a former grandeur. He was what Jack Cotton used to call somewhat cold-bloodedly 'one of the living dead', by which Cotton meant a businessman, who was going through the motions of being actively present in a room, of taking part in a meeting, of listening to a discussion, but who in reality was detached, cut off. Something within such men has been severed, probably by a doctor's death sentence, a business crash, a betrayal, a shock. On the mercifully rare occasions when Cotton's searchlight antennae gave him the signal, he would observe with regret, but with finality after such a person departed, 'That man is dead'. On the first occasion I heard this morbid lapidary sentence, I asked, 'How do you mean dead?' Cotton replied, 'He is dead because something in his brain has cracked. You can see it in the eyes. You can see he is one of the living dead.' And when most ironically and most tragically it happened to Jack Cotton himself, when something in that decent frame broke, when there was no expression in those honest coal-black eyes, I was struck by an overwhelming feeling of sadness when I realised that lovable Jack Cotton had himself become one of the living dead.

Jack Morrison was now one of Cotton's living dead: something had disconnected, something had severed. Stricken amongst his family and his colleagues, he appeared a brittle, almost wax-like figure. The matriarch, not one to show her feelings unduly, would have been moved to tears if she had seen him in this state, but she would certainly have been sustained by a feeling of pride in the way he comported himself. Later when I learnt from Michael that Jack had particularly wanted Ziff to be with them, it was only then that I fully appreciated how agonising had been the level of his despair, how desperately the genuine family man had needed his nearest and dearest around him. Only three weeks earlier just after the flying jaunt to Scotland, in buoyant happy mood, feeling on top of the world, he had left for New Zealand. Effervescent, if not self-satisfied, he had gone for business and pleasure; for business to see the Phoenix people in Auckland – the beginnings of an antipodes joint venture; for pleasure, another trip, another cruise, perhaps another lady. Then the bolt from the blue. The terrible phone call from Michael. The immediate flight back to London. In black misery. Deposit run? What deposit run? How? Why? He had departed from London the happy, smiling multimillionaire, the chairman of a thriving City bank, the head of a prosperous happy family – and then the voice of his son, thousands of miles away, the voice Jack knew and loved best of all. Something in him snapped.

He was now sitting, baffled and uncomprehending in a waiting room in the Bank of England. He was placed at the head of the oval table. The entrance to the room was on his left. On his right were Fischer, Ziff and Watt. Michael was on his left, then Ahmed, then several empty chairs, then Glass, then Edward, Grinling, Eames, Johnston, Bailey and Stanley. When visitors entered the room, the first person they would see would be Jack with his enlarged family sitting closely around him.

They had their first visitors: Gillum and Sadleir, their advisers from Samuel Montagu. Gillum was courteous, and he explained: the institutions and their advisers are meeting upstairs in the Bank, they have agreed to mount a rescue, discussions are proceeding, everyone concerned in the rescue is here in the Bank. The institutions have brought in Hambros to advise them. I will come down as soon as an agreement is ready. Gillum and Sadleir departed. The executive directors were thoroughly non-plussed.

Then David Higginson came in with David Bolton. Higginson had been an extremely unhappy man since the deposit run and, if it were possible, even more unhappy since his arrival at the Bank with Sadleir and Horner. He knew the Morrisons well and he liked them. From the earliest days of Cedar, his firm Herbert Smith had been involved in all the corporate legal work – the agreements with the institutions, the public quotation, the loan and debenture agreements. Herbert Smith had a very good name: Herbert on its own was old-fashioned Victorian, Smith was well, Smith, but Herbert Smith evoked an immediate respect for a great City law firm with a first-class name.

Higginson was now a senior partner and, from the beginning of his association with the Morrisons, he had made a point of acting personally on all the Cedar legal matters, rarely passing anything on at Pall Mall to anyone other than to Bolton. As his relationship with the Morrison family matured and became closer and more cordial, especially with Michael Morrison, it was part of the natural course of events that he would be invited to become a trustee of their family trusts, a position he later shared with Gerald Drew, a partner in Coopers and Lybrand. Higginson became an elder uncle figure to Michael. He had the air of the benevolent shrewd family lawyer. He was a man of undoubted integrity, a pillar of a City law firm, his staunchness to his clients unquestionable. He had immediately sympathised with the Morrisons in the devastating and abrupt way they had been flung into the pit of fear. Since the start of the deposit run he had been in constant touch, becoming increasingly anxious about the emotional effect it was having on Michael. And what about Jack? The poor man having been yanked back from the other end of the world to face all this.

Higginson was a man of moderation, of sympathy, of steadfastness. He was available at all times to help a client, particularly a client in distress. The Morrisons were very much in distress and he accepted why Michael in these recent desperate days had constantly tele-phoned, sometimes incoherently, sometimes very much to the point, especially when he stressed the extreme vulnerability, the potential insolvency of the family trusts. The trusts were certainly in extreme danger; possibly so were the trustees. But what had to come first was an end to Cedar's predicament. For that reason he had been, on Cedar's behalf at Barclays that afternoon with Sadleir, to obtain support from the bank. He had been there in great part because of his deeply ingrained professionalism which was based on the tenet that one always helped one's client as best as one was able.

Facing the Morrisons, Higginson began to tell them what was happening upstairs, but the atmosphere was edgy. Speechless before with Gillum, Michael and David now gave vent to their outrage. Their colleagues were upstairs. Why? They were downstairs. Why? What was going on? Why the separation? Higginson tried to explain. Michael, with frequent excitable interjections from David, continued to fulminate; eventually he subsided. Higginson continued patiently. The institutions had to be upstairs. They had to agree terms between themselves, not only with Barclays. The institutions had not been keen to do anything. That was why it had taken such a long time. There had been real problems. There had been great difficulties before they had ultimately even agreed to mount a rescue. They had been in the Bank since early morning. What? The Morrisons and the executive directors were taken aback. Since early morning? Yes, since early morning. He had himself been at Barclays with Sadleir when Gillum had telephoned. Barclays were being extremely unhelpful. The rescue was by no means a certainty. He had to leave to get on with the negotiations.

Those left downstairs could not believe what they had been hearing. They had come to agree a rescue operation and had assumed it was just a matter of rubber stamping; they now learnt that the institutions had been there all day. They began to feel that in some way they were tainted, that some form of quarantine had been imposed. The non-family executive directors said very little. The 'enlarged family' was not talking to Glass. He had already gone over to the other side. He had crossed the floor. Had he perhaps also known that the institutions had been there since the morning? How much did he know? Neither Michael nor David deigned to ask Glass himself.

An incident of pathos occurred. Jack Morrison came to life. There was a lull in the conversation. The chairman had been thinking and he said to no one in particular, 'We don't really have anything to worry about. All we need to do is to stop lending for a few days then the position will improve'. No one made any response. Michael leant foward and was seen to murmur quietly to his father.

Amongst Michael's clearest recollections were how they were huddled together, how they were on the receiving end, how they were waiting for something to happen, waiting for someone to appear, someone to tell them how things were going, or were not going, how things were to be settled, how noble the institutions were. Events were taking place elsewhere, decisions were being made by others; he said he felt impotent and powerless.

At this juncture with no sign of any rescue, as time wore on, past 7 pm, past 8 pm, past 9 pm, Michael began to consider the possibility that there might not be a rescue at all or that the rescue might be attached to dangerous conditions, dangerous to him personally. When he had first arrived at the Bank, David kept saying to him, 'Don't worry. It's going to work out,' and, at first, he had been inclined to agree. The rescue was a relatively simple matter of putting up some further money; £25 million had already been advanced, and a further sum was required to be injected or committed to restore confidence. The business was sound, he knew that only too well: no real problem existed other than stemming the deposit run. The loans to its customers were also sound; it was in fact a good loan book. There was ample security for further commitments; on the initial £25 million only property had been charged, the second mortgage loans were unencumbered.

Cedar's bad debt history had been exemplary and, though standards of lending may have dropped, though some of the advances made may not have been approved in the earlier years, any possible bad or doubtful debts would eat only marginally into profits. As for the properties in Amal, they were mostly investment properties, let to tenants of good standing. The only major development was Buckingham Gate, and that was a real prize, in a first-class location, and certainly worth a lot more than its cost. It had already cost several million pounds, a considerable amount – site acquisition and assembly had not been easy, neither had the planning – and it needed several additional millions to be completed, a problem yes, but nowhere near insurmountable.

The only problem was temporary illiquidity. Michael and David had gone over this dilemma every day for the past three weeks. They had discussed the deposit run incessantly with the institutions and with the advisers, and had studied interminable schedules and projections and estimates until the figures had come out of their ears. Cedar was sound, it was solid: there was only a liquidity problem and a temporary one at that, he was sure. Cedar could not be compared with London and County, and look how quickly that scurrilous lot had been saved. Certainly all the family money was in Cedar. Certainly the family trusts were in jeopardy. Cedar had to be saved. But why were they taking such a long time upstairs?

Michael really started worrying. There must be something wrong. The delay could not only be due to Barclays. There was something fundamentally unpleasant behind all this, and he was now sure that there was a dangerous chasm between the institutions and his family. Things which were unimportant before were now important, loans to the Morrisons, the private jet; the institutions must be thinking there were hundreds of skeletons in the cupboard, of which they knew nothing, or on which they had been misinformed. This was when he felt on very weak ground, that there was no longer any trust. It was demonstrated in the way they were not all meeting together; they were not even in adjacent rooms. It was not just bad manners, and it was not just degrading and humiliating, it was now a matter of them and us, and 'they' were against 'us'. Yesterday they had put off the board meeting. Cedar was no longer their family bank. They were going to be carved up. Those fellows up there were no friends. His father had always been suspicious about them. Jack had been right all along. The family should have its own lawyer. It should have independent advice.

*   *   *

The door opened, Ray Simpson stood aside and the party, led by John Gillum, his tall slim figure emerging first, followed by Bill Sadleir, David Higginson, David Bolton, and Michael Richardson, entered. They greeted the Morrisons and the other directors. Gillum had a sheaf of papers in his hand. He sat down on one of the spare chairs by the door, with Sadleir beside him, one or two stood by the door. Gillum put his papers on the table in front of him. From his first remarks the Morrisons and the executive directors could not have been more shocked.

'The institutions no longer have confidence in Cedar,' said Gillum. 'They only decided to go ahead with the rescue after a great deal of discussion between them and they are doing so with great reluctance. They are not concerned with the shareholders but with the depositors. The amount involved exceeds £70 million. The Bank has suggested that the whole of the left-hand side of the balance sheet is to be underwritten. Our talks with the institutions and Barclays have not been easy. It has been an extremely difficult negotiation. I am pleased to say we have now finally got an agreement.

Michael and David were speechless. Jack shifted in his chair as if he were coming out of a coma. Dotting the 'I's' and crossing the 'T's'. Yes. Shoring up the deposits. Yes. Arranging a short-term facility whilst the temporary illiquidity was being sorted out. Yes. Taking security of some sort. Yes. Taking a larger shareholding in return for a facility. Yes, perhaps even that. But to write off the equity. No! No! No!

They looked with concentration at Gillum. He peered over his half-glasses. These are the terms: 'The total amount of the rescue comes to £72 million. First, Barclays will provide an immediate facility of £22 million. Second, this will be underpinned by the four institutions. Third, the institutions will pledge a total of £12.5 million each, £50 million in all, of which £25 million has already been advanced. This £72 million, together with Cedar's cash and near cash, underwrites the whole of the left-hand side of the balance sheet. Fourth, the institutions will purchase properties in order to reduce their advances and assets will be sold. Fifth, one new share will be issued to each institution. Each of these four shares will carry 10 million votes. Sixth, the directors will sign undated letters of resignation. Seventh, the directors will sign letters renouncing any claims against the company. Eighth, no new business will be taken on.'

Michael could stand it no longer. He jumped up. 'It's unfair. You are giving the company away for nothing.'

'I am afraid this is the best deal we can negotiate.'

'They have not had good advice.' A Yorkshire voice.

'Who are you?' Gillum asked sharply.

'I am Arnold Ziff.'

'What are you doing here?'

'I represent the Morrison family shareholdings.'

'You are not an officer of Cedar and you have no right to be here. If you intervene again, I am afraid I shall have to ask you to leave.'

Questions were hurled at Gillum, mostly from Michael. How would the special voting shares work? Reply: they are for control, not for extra shares. There is one share for each institution and each share has ten million votes.

What was Barclays doing? Reply: putting up £22 million. It will have a first charge ranking in front of the institutions.

Why must we sign undated letters of resignation? Reply: a normal requirement of these circumstances, and the institutions have insisted upon it.

How will the properties be valued? Reply: they will be valued as between willing buyer and willing seller.

What about Buckingham Gate? Reply: it will be valued on the same basis.

What about its value? Reply: it needs finance to complete it, so that has to be taken into account when it is valued. This means it will have a lesser value than a completed property. 'Or nothing,' an interjection, it was thought, from Grinling.

'No new business?'

'That's right,' said Gillum, 'no new business.'

At this point Michael Richardson, the consummate negotiator, poured some oil on the interchange. Like the rest of the group from downstairs he could see it was not going at all well. He declared that in general terms, taking into account all the difficulties, it was the best possible deal for the company. The Morrisons were halted a little, as they had learnt to listen to Richardson when he had anything to say, but on this occasion they were too upset, too angry to take heed of any soothing explanatory comments. As Richardson put it later, 'They could only see a black pit in front of them'.

The most pertinent questions were on the property values and the property sales. This clearly was the crux. If a full value was put on the properties – particularly on Buckingham Gate – the shares of the company would be worth something; if a low value were put on the properties, pariticularly if a low value were put on Buckingham Gate, the shares would be next to worthless.

After Richardson's interjection, whilst Gillum was answering questions, Ahmed, sitting next to him, tried to advance alternatives to the terms. Richardson listened to him politely and gave his view that he did not think the institutions would consider any changes. Ahmed tried another tack. He asked Richardson whether the institutions would consider a fundamentally different plan. Richardson told him 'One can always ask'. Ahmed then quickly showed Michael his calculations based on an alternative plan, whereby the institutions would agree to buy all the shares at a very low price, say at 10 pence or 20 pence per share.

Michael whispered to Ahmed, 'Yusuf, we cannot sell the shares at too low a figure.'

The penny dropped. Ahmed realised for the first time the precise nature of the family's frightful predicament. Of course, the price of the shares were all important to its net worth and to the trusts. If the shares were sold below a certain price they would be insolvent. What the Morrisons were fighting for was to obtain a high price or no price. If the shares were not priced it would give them a chance. If sufficient time was provided for a recovery, the shares might then have a value and the Morrisons might then be able to restore their fortune, or at any rate salvage something. Everything depended on how the properties were to be valued, which also applied to Ahmed and the non-family executive directors, although their viewpoint was somewhat different. It was not only that their 'incentive' shares and convertibles could be basically worthless, but nothing had been said about the moneys they had borrowed in order to take them up. These loans would have to be repaid. But how and when? Surely loans to the executive directors should be written off as part of the rescue agreement. But then how could they be, if the loans had been made to the directors, including the Morrisons 'in the ordinary course of banking business?'

Gillum was explaining a point when he was suddenly interrupted by Michael. 'We need legal advice.'

'There is your legal adviser,' said Gillum, pointing to Higginson.

Michael turned brusquely to Higginson. 'I don't want your advice. I want independent advice.'

David Higginson was in a delicate position. He was present as Cedar's legal adviser, but he was also a trustee for the Morrison trusts. He had in effect two separate daunting tasks, made more so by the mutterings of directors' loans and extravagance and whispers of a private jet. Certainly on the proposed rescue terms, the trusts were seriously underwater, a state of affairs which should not have been allowed to occur in any family settlement; to have a nil value was one thing, but to have a liability of a million pounds, to have a family trust that was insolvent, that was untenable. He and his co-trustee Gerald Drew could be in personal peril for having sanctioned the debt, and their own firms could be involved. It would be indefensible to claim that the loan was taken up because the beneficiaries were enthusiastic and because the same beneficiaries had negotiated the terms of the loan with the Bank. The trustees of a family trust with a single asset should be very reluctant, if not opposed, to creating a liability in order to increase the investment of the same single asset. The ghastly implications to the trustees of insolvent Morrison trusts had not entered his head with anything like the same force that it had entered and clouded Michael's.

Higginson was concentrating on saving Cedar's depositors, and the interests of the shareholders had to come next. Michael gave as much prominence to saving the shareholders' interests as he was to saving the depositors' money. There was a clear difference of emphasis. A lawyer of any school, not only of the old school, when confronted with a rich and important client who has suddenly been smitten, undergoes one of the more unpleasant experiences to which he can be exposed; what was more distressing and more poignant to Higginson, was that he knew the Morrisons had virtually no assets other than Cedar, that a Cedar collapse was not a partial but a total disaster for the Morrisons.

Michael's single outburst, 'I don't want your advice, I want independent advice', immediately broke their relationship of ten years. This was not because Michael wanted independent advice; he was of course entitled to that and Higginson would have encouraged it. It was the way Michael had put it. Higginson slumped further into his chair. Neither he nor David Bolton made any further comment.

One of the executive directors then asked, 'Why don't we break up now? Why don't we go home and meet tomorrow morning?'

'Absolutely not,' said Gillum 'we have to agree now. No one is to leave the Bank until we have an agreement.' He looked at the Morrisons clustered together. There were fervent whisperings.

Suddenly Michael said, 'We refuse to sign.'

The family had not conferred with the other non-family directors, and not one of them made any comment.

Gillum, Sadleir, Richardson, Higginson and Bolton rose to leave. There was nothing more to be said. They had been there for well over an hour. It was getting on towards midnight.

*   *   *

After they had departed, the downstairs atmosphere changed very much for the worse. There were signs – the first – of desperation. Michael, the family spokesman and the spokesman for the executive directors, had with some vehemence said 'No!' A dejected Gillum had left with his papers.

The family talked intensely to each other. From time to time Ahmed, never one to give up, still tried to go over the figures with Michael; there was little point and Michael was too disturbed to listen. He talked to Watt. They both considered that Ziff's constant exhortation not to sign anything was the best advice to follow. Watt was already concerned about the property valuations. In the normal transaction, valuations were not easy to agree as between borrower and lender. This was no normal transaction, he already smelt an element of firesale about it which he did not like. Fischer, his large bald forehead glistening with sweat, curiously less emotional than Michael during most of this night, was now betraying signs of panic, his eyes, normally wide and knowing, were blinking with fear. Jack, was again sphinx-like and immobile. There were signs that Michael was losing control. His voice, normally a shade over-loud, was nearer shouting level; unable to sit still, he kept shifting about. He got up, he walked around, he sat down. He was frightened, it showed and he did not care. The family had put all its eggs into the Cedar basket, its family trusts were in debt, he himself had incurred personal loans which he had applied entirely to increasing his holdings in Cedar. The terms from the so-called rescuers upstairs were not unfriendly, they were vicious. Could he be made personally bankrupt? It was too terrible that he had to even ask himself such a question.

Most of the executive directors were also asking themselves the same terrible question. They owed money to Cedar secured against the Cedar shares. The shares were very probably worthless under these rescue conditions. If they fought the institutions, they might be forced under. The spectre of bankruptcy had already started hovering in the forefront of their minds. If they agreed to the terms, even if their loans were not going to be written off, they might be offered more gentle terms of repayment. Some of them harked back to the initial arrangements made for the loans, orginally granted to them by Samuel Montagu, then, in some mysterious way after the acquistion of Amal, they had been switched over to Cedar without discussion. If they had still owed this money to Samuel Montagu, might they not now have been better off? The room was getting colder. The temperature outside was dropping. Some were still wearing overcoats: one or two who had discarded them earlier now put them on. The prison shades were darkening.

Suddenly they heard a shout from Michael directed to David. 'We must have our own lawyer. Get hold of Lord Goodman. Do you know his number?'

'Of course I know his number,' Fischer shouted back. 'It's in my flat.' He picked up the only telephone in the room. Everyone looked at him. He told his Portuguese manservant, 'Look for Goodman in my address book'. There was a long pause. 'Goodman. Lord Goodman.' Another pause. 'Look under G. G for George.' David's voice rose feverishly. 'G for George. O for Oliver.' There was a further pause. 'What do you mean an Olive? O is for Oliver.' Then a screech: 'G for George and O for Oliver and another O is for another Oliver'.

Michael blew up, purple with frustration. He put his head in his hands and bawled 'Doesn't anyone there speak English?' There were suppressed gasps and even one or two nervous giggles; tension and anxiety was heightening the latent hysteria. Fischer, tears coursing down his cheeks, put down the receiver. They did not get Lord Goodman's number; Lord Goodman did not get their phone call; they did not get independent advice. There was silence in the room. Some of the others looked away in embarrassment. Michael still held his head in his hands. He was in tears; he seemed to be giving up.

Michael then got up and walked around the room. From time to time he shrugged his shoulders and was seen to shake his head from side to side as if he could not believe the reality of the nightmare he was going through. He returned to sit beside his father. He began to recover some of his composure. He whispered to Ziff and to Fischer.

He and his father talked closely to each other. He had said no to Gillum. He had said, we refuse to sign. The terms were awful, hopeless. There had to be a real improvement. Not all was lost. He was not going to give up. He would fight on.

Months later, I listened to Michael's vivid and emotional description of that night, his memories still raw, his wounds still alive and fermenting. He still could not understand why they had sat there so meekly, why they had been so submissive, why they had always remained isolated and on their own, why they had not insisted upon a combined meeting. In describing the scene, he kept asking himself the same questions. Why were they always at the receiving end? Why had they not just walked out? Why had they not listened to Ziff? And why the hell didn't they get through to Goodman?

THIRTEEN

The Upstairs

Upstairs the others waited whilst Gillum and party did not come back and did not come back. Eventually they reappeared. Gillum had said, 'They refused to sign,' and there was an audible gasp.

Here they all were in this evocative monument of a building, a number of fairly to very important people, late at night, close to midnight, many of them having been in the building since early that morning; it was not only late, it was also cold, many had not eaten since lunch, and some had not even eaten since breakfast. And those bloody people downstairs refused to sign. It was outrageous. What on earth did they think they were about? How dare the Morrisons refuse help? Were they so rich, did they have such substantial resources outside Cedar? Any traces of patience were stamped out, tempers flared, nerves already frayed, showed more of their sharp edges. Dawn and tomorrow's business hours were looming nearer and, underlying the executive directors' refusal to sign, was the reality that none of them could leave the Bank until there were signatures on a document. They might be there all night. It was a horrible thought.

It had never crossed anyone's mind that those about to be rescued would in effect say, 'Get lost.'

In the overall consternation and disgust, one man who showed his feelings most and was patently not bothering to conceal them was Tim Bevan. He had what Kenneth Cork, the liquidator described as his spaniel look of petulant indignation. Cork had been sitting subdued most of the evening beside Bevan. When those upstairs heard Gillum say 'they refused to sign' they were all astonished – all except the liquidator. Rather, he would have been astonished only if the directors had signed. Since he had been extricated by Bevan from his meeting at Barclays several hours earlier, and had arrived at the Bank in some puzzlement and more curiosity, Cork had listened unbriefed but intently whilst the terms for the rescue were being hammered out between the protagonists. Cork had noted the reactions of Gillum and Wheeler, the respective lawyers and their clients. His general evaluation was respect for many of the professionals involved, by no means for all of them, but he felt disquiet, and on one or two vital matters he was in distinct disapproval. He knew the outcome and had known it from the beginning: those chaps downstairs would never sign this sort of agreement.

Experience, earned after many weary years, told him that what the institutions were seeking – a realisation agreement encompassing no immediate hope for the executives and no future for the company – could not possibly succeed. Why should the Morrisons sign their own death warrant? Receiverships and liquidators ran in Cork's blood, and the initial rule he knew from his father, almost from his schooldays, a rule he had subsequently instilled in his own staff, was do not kill off what can be kept alive. In a near-terminal situation, which is how he would ruefully define the menacingly vague borders of his profession, the emphasis was on the word 'near', for whilst the corporation or individual was still alive, was still breathing, it must not be regarded as a corpse.

Cedar was not terminal, but near-terminal, and one had to go in as a doctor or a surgeon to improve the health of the patient, not go in as an undertaker; undertakers were for corpses, not for something still breathing. One had to look at the body corpus as a medical practitioner; it was a virtue, a true cash virtue, to keep a patient alive, though sometimes it was necessary to cut off an arm here and a leg there. Cedar was not dead; it was nowhere near coffin time, and these participants sitting within the country's final resuscitation centre should be reminded that Cedar was not dead, it was still in respiration.

But Cork had no standing; he was not allowed to say anything, he was there purely at the invitation of Barclays, he had no role except to advise Barclays, and only then when specifically requested by them. He was silent as instructed by his clients, who had said, 'Don't talk, just listen'. So listen he did, his small gimlet eyes roaming around the table, taking in everything, taking in the special qualities of the great room, the special qualities or lack of them of the participants themselves, on each of whom he had reached his own assessment hours earlier. Cork knew full well that most of them wondered what on earth he was doing there. This did not bother him. He knew from of old that when a receiver was called in, a bomb was ticking, he was on the scene as a bomb expert, to defuse it or to blow it up. Having diagnosed the situation and the characters, he knew, without any doubt, that sooner or later, as the expert, he would be asked to deal with it, one way or the other.

As the stark impact of Gillum's bulletin took effect, several got up from their chairs. They looked for refreshments, whisky was favoured, they spoke to each other in small groups, there was no laughter, no smiles, only resentment. It was getting colder and, like the downstairs group, some had worn their overcoats throughout, others were putting them on again. Burton Johnson was fatigued but not worried; he remembers murmuring to George Cumming beside him that he was convinced that the Morrisons would change their minds, they would have to agree, they personally had far too much at stake. If they had not quite got the message so far, he surmised, they certainly would if that liquidator chap sitting next to Bevan ever appeared downstairs.

Though Gillum was dejected, he refrained from showing it. It was a tough slog. All in a day's work, and now all in a night's work. But far more so. It was his definite judgement that they had got the best deal possible, which is why he recommended his clients to accept it. Would they ever sign, what would make them sign? He had the same thought as Burton Johnson. He looked across and said to Cork. 'Would you care to talk to them?' Cork turned to Bevan. 'I'm here for you and for Barclays. What do you want me to do?' 'Do?' snorted Bevan. 'Do anything to get this thing settled. It's ridiculously late.'

Cork surveyed the table. At last he could talk. At last he could express his views. As his father had taught him, take immediate control and the most difficult lot of any to control are creditors. His thin sloping nose had already smelt that peculiar but familiar creditors' aroma of final exasperation. He knew exactly what he was going to say and how he was going to say it.

Kenneth Cork, born just before the First World War, was the youngest son of the celebrated W. H. Cork. His father had prospered, concentrating almost entirely on insolvency liquidations and trustee-ships mostly in the provision trade – this being the quaint late Victorian description for food supply, for the provision of daily sustenance via the grocers or grossers who purchased gross in sacks and tea chests, and then sold in small quantities to their pennypinching, near penurious ever-watchful customers. The growth of the Co-ops, the Cullens, Liptons, Maypoles, the multiple grossers had put thousands of small shopkeepers out of business. Father Cork consolidated his rising reputation by becoming a liveryman and an active member of the Eastcheap ward of the City Corporation. To substantiate his increasing eminence and to publicise his talents with an up-grading flourish, he became the owner of an outsize Rolls Royce which sent tremors across the backs of his targets – his competitors, who when they saw this missile parked outside a creditors' meeting were almost disposed to giving up and going home.

The key to insolvency work, as he told his three sons, was the ability to attract rapid attention at a creditors' meeting. In these manoeuvres, W. H. Cork was a master. As described by Kenneth, 'He had to make a quick and lasting impression at meetings of creditors by the force with which he was able to express himself, by the questions he asked, by possessing a natural stimulating presence. In his case this was very natural, and it made people sit up and take notice. The creditors, their accountants, their representatives filled the room as equals at the beginning, but by the end of the meeting one of the accountants or representatives would emerge as the dominating personality'. More often than not the dominating personality who emerged, as his son told me proudly, was W. H.

The sons inherited their father's commercial savvy, each sibling slotted with astute if not opportunistic synergy into their appointed careers. Leslie, the eldest, went into law as a City solicitor, able to increase the interaction between the legal and insolvency aspects; Norman, the middle one, remained unqualified so that he could advertise the sale of businesses and assets, something forbidden by the professional bodies; Kenneth, the youngest, inheriting more than his share of the family genes, qualified as a chartered accountant in 1935 and learnt the ropes of the fashion of the times, not only from his father, but also from his father's cronies.

One of these cronies was Harry Gully, and both Cork and Gully decided to fortify their connections by starting a new firm bringing in Kenneth as the third partner; it was called W. H. Cork Gully. Profits were shared, one-third to W. H. Cork, one-third to Harry Gully, and one-third to young Kenneth, newly qualified and newly married. Soon after the beginning of the War, W. H. died, and Kenneth having himself reached the rank of Lieutenant Colonel (on active service in the catering corps, he was just the man to dole out rations under fire), set out to get his career going again. He used his war gratuity plus borrowings to buy out everyone else, and he paid for his previous partners' shares in instalments, so he was not only the sole owner of W. H. Cork Gully, he was, in his own wry admission, also technically insolvent. He restarted his business with a realistic understanding of the workings and motivations and emotions of this most pitiful sector of the commercial scene, and so commenced the colourful and distinguished mainstream career of the greatest liquidator the country has ever known.

The name of Cork Gully became pre-eminent. Its strength lay in its professionalism, its integrity, and its innovations; but the cleverest ploy, W.H.'s, not Kenneth's, which gave his firm immense prestige, was that, from the beginning, it had been set up as a City firm, never to be confused with lesser lights outside the square mile, some of whom were very shady indeed.

Kenneth Cork explains the essence of his craft thus: 'There are two types of businesses in insolvency; the dud business and good business. The dud business is one which no kind of aid can make profitable; the good business is one which has run into trouble for a particular reason. As soon as an insolvency expert is called in, he has to ask himself: is this a dud or a good business? If it is a good business, can the problem caused by that particular reason be surmountable? That question is the key to a successful insolvency job. It is vital that one provides the answer right there, quickly and immediately'.

Cork normally sat on the platform representing the receivers, invariably a bank which had foreclosed on its loan, whilst the unsecured creditors, sat in the body of the hall. It was the receiver's duty to extract the most amount out of the assets for the preferred creditors and it was the unsecured creditors who had the right to put the company into liquidation. As the name and fame of W. H. Cork Gully spread, 'more of the unsecured creditors', Kenneth Cork declared without false modesty, 'reached the very simple conclusion that they wanted my firm as the liquidators in preference to anyone else'. In the 1950s and 1960s Cork Gully handled most of the more celebrated insolvencies: British Commercial, the first big insurance company to go under since the war; Waller & Co, the big Smithfield meat distributors and retailers; Savundra, the notorious Sri Lankan insurance villain; Handley Page, the Rolls Razor washing machines.

Banks needed to retain the services of an insolvency professional who would know how to deal with loans seriously at risk. A bank's first choice of receiver in this problem area was usually Cork Gully, and if it was Cork Gully, it was Kenneth Cork. By the beginning of the 1970s whenever Barclays Bank had a problem, there was never any hesitation – call Kenneth Cork.

On Wednesday, 19 December 1973, Barclays had a unique problem, for somehow the Bank of England was involved. Call Kenneth Cork. Where was he? Appropriately he was at its head-quarters at 54 Lombard Street having a meeting with a high official on another problem. During the meeting Bevan's call came through. The instruction was clear. I want Cork. Here. At the Bank of England. 'At the Bank of England? Good Lord. What about our meeting?' asked Cork. There was an amused timbre in the reply, 'Kenneth, when the head of Barclays UK says he wants you, that's it. This meeting is at an end'.

Cork, thinking he was only required for a short period, disregarded his chauffeur and car and walked the short distance down Lombard to the Bank. He entered the Court Room. Bevan told him to sit down beside them. There was an implication or an order, he cannot remember which, that he had to keep quiet and listen.

Cork had come across some of the participants before. Herbert Smith had been supporters from his father's day, Higginson was a familiar figure, so was Keogh, whom he perceived shuffling in and out, sometimes alone, sometimes with colleagues. Gillum and Wheeler he had met before. He did not know any of the men from the institutions. He said nothing. He listened. He was in the role firmly assigned to him; he had to advise his clients when asked. Was his presence a Barclays ploy to subdue the others? He did not know. If that was the reason for him being there, fine and good. He would do his job, which put as simply as possible was to advance the best interests of his clients.

The advisers and the lawyers had been closeted for hours in the Octagon Room. From time to time Wheeler or Boyce would emerge to go over some point with the institutions, who would then confer with each other, sometimes the Barclays men would whisper amongst themselves, sometimes with Gillum and Wheeler, and sometimes it seemed as if several different meetings and discussions were taking place at the same time not only in the Court Room and Octagon Room, but also in the anteroom.

No one spoke to Cork apart from the occasional aside from the Barclays men. He spoke to no one except on the occasions when

Keogh would beckon him to one of the serving rooms where he seemed to have a personal bar and he would be offered a glass of refreshment. He assiduously followed the instructions from his Barclays' masters. He thought Bevan was being unduly tetchy and abrasive, was surprised that he was being so narrow and rigid, and more than surprised that he did not seem to realise that he was irritating many of the participants.

Nevertheless, as the silent expert, Cork already knew the answer: Cedar was very much alive, it was a good business not a dud business. It was nowhere near coffin time. Gillum had gone downstairs with his party. They had all waited upstairs, and he didn't come back and he didn't come back. Then he came back and told them they refused to sign. He was not surprised when Gillum asked him if he would like to have a go. Any self-respecting merchant banker should have a brain which works well if not better under pressure, especially in a confrontation or a battle. Gillum, Cork realised, had a good brain, he had the disposition to match his task, he was self-reliant and, though not over imaginative, he was resourceful and also articulate. Cork was already of the opinion that if Gillum had elected to sit downstairs through the negotiations, he would have had one or two extra cards to play.

Cork knew that Gillum had been far more jolted by the executive directors' refusal to sign than he cared to admit. He knew that Gillum and all the others had taken in the implication of his presence. His clients, Barclays, had played this card well. He might represent a bleak symbolism, but he might also be a possible solution to its predicament. It had been an enterprising thought of Gillum's to ask for his involvement and he was amused by the manner in which Bevan had expostulated his approval. He could see John Gillum sitting back in his chair with a self-satisfied but apprehensive look in his eyes, and he noted that all the participants had returned to their seats. All eyes were upon him.

Cork focused on the situation. All right, it was like a creditors' meeting, but of all places what a room to hold it in, the directors room of the members of the Court of the Bank of England. He relished the prestigious venue, it appealed to his sense of occasion.

Kenneth Cork had the same upper-class cockney accent which is still found in some peers who serve an over-long apprenticeship during their father's last relentless years, and also found in accountants and solicitors who serve a long apprenticeship straight from school under the waspish tutelage of a qualified senior. Cork's delivery was well accented, each word was unambiguously enunciated. Over the years he had addressed dozens of creditors' meetings, some of them very arduous. He had dealt with countless frightened people going through difficult times and had been in numerous situations where creditors had found themselves in sudden extreme danger or when rich individuals had found themselves in sudden extreme penury. He knew perfectly well how normal sane businessmen flinched when exposed to unexpected ugly financial pistols held at their heads.

Cork sympathised with the people around the table. Not one of them really understood the shockwaves of the downstairs situation. He knew exactly what the Morrisons were going through, and what they and the executive directors downstairs needed: it was hope. They needed to know that they were in an ongoing situation, that they were not being asked to sign their own burial certificates. He had learnt more than enough during the evening to know that Cedar was not a dud business, that its loans were safe. The properties were the key to any agreement and they should be perceived as assets to provide security, not as assets to be sold. What had to be got across, above all to the Cedar directors, was that they were being offered a future: without it, they would never sign.

He started talking. Suddenly the weary men in the Court Room were alert. No one coughed. No one rustled any papers. The 'creditors' had been totally dominated.

'There is all the difference between a liquidator and a manager, between temporary illiquidity and terminal insolvency. Cedar is illiquid. It is not insolvent. Cedar must be looked at as a continuing business, not one to be frozen and dismembered. Why otherwise should the executive directors downstairs sign any document? They had to be given hope and that could only be done if they felt the business was going to be kept alive.'

Cork then explained what had happened to Rolls Razor, a celebrated insolvency case arising from the direct selling of washing machines to the public. There were similarities with Cedar, said Cork. In Rolls Razor the members of the public who had purchased the washing machines had made arrangements to repay by instalments. If he had merely liquidated the Rolls Razor assets, most of the money would have been lost. 'The British public, the man in the street, always expects to repay what he has borrowed,' declared Cork. 'Cedar is owed a considerable amount of money, tens of millions of pounds and its borrowers will repay. They are ordinary men in the street who when they incur a debt have every intention of paying it back.'

Cork looked around the table. All eyes were upon him. The proverbial pin dropping could be heard. 'You won't lose any money on Cedar. Its business is about personal debts, all from the man in the street. If you want them to sign, they must have a definite element of hope. You have to give them something to hold on to. You can't take it all away from them.'

Jenkins: 'Cork was absolutely first-rate. He quickly got down to the basic essentials. Without him it would not have got going.' Stenham: 'The greatest strength in all of this, when a degree of sanity came into the proceedings, was when Kenneth Cork arrived and he knew exactly what he was doing.' Burton Johnson: 'Cork was highly professional and highly practical. He had this most magical way of saying something which simplified difficult issues. I was very impressed.' Ron Bishop: 'He was the man of the moment.' Bevan, no doubt, felt some pride that it was his man who had caused this stunning effect. The atmosphere had changed completely. Michael Richardson: 'He cut out all the cackle'.

'I will go down and speak to them,' said Cork. 'But I want to see them on my own.'

There was no dissension. On the contrary, there was visible relief as Cork got up. W. H. could not have performed more admirably than his youngest son. No longer a lad, now sixty years old, in the prime of life, soon to be Lord Mayor of London, Kenneth Cork with a slight academic stoop to his narrow shoulders left the great Court Room.

It was now his turn to go downstairs.

FOURTEEN

The Signing

The parlour steward opened the door and a man whom none of the executive directors had ever seen before, entered.

'Who are you?' barked Michael Morrison.

'I am Kenneth Cork of Cork Gully.'

'Oh no!' gasped Michael. If he had seen Banquo's ghost he could not have been more terrified. Kenneth Cork. Cork Gully. Bankruptcy. It was staring him in the face. But this was no apparition. It was the notorious liquidator himself.

Cork was undismayed. He was used to this kind of physical and emotional reaction. He appreciated that Cork Gully could sometimes strike terror. His urgent task, however, was to obtain the confidence of these people, to persuade them to face the realities of a failed rescue, to persuade them of his own sincerity.

Cork disdained a chair and stood up just inside the room by the door. It was an instictive thing for him to do, part of the technique of dominating the proceedings, of being in control.

'The situation is very serious,' he said, looking levelly around him. 'If there is no rescue, the company will go under and a lot of people will be in distress. If an agreement is not signed, some of you here will go bankrupt.' He paused, knowing the use of the dreaded word would have the effect he desired. He guessed that the 'Who are you?' came from Michael Morrison, and that the older man was the chairman, Jack Morrison. He specifically looked at Michael and he knew immediately that the word bankrupt had unnerved him.

Cork went on, 'Let me say straightaway that I am not in the least surprised that you refused to sign. I think the agreement should be altered.' The tension visibly eased, his words hit the bullseye on the first round. He went on to insist that an agreement should nevertheless be signed. Of that there was no doubt. If it were not signed, there would be no rescue and that would be the end of Cedar and everything would be lost.

At this juncture a loud clear North country voice was directed at Michael and Jack Morrison. 'Don't sign anything.' Ziff was as consistent as ever, still exhorting his father-in-law and brother-in-law. Cork took no notice but he was concerned, because he perceived that Ziff was by no means rattled. He considered that Ziff was far more of an adversary than the Morrisons, that he was clearly a man who carried weight and Cork hoped that he would not carry sufficient weight to stop his in-laws from signing. 'We have got to regard Cedar as an on-going situation with you, its directors, still carrying on. The chairman will still be Jack Morrison. As you can see, the institutions are prepared to help, so is Barclays bank, whom I represent. The present proposal is not the best one, particularly on the way the properties should be valued. I am prepared to alter the proposal into a form with which I would personally be happy and with which I believe the others would also be happy.'

Cork was not sure whether he had them on his side but he could tell they were not against him. 'Do you agree that I should do this?' The non-family directors turned towards the family. Having seen Banquo's ghost, Michael, very white and shaken, was now observing a liquidator who appeared to be more like that of a reasonable businessman. He nodded in agreement. So did the others. 'In which case I will prepare a redraft,' said Cork. It was now past midnight.

Kenneth Cork returned upstairs. How did it go? What they are prepared to do is to consider a revised agreement, do you approve? Yes. I would like to draft it in my own hand, do you agree? Yes please.

Cork started drafting the new agreement.

Downstairs there had been a curious change in the Morrisons. They no longer talked like owners, and this had already been noticed by the other executive directors. One glance at the chairman was enough, he was catatonic and immobile, hardly aware of his surroundings. Fischer sat silently, though showing signs of fear; he seemed to have accepted the inevitable, that everything was lost. Only Michael was still vociferous, still charged up with emotion, still at times incoherent. The change, in effect, was that the Morrisons were not any longer just fighting for Cedar's survival, but for their own survival. Ziff was consistent: he kept on saying that nothing should be signed.

Whilst Cork was drafting, certain visitors appeared from upstairs. First Higginson accompanied by David Bolton. Higginson's large frame was crumpled, he was tired and uneasy as before, only more so. Michael's abrupt expostulation about seeking another lawyer had torn the texture of their long-term relationship. It would never be the same again. The gap between him and the Morrisons had widened irreparably. Now stooping and with his shoulders hunched, his head bowed, Higginson soon left the room. When he returned upstairs he announced that the Morrisons would like to see William Broadfield. Stenham did not move a muscle.

Broadfield got to his feet and went off full of trepidation. He was sickened by what the Morrisons were going through, by the treatment being meted out to them. It was as if they were near-criminals, as if they had committed some offence. He hated his own timidity. He wished he had the nerve to say so, to stand up for them. He felt guilty and embarrassed. When he entered their parlour room, he was dismayed by the atmosphere which was like a railway waiting room, the arrival of the train unknown. Michael and David Fischer were genuinely pleased to see him. Confronted by their isolation, Broadfield felt more guilty, particularly when Jack himself greeted him warmly; Broadfield's friendly face had perked up the old man's spirit. 'We are doing all we can,' Broadfield muttered to them. Michael did not notice Broadfield's discomfiture, as the mere sight of his old friend had heartened him instantly, his obvious sincerity and goodwill clearly warming.

George Cumming was another visitor. He sat by Michael trying to explain the terms, urging him and David to accept and discovering that it was not only the valuation of Buckingham Gate which was sticking in their throats but the undated letters of resignation. Michael Richardson also visited. He felt it was necessary to explain and answer any technical queries on the Stock Exchange implications. The Morrisons were not interested in the stock exchange implications or any technicalities. There were awkward moments.

Cork, sitting in the Octogan Room, was near to completing his draft. The general atmosphere was of a listless open-ended weariness, a widening disgruntlement and a growing animosity towards the Morrisons. An element of disorientation wafted in. When would this ever end? Would it ever end? For those who had arrived in the morning, like Jenkins and Burton Johnson, their last proper meal, aeons before, had been a hurried breakfast. They had gone through the morning and most of the afternoon without realising that they had missed lunch. They had gone through the late afternoon, the early evening and the rest of the night well past the dinner hour without anything more than coffee and biscuits, and some sandwiches and whisky. Jenkins did not realise until the next day that he had not had a meal all day. It was getting towards 1 am. The clocks chiming every quarter of an hour seemed louder, as if to remind them that they had less and less time to lose.

When tension has numbed the senses, and time has stretched in all directions, when one has almost forgotten the reason why one had to persevere in what one is doing, when one has an overwhelming and desperate urge to go home, at this sort of juncture, one could almost agree to anything.

As the hours advanced it had got even colder, the heating was obviously not functioning as well as it should during the night. They were a motley collection, striking up desultory instant friendships forced upon them by propinquity, like diverse travellers forced by circumstance to be together, unique circumstances in a unique place, circumstances encompassing a common objective which was taking far longer to achieve than anyone had imagined, circumstances now producing a back-breaking *ennui* interspersed by humorless vapid laughter and trite rejoinders and echoes of unrequited activity.

Yet the Bank retained its pervading authority; there was a sort of decorum, despite the steady consumption of whisky, the refreshment most readily available and increasingly welcome, its influence apparent in their over-jocular over-enthusiastic rejoinders. Perhaps the decorum was due to the special magnificence of the Court Room, perhaps because in the early 1970s the niceties of behaviour and dress were still maintained, so whisky and weariness may have loosened some of their tongues but not their ties; appearances were straitlaced to the last, despite the strain; but sporadic conversational asides were beginning to show the growing pressure. Through the windows the garden court was black and there was an impression that this long December night of unmitigated starkness, the longest of the year, the longest of their lives, would never end.

A sprawl of people, slightly disoriented, slightly disorganised, a common aim, a specific task, each of them knowing that he could not leave until that task was completed, wondering above all else, whether those intractable people downstairs would ever sign. Thank the Lord for Cork. If he could not get them to do it, no one could.

There was suddenly some activity, some movement, a little coughing. Cork emerged and was ready to read out the new draft. Those who were standing by the Court Room windows or by the vast chimney pieces or in the anteroom or in the corridors, returned to their chairs.

Cork looked over his half-glasses. He started reading from his manuscript. He was now ready to detail his points. He had not altered the basic terms but he had changed the emphasis. He had been quite dexterous. There was more stress on the directors staying on, more stress on the future of the company, more stress that it should, as soon as possible, be operated as a viable business.

On the most sensitive issue, the bone of contention, how to value the properties, Cork's most significant wording, though still vague, had shifted the method of valuation, to what the properties were worth before the collapse. This would particularly benefit the valuation of Buckingham Gate. The wording was sufficiently vague, its large print probably large enough to quell anxieties on either side. As Cork read out the points, some of the listlessness, some of the sluggish apathy, some of the torpid defeatism receded. The atmosphere was more attentive, more wide awake. When he had finished, there was no dissenting comment: on the contrary there was a spirited and lively assent.

'Let's try it on the dungeon. They should certainly accept this,' was one ribald response.

Possibly because Jenkins was the youngest institutional man there and more of an age with most of the executive directors, possibly because his forthright character had shone more brightly during the long day and night, he was selected to go down with Cork and Gillum on this second trip, the party to be completed by those who had accompanied Gillum on his previous abortive descent. The mosaic stone staircase underlit at the best of times, threw shadows on to the stone walls and ceiling as if it were candlelight held up by a janitor, the staircase took on the look of a medieval prison, of a dungeon; the Count of Monte Cristo could not be far away, was the thought of one of the group.

The party descended into the depths. Would they all fit into the room? They crowded in. The exececutive directors looked up with rapt attention, particularly at Cork.

Cork read out his draft, divided into what was now ten points. He was conscious that he had everyone's concentration, conscious too, that Arnold Ziff was glaring at him. No one interrupted. Cork read out the separate points in his clear explicit manner, occasionally glancing up as was his normal professional custom to monitor the response of his listeners, to measure and size up their reactions, to convey an aura of domination. When he finished, he stared down at his papers, pausing for a while. Then he looked up sharply, throwing a glance at each of the faces in front of him.

This was the crucial moment. Would they agree to sign or would they refuse? He gave it no more than a 50/50 chance. Earlier that night in his first encounter he had given it only a marginal chance; what he had achieved then was to bring them round from a hostile to a neutral posture. It was now a question of when push would become shove. There was silence. But only for a moment.

For one of the executive directors was seen to be getting up from his chair. It was Alan Glass. He had decided to speak.

Glass was thirty years old. Slim, neat, of medium height, very tidy even at this hour in his well-cut suit, a slightly pointed face, a long unlined forehead, wavy crinkly hair with none of it out of place, his eyes though alive had no expression, perhaps because they were trying not to display visible nerves. Conscious of the charged atmosphere, his voice as he uttered was quiet and almost sibilant, and he gave the impression that he was in full control of his emotions. With one hand in his jacket pocket he turned a little towards the Morrisons in an old-fashioned gesture of acknowledgement. As he spoke, his listeners were aware that here was a man who had his own personal sense of judgement, who could think ahead and with clarity, who knew how his second sentence would end before he had finished his first.

'I have not been with Cedar for very long, but I've grown to have great respect for the family, for the Morrisons. They may or may not agree or indeed they may not like what I am going to say, but there comes a time when one has to be counted, and I am prepared to be counted. One has to make one's own views clear to ones colleagues. This is a desperately difficult situation. It is particularly fraught for the family. Everyone as far as I can see is doing his best to reach a possible conclusion. The first proposals had weaknesses but I believe that this proposal we have just heard from Mr Cork is not only the best available but also I think fair to all concerned, to the large and small shareholders, to our customers and depositors and to ourselves. We may or may not like it, we may or may not lose our jobs, but our first consideration must be to open our doors to our customers tomorrow morning.'

Cork knew then that they had won. This was what was required, a strong coherent endorsement from an exective director. It was not only marvellous the way Glass had stood up, it was bloody lucky. The others, Gillum, Richardson, Jenkins, Sadleir, Higginson, Bolton, were deeply affected as were most of the other non-family executive directors.

But Michael Morrison was white with fury. This man was a Judas.

The executive directors started talking at the same time. Ahmed asked: 'Why don't we leave it till the morning?' 'Absolutely not' said Gillum. But Ahmed insisted. 'We still have some money in the kitty for tomorrow.' Cork intervened. 'Show me your current account.' Cork then turned to the executive directors and said: 'Well if you listen to Mr Ahmed tonight and ignore the withdrawals, I will say you are very brave men. If I were in your shoes, I would not take the slightest risk of going under.' Then Gillum, sensing the right moment, addressed Jack Morrison, 'You are chairman, sir, there ought to be a vote.' Jack nodded.

Gillum went round the table. He asked each director in turn.

Glass: 'Yes.'
Edward: 'Yes.'
Grinling: 'Yes.'
Eames: 'Yes.'
Johnstone: 'Yes.'
Watt: 'No.'
Fischer: 'No.'
Michael: 'No.'
Ahmed: 'No.'

It was over. There was a clear majority amongst the non-family directors. The family was beaten.

Gillum spoke to Jack: 'There you are, sir. That is your board's decision.'

Jack nodded.

Michael, in a passionate tirade, immediately turned to the executive directors who had voted yes. 'You are mad to vote for this. The institutions will throw you out. They are against you as much as they are against us. Do you think they will look after you? Never! Let me tell you it is curtains for you as well as for us.' No one made any comment. His intemperate emotional outburst had expressed darker thoughts.

Gillum said, 'We shall have copies typed for signing.' Jack nodded.

Glass was impervious to Michael's hostility. Ziff was silent. Watt thought about the valuations of the property. Ahmed looked at his schedules, loathing Glass for standing up like that. Without his intervention he was sure they could have stuck out for improved terms. Would there otherwise have been a vote? To this day even Alan Glass himself is not sure. Cork is not so uncertain: 'Without that plucky young accountant standing up in that room,' he said, 'we may have been there for ever.'

On Cork's return upstairs there was no jubilation in the Court Room, but an immediate flurry of phone calls from any available telephone. It was past 1 am, and most were telling their wives that they would be home soon, perhaps in an hour. As anyone knows who has been involved in a difficult negotiation between various different parties, when the final negotiations have been long and arduous, when accord has been reached, the actual signing of the agreement is rarely a simple swift matter. Mindless fatigue has taken over from over-tiredness, even affecting those who have to do the typing and copying. People are slower, brains which have moved on to a siding have to be jolted on to track. Each crossing out of a word or a comma has to be looked at by each lawyer and has to be assented by each principal. The papers themselves become gremlins and put themselves into disorder. Lawyers looking down their spectacles, exercising their expertise with infallible omnipotence and with forced concentration, though on familiar terrain, take longer to dot and to cross.

Just at this moment the copying machine jams. The right person is in the wrong place. The key to a stationery cabinet is mislaid. The wrong person is in the right place. A typist flies into a rage with her machine. There is a disordered mêlée, rising impatience, inane talk from those whose only fuction now is to sign their name on a document. The clocks tick away, a mechanical sip is taken of weak watered-down whisky, a biscuit is nibbled half-heartedly, some of it spills on to the paper and is brushed off perfunctorily. There is a desperate yearning to get home, the forced hours together, the long unsolicited intimacy, brings out the best and the worst, and the worst is banal beyond the normal boundaries of social niceties, one never wants to see certain faces again.

As the papers begin to take shape, as the documents are collated and made ready, as the moment of signing is nigh, there is a *bonhomie*, a feeble stale cheerfulness, weak jokes are made and laughed at, good ones produce daggers, this is not a time to be witty or clever.

The papers comprising the heads of agreement, the board resolutions, the undated resignations, are now ready and have been placed on the Bank of England's board table; one for Barclays Bank, one for each of the institutions, one for Cedar and one for the Bank. Relevant designated persons have to sign each of the sets of papers. Four sheets of typescript make up a full set. Each set requires eighteen signatures. Higginson, Bolton and Sadleir make their way downstairs for the signatures of the Morrisons and the executive directors.

All is now signed. It is nearly 3 am on Thursday morning. It has been eighteen hours, some would say eighteen weeks, or eighteen years, since the Governor held his first meeting in the early morning of the previous day. Not at any time is there a suggestion that those on the first floor and those in the nether regions should all get together. It is all over. Everyone can go home.

But no, wait a moment! What about tomorrow morning? Tired and drained, but a little elated, they have forgotten the dawn, they have forgotten that tomorrow morning is now this morning. The newly-rescued Cedar will be opening its doors for business in a few hours. Who is going to start it off? Who is going to run the show? They all look in one direction: Kenneth Cork.

At this first meeting of Cedar, at number 60 Pall Mall, with the institutions in control, Cork was to be in charge. The Morrisons had lost their management positions, they had lost control, they had lost their money; but they had not lost everything. Jack Morrison, dignified to the end, had indicated that he and his son and his nephew would attend that first meeting in a few hours time.

FIFTEEN

The Exit

The Morrisons left together. One of the executive directors, watching them as they made their way, by no means a sentimental person, had a lump in his throat. He firmly believes that he was not the only one.

Yusuf Ahmed left with Bailey who drove him to his north London home. Alan Watt was staying the night in the company flat in Hertford Street and went there by taxi.

Philip Johnstone's homecoming was by no means easy. His wife had driven from Esher to collect him. He tumbled into the driving seat. The car would not start. It took a long while to find a taxi. They did not get home until after 5 am.

Alan Glass lived in Radlett in Hertfordshire, near Douglas Horner of Barclays. They drove home together in a car which Glass had ordered. Eames, Edward and Grinling made their own way home.

Higginson and Boyce left together.

Michael Richardson's London home was in Eaton Square. David Bolton, whose wife worked at the Belgian Embassy which was in Eaton Square and who had the use of an embassy flat, shared a taxi with Richardson.

John Gillum lived in Hertfordshire. He had come up as usual by train the previous morning. Ray Wheeler offered to put him up in the spare bedroom of his Chelsea flat. He accepted with gratitude. William Sadleir went to his home in Dulwich by taxi.

Hugh Jenkins left with David Clement. As a heavy smoker, Jenkins had arrived well prepared with his usual two packets of cigarettes, plus one extra emergency packet, never used before. The last eighteen hours had been an emergency. He smoked all three packets, running out just before the signing. Since that night he has not smoked a single cigarette. Aversion therapy is what he calls it.

William Broadfield's wife, Sheila, had been waiting outside at the Lothbury entrance. The Broadfields lived in Palmers Green. Ronald Stanley, the secretary of Cedar, lived in neighbouring Enfield. Sheila drove and they dropped Stanley at his house. Only then did William tell her of his deep regret in not having done something more to demonstrate his personal sympathies for the Morrisons.

Cob Stenham lived by the Albert Hall in Queen's Gate. His Unilever driver took him to Blackfriars. Conscientious to the end, he wrote out a summary for his colleagues and was then driven straight home; he sat in the car working on his papers. Thursdays were more than usually busy at Unilever. In his own mind he had already wasted one day and one night and he wanted to catch up.

Lord De L'Isle had suggested to Ron Bishop that in order to catch his last train to his home in Amersham, he should leave early. This he did as he was not required for the signing. The two quiet gentlemen from Electricity, Burton Johnson and George Cumming, departed together. On their way out, De L'Isle said to Johnson, 'Thank you for your support'. Johnson replied: 'Thank you for your leadership.' Lord De L'Isle was taken to his London flat by his driver.

Bevan left with Vander Weyer. Bevan's parting remarks to Cork were, 'My grandfather was a banker, my father was a banker, I'm a banker. But in their day when anyone went bust they did it during working hours'. Cork knew better.

Cork left with Keogh. They walked along the stone corridor together. Before they reached the front door Keogh said to Cork, 'Put up your collar so that you can't be recognised. If anyone sees you coming out now, people might think the Bank of England has gone bust'. Cork smiled but nevertheless he put up his collar because, he claims, it was cold. His car was outside and he got in beside his chauffeur. This faithful retainer had first driven him to Lombard Street the previous Wednesday afternoon. He had waited there until he learnt that his master had walked to the Bank of England. He had driven there unbidden, and had waited patiently ever since.

Ray Simpson was immaculate to the last. He cleared up after everyone had left. He would be staying the night in the staff room. Before settling down he reheated some coffee, poured it into a silver coffee pot, and served himself from the usual silver tray and Wedgwood china. It had been the longest day and night of his life. He was in perfect attire except that he had taken off his pink frock-coat and had hung it carefully on a hanger in the wardrobe. He was still on duty and could have served the Governor, if necessary, even at that hour.

*   *   *

That hour was 4 am.

Epilogue

Spring 1988, fifteen years later
The great English cathedrals, unlike Chartres, Seville, or Milan, radiate a special quality which derives from the distinctive fabric of English social life; it is a quality of friendliness, which is embedded well within the social order of its tolerant adherents, rather than arising from a somewhat more demanding religious order. To this English order of things it is not surprising that the most moving, intimate and poignant love poems in the language were created by a cleric, John Donne; but he was not enflamed or excommunicated or compelled to demonstrate public repentance for describing private joys. Another cleric, a most celebrated humorist, was the much-loved Reverend Sidney Smith who, for nearly half a century, from pre-Pitt to post-Melbourne, made the élite of his country laugh until they ached at their dinner tables. Still another cleric, David Sheppard, the current Bishop of Liverpool, was a superb sportsman who captained England's cricket team with a God-like straight bat.

Jane Austen's descriptions of rural society would lose half their magical resonances without her vivid evocations of the parsonages and their incumbents. The village church, with its peaceful chimes and age-old mellow stone and informal grassy graves and peeling tombs, is a permanent anchorage entwined in the more precious memories of each succeeding generation. The clergy, not endowed with any celibate powers, were in every way like the members of their flock, from the lowliest prelate to the archbishop, and having fulfilled their pastoral duties on the Good Lord's behalf, they retired from their livings, their social and spiritual lives not altered perceptibly in any way: one can no more separate the Church of England from the State, than one can separate its parish churches from the Vale of Evesham.

Likewise one cannot feast one's eyes in Salisbury upon the most beautiful spire in the world without the deepest feelings of gratitude that its serene high-steepled slenderness, overlooking a domain unchanged for hundreds of years, of cloisters and naves and streams and rich cow-sodden Sarum pastures, can still project a wonderful warp of timeless continuity, can still spellbind the dutiful prelates, the fluttering garbed choirboys, the shepherding beadles, the everyday strollers and visitors and, those most fortunately placed of all, the neighbouring houseowners.

There are few more elegiac sanctuaries in all of Europe in which to spend the evensong of one's life, than by the meadowed cloisters of Salisbury Cathedral. One such happy soul, and its most distinguished riverain, is Edward Heath who, though more than three score and ten, considers himself with some justification to be in his prime. He would also claim that any person, not only a passionate music-lover, on first hearing the soft sacramental sounds percolating through those ancient stones towards Constable's immemorial trees, might come to believe that they were listening to the beguiling murmurs of an incomparable English heaven.

Heath's serene house is one of several by Salisbury Cathedral Close, and it was in the course of a visit there that I made an ardent, perhaps too ardent, observation to him about Lord Richardson. It was some fifteen years after the banking crisis, the spring of 1988, after a sumptuous and spirited lunch, our host was in an armchair, relaxed in his airy drawing room, the other guests were looking at his pictures or walking in the medieval garden. I was sitting deeply in an adjoining chair balancing my coffee cup and chatting about my preliminary work on this book. 'Gordon Richardson,' I said, 'looms more and more as a great figure,' adding, 'and I have come to believe that your appointment of him as Governor was one of the best you made as Prime Minister.'

Heath listened to this comment with its overtone of hyperbole in his usual intent manner. Whilst never disdaining a positive view of any of his achievements he was always quick to reject anything if it were inaccurate, and even those far better acquainted with him than I would have found it hard to interpret his characteristic honest stare of non-committal. He made no rejoinder other than to take a baleful sip of coffee with a gentle frown, which signified that he knew I wasn't making anything like an idle comment.

Later, Nadia and I walked through the meadows and amongst the trees. The sceptred beauty of the spire pierced the sky. A light breeze ventilated the tranquil Salisbury afternoon. We were at the melancholy end of the great Thatcher boom. Edward Heath's era had long since passed and it seemed more like fifteen decades than fifteen years since Gordon Richardson and Jasper Hollom had been digging in at the Bank of England to do battle with that ferocious financial storm – a storm of force 10 still rising.

Thursday 20 December 1973: The first day after the rescue
The new régime, led by Kenneth Cork and accompanied by Douglas Horner and assistants from Barclays Bank, arrived at 10 am. The atmosphere, said one director, was like a morgue. What was immediately apparent to them all, was that it was not a family bank, the Morrisons' bank. It was no longer even a bank, but a corporate body ready for dismembering. The night before the gloves had been off and there had been some pugilism; now it was time to don the surgeon's gloves. The new men with their scalpels were the liquidators and bankers, impatient to start their incisions, perhaps a little too eager for the cut and thrust.

Before the meeting Cork, noting the presence of the Morrisons with slight surprise and more than slight respect, took father and son aside and administered a dose of anaesthetic. This was his pain-relieving routine for the months to come, a calming chat with the Morrisons before the process of dismembering.

Immediate changes were made. Alan Glass became *de facto* managing director. Grinling gave Cork his letter of resignation, saying, 'I will stay on if you want'. Cork brusquely replied, 'Your resignation is accepted. You can go.'

Having cleared the decks, Cork's first priority was to inspect the money book and to make arrangements to deal with the deposits on an hourly basis. There would now be continuous contact with the no-nonsense Barclays minders. The next priority was to decide what to sell. Top of the list was the beautifully crafted athlete eating its head off in the hangar. Cork went through the separate items methodically. When he came to new business, Eames was told what to do: no new business; tell the brokers; now, pronto. There was chaos at this sharp end, at the brokers' end. Eames and his assistants, soon to be deprived of their Jaguars and their jobs, telephoned each of Cedar's brokers to say that no new business could be underwritten. They could provide no answer on what to do with business in the pipeline, and no answer on the commissions owed. Many of Cedar's brokers suffered grievously as a result.

There was another early-morning meeting: this time of the City advisers. This took place at Hambros Bank and included Michael Richardson, John Gillum, William Sadleir, Ray Wheeler and his assistant Michael Sorkin. They quickly (but not that quickly) agreed the announcement of the rescue which had to be made to the Stock Exchange. It was brief, stating:

> The Board of Cedar Holdings Limited announces that the institutional shareholders, in association with Barclays Bank Limited, have made arrangements which, on the basis of information provided by the company, are designed to ensure that the depositors and the account holders can be repaid as their moneys become due. The necessary legal and other requirements are now in course.
>
> The institutional shareholders are Electricity Supply Industry Pension Funds, National Coal Board Superannuation Pension Funds, Phoenix Assurance Company Limited and Unilever Superannuation Funds.
>
> The company is requesting the Council of the Stock Exchange to suspend the quotation of all the listed securities of the company and of its subsidiary, Amalgamated Securities Limited.

The shares of Cedar were immediately suspended. After the nail-biting agonies of the night before, after the most stretched hours the participants had ever endured, this was the anodyne statement which informed the City that Cedar had been saved, this was the terse statement which informed the unaware nation that the City also had been saved.

The announcement of the Cedar rescue and the suspension of its shares sent shudders through the entire secondary banking sector and beyond. Sharp falls were recorded – a full third of market value, with tens of millions of pounds wiped off the share prices.

On this first morning (and for several further mornings following the Cedar rescue) the money market professionals, without any exceptions, withdrew deposits as they became due. There were no renewals and as moneys became due they were promptly paid. The mechanics were in place. The immediate surgery was effective.

That same afternoon at 3 pm there was a meeting at Samuel Montagu. This time the lawyers were in pairs: Higginson and Bolton for Cedar; Boyce and Coleman for the institutions as a whole; Peach and Widdowson for Coal itself, and still ark-ridden, a further twosome for Electricity, for Unilever, and for Phoenix. The heads of agreement had to be put into proper legal form although it eventually took months before it was sewn up. One of the major legal difficulties, the most contentious in the heads of agreement, was that the purchase price was blind; the institutions had agreed to purchase the properties but no exact price was agreed and the lawyers found this arrangement extremely difficult to draft.

Friday 21 December: The second day after the rescue
This day marked the real beginning of the Christmas break as many of the offices closed at midday, not opening again until the New Year. There was little enthusiasm to work during Christmas, what with restricted TV, little lighting and heating, coal and rail go-slows; why keep the offices open? The economy was in shreds, there was turmoil in Westminster, in Whitehall, in the City and throughout the manufacturing industry. And there was now, of all things, a travel boom – anything it seemed to get away.

But not everyone could get away. For on this Friday there was a further meeting of the clearing bank chairmen held at the Bank, just two days after their first secret meeting. This time they were joined by the senior managers. There were little or no recriminations that one or two clearers had been more sympathetic and more friendly towards the fringe banks than the others; and general agreement to establish a support pool for the troubled fringe banks was soon met. What proved to be a momentous decision was quickly announced to the press, and it achieved exactly what it set out to do.

Christmas 1973
The City was empty on Saturday and Sunday. It was also deserted on Monday, Christmas Eve, as it was on Christmas Day and Boxing Day. The mood was far from cheerful. Richardson told me that he couldn't recall a more miserable Christmas; I thought that he must have had some pretty rough ones during the war. When the emergency measures were imposed some weeks earlier, the Prime Minister, in a fraught national broadcast, said, 'In terms of comfort, we shall have a harder Christmas than we have known since the war'.

Thursday 27 December: A week after the rescue

The first working day after Christmas and a trickle of people returned to their offices. Amongst them were the clearing bank chairmen who requested to meet the Governor again, the third time in a week. This encounter marked the precise moment when the Lifeboat was officially launched. It was agreed that the Scottish clearers would be invited to join in and that meetings would take place in the Bank of England, chaired by Hollom. As a matter of simple procedure each clearing bank would in the first instance look after those of its own customers in trouble. The Governor agreed that a 10% stake would be taken by the Bank in the support pool. The Bank would also be the coordinator and it would inform each clearer each day – based on its comparative deposits – how much cash from each was required; the first call to take place to be the next day.

What was remarkable was that no upper limit for contributions was fixed, which was another example of the effect of the Richardson method of consensus. There had been no legal sanctions, no demands, no ultimatums. It had all been done by consensus, the symbiosis of like minds and actions. It was the way Richardson worked; everything was clear to, and agreed by, the relevant people. It was a team effort and perceived to be so.

Friday 28 December

The first formal meeting of the Lifeboat committee took place. It was held in the Octagon Room of the Bank and was set up like an emergency war committee geared to making immediate decisions. Jasper Hollom was in the chair and Roger Barnes acted as secretary. It operated continuously during every working day under Hollom's chairmanship, and it wasn't until a full year later, by which time £1.2 billion had been committed – 40% of the then combined reserves of all the clearing banks – that the clearers questioned the need of an upper limit, the Bank itself agreeing to provide any additional amounts required.

The pattern of priorities for the long campaign had been slotted in with what looked like sublime skill. Cedar, being the first vital part of the operation, had been despatched off the field in the early hours of Thursday 20 December and the first meeting of the chiefs of staff had taken place the same day in secrecy; their second meeting took place on Friday 21 December, also in secrecy; their third meeting plus adjutants took place on Thursday 27 December, again in secrecy, with Christmas having intervened. And now the plan of campaign settled, with no time to be lost, the adjutants with the chiefs of staff assembled the next day, on the Friday, to draw up the battle lines. The contingency plans were in place.

It was recognised that the offensive would produce some carnage, though it would have been considered unduly pessimistic to have prophesied that, a year later, a clearer, in fact one of the original big four initiating the rescue, would itself have to issue a denial that it was in trouble.

The night of the Cedar skirmish, however, had not been easy, being too close to the brink of failure, hair-raisingly so. A certain amount of pressure had been applied, some would say a pressure which had a trace of guerrilla tactics; others would say no harm in that, as the City *had* to be saved, the end justfied the means.

January 1974

In the United States the greatest financial horror of all time was the collapse of the banking system in the 1930s resulting in the Great Depression. *Barrons*, the influential New York finanical journal, in referring to this current UK banking crisis did not mince its words, declaring that it was the worst since the 1930s. Later in the month Cedar had to deal with the formal approval discreetly received from the New York Federal Reserve to its proposed acquisition of the Chester National Bank. Alan Glass wrote to them, stating, 'Facts regarding Cedar's situation have changed substantially since the takeover was approved'. The understatement of the year, was the observation of one of the Fabulous Four.

February

The slow seepage of the miners' go-slow had seriously weakened the Government's chance of a settlement. The miners had cleverly manoeuvred themselves into a direct confrontation and, after weeks of the painful drip of the go-slow, they announced their strike on 4 February. Seconds were now out of the ring. At long last Heath decided to go to the country. The General Election would be held on 28 February. His theme: 'Who governs the country?' The miners had certainly decided it wasn't going to be him, and the mere posing of such a question was enough to make them self-important, more militant and more confident. Heath had made an elementary error; a man in charge who has to ask *who* is in charge, is not in charge.

*   *   *

The property world was showing alarming signs of falling apart. I went to see my friend Harold Samuel at Devonshire House, the chairman of Land Securities, the great man of property himself. He was quietly self-contained and exuded, as always, an immaculate neat trim strength. We had morning coffee and looked out through the window in his office, overlooking Green Park and St James's Park. 'Do you know,' he mused without boasting, 'many of the buildings you can see from here belong to us.'

It was a verdant vista, high up. London was confidently spreading some of its wares on a green carpet, the near invisible traffic was far away and silent; tower blocks stood out, Roebuck House, the other new buildings on the old Stag brewery, the pre-Home Office; while Buckingham Palace was hiding furtively amongst the thin winter trees. 'Harold, I'm not looking at the Palace,' I said. He smiled, but not before giving it a sidelong glance.

We discussed his notorious second property revaluation. Why had he done it? He had never been an opportunist, he was a property strategist of genius. Our discussion was unsatisfactory as he would not agree that this second revaluation in a year was itself a serious symbol of property overheating. We also discussed the fringe bank crisis and the general financial situation. To my astonishment he said that he was buying in his convertible stock. You are using cash at a time like this? Yes, he said. Then you can buy my property portfolio, I suggested, at half its asset value. Don't panic, Charles, he said, it will all work out. This was another rare occasion when Harold Samuel had seriously misjudged a situation. I became even more worried.

*   *   *

In the General Election on 28 February the miners won on points; it wasn't a knock-out. No party had a clear majority. Jeremy Thorpe, the Liberal leader, was invited to number 10. His party was given the chance of joining the Conservatives. The offer was declined: the decision deprived Thorpe of a cabinet post and his party once again of playing an important political role.

March
Ted Heath moved out of Number 10 on 4 March and Harold Wilson moved in. Wilson's first decision when he walked through the door

was to invite Joe Gormley, the miners' leader, to see him. Wilson gave Gormley everything he wanted, including his favourite brandy. Gormley smacked his lips. He could not ask for more. Soon after, the miners' strike was settled, although not without some tricky bargaining between Ezra and Gormley.

*　　*　　*

I bumped into Michael Morrison and David Fischer, by chance, in Motcombe Street, the link between Belgrave and Lowndes Squares. If asked to name one of the more picturesque streets in London I would unhesitatingly include Motcombe, which for many years was my London village street. The buildings are early nineteenth century, two and three-storey terraced houses, art galleries and shops on the ground floor, flats and offices above. It has London's first pantechnicon and the once captivating Halkin Arcade, designed in 1830 by Joseph Jobling, joining Motcombe to West Halkin, which also has its seductive façade of terraced houses and shops. At this Halkin end, opposite the arcade, by the corner of a lane which leads fitfully to the eighteenth-century Star Tavern, was situated the Shirley James Travel Agency, which is now an antique shop. Old Shirley James was an acquaintance of Nadia's father and of other travellers from South Africa. After he died, urged by David Fischer, who learnt that the agency was for sale, it was bought by one of Michael's trusts. This was an astute business move, for the Morrisons' travel requirements could alone have kept it going. After the Cedar rescue, Michael and David, no longer able to use their offices in Pall Mall, based themselves in the travel agency until that too had to be sold.

As soon as he saw me, Michael threw his arms joyfully into the air. 'It's wonderful to see you Charles. We must talk.' I looked at David Fischer; he didn't attempt to say anything in case I walked on, but his eyes were clearly imploring me to forget my enmity towards him. It was almost three years since we had last set eyes on each other. I looked at Michael; he was blubbing. That did it. I put my arm round his shoulder and he and I strolled back to the Lowndes Hotel, and over tea – whatever other arrangements I had were put firmly into the background – I listened to Michael's torrent of words, occasionally interspersed by Fischer, who was on his very best behaviour. Michael told me in graphic detail of 'the terrible things' that had happened to them, describing particulary the event at the Bank of England. He was quite unashamedly in tears. My wellspring of friendship with Michael ran to the surface. I, too, was overcome by emotion, not only because of Michael's overwhelming sincerity, but over the ordeal in the Bank. Until then I had heard accounts of what the Morrisons had gone through, but these versions, either first- or secondhand, were garbled by the teller's own version; this was the account of the chief actors. It was a true horror story and, at times during the telling, Michael would occasionally interrupt himself, in his exuberant, volatile, sincere manner, to repeat how thrilled he was to see me and how I was the one person he had desperately wanted to talk to. I was not in any way flattered, although I am an easy target, but I was exceedingly moved. The afternoon wore on. Michael insisted that we meet again the next day. We did, and on a number of further occasions.

During this period, when the real estate market collapsed, the level of my own net assets was eroding from millions to not very much more than nil. Despite a friendly call from Harold Samuel and several others, I felt also as if I were walking on quicksand. But that was a different horror story.

April

Nearly four months after the rescue, the heads of agreement were signed, after almost four months of non-stop meetings,* the detailed terms were finally agreed by the parties at 5.30 pm on the Thursday before Good Friday.

The documents circulated to the shareholders stated that if the proposals were not accepted, the company would almost certainly have to go into liquidation. They also disclosed that the Fabulous Four had exacted their full toll. The feature of the proposed issue of four redeemable preference shares, one to each institution, each share carrying 10 million votes caught the interest of the press. Never before had so few shares been issued to so few shareholders with so many votes. The *Daily Telegraph* was particularly vitriolic: 'The issue of four

---

* All those concerned with formalising the heads of agreement have stressed the inordinate amount of time they spent (particularly the lawyers) in the first four months of 1974. Fortunately the time spent didn't have to be fully costed. Alan Urwin, tidy and precise as always, commented on his Cedar involvement during that period: 'My Cedar meetings board or otherwise, were as follows: January 8, 10, 11, 15, 21, 24, 29, 31. February 4, 7, 11, 12, 14, 18, 21, 24, 28. March 1, 4, 5, 7, 11, 14, 19, 21, 22 25, 26. April 2, 4, 9, 17, 18, 22, 25, 30. Of course one must add to the above meetings the internal discussions to brief me on the past, to discuss action, to talk with my in-house legal advisers, and particularly in the beginning of the year there were also, I am certain, unrecorded meetings arranged ad hoc at the last minute on the phone. Meetings were well attended!'

new preference shares with 10 million votes per share, giving the four institutions voting control of Cedar, could scarcely have been designed with more cynical disregard for the private shareholder than if it had been the object of the exercise.'

The documents also disclosed that the loans to the Amalgamated directors might have been improper. It was the old story of whether loans to directors of a bank were made in the ordinary course of banking business. Apparently not.*

The lawyers had never had so many field days. The Morrisons became increasingly anxious about the outcome. In money terms, for them it was life and death, and they fought tenaciously for a full property value, especially in respect of Buckingham Gate.

Board meetings were inevitably strained. Jack was still taking the chair, but went through the agenda like a man programmed to do so. Michael and David, who had previously called all the shots, now had to listen; it didn't stop them talking, but they had no say. They were like dispossessed previous owners of a house, neither welcome nor unwelcome, wondering whether the proceeds of a forced sale would leave anything over after the banks had taken what was owed to them. Everything depended on the property values: it was a continuous bitter argument. The two professional property men on the board, Jenkins and Watt, saw eye to eye on their mutual respect for each other, but not at all on their different perceptions of the values. The Morrisons, having only one asset, had only one objective and that was to obtain the highest possible value for the properties. They fought month after month; they fought before the board meetings, and at the board meetings they lobbied anyone they could, or rather anyone who would listen to them.

Many questioned why they didn't just pack it in. Why were they enduring this slow death? But they were not to be deterred. If they won

* The detailed note to the accounts was as follows: 'These loans were made in August 1973 for the purpose of refinancing loans which were made to another bank [Samuel Montagu] at the time of the merger with Amalgamated Securities to enable these persons to pay off the balance of the subscription moneys which became due, as a result of the merger on the partly-paid ordinary shares of Amalgamated Securities previously issued under the company's Executive Share Incentive Scheme. The directors had subsequently been informed that the above mentioned financing arrangement for the directors may have been in contravention of Section 190 of the Companies Act 1948 in so far as such arrangements may not have been made in the ordinary case of business of the bank.'

their battle over property values, there would be something left over. But whatever the basis of valuation, values were declining rapidly by the day: the property market was in freefall.

Kenneth Cork was none too happy over these arguments in Cedar over the property values. In these intervening months since the rescue, the property market had curled up and died. He declared later: 'What I learnt that night was not to put a price on property'. He had developed the view that owners forced to sell should postpone formal valuations until the property market had regained some semblance of normality. Later he organised an operation whereby the banks or any other forced owner would not seek a valuation, no selling prices would be mentioned, nothing would actually be for sale, offer prices would be unsolicited, and if offers were received they would be rejected or accepted. It worked with stunning effect, creating an orderly disposal and not a firesale under neurotic selling conditions. It was later known as the Cork Syndrome.

May

A minor sensation was caused when it was announced that First National had gone into a 50/50 partnership in a formal arrangement with the Bank of England to operate the banking rump of London and County. It was considered a 'smart move' by Pat Matthews, and an insurance policy for his own group – it isn't every day that one has a joint company with the country's central bank. The *Evening News* wrote, 'Not a Rothschild nor a Baring has been paid such a compliment by the Bank. It is a compliment that other banks must envy.' The *Evening Standard* expressed disagreement with its rival, 'The Old Lady of Threadneedle Street moved in with First National with a joint rescue of London and County just over a month ago – since when, its shares dropped from 40 pence to a low of 20 pence. So First National variously described as a property bank and a bank somewhere between the fringe and the centre, has been subjected to the same speculative selling as others in this field, despite the Bank of England's seal of approval.'

If Matthews thought he could earn valuable brownie points he was, it seemed, mistaken. Later his own company was ravaged by the crisis, and he had to go cap in hand to the Lifeboat: joint partners with the Bank of England or not, First National's application to the Lifeboat was examined as searchingly as any other and, in his case, to the extent that the committee considered that it should seek an independent report (from Kleinwort Benson) before it could consider a commitment. In the event First National and United Dominions Trust (both of which had received their prestigious Section 127 authorised seal of banking approval on the same day, 6 December 1973) became the two largest recipients of Lifeboat support.

Well-known property enterprises were crashing, two big fish, Ronald Lyons and William Stern, amongst them. The king of liquidators was appointed for both, and the Cork Syndrome was applied. Many of the secondaries had been big lenders to these two – Keyer Ullman, the British Bank of Commerce and First National Finance. The shares of First National fell to a fresh low of 16 pence before steadying at 20 pence as rumours ran around the market. Pat Matthews was forced to make a press statement: 'I have never heard such rubbish. I do not know where these rumours come from. We certainly have no liquidity crisis'.

*   *   *

The amount drawn under the rescue terms had moved up to £53 million. The Barclays £22 million was beginning to be tapped. This was the highest level of the £72 million support. By August the figure dropped to £48.6 million.

June

Amongst tremors of a possible international banking crisis the Herstatt Bank crashed, Hans Gerling's bank. He owned most of the shares. It was a Friday afternoon, before the end of banking hours, and many payments were *en passage*. This did not deter the German authorities who closed shop in a distinctly messy way which sent reverberations throughout the international banking system. This was not at all to the taste of its fastidious owner. The bank was Hans Gerling's intellectual hobby, for his principal business was the Gerling Konzern, one of Germany's largest insurance companies of which he was the sole owner.* Herstatt had a proud history as a private bank in Cologne, and Hans, a business aristocrat, who extolled the familiar German attributes of integrity, of attention to detail, of reliability, took particular enjoyment in discussing banking philosophy with its top management.

---

*Hans Gerling has since died. His son Rolf runs the Konzern which is 70% owned by him and 30% by the Deutsche Bank.

Gerling was tall and had the bright eyes and intelligence of a Senior Wrangler. He was a man with a brilliant mind, an internationalist and a perfect host in whatever country – the Gerling office in Paris by the Etoile was more like a palais, and as Cologne is the only major German city on the French side of the Rhine, it was not surprising that Gerling had a slight whiff of Gallic charm. His city is a city of culture, celebrated not for its water, but for its architecture, its cathedral, its opera, and of course for its Gerling Konzern, the city's largest homegrown family business. It is also known for its art galleries, one of its best designed owned and run by Irene Gerling, herself as beautiful as the most statuesque of Rhinemaidens and the proud mother of their four children. The gallery showed a wide stretch of contemporary art and we still have several pieces of sculpture, first viewed there, some of which she gave us. With his fine feeling for architecture and design, I always suspected that the gallery was designed more by Hans Gerling himself, than by the accredited architect.

And then there was the Gerling furniture, dark gleaming burnished laminated wood, strong and slender and immensely elegant. I first saw an example in Hans's study in his home in Cologne; it was his desk and it was sensational; the desk top floating on a solid curved perspex slab. It was a beautiful piece. Later Irene had a similar one made for me for my office in Old Jewry and later still the whole of the Spey offices were filled with glittering redwood Gerling furniture, and even design-struck architects from Madison Avenue said that they hadn't seen anything so handsome and were soon wending their way to Cologne.

At the time of the Herstatt crash, Hans was one of the richest men in Germany, also one of the most refined, more at home in a Proustian salon than in a Dusseldorf restaurant, more at ease looking at first editions and, though he was a most literate student of balance sheets, more happy admiring a piece of sculpture than a steel mill. He was of a different cast from his fellow German magnates, many of them were envious and jealous; Hans seemed to them too arrogant, too proud, too different, too grand, and even in Cologne there was always the emblem of his house, the old Gerling family house, like a miniature Sandringham set almost in the centre of that great city. And then the Herstatt Bank crashed and collapsed and all the pent up jealousy from many of his rivals came thundering around him.

We had met the Gerlings some years earlier through our friendship with Frank and Cella Roberts when we stayed with them in Bonn. Previously Frank had been our Ambassador in Moscow where he and

Cella had entertained Nadia when she was a guest ballerina at the Bolshoi and the Kirov* before the Royal Ballet itself had set foot in Russia. During that visit, apart from the Roberts, Nadia made and renewed many friendships, notably Galina Ulanova, whom she had first met during the Bolshoi's historic visit to Covent Garden in 1956. Another was Raissa Struchkova, who had danced with such grace partnered by her husband the great Lapauri. Yet another was Yuri Faier, the near-blind Bolshoi conductor who held Nadia's hand during rehearsals to feel the rhythm of her musical phrasing (Nadia regards him as the greatest ballet conductor of her experience). Then, of course, there was the wonderful Nicolai Fadayechev, who partnered her poetically in Moscow and who had been allowed out of Russia a year or two earlier during the iciest period of the Cold War, to dance the historic Nerina/Fadayechev *Giselle* on BBC television, the first ever full-length ballet classic danced live in a TV studio and all the more memorable for that. Nadia's Bolshoi visit, followed by an equal triumph in Leningrad where she was partnered by Constantine Sergeyev and looked after by his wife, Leningrad's most exalted ballerina, Natalia Dudinskaya, was a highlight in many ways, of which the forming of lasting friendships was paramount. Of these continuing friendships one of our most treasured, was with Frank and Cella Roberts, he unquestionably amongst the most talented diplomats since the war; she amongst the most beautiful women of her generation.

During our stay at the Embassy, which resembled a large Victorian Scottish fishing lodge, but facing the Rhine rather than the Spey, the Roberts took us one night to the Cologne Opera for the *Magic Flute*, with Hans and Irene Gerling making up the party. We went to their house for supper after the performance and this is when I saw Hans's desk in his study.

And then, six months after the UK secondary bank crisis, the international banking community trembled when Herstatt collapsed. Its management had over-extended itself and Hans Gerling was blamed. From the first he fought back with such controlled intensity that he eventually won back his ownership of the Gerling Konzern, but he was to go through purgatory first. The fact that Herstatt was in trouble and Hans had lost his entire investment was not enough for the Germans. He had to be brought to account personally. He had to

---

* The Kirov has reverted to its traditional name of Maryinski as has Leningrad to St Petersburg. Moscow, in almost every way, is still, alas, Moscow.

support the bank personally and with huge sums, and so he had to lose control of the Gerling Konzern. His compatriots were not going to let him off lightly, they were not going to forgive him for preferring claret to beer, for being a man of culture first and a man of business second, for being a European first and a German second, and when he eventually regained his original 100% I am sure he and Irene paid a visit to Le Grand Vefour, their favourite Paris restaurant, to savour a well-deserved victory sip of Margaux.

July

In this month a piquant event at the Bank of England, the celebrated Principal of the Discount Office, Jim Keogh, took premature retirement. There were some tears but not that many.* The new head was Rodney Galpin and his deputy was Roger Barnes,† with whom he had shared an office next door to Keogh.

The only satisfaction Keogh may have had was that the Bank had decided to take banking supervision more seriously. His staff had numbered fifteen. It was now seventy strong. (Today it is nearly 200). There was no longer one senior interface between the Bank and the banks. Proper reporting procedures were laid down which had never existed before. The Bank was confident that the new measures would provide sufficient early warning signals to avoid any future banking disaster. The Bank was going to be a little bit more like the Treasury (something it would never admit) which considers that verbal messages and verbal reports are not worth the paper they are not written upon. No more nods and winks; it was filing cabinet time. On this

* An extract from one of the best City commentators, Christopher Fildes – who appears every Thursday in the *Spectator* and is proudly reprinted by its same proprietor every Saturday in the *Daily Telegraph*. Fildes wrote after Keogh died in May 1991: 'I knew there was a crisis when I went to see Jim Keogh at the Bank of England and came away to write that fifty banks were at risk. How bad it must be, I realised a few hours later, when the bank's press office rang me up to ask me to tone down my headlines. It might, the spokesman murmured, give a false impression – or worse (I reflected) a true one. This was the fringe bank crisis, the gravest of the century and Keogh was the Bank's man at the eye of the storm – until ruthlessly and arbitrarily he was thrown overboard.'
† Galpin is now the very able chairman of the Standard and Chartered Bank and Roger Barnes is now the very able head of the supervisory division of the Bank of England.

matter the Crown Agent's Report* published eight years later in 1982, itself a deeply-flawed document, was vigorous in its criticism of the Bank, stating that much of its work 'was done orally and informally, was even not recorded at all, or worse, recorded only in a brief manuscript note scribbled at the top of a minute and often not copied to all concerned'. A wonderfully bland Treasury friend known for his elegant use of the language, on reading this, came out with the most non-Treasury response I have ever heard, 'Cor blimey'.

August

A most tempestuous meeting took place at Samuel Montagu; the man who caused it was Henry Benson (now Lord Benson), the senior partner of Coopers and Lybrand, the auditors of Cedar, one of whose partners, Gerald Drew, was a Morrison trustee. This was the rub. The Morrison shares were owned by the trusts, the trustees were Higginson and Drew; only the trustees could vote the shares, and whether Michael as the principal beneficiary agreed with them or not, he was intrinsically powerless, the trustees always acting and voting in what they considered was in the best interests of the beneficiaries and not what the beneficiaries thought was in the best interests for themselves. If Michael had owned the shares in his own name, he could have voted them as he thought fit, and there is little doubt that if he had had the power to vote, he would have voted against many of the subsequent approvals required from its shareholders.

* The *Report of the Tribunal appointed to inquire into certain issues arising out of the operation of the Crown Agents and financiers on own account in the years 1967–74* was published in May 1982. It is written in the manner of a financial soap opera, except that there are no heroes. The history of its involvement is as bizarre as the series of government reports and committees set up to investigate what, how and where the Crown Agents had acted as financiers in the secondary banking sector. The Report is particularly interesting on the relationship between the Crown Agents' then director of finance, Alan Challis, and First National. Challis had left the Crown Agents in November 1973 to join First National as joint managing director with Pat Matthews. At the time of his joining, the Crown Agents were owed getting on for £20 million – up from £13 million in September 1973 – by First National, apart that is from the cost of its 9% shareholding. Challis resigned from First National in December 1974 after adverse publicity following the government's announcement of its financial support for the Crown Agent. Margaret Reid, who later wrote an excellent thesis on the secondary banking crisis, covered the Challis episode for the *Financial Times*: her coverage together with the Report of the Crown Agents' Tribunal are essential reading for those who wish to learn more about this extraordinary situation.

Michael Morrison and David Fischer had complained to Benson (who was in the country on holiday) about Samuel Montagu, saying that the valuations of the properties were ridiculously low, and that at these levels the trusts were insolvent. And if the trusts were insolvent what about Gerald Drew's position as trustee?

Benson demanded a meeting. He was accompanied by Michael Morrison, David Fischer and Gerald Drew. As John Gillum was absent on holiday, present were William Sadleir and his colleague Ian Mackintosh, himself an ex-Coopers man from Samuel Montagu. Benson became more and more irascible as the meeting proceeded. Suddenly he said he would have no more of the discussion, and abruptly left the room. But the matter could not be left like this. Mackintosh got Benson to agree to have a talk later in the afternoon. It did not include Michael and David. Benson, when he heard the full story, did not apologise but said that he had been badly briefed, and he just about managed to summon up the courtesy to shake hands with the Samuel Montagu men when they departed. Sadleir believes Benson lost his equilibrium because Gerald Drew was under pressure as a trustee. During the Spey confrontation, when it was known that I was having a row with Henry Benson, a distinguished ex-partner of his, who was successfully running a major enterprise phoned me to say that he had heard that my opinion of Benson was the same as his own and that if I required anything from him he would be glad to oblige at any time of the day. I was grateful more for the reassurance that I was not the only one who disliked Benson than for the kind offer. I believe that on this occasion Benson lost his cool because he had only heard one side of the story and also because he could not influence Mackintosh and Sadleir. The episode demonstrated the running sore of the basis of the property valuations, particularly Buckingham Gate. Michael and David's emotions were still riding high. The proposed reorganisation of the capital and the board of Cedar was nigh and Michael was still fighting for his financial life. But if Michael had asked me I could have told him from bitter personal experience that Benson had few equals as a steamroller.

September
The accounts of the Unilever Pension Fund for the year ending 31 March 1974 were published. The report of the trustees included an intriguing paragraph and Stenham's logic that the pension fund

should be protected by Unilever Limited, had the resounding ring of a positive conclusion. This is the extract:

> The difficulties in the secondary banking sector mentioned earlier, affected the Fund through its substantial investment in Cedar Holdings. The Trustees came under pressure to be party to a support operation to protect depositors in that company. The Trustees did not feel justified in using the Fund's resources for this purpose and Unilever Limited agreed to provide the amount required by ways of loans to the Fund. The balance sheet headed 'Special Deposits' shows the advances made under this arrangement. No loss is expected to result but in the event that a loss occurs it will be borne by Unilever Limited.

What transpired as the first stage of a reorganisation at Cedar, was announced. Ahmed, Eames, Johnstone and Watt resigned from the board but retained their executive duties. Michael and David stayed on as directors but were to give up their executive duties. Jack was to remain as chairman, but only until a replacement was found.

October

Another General Election was called and this time there was a slight improvement in Labour's majority. But it was still a hung parliament and Harold Wilson was still Prime Minister.

November

Soon after the Herstatt crash, the *Economist* had asked whether there was a serious danger 'within the next few weeks of a big international banking crisis like that of the Credit Anstalt in 1931?' Arising from Herstatt and also the lessons learnt from the UK financial crisis, the international Lifeboat was initiated, inspired by Richardson. The Banking International Settlements in Basle, established its own Lifeboat committee, known as the Blundell committee. Blundell was the Bank of England man who was designed by temperament and character to solve problems. The committee established the new important principle that the parent of a bank had to be responsible for any of its branches, even those operating overseas.

December: A year after the rescue

The annual party of Edward Erdman and Co., was the one I always enjoyed most among the many thrown – some might say jettisoned because of their casual plonking standards – by the larger real estate agents. In the 1980s Edward Erdman's partners dropped the 'and Co.', thus prematurely embalming its founder, a titan of his profession, who was still very alive and very much loved. Erdman, a friend of many years standing whom I had personally invited to join the Board of Bishopsgate Property, was not bothered by this corporate burial. I was, though, and in response said I was not disposed to doing business with his partners again; this in turn would not have bothered his partners. The party itself was held in the Hilton Hotel ballroom in Park Lane and its most agreeable feature was the way the bird-like Eddy – he has the figure of a sparrow and is just as spritely – arranged and rearranged his hundreds of guests; everyone of note in the property world was there or would have been there but for previous engagements.

Clore and I were together. Like moths, several of the brighter young luminaries, including Jeffrey Sterling, buzzed around him. Sterling was saying that he now saw his role as chairman of his company Town and City,* as a controlled liquidator of assets for at least three or four years ahead. It was a very bearish timescale even in those days, though if anything it proved optimistic. Walking afterwards down Curzon Street towards Marks Club to join the rest of our party, Clore who was in a good mood because he always felt at home in the Hilton as if he were still the true owner, said, 'That man's clever'. 'What man?' 'Who else but Sterling, you idiot. Did you know he used to work for Isaac?' I mumbled something about the difficulties of people having the same name as a currency – it was confusing. Clore said, 'You watch him, I would buy him forward any time.'

What no one ever thought could happen, happened. On Monday 9 December, from the gilded parlour of a major UK clearing bank, the National Westminster, to its branch managers, a letter from Alec Dibbs, their chief executive, denying rumours that the bank was in trouble. This was a double digit on the Richter scale; every other clearing banker quailed and quaked. There was no comment from the Evergreen Lady. Richardson and Hollom knew the worst was over, that this shock-inducing NatWest note was the final signal.

---

* Sterling is the formidable chairman of the P&O which is now the parent company of Town and City.

Christmas

At Charles Clore's usual large Christmas party at Stype, with the usual guests, the usual huge Boxing Day shoot with over forty people for lunch at a long table by the swimming pool. Halfway through lunch, a friendly wager on the number of birds bagged, everyone chipping in. The man who suggested it was an excellent shot and shrewd, the two go together. His guess was the highest, ten more than anyone else; I therefore made mine five more than his and I won. It was the only money I made that year.

Clearly for some it had been another decidedly unseasonal Christmas like the year before, for, on the next day, it was announced that the Bank of England had come to the rescue of Burmah Oil. Its shares had dropped from about 80 pence to 20 pence since the beginning of the year. After lunch, walking past the orchid house to the stud, Clore and I discussed the implications of the announcement. He was exceedingly gloomy. I said that at this level the Stock Exchange indicated that the country was bust which was sheer nonsense; blue chips could only go up as their prices were discounting every disaster known to man. Clore said that, in that case, why didn't I act like a man and do something about it? I said I was far from liquid and he knew it. But you must have something in Switzerland, everyone has, he insisted. Not me, I said, and then came the only time I asked him for money. 'Let me have £5 million. I want to buy into Jeffrey's company. We can share profits and losses.' Town and City, once highly valued, was now a penny stock. Sterling was struggling for survival. (I did say it was confusing.) Since Eddie Erdman's party I had studied the data and made a thorough analysis of his company, finding it was not shaky even on a worst position scenario. The fact that the Prudential had also announced its support meant that there was a floor to the share price. That was good enough for me, but it wasn't good enough for Clore. A few months later when the share price had soared, he told me, 'You should have insisted, we could have made a killing'. I told him he would be better off in another currency. 'Don't sulk,' he said. 'Let's have another drink – I'm a *Potz*. You're a *Potz*.'*

---

* Clore's vernacular was economical, taciturn and a resonance of his East End Yiddish boyhood, the exact meaning of key words, depending on the context and on his mood. His main expletive was *potz*. It could mean a *schlemiel* who was an idiot who knew not better, or a *schmock* who was a *schlemiel* who should know better, or it could be an affable nonentity who has gone astray, like a man allowing his daughter to marry a *schlemiel* or a *schmock* or indeed a *potz*. To Clore the whole

The Burmah rescue was a watershed; it was the turn-round of the markets. The day of the announcement the FT index stood at 161.4. By the end of 1975 it had risen to 375.7.

New Year's Eve
A year since the beginning of the crisis, and a year since the Lifeboat had been launched. During the year retail prices had increased by 19%; wages had increased by 29%. Inflation had reached 16.9%.

March 1975
Some fifteen months after the rescue, documents were circulated of the second and final stage of the board changes and of a capital reconstruction scheme.

Jack, Michael and David were to resign, as were most of the other directors, including Broadfield who, notwithstanding Stenham's bite and Roger's involvement, had stayed on as a transparent nominee for his fund. Jack was voted £5,000 per year as a life pension, but this was only after strenuous pleas by Michael who had to emphasise that his father was totally without resources. Michael and David were to receive a single payment of £5,000 apiece. The level of these amounts could have been construed as a gratuitous insult, but Broadfield had to fight hard behind the scenes to obtain board approval, and though the payments were a pittance compared to former affluence, they were still received, if not with gratitude, with some relief.

Alan Glass was to continue as chief executive and the sole institutional director on the board was to be Oram. Broadfield, the longest serving institutional director, was leaving after ten years; two years later than he would have done if he had resigned when he wanted to, at the time of the Amal merger. The new chairman to replace Jack was to be one Simon Coorsh, a long-distance runner from the Wolfson stable, recommended by Kenneth Cork, who thought this provenance might soften the withdrawal pains of the Morrisons. It had the reverse effect, the Wolfson resonance provoked a response of sour anguish.

---

world was made up of *potzes* of one sort or another. His other favourite word was bastard, which included any one who stood in his way – a waiter or a telephone operator or a competitor. I'm a *Potz* came from a well-known Houston story emanating from a rich, well-heeled couldn't care less Texan, called Hogg, who gave his three children the first names of Ima, Yura and Hisa.

The capital reconstruction scheme was not overly complicated. In essence, after extraordinary losses of £22.0 million of which £15.5 million derived from property write-downs and £6.7 million from losses on the sale of assets, such as the Hawker Siddeley, a deficiency of over £6 million of shareholders' funds thrown up. This sum was to be eradicated through the capital reconstruction by way of the institutions converting some of their loans with the ordinary shareholders being severely diluted: the institutions then would own roughly two-thirds of the company.

As to properties, the institutions would purchase the portfolio (excluding Buckingham Gate) for £16 million against the December 1973 book figure of £24 million. Buckingham Gate would be sold to them for £1.5 million against the book figure of £9.2 million (which included the revaluation surplus of over £4 million). Their purchase price, including further costs of completion, was estimated to be £8.5 million in all. The *Investor's Chronicle* was highly critical: 'There can be little justification for the harshness of this property deal'.*

April

Shareholders were invited to a meeting on the 8th to vote on the capital reconstruction scheme and on the property proposals. The day of the meeting marked the end of the Morrisons' formal association with Cedar. In all only seventeen people turned up to vote, including one each from the Fabulous Four and one representing the Morrison family trusts. On the capital reconstruction, a majority of 75% was required and this was easily carried with the institutional vote of over 50% and the Morrison trusts of over 25%. The property proposals required a simple majority and the institutions being the buyers didn't vote. The Morrison trusts owned nearly half of the balance. If the trustees voted in favour, the property proposals would be assured. The trustees voted in favour.

The Morrisons had fought hard to retain something. There was

---

* The purchase consideration was based on a price which would be 15% less than the lower of the valuation figures produced by the two independent valuers. There was a wide disparity between Healey and Baker's figure (acting for the institutions), which was well below Jones Lang Wootton's figure (acting for the company). I asked my friend Norman Bowie, a former senior partner of Jones Lang Wootton and the first chairman of the prestigious Asset-based Valuation Standards Committee of the Royal Institute of Chartered Surveyors for his comments. His succinct reply was: 'Valuation is an art, not a science, and one valuer's view is therefore most likely to be different from that of another valuer'.

nothing left. The fight was now over. The Chinese torture had ended. The Morrison relationship with Cedar had been terminated.

May

The last occasion I was ever to see Jack Morrison was a crisp afternoon in Charles Street, Mayfair. It was after lunch. I was coming out of Marks Club and he and Michael were walking down towards me by the English Speaking Union. Jack was leaning heavily on his umbrella and Michael was holding his other arm. Jack wore a navy-blue cashmere coat, a scarf and a matching blue trilby. He still looked elegant, but frail. It was the trilby rather than his weak appearance which gave me a jolt, for he had always enjoyed wearing his hat with a jauntiness which gave his walk a pleasant swagger. Now it was fixed firmly on his head like that of a child. Instead of the swagger there was an old man's shuffle. Michael greeted me with warmth. Turning to his father, Michael said, 'It's Charles'.

I looked at Jack. There was a long pause. At first he didn't appear to recognise me. Then he focused. He gave me a look of questioning uncertainty, and then said, 'Please give your mother my best wishes'. 'Yes Jack, I will'. As they passed by, I turned round and watched until the two figures, father and son, merged into the shadowy landscape of Berkeley Square.

June

The EEC referendum: 67% voted yes. In this month, too, North Sea oil was landed for the first time. Amongst the many celebrants was Michael Belmont of Cazenove, the City's godfather of North Sea oil financing. He had many toasts, including one from the author.

September, Zurich

We drove into the forecourt of the Baur au Lac. As soon as he saw me, Erwin, the doorman broke into tears. 'Excuse me for crying,' he said, 'we still miss your father. He was such a happy man and so full of life.' Nadia gave me a misty look. We hadn't been to the Baur au Lac since my father had died there ten years earlier. I had then cynically observed that the staff had always admired him more for his generosity than for anything else; but before Nadia could say anything – she wouldn't have anyway – I said that I would eat my words.

Though Zurich was one of my favourite cities, I found after my father's death, I was disinclined to visit, so I resigned from those boards which met there, returning for the first time these many years later, to be greeted by the sincere weeeping Erwin.

A decade earlier, shortly before his untimely end at only seventy-one, my father had telephoned me at Hambros Bank.

Whenever he did phone the routine, going back to my Cambridge days, was always the same. His long-standing secretary, first Marjorie Corbett and later Deborah Lever, was on the line first, 'Your father would like to speak to you'. Then, 'How are you my son?' Before I could reply there was the second inevitable question, 'Are you short of money?' Short or not I invariably said yes: I was not one to spoil his pleasure, or mine for that matter. After Nadia and I married, his second question in Russian was, *'Kak pozhivaet Nadyanka?'* To which I would reply, *'Chorosho – spaseeba'*; his traditional enquiry about my cash position relegated to third place. By this time when I was rich by some standards, but clearly not yet by his, although I had got into the habit of buying my mother expensive presents as a hint of my increasing affluence, I would respond to the effect that I was OK thanks, but would let him know immediately if I needed any. Satisfied, he would get to the point of his call. 'Are you free for lunch?' Dinner *à quatre* or more was always through the ladies. For our lunches, I would say yes unless I had an 'unbreakable', and I would then ask what time and where? I needn't have bothered as it was always the same place and the same time. Les Ambassadeurs at 1 pm. Their bortsch was of truly authentic quality – this was the attraction, not the baroque furnishings, a relic of its Park Lane Rothschild origins, or the other patrons, mostly hirsutes from Beverly Hills or Elstree. No, it was the bortsch; dark amber, mauve and purple, a slight tincture of vinaigrette, the pomme vapeur al dente, the cream half sour and thick, on the side. It was his favourite dish and mine too. We would start by nibbling peroshkis, savouring the bortsch as the main course.

We arranged ourselves at the table looking completely unlike father and son – he was bald and fat, I was thick of mane and thin – both pleased to be together, both more interested in imbibing, conversation was later, when we had our lemon tea. On this occasion he started with a stunner. 'I'm going to pop off soon.' 'Oh yes,' I said, looking calm. 'Well, don't be so blasé about it', he said, not entirely mocking. 'I know that I am going. I'm not ill or anything, I just feel it's not long away.' I had noticed a recent weariness, but nothing more; a man of abundant humour, intellect and energy, he had somehow sensed his end. He went on, 'I would like you to promise me something.' 'Anything.' He beamed with the contentment of a father whose friendship with his eldest son had deepened as had his affection for his daughter-in-law. 'I want you to promise to become chairman of Dixons after I go.' Dixons was the family engineering company. 'I promise,' I said, without any further comment. 'What about a vodka?' he asked. 'Yes please, a large one.' We both needed it.

He 'popped off' a few months later as he said he would. He had often observed that if he was not to die at home, he would like to die at the Baur au Lac. And he did. I used to think that he opened a European sales office in Zurich because of his affection for the hotel and its staff. He died in a trice from a cerebral haemorrhage on a Friday afternoon. I was at Pall Mall having a talk with Jack Morrison. The phone rang. 'It's for you,' said Jack. I took it and told Jack that I had to go straight to the airport

We flew to Zurich, my mother, Nadia, sister, brothers, their wives. The Baur au Lac put us all up, how I do not know as it was always full; perhaps with ultimate Swiss efficiency they always kept back rooms for just such need. We went to see him at the clinic; it was spotless and efficient. There was a suggestion of a smile on his face. Was it his last laugh, was it because he had made his final exit at the Baur au Lac, or was it because he had left me with a headache, knowing I did not particularly care for one or more of his siblings? The next morning Jack Morrison telephoned me in Zurich to express his condolences. I have always remembered his solicitude, as I have always remembered the name given him by my father.

April 1976

Two political parties changed their leaders. Jeremy Thorpe resigned as leader of the Liberals and Harold Wilson resigned as Prime Minister in favour of James Callaghan. Harold Wilson had decided enough was enough, and Jack Morrison's closest political friend took office. In balmier days, if Jack hadn't already received his knighthood, he may now have been a delighted recipient. At his seventieth birthday celebration at Claridges in 1972, James Callaghan was the guest of honour and, as the chief speaker, made the most laudatory remarks about his friend.

August

In advance of what was to be the 1979 Banking Act, a white paper was published, outlining a proposed two-tier banking system. The first tier would be banks in the true sense, in the Bank of England sense; the second tier would be near or non banks, to be called Licensed Deposit Takers.

December: Three years after the rescue

Cedar's indebtedness to the institutions, including all interest payments, was now down to £13 million. This figure did not, of course, include any surplus on properties purchased by the institutions from the company. By the following September the indebtedness was down to £6.3 million.

August

Jack Morrison died on Sunday 28 August. It was very sudden and later I was given the cause of death. Born in January 1902, he was seventy-five. In his will he left everything to his son Michael absolutely. What he left was just over £6,500, about a twentieth of his yearly donations to charity before the Cedar collapse.

January 1978

Gordon Richardson's verbal evidence at the Parliamentary Select Committee on Nationalised Industries, referring to the fringe banking crisis, was illuminating.

His preliminary observation was:

'We managed in the years since 1973, which have seen certainly the worst financial crisis since the 1930s, successfully to contain and then to overcome the collapse which threatened, and which, if it had happened, would not merely have damaged financial institutions but would have spread out into the whole economy with consequences both domestic and international. I have in the course of recent months, reflected on all these support operations with the benefit of hindsight, and, as I say, especially looking back in the tranquillity of our present transformed situation and in minor degree there are no doubt things one would have done differently with the benefit of hindsight. But I have absolutely no hestitation in saying that, faced with the same circumstances again – regrettable though they were – I would take the same strategic decision and would act in the same way.'

And in answer to one question, he replied,

'What you got at the end of 1973 and early 1974 was, so to speak, a contractionary spasm when, after one of the early collapses, people who had deposited sums of money with these institutions suddenly took fright and had a fit if you like, of collective prudence – and indiscriminately withdrew demand deposits from them, and if these had not been replaced, those institutions would have collapsed immediately.'

And his reply to another was,

'If I might put it this way, shortly before Christmas 1973 – and it is a time I shall never forget – we saw and felt the contagion of fear beginning to take effect and I with the Deputy Governor, gathered together the chairmen of the London clearing banks and put the situation to them, substantially in the terms I have put to you this afternoon, and said that in my judgement there was the threat of the collapse of confidence and in those circumstances we must act together.'

On Thursday 26 January, as it happened the day after his second appearance at the Select Committee, Gordon Richardson was re-appointed Governor of the Bank of England, for a further five-year term.

May

Eric Rogers of Unilever, William Broadfield's immediate superior and the man asked by Cob Stenham to take charge of Cedar after the rescue, asked me if I would attend a meeting at Blackfriars. It was something very hush-hush about Cedar, and also at the meeting was to be my old friend Hugh Jenkins. The story was that Phoenix was interested in acquiring control of Cedar, and Rogers and Jenkins thought the price being offered was too low, while the men at Electricity were neutral. The institutions thought I should be consulted. What did I think? Discussing the figures, it was clear that the price was low.

I told them I thought a third party should be approached and my immediate suggestion was that I would like to talk to Geoffrey Rippon, chairman of Britannia Arrow, the old Slater Walker company, now being operated under its new name and under new management. I thought it was something Britannia Arrow might well consider seriously. I subsequently spoke to them. They were interested, very interested; their managing director, Brian Banks, a talented investment brain, was enthusiastic and so was his board. They even agreed a price. Anything pertaining to Slater Walker was sensitive, the Bank itself having appointed two merchant banks to act as financial advisers who, on being consulted, were adamantly against this purchase. In the face of this opposition, the bid had to be dropped, and Brian Banks resigned in disgust.

July

Charles Clore died at the age of seventy-four in a London clinic. The hard granite had crumbled. He fought, as he always fought, to the death. During the last years of his life our friendship had deepened considerably. One of my modest compensations was his rising lack of esteem for Sainer, especially over Sainer's machinations to get Pat Matthews into Sears – Clore's industrial group which controlled *inter alia* Selfridges, the Lewis stores group and the British Shoe Corporation, Europe's largest shoe manufacturer and retailer. Sainer had gone on to the First National board in June 1971 just days before he had advised me on the Spey situation. 'If we had taken over First National, we would have gone down the spout,' Clore said to me. I agreed with him, but didn't agree that on Spey it was all Sainer's machinations.

November: Five years after the rescue

On 11 November a press announcement was made: 'Cedar has received an approach which will lead to a cash offer'. Electricity owned 20.6%, Coal 17.8%, Phoenix 10.9%, Unilever 10.1%: in total 59.4%; Coorsh owned 400,000 shares and Alan Glass owned 105,000 shares. The original shareholders, including the Morrison trusts, had been diluted to virtually nil. The approach was from Lloyds and Scottish, which offered 26 pence per share valuing the company at £9.6 million. Its chairman, George Duncan, had been one of my senior assistants in Bentworth some twelve years earlier. I congratulated him on his fabulous purchase. Geoffrey Rippon, having lost both Cedar and Brian Banks, sacked his company's two financial advisers.

*   *   *

Kenneth Cork became Lord Mayor of London. The great liquidator was the sixth hundred and fifty-first Lord Mayor since Dick Whittington. He received the customary Lord Mayor's knighthood. He was now Sir Kenneth Cork; his special pleasure, he told me, was knowing how proud W. H. would have been.

January 1979
In the *Financial Times*, Lex observed, 'All of a sudden fringe banks are back in fashion. This sudden burst of popularity is rather puzzling. The two biggest victims of the fringe bank crisis, First National and United Dominions Trust, continue to wallow in the Lifeboat. However hope springs eternal in the minds of some punters and the City was alive with rumours last week that somehow a magic wand can be waved.'

March
Buckingham Gate was fully let on 16 March, all the 50,000 square feet of office space. A Rolls Royce building for a Rolls Royce tenant; the tenant was Rolls Royce. The owners were PECU, an acronym for Phoenix, Electricity, Coal and Unilever, and the value of the building was put at over £16 million. The total cost to PECU was approximately £8.5 million. Arnold Ziff, in his forthright Yorkshire manner, had pleaded unavailingly with father-in-law and brother-in-law and had kept saying: 'Don't sign'. Two of the executive directors to this day, Alan Watt and Yusuf Ahmed are convinced that if Jack and Michael had taken more of Ziff's line, the terms would certainly have been more favourable to them and to the executive directors. They did not, however, take into account Jack and Michael's fear of bankruptcy – a fear convincingly exploited by Cork, whose cool well-chosen words sapped Michael's remaining fighting spirit.

April
On 4 April, the Royal assent to the first-ever Banking Act which contained the very first legal definition of a bank. The supervisory role of the Bank of England was now defined by statute, and the assumption was that, with proper supervision and early warning signals, no bank could become illiquid or insolvent because the Bank of England would be able to intervene in good time. It was considered that depositors would be safer and that the sanctity of the word 'bank' would be maintained.

May
There was a General Election on 3 May and Margaret Thatcher became Prime Minister. Ted Heath began what many have thought was the greatest and longest political sulk of all times. In his prominent tent on the front bench, no Patrocles in sight, he waited for the day

when his intractable opposition to his successor would be vindicated. He had to wait eleven long years.

June

Izzy Walton died on 29 June. It was the end of the delightful chortle. The one-step-forward man, of caution first and caution second, the man who studied the small print and then studied it again. Above all, as he had often asserted, one should lead a charitable life; he had given millions to charity and he left millions, his family trusts were ample, how ample I did not know, because to his bemusement I had declined to be a trustee because of the small print.

September

Michael Morrison, with the help of Arnold Ziff, had started a new business supplying packaged nuts to supermarkets and hotels. He was liking it, particularly the marketing end. He telephoned me out of the blue. He was as exuberant as ever and told me how his new business was progressing. No longer a Rolls, he had a Citroen and in London he would make deliveries himself, sometimes to the trade entrance of a West End hotel. His Siamese-twin relationship with David Fischer had at long last been severed. It was not a surprise, or rather it was surprising how long it had lasted. It had ended, soon after they had both resigned from Cedar in 1975, with a furious terminal row, in Ian Pitt's boardroom in Albemarle Street. Pitt was chairman of Cedar's advertising agency and, having become a friendly supporter of Michael, was now helping him out on his new venture. On that terminal day the two cousins were heard screeching at each other. David insisted that he should be an equal partner: Michael said 'no'. David stormed out of Albemarle Street and very soon afterwards stormed out of England for America. It was noted that Michael was a perceptibly happier person after Fischer had departed.

October

Exchange control was abolished and about six hundred valiant Bank employees in the exchange control department, one of the largest departments of the Bank of England, suddenly found that they had nothing to do. Most were dispersed to other departments. The tradition of the Old Lady looking after her own still persisted. But for how much longer?

January
The *Investors' Chronicle* was still gnawing at the Cedar property bone, still determined to point out that the institutions had not come out too badly in the rescue of Cedar, as had other shareholders. This month the institutions sold *en bloc* the balance of the properties which it had purchased from Cedar in April 1975. The *Investors' Chronicle* calculated that they 'seemed to have made a neat £10 million profit' including Buckingham Gate not including interest and income earned nor the £6 million received on their portion of the sale of Cedar to Lloyds and Scottish. The *Investors' Chronicle* had not however taken into account the institutions' original cost of their Cedar investment. One of the institutions has calulated that they came out just on the right side of evens. My own calculation is they they did a little bit better than that.

August
A painful situation emerged concerning two of the most honorable men in the pension fund world, Alan Urwin (who joined Electricity Supply pension fund as pension fund manager in January 1974, going onto the Cedar board the same month) and Bill Lund his deputy in charge of property. They had been suspended from their duties arising from a transaction with Boris Marmor the original head of Spey's old property company. These two well-liked and universally respected institutional dependables were not accused of any impropriety, but had taken early retirement. Cork Gully had been instructed to make the report and when I asked Kenneth Cork about this many years later, saying that all of us who knew these two men were incensed over what had happened, he told me the wrong men had taken the flak.

November
During this month, the pound rose to $2.45 which was the highest since 1973, unemployment was over two million, and James Callaghan, a year into Margaret Thatcher's reign, resigned as Labour leader. Michael Foot was elected as leader just ahead of Dennis Healey.

June 1981
At the invitation of Michael Richardson who had earlier left Cazenove for N. M. Rothschild, Gillum left Samuel Montagu to join him at NMR. Richardson had been instrumental in transforming Rothschilds into a leading merchant bank, on its corporate finance business

especially on government privatisations, for which he was later to receive a knighthood. When Gillum departed, Bill Sadleir, who took over from him as Samuel Montagu's poet in residence, uttered a fulsome poem at Gillum's leaving party. Two short extracts appear below:

'John Gillum's words and deeds and metaphors,
Bids, issues, deals and loyalty to the cause
Of clients in a high or a low condition
Who, on the road to heaven or perdition,
have sought from John a proxy at the gate
And God's view of the long-term interest rate'

'We respect him for his wit and style if not always quite *at idem*
It's *au revoir* and not *adieu* as we affectionately bid him
Farewell: he'll be a brightly shining star
With Michael, Luke, and Evelyn in the house of NMR.'*

July 1982

Jasper Hollom retired from the Bank after what was universally considered an outstanding tenure of ten years as the Deputy Governor. Sir Kit MacMahon, a distinguished economist, ex-All Souls, a powerful intellect in the Bank, was appointed in his place. MacMahon, the true hero of the later merger between the Hong Kong and Shanghai Bank and the Midland Bank, chaired the latter for a while after he left the Bank of England.

After much acrimony the long-running rail strike was defeated. In November, the miners voted against a strike. In December, the National Health unions voted to end their thirty-three week dispute. The union bosses had begun to lose their power; democracy was returning to the members – just what Heath had been striving for, ten years earlier.

June 1983

Gordon Richardson reached the end of his five-year second term and retired. He was created Lord Richardson of Duntisbourne. History will no doubt decide that he was one of the great Governors of the Bank.

* Sir Michael Richardson, Luke Meinetzhagen previously senior partner of Cazenove and Sir Evelyn de Rothschild chairman of his family bank.

April 1984

Death of Michael Morrison. It was cancer and it was quick. He was fifty years old. He, Angela and Juliet had moved from St John's Wood to a mews house off Eaton Square. Nadia and I went there for a service and it was filled to overflowing with family and friends. Greeting Angela I found I was very moved. An abiding comfort to her husband, always having been his mainstay, she had supported him through thick and thin; they had had a very deep affection for each other. Now she was a sudden widow, greeting her family and friends at the service with immense dignity, Juliet by her side. Somehow I felt, she would, with her quiet strength, manage to cope in the future, as she had always done in the past.

Harold Samuel died at the age of seventy-two. As a minor mark of remembrance and respect I walked through Green Park to Queen Anne's Gate. Before reaching the small dedicated Queen Mother's Garden by the lake, I turned to Devonshire House from where ten years earlier Harold had directed me to view the park and his buildings surrounding it. I then looked up at Buckingham Palace and recalled his smile.

May

Cedar had a new chairman. The man elected to the position – Alan Glass, Kenneth Cork's plucky little accountant.

April 1986

Cedar's profits before tax, for the year of 1985, were nearly £6 million.

January 1988

Cob Stenham left Unilever to become chairman of Bankers Trust Europe. At last he was the man in charge, at any rate in Europe.

Thursday 31 March 1988: Fifteen years after the rescue

The 'Marie Hall' Stradivarius was sold today by Sotheby's for nearly £500,000 – a world record. It was a beautiful instrument, so light it seemed to float in one's hands. At close range the S-bends, the curlicues, the scroll, the neck, the throat, the wonderfully rounded mature, womanly, rather than feminine curves, are sensual and pressingly tactile. A Stradivarius, like a woman who is truly compliant and yielding, will not allow itself to be forced and will withdraw affronted after a strong attacking fortissimo, but treated lovingly will emit a thrilled virtuous tone of its own free will. Most of the greatest violinists, refined and responsive instrumentalists and ever sensitive to the deepest rhythms, aspire to possess a Stradivarius within their subtle control, wanting to convey their love and affection within the exultant musical phrasing of the very finest sounds. The violin's copious cousin, the big-bellied cello belongs to the women instrumentalists; betwixt their legs it is a different sort of love duet caught beautifully by Augustus John in his masterly portrait of the great cellist, Madame Suggia, characterised as a forceful woman dominating the object of her love with her wary no nonsense command, her bow-stricken lover too frightened to upset the rhythm. The violin is more intimate, more poetic, less languorous, more urgent, more vibrato, yet it was known that Marie Hall, for whom Vaughan Williams composed his 'The Lark Ascending', was one of only a few outstanding women violinists who, in her day, had a tone unsurpassed for clarity and gentleness. Stradivari had created the instrument in 1709 and, according to one expert, it was the most handsome he had ever ever seen, the varnish beautiful and golden brown and wonderfully intact, the form of the instrument remarkable for its strength, for its boldness of outline and, like all Stradivari's creations, it had an unequalled combination of strength and elegance.

Originally used by Viotti on his first concert in Paris when he took the French capital by storm, it passed through various ownerships until in 1905 it came into the possession of Marie Hall. In 1968 through her daughter it came up for sale at Sotheby's. It was purchased by an ecstatic Jack Morrison.

As a man who all his life had loved the violin, he would have known many of the violin and cello dealers, a rare breed, in that the best amongst them are not merely dealers but tonal experts and musicologists. They are in fact a very special cognoscenti, knowing the calibre of the past and present virtuosi as well as any music critic. They are never reluctant, if anything they are enthusiastic, to express their opinions on the different tonal qualities, on the sensitive finer nuances brought out by great instrumentalists, on the particular physical features of the different instruments – which they regard as works of art. Unquestionably one of the most notable of these beautiful works of art is the Marie Hall and these cognoscenti, being passionately interested in the status of a Stradivarius, would question the worthiness of a new owner. They all approved of Jack Morrison. To them he was a worthy owner.

In one of his darkest hours, Jack had to sell his Marie Hall. His dealer told me they were both in tears, it was a harrowing moment. One wonders whether this was when Jack Morrison's strings finally snapped? Or was it when he received that terrible phone call from Michael? Or was it when he sat immobile, like one of Jack Cotton's living dead, for hour after hour at the Bank of England? Or was it, finally, when he committed suicide?

Index